Student Guide
and Review Manual

Cost Accounting

A Managerial Emphasis

John Harris
University of Tulsa

With the assistance of

Dudley W. Curry
Southern Methodist University

Student Guide and Review Manual

Cost Accounting

A Managerial Emphasis

EIGHTH EDITION

Charles T. Horngren

Stanford University

George Foster

Stanford University

Srikant M. Datar

Stanford University

Prentice Hall

Englewood Cliffs, New Jersey 07632

Production Editor: *Naomi Nishi*
Acquisitions Editor: *Bill Webber*
Supplement Acquisitions Editor: *Diane deCastro*
Production Coordinator: *Herb Klein*

 ©1994 by Prentice-Hall, Inc.
A Paramount Communications Company
Englewood Cliffs, New Jersey 07632

Printed in the United States of America

10 9 8 7 6 5 4 3 2 1

ISBN 0-13-184730-9

Prentice-Hall International (UK) Limited, *London*
Prentice-Hall of Australia Pty. Limited, *Sydney*
Prentice-Hall Canada Inc., *Toronto*
Prentice-Hall Hispanoamericana, S.A., *Mexico*
Prentice-Hall of India Private Limited, *New Delhi*
Prentice-Hall of Japan, Inc., *Tokyo*
Simon & Schuster Asia Pte. Ltd., *Singapore*
Editora Prentice-Hall do Brasil, Ltda., *Rio de Janeiro*

Contents

To The Student   vii

Student Comment Form   ix

1   *The Accountant's Role in the Organization   1*

2   *Introduction to Cost Terms and Purposes   9*

3   *Cost-Volume-Profit Relationships   23*

4   *Costing Systems in the Service and Merchandising Sectors   37*

5   *Costing Systems in the Manufacturing Sector   49*

6   *Master Budget and Responsibility Accounting   65*

7   *Flexible Budgets, Variances, and Management Control: I   77*

8   *Flexible Budgets, Variances, and Management Control: II   93*

9   *Income Effects of Alternative Inventory Costing Methods   111*

10   *Determining How Costs Behave   125*

11   *Relevance, Costs, and the Decision Process   143*

12   *Pricing Decisions, Product Profitability Decisions, and Cost Management   159*

13   *Management Control Systems: Choice and Application   173*

14   *Cost Allocation: I   183*

15   *Cost Allocation: II   195*

16   *Cost Allocation: Joint Products and Byproducts   209*

17   *Process-Costing Systems   221*

18   *Spoilage, Reworked Units, and Scrap   231*

19   *Operation Costing, Backflush Costing, and Project Control   241*

20   *Capital Budgeting and Cost Analysis   253*

21   *Capital Budgeting: A Closer Look   263*

22   *Measuring Mix, Yield, and Productivity   275*

23   *Cost Management: Quality and Time   293*

24   *Inventory Management and Just-In-Time   305*

25   *Systems Choice: Decentralization and Transfer Pricing   317*

26   *Systems Choice: Performance Measurement and Compensation   329*

TO THE STUDENT

This *Student Guide and Review Manual* is a self-study aid designed for use with the eighth edition of Horngren, Foster, and Datar's *Cost Accounting: A Managerial Emphasis*. The purpose of the *Student Guide* is to help you systematically study cost accounting in an effective and efficient manner. For each textbook chapter, there is a corresponding *Student Guide* chapter that contains four sections:

- *Main Focus and Objectives* – introduces the chapter, provides the overall learning objective, refers to the specific learning objectives in the textbook, and identifies concepts and techniques that deserve special study.

- *Review of Key Terms and Concepts* – is a comprehensive outline featuring (1) references to textbook exhibits and examples, (2) the Terms to Learn, and (3) references to the specific Practice Test Questions and Problems that illustrate important concepts and techniques.

- *Practice Test Questions and Problems* – includes an average of 10 fill-in-the-blank questions, 14 true-false questions, 9 multiple-choice questions, and 4 problems. **Check figures** are given immediately after each problem. An average of 5 **CPA/CMA questions** are included per chapter.

- *Solutions to Practice Test* – provides (1) explanations for all true-false and multiple-choice answers and (2) easy-to-follow solutions to the problems. These solutions, which are located immediately after the Practice Test, give useful feedback for mastering the textbook material.

All four sections are sequenced in order of the textbook presentation.

How to Use the Student Guide

In your study of cost accounting, it is essential to develop a clear understanding of terms, concepts, techniques, and relationships. This task requires much more effort than mere memorization. The *Student Guide* can help you obtain the clear understanding required.

There are many different ways to use the *Student Guide*. Choose whichever way works best for you. The approach we recommend is as follows:

1. Read the Main Focus and Objectives section of the *Student Guide* to get an overview of the chapter.
2. Study the chapter in the textbook.
3. Read the Review of Key Terms and Concepts section of the *Student Guide*. *Note: Some students prefer to reverse the order of steps 2 and 3. This approach, in effect, gives you an "executive summary" of the chapter before studying the textbook.*

4. Complete each of the statements in Practice Test Question I and check your answers against those in the Solutions. Incorrect answers are a signal to review the appropriate sections of the textbook to clarify your understanding.

5. Make "a good college try" to solve the remainder of the Practice Test Questions and Problems *before* looking at the Solutions. **Caution**: If you look at the Solutions before preparing your own answers, you are likely to develop a false sense of confidence and your understanding could be limited.

   a. When you finish the true-false items in Question II and the multiple-choice items in Question III, check your *letter answers* against those in the Solutions. In the case of incorrect answers, make a **second try** *before* looking at the *Explanations* provided for the letter answers.

   > If you have a tendency to select the incorrect answer to true-false or multiple-choice questions, diagnose the reason as early as possible. Four common mistakes are (i) misreading the question, (ii) failing to recall a fact, (iii) making a careless error in computation or interpretation, and (iv) failing to understand a concept or technique.

   b. When you finish each Test Problem, compare your answers against the Check Figures at the end of the Problem. Again, if any of your answers are incorrect, make a **second try** *before* looking at the complete Solution.

   c. When you do not answer a question or solve a problem correctly on the first try, place a check mark beside it. These marks will help in your review for exams.

6. Solve the homework problems assigned in the textbook.

7. Review for exams by reworking some or all Practice Test Questions and Problems. The check marks from your initial study will help you allocate review time wisely.

Student Comment Form

Over the years, comments, suggestions, and corrections from students have been very helpful to us in writing this *Student Guide*. If you have feedback, we encourage you to use the tear-out Student Comment Form on the next page.

Acknowledgements

For ideas and assistance, we are indebted to Charles Horngren, George Foster, and Srikant Datar of Stanford University, Linda Bamber of the University of Georgia, Jim Payne of the University of Tulsa, numerous students (especially Lisa Brown of the University of Tulsa), Judith Harris and Steve Kovzan of Amoco Corporation, and Bill Webber and Diane deCastro of Prentice Hall. We thank Barbara Sain for her expertise in preparing the camera-ready copy. We are grateful to the American Institute of Certified Public Accountants and the Institute of Certified Management Accountants for permission to use their exam materials.

John K. Harris and Dudley W. Curry

STUDENT COMMENT FORM

SEND TO: John K. Harris
                College of Business Administration
                University of Tulsa
                Tulsa, OK 74104

FROM: _____

               _____

               _____

DATE: _____

SCHOOL: _____

SUBJECT: Comments and suggestions on the *Student Guide and Review Manual* for *Cost Accounting: A Managerial Emphasis*, 8th Edition

1.   My favorable comments are:

2.   My unfavorable comments are:

3.   My suggestions for improvement are:

CHAPTER 1

THE ACCOUNTANT'S ROLE IN THE ORGANIZATION

MAIN FOCUS AND OBJECTIVES

Welcome to the study of cost accounting. This preview chapter emphasizes the intertwining roles of managers and accountants in planning and controlling the operations of an organization, whether for profit or nonprofit purposes. Unlike the remainder of the textbook, this chapter has no "number crunching" – its purpose is to provide a framework for studying cost accounting. Your overall objective for this chapter is to understand how accounting can assist its internal and external information customers. Eight learning objectives are stated in the textbook (p. 2). Give special attention to:

- the set of business functions in the value chain
- the five important themes of the modern management approach that shape the evolution of management accounting systems
- the cost-benefit approach
- the roles and functions of the corporate controller
- the standards of ethical conduct for management accountants

Also, be able to distinguish clearly between:

- management accounting and financial accounting
- cost accounting and cost management
- planning and control

REVIEW OF KEY TERMS AND CONCEPTS

A. An accounting system provides information for use both within and outside the organization.
   1. *Internal customers* – managers – use information for three broad purposes:
      a. Planning and control of operations and performance evaluation of people and activities.
      b. Routine decisions on resource allocation and pricing, based on the profitability of products, customers, distribution channels, and the like.
      c. Nonroutine strategic and tactical decisions such as new product development and investing in equipment.

> **Management accounting (also called modern cost accounting) reports information to assist internal customers in fulfilling the goals of an organization. Management accounting ties management with accounting.**

2. A central theme of management accounting: each of the three broad purposes can require different information, "*different costs for different purposes.*"
3. The success of management accountants depends on whether managers' decisions are improved by the accounting information provided to them.
4. *External customers* — stockholders, creditors, government authorities, and other parties outside the organization — use information in the financial statements and other reports.
5. *Financial accounting* provides the financial statements to the external users, its customers.
6. Note these key differences:

Financial Accounting	*Management Accounting*
• Constrained by generally accepted accounting principles (GAAP)	• Not constrained by GAAP: guided by the cost-benefit approach (covered in section E of the outline below)
• Takes a historical perspective (that is, reports on past events)	• Emphasizes the future: utilizes budgets and other projections in addition to historical information

7. Both managers and external parties use cost accounting information.
8. **Cost accounting**: management accounting in its entirety plus a part of financial accounting.
9. **Cost management**: actions by managers to satisfy customers while continuously reducing and controlling costs.

B. Management accounting helps internal customers manage the value chain of business functions.
1. **Value chain**: the sequence of business functions in which utility (usefulness) is added to the products or services of an organization.
   a. Research and development
   b. Design of products, services, or processes
   c. Production
   d. Marketing
   e. Distribution

f. Customer service

g. Strategy and administration

> **Textbook Exhibit 1-1 shows that management accounting provides information to managers throughout the value chain.**

2. In Exhibit 1-1 note that the strategy and administration function spans across the other six business functions.
   a. Strategy and administration includes (i) senior executives charged with the overall responsibility for the organization and (ii) general administrative tasks such as human resources management.
   b. *Note that for convenience the strategy and administration function will not be included in the visual presentation of the value chain in subsequent chapters of the textbook.*
3. Do not misinterpret Exhibit 1-1.
   a. Managers should not proceed sequentially through the value chain.
   b. Important gains can occur when managers of the various parts of the value chain work together as a cross-functional team.

C. The design and operation of management accounting systems are shaped by newly evolving management themes.

> **Five important themes of the modern management approach:**
> - **Customer satisfaction**
> - **Key success factors (cost, quality, time, innovation)**
> - **Total value-chain analysis**
> - **Dual internal/external focus**
> - **Continuous improvement**

1. As Exhibit 1-2 shows, *customer satisfaction is the dominant theme.* All the other themes are directed toward increasing customer satisfaction.
2. Terms to learn related to the modern management approach:
   a. *Quality*: conformance of a product or service to a preannounced or prespecified standard.
   b. *Extended value chain*: all the business functions (both within and outside the organization) related to a product or service (see Exhibit 1-3).
   c. *Continuous improvement* (called *kaizen* by the Japanese): a never-ending search for higher levels of performance of the organization.
   d. *Benchmarking*: the continuous process of measuring products, services, or activities against the best levels of performance that can be found inside or outside the organization.
3. *See Practice Test Question IV.*

D. Management control systems encompass planning and control, two distinct functions that go hand-in-hand.
   1. **Planning**:
      a. Choosing goals
      b. Predicting results under alternative ways of achieving those goals
      c. Deciding how to attain the desired results
   2. **Control**:
      a. Implementing planning decisions
      b. Using feedback to evaluate performance of personnel and operations
   3. **Feedback** involves managers examining past performance and systematically exploring alternative ways to improve future performance.
   4. Accounting tools for planning and control:
      a. **Budget**: a quantitative expression of a plan of action and an aid to the coordination and implementation of the plan.
      b. **Performance report**: a comparison of actual results with budgeted amounts (see Exhibit 1-5).
      c. **Variance**: the difference between an actual result and a budgeted amount.
      d. **Management by exception**: the practice of concentrating on areas that deserve attention and placing less attention on areas operating as expected.

   > **Carefully study the comprehensive diagram in Exhibit 1-4. Note the feedback loop from control back to planning.**

   5. In no case should control mean that managers cling to a plan when changing circumstances indicate the likelihood that another plan would offer better results.
   6. Unless otherwise stated, the textbook uses control in its broadest sense to denote the entire management process of both planning and control.
   7. Management control is primarily a *human activity* to help individuals do their jobs better.

E. The **cost-benefit approach** is a conceptual way to choose among alternative accounting systems.
   1. As an example of applying this approach, think of budgeting systems as economic goods.
   2. Compare the expected costs of a new budgeting system with its expected benefits.
      a. Expected costs of this system include personnel and computer time as well as user education.
      b. Expected benefits of this system, such as compelling managers to plan ahead more formally, are the collective set of decisions that will better attain organization goals.
      c. Measurement of these costs and benefits is seldom easy.
   3. Choose the system with the largest excess of benefits over costs.

   > **No one particular system is necessarily the best for all organizations. Why? Because the collective personalities and cultures differ among organizations.**

F. Management accountants typically are found in all the areas labeled "staff" in Exhibit 1-6.
  1. Line management and staff management designations are best thought of as polar extremes.
    a. *Line management* is directly responsible for attaining the goals of the organization.
    b. *Staff management* provides advice and assistance to line management.
  2. As organizations use cross-functional teams for attaining their goals, the traditional distinction between line and staff management becomes less clear-cut.
  3. The *chief financial officer (CFO)*, a staff function, has responsibility for overseeing the financial operations of the organization: controllership, treasury, taxes, and internal audit.
  4. The **controller** is primarily responsible for *both* management accounting and financial accounting.
  5. The *treasurer* is primarily responsible for obtaining investment capital and managing cash.
  6. *Internal auditing*: the function responsible for the integrity of financial records of the organization and, in some cases, also responsible for promoting operating effectiveness and efficiency.
  7. *See Practice Test Question V.*

G. The controller performs two roles simultaneously.
  1. *Watchdog role*:
    a. **Scorekeeping function** accumulates and reports operating data to all levels of management.
    b. Examples: general accounting such as payroll and billing, maintenance of cost records.
  2. *Helper role*:
    a. **Attention-directing and problem-solving functions** support the routine and nonroutine decisions of managers.
    b. Examples: interpreting performance reports, designing budgeting systems.
  3. *See Practice Test Question VI.*
  4. At the corporate headquarters' staff level, the controller reports directly to the CFO.
  5. At the division level, the controller reports in a manner that emphasizes either the helper role or watchdog role.

> **Exhibit 1-7 is an actual organization chart highlighting the CFO and corporate controller. Note the controller's primary (hard-line) reporting relationship and secondary (dotted-line) reporting relationship.**

H. Accountants consistently rank high in public opinion surveys on ethical conduct.
  1. Both *Certified Management Accountants (CMAs)* and *Certified Public Accountants (CPAs)* have codes of professional ethics to which they must adhere.
  2. Exhibit 1-8 describes the **four standards of ethical conduct for management accountants**:

a. Competence
b. Confidentiality
c. Integrity
d. Objectivity
3. Many companies and government agencies have their own codes of ethical conduct.

PRACTICE TEST QUESTIONS AND PROBLEMS

This section is designed to help you find out how well you have mastered the material in the textbook. Try to answer all of these questions and problems without using your textbook. Follow the guidelines in "To the Student" (p. viii). After checking your answers with the solutions that immediately follow the practice test, you can determine if any sections of the textbook chapter need to be restudied.

I. Complete each of the following statements.

1. The accounting system provides information to its _____ and _____ customers.
2. The actions of managers to satisfy customers while continuously reducing and controlling costs is called _____.
3. The value chain is the sequence of _____ _____ in which utility (usefulness) is added to the products or services of an organization.
4. Of the newly evolving management themes, _____ is the top priority of organizations.
5. The continuous process of measuring products, services, or activities against the best levels of performance that can be found inside or outside the organization is called _____.
6. The comparison of actual results with budgeted amounts is called a(an) _____ _____ report.
7. The differences between actual results and budgeted amounts are called _____.
8. The management practice of concentrating on areas that deserve attention and placing less attention on areas that are operating as expected is called _____ _____.
9. The _____ approach is a conceptual way to choose among alternative accounting systems.
10. In the helper role, the controller performs the _____ and _____ functions.
11. CMA stands for _____ _____.

12. The four standards of ethical conduct for management accountants are _____ _____.

II. Indicate whether each of the following statements is true or false by putting T or F in the space provided.

____ 1. Management accounting reports information to assist internal customers in fulfilling the goals of an organization.
____ 2. A central theme of management accounting is "different costs for different purposes."
____ 3. Management accounting is constrained by generally accepted accounting principles.
____ 4. Cost accounting is a part of management accounting plus a part of financial accounting.
____ 5. Managers should proceed sequentially through the value chain of business functions.
____ 6. Control is defined as the process of setting maximum limits on expenditures.
____ 7. Feedback is an integral part of a management control system.
____ 8. In using the cost-benefit approach for redesigning a budgeting system, the benefits are the collective set of decisions that will better attain organization goals.
____ 9. Staff management is directly responsible for attaining the goals of the organization.

___ 10. The treasurer is regarded as the chief management accountant.

___ 11. Maintaining the general accounting records of an organization is part of the controller's helper role.

___ 12. The attention-directing function is included in the controller's helper role.

___ 13. If the division controller reports to the division president in a primary (hard-line) mode and to the corporate headquarters' controller in a secondary (dotted-line) mode, these relationships emphasize the watchdog role of the division controller.

III. Select the best answer for each of the following multiple-choice questions and put the identifying letter in the space provided.

___ 1. One of the newly evolving management themes is called key success factors. Which of the following is not a key success factor?
   a. time
   b. total value-chain analysis
   c. cost
   d. quality

___ 2. The control function includes:
   a. choosing goals.
   b. implementing planning decisions.
   c. deciding how to attain the desired results.
   d. preparing budgets.

___ 3. The functions of the controller include:
   a. managing cash.
   b. overseeing the financial operations of an organization.
   c. financial accounting.
   d. obtaining investment capital.

___ 4. Maintaining records on traffic tickets issued by the city of Atlanta is a:
   a. scorekeeping function.
   b. attention-directing function.
   c. problem-solving function.
   d. benchmarking function.

___ 5. The code of ethical conduct for management accountants includes standards on:
   a. competence and responsibility.
   b. integrity and professionalism.
   c. objectivity and responsibility.
   d. competence and confidentiality.

IV. Distinguish between the value chain of business functions and the extended value chain.

V. Explain why the traditional distinction between line and staff management is less clear-cut today than it was a decade ago.

VI. For each of the following activities within an organization, identify the main function that is being performed.

   SK: scorekeeping
   AD: attention directing
   PS: problem solving

___ 1. Preparing a monthly performance report of fuel consumption by buildings for a large university

___ 2. Recording the costs of a sewer project on the books of the construction company

___ 3. Analyzing the costs and benefits to a school district of using school buses offered for sale by three competing manufacturers

CHAPTER 1 SOLUTIONS TO PRACTICE TEST

I. 1 internal, external; 2 cost management; 3 business functions; 4 customer satisfaction; 5 benchmarking; 6 performance; 7 variances; 8 management by exception; 9 cost-benefit; 10 attention-directing, problem-solving; 11 Certified Management Accountant; 12 competence, confidentiality, integrity, objectivity.

II.

1 T	5 F	9 F	13 F
2 T	6 F	10 F	
3 F	7 T	11 F	
4 F	8 T	12 T	

Explanations:

1 Management accounting, also called modern cost accounting, ties management with accounting. (T)

2 Managers use information for three broad purposes (see section A(1) of the chapter outline). Each of these purposes can require different information. (T) Note that Chapter 2 will provide numerous examples of the central theme "different costs for different purposes."

3 Financial accounting is constrained by generally accepted accounting principles. In contrast, management accounting is guided by the cost-benefit approach. (F)

4 Cost accounting is management accounting in its *entirety* plus a part of financial accounting. (F)

5 The statement is false because important gains can occur when managers of the various parts of the value chain work together as a cross-functional team. (F)

6 Control has two aspects: implementing planning decisions and using feedback to evaluate performance of personnel and operations. (F)

7 Feedback is an integral part of the entire management process of both planning and control, which is called a management control system. Feedback involves managers examining past performance and systematically exploring alternative ways to improve future performance. (T)

8 One example of a benefit is compelling managers to plan ahead more formally. Measurement of such benefits is seldom easy. (T)

9 Line management is directly responsible for attaining the goals of the organization. Staff management provides advice and assistance to line management. (F)

10 The controller is regarded as the chief management accountant. Both the controller and treasurer report to the chief financial officer. (F)

11 Maintaining the general accounting records of an organization is part of the controller's watchdog role. (F)

12 The controller's helper role consists of the attention-directing and problem-solving functions, whereas the watchdog role is embraced by the scorekeeping function. (T)

13 The relationships described in the statement emphasize the helper role of the division controller. (F)

III. 1 b   3 c   5 d
         2 b   4 a

Explanations:

1 There are four key success factors: cost, quality, time, and innovation. Total value-chain analysis is regarded as a separate, newly evolving management theme. (b)

2 Choosing goals and deciding how to attain the desired results (including preparing budgets) are parts of the planning function. (b)

3 Managing cash and obtaining investment capital are functions of the treasurer. Overseeing the financial operations of an organization is the function of the chief financial officer. Functions of the controller include internal and external reporting. (c)

4 Keeping accurate and reliable records is referred to as scorekeeping. (a)

5 The code of ethical conduct for management accountants has four standards: competence, confidentiality, integrity, and objectivity. (d)

IV. The value chain of business functions consists of (1) research and development, (2) design of products, services, or processes, (3) production, (4) marketing, (5) distribution, and (6) customer service. In addition, the function of strategy and administration spans across the other six functions. The extended value chain embraces the idea that "upstream" parties such as suppliers and "downstream" parties such as customers are essential parts of total value-chain analysis. See Exhibits 1-1 and 1-3.

V. Line management is directly responsible for attaining the goals of the organization, while staff management provides advice and assistance to line management. This distinction becomes less clear-cut as organizations use cross-functional teams for attaining their goals—a practice that has gained popularity in recent years.

VI. 1 AD   2 SK   3 PS

CHAPTER 2

AN INTRODUCTION TO COST TERMS AND PURPOSES

MAIN FOCUS AND OBJECTIVES

This foundation chapter introduces the language of cost accounting. The focus is on basic terminology, especially different types of costs:

- direct costs and indirect costs
- variable costs and fixed costs
- total costs and unit costs
- capitalized costs, inventoriable costs, and period costs

Your overall objective for this chapter is to understand how these different costs are used to serve different cost accounting purposes. Eight learning objectives are stated in the textbook (p. 26).

Also give special attention to many related concepts:

- cost object
- cost assignment, cost tracing, and cost allocation
- cost driver
- relevant range
- components of manufacturing costs
- three different meanings of product costs

Carefully study the key textbook Exhibits 2-9, 2-10, and 2-12. They present comparative income statements and diagrams to help you understand important distinctions in accounting for service, merchandising and manufacturing companies.

REVIEW OF KEY TERMS AND CONCEPTS

A. **Cost** is the monetary measure of a resource used or forgone to achieve a specific objective (for example, the cost of acquiring a machine).
   1. **Cost object**: anything for which a separate measurement of costs is desired.
      a. Exhibit 2-1 illustrates eight common cost objects.
      b. Cost objects are chosen to help decision making. For example:
         (1) What selling price should be charged for a product or service?
         (2) Which customers contribute most to a company's profits?
   2. A **costing system** accumulates costs by some natural classification (such as materials, fuel, advertising) and assigns these costs to cost objects.
      a. *Cost accumulation*: the collection of cost data in some organized way via an accounting system.

b. **Cost assignment**: a general term that encompasses *both* tracing and allocating accumulated costs to the chosen cost object.
3. Exhibit 2-2 shows how cost accumulation, cost objects, and decisions are interrelated.

> *Question*: **For a given cost object, what is the distinction between direct costs and indirect costs?**
> *Answer*: **Direct costs are traced to a given cost object and indirect costs are allocated to it.**

4. **Direct costs**: costs that are related to the cost object and can be *traced* to it in a cost-effective way.
   a. Example: the company president's salary if the company as a whole is the cost object.
   b. **Cost tracing**: assignment of direct costs to the chosen cost object.
5. **Indirect costs**: costs that are related to the cost object but cannot be traced to it in a cost-effective way (that is, indirect costs are *allocated* to the cost object).
   a. Example: the company president's salary if one of the departments in the company is the cost object.
   b. **Cost allocation**: assignment of indirect costs to the chosen cost object.
6. Managers have more confidence in the accuracy of direct costs than indirect costs, so they prefer direct costs for decision making.
7. What determines if costs can be traced to the cost object in a *cost-effective* way? It's a matter of judgment.

B. *Cost management* occurs when managers take actions to reduce costs.
   1. Two key areas of cost reduction:
      a. Doing only *value-added activities*: those activities that customers perceive as increasing the utility (usefulness) of the products or services they purchase.
      b. Efficiently managing the use of the cost drivers in value-added activities.
   2. **Cost driver**: any factor that affects costs.
      a. A change in the level of the cost driver will cause a change in the total costs of a related cost object.
      b. Examples of cost drivers: number of units produced, number of products sold, sales dollars, number of service calls, and many others listed in Exhibit 2-3.

C. Two basic types of cost behavior patterns are variable costs and fixed costs.
   1. Suppose a manufacturing company increases the number of units produced (the cost driver).
      a. *Question*: How are variable costs and fixed costs affected in this situation?
      Answer:

Type of Costs	Total Costs	Unit Costs
Variable	Increase	No change
Fixed	No change	Decrease

b. The logic that supports these answers is tied directly to the definitions of these important types of costs.

 2. **Variable costs** change *in total* in proportion to changes in the level of a cost driver.
   a. Variable costs do not vary on a *per unit basis* as the level of a cost driver changes.
   b. Examples: direct materials, sales commissions.
   c. Exhibit 2-4 shows graphs of two variable costs.

 3. **Fixed costs** do not change *in total* in response to changes in the level of a cost driver.
   a. Fixed costs vary inversely on a *per unit basis* as the level of a cost driver changes.
   b. Examples: executive salaries, insurance.

 4. **Relevant range**: the range of the cost driver within which variable costs and fixed costs behave according to their respective definitions. Exhibit 2-5 illustrates the relevant range.

 5. Underlying assumptions regarding cost behavior:
   a. The cost object must be specified.
   b. The time span must be specified (such as months or years).
   c. Both variable costs and fixed costs when graphed on a *total basis* (as distinguished from a *per unit basis*) are linear (straight lines).
   d. Only one cost driver is used for a given cost.
   e. The relevant range of fluctuations in the cost driver must be specified.

 6. The two major cost classifications discussed above—direct-indirect and variable-fixed—can be considered simultaneously. Carefully study the examples of the four possible combinations of these cost classifications in Exhibit 2-6.

D. Consider this cost matrix:

Type of Costs	Total Costs	Unit Costs
Variable	I	II
Fixed	III	IV

 1. *Question*: When making predictions, should variable costs be thought of as I or II? *Question*: When making predictions, should fixed costs be thought of as III or IV? *Answers*: II and III. Why? Because as the level of a cost driver changes within the relevant range, no change is expected in variable costs per unit or in total fixed costs.
 2. **Caution**: For decision purposes, unit costs are often useful, but they must be interpreted with care if they include a *fixed cost component*.
 3. See the textbook example of hiring a musical group (p. 33).
 4. *See Practice Test Questions III (items 3 and 4) and Problems V and VI.*

E. Key differences among service, merchandising, and manufacturing companies center on the nature of outputs and inventories.
 1. Exhibit 2-8 summarizes those differences.
 2. Because of the differences, income statements for the companies are not alike.

3. See the income statement for a **service company** in Exhibit 2-9 (Panel A). Note these characteristics:
    a. Revenues − Operating costs = Operating income
    b. There is no line item for cost of goods sold. Why? Because there is no inventory.
    c. Labor costs usually are the largest cost category.
4. See the income statement for a **merchandising company** in Exhibit 2-9 (Panel B). Note these characteristics:
    a. Sales − Cost of goods sold = Gross margin
       Gross margin − Operating costs = Operating income
    b. There is *one* type of inventory: merchandise inventory.
    c. Cost of goods sold = Beginning merchandise inventory + Purchases of merchandise − Ending merchandise inventory
    d. Gross margin and gross profit are synonyms.
5. See the income statement for a **manufacturing company** in key **Exhibit 2-10**. Note these characteristics:
    a. There are *three* types of inventories: direct materials, work in process, and finished goods.
    b. Only the cost of goods sold section differs from the income statement of a merchandising company.
    c. Cost of goods sold = Beginning finished goods + Cost of goods manufactured − Ending finished goods
    d. **Cost of goods manufactured**, the counterpart of "purchases" for merchandise companies, refers to the goods brought to completion, whether they were started before or during the current accounting period.
    e. Exhibit 2-10 (Panel B) shows how direct materials and work in process inventories are used in the computation of cost of goods manufactured.

    > **See Practice Test Questions III (items 6 and 8 - 11) and Problem VIII.**

F. Three cost concepts—capitalized costs, inventoriable costs, and period costs—are important in preparing the financial statements of all types of companies.
    1. **Capitalized costs**: costs that are recorded as an asset when incurred and then later become an expense.
    2. **Inventoriable costs**: a specific type of capitalized costs associated with purchase of goods for resale by merchandising companies or associated with purchase of direct materials and their conversion into finished goods by manufacturing companies.
    3. **Period costs**: the sum of the portion of capitalized costs expensed this period and costs expensed as incurred.
    4. Exhibit 2-11 clarifies the distinction among these three cost concepts in service, merchandising, and manufacturing companies.
    5. *See Practice Test Question IV.*
    6. Two basic ways of accounting for inventories:
        a. *Perpetual inventory*: continuous record of inventory transactions, which is now more cost-effective in both merchandising and manufacturing companies because of advances in information technology.

b. *Periodic inventory*: actual physical counts of inventory.
c. Perpetual and periodic inventories can result in the same figure for cost of goods sold, as shown in Exhibit 2-13.

> **Carefully study Exhibit 2-12. In particular, notice the similarities and differences between merchandising and manufacturing companies.**

G. A widely used *three-part classification* of manufacturing costs is direct materials, direct manufacturing labor, and manufacturing overhead.
1. **Direct materials costs**: the acquisition costs of all materials that eventually become part of the manufactured products and that can be traced to the products in a cost-effective way.
2. **Direct manufacturing labor costs**: the compensation of all manufacturing workers that is considered to be part of the manufactured products and that can be traced to the products in a cost-effective way.
3. **Manufacturing overhead costs** (also called *factory overhead costs* or *indirect manufacturing costs*): all manufacturing costs that are not direct costs of manufactured products.
4. Examples:
   a. Direct materials costs — wood, cloth, and hardware for making furniture.
   b. Direct manufacturing labor costs — compensation of machine operators and assembly workers.
   c. Manufacturing overhead costs — power, indirect materials, indirect manufacturing labor, plant depreciation, plant rent.
5. Some manufacturing companies do not use the three-part classification. For example, a *two-part classification* might be used if direct manufacturing labor becomes a small proportion of total manufacturing costs (which can be caused by increased automation).
6. **Prime costs**: all direct manufacturing costs.
   a. In the three-part classification, prime costs are direct materials costs and direct manufacturing labor costs.
   b. In the two-part classification, prime costs are only direct materials costs.
   c. Additional direct cost categories might be used, such as metering power costs to machines dedicated totally to particular products.
7. **Conversion costs**: all manufacturing costs other than direct materials costs. These costs are for *converting* direct materials into finished goods.
8. *See Practice Test Problems VII and IX.*
9. Payroll fringe benefit costs of direct manufacturing workers are classified by some companies as manufacturing overhead, while others classify them as direct manufacturing labor.
   a. The latter approach is superior. Why? Because these payroll fringe benefit costs are a fundamental part of acquiring the labor services.
   b. These costs often exceed 25% of the payroll in companies around the world.
   c. To prevent disputes, contracts and laws should be as specific as feasible regarding accounting methods and cost classifications for items such as payroll fringe benefits. See the textbook example (p. 45).

H. An important theme of the textbook is "**different costs for different purposes**."

> *Question*: **What are three different purposes for which costs are assigned to products?**
> *Answer*: **(1) product pricing and product emphasis decisions**
> **(2) contracting with government agencies**
> **(3) external financial reporting**
> **See key Exhibit 2-14 for a useful diagram of different product costs for different purposes.**

1. Distinguish between product costs and inventoriable costs.
    a. **Product costs**: the sum of the costs assigned to a product for a particular purpose.
    b. Inventoriable costs are *a specific type of product cost* used for financial reporting under generally accepted accounting principles.
2. A convenient summary of the major classifications of costs is given in the textbook (pp. 46-47).

PRACTICE TEST QUESTIONS AND PROBLEMS

I. Complete each of the following statements.

1. Anything for which a separate measurement of costs is desired is called a _____ _____.

2. For a given cost object, direct costs are _____ to it and indirect costs are _____ to it.

3. Any factor that affects costs is called a ____ _____.

4. The range of the cost driver in which variable costs and fixed costs behave according to their respective definitions is called the ____ _____.

5. For decision purposes, unit costs are often useful, but they must be interpreted with care if they include a _____ cost component.

6. Sales minus cost of goods sold is equal to _____.

7. The three types of inventories in a manufacturing company are _____ _____.

8. All costs of a product that can be regarded as assets under generally accepted accounting principles are called _____ _____.

9. Two basic ways of accounting for inventories are _____ and _____.

10. All manufacturing costs other than direct materials costs are called _____ _____.

11. Different costs are allocated to products for different purposes. Three of the purposes are: _____ _____ _____ _____.

II. Indicate whether each of the following statements is true or false by putting T or F in the space provided.

___ 1. A cost object is a target level of costs to be achieved.

___ 2. The main purpose for using a cost object is to compute inventory costs.

___ 3. Cost accumulation is a general term that encompasses both tracing and allocating costs to a cost object.

___ 4. A given cost item can be both a direct cost and an indirect cost.

___ 5. Managers prefer to use direct costs for decision making.

___ 6. Examples of cost drivers are sales dollars, number of products sold, and number of units produced.

___ 7. When graphed on a per unit basis, both variable costs and fixed costs are linear within the relevant range.

___ 8. In general, if unit costs are multiplied by the number of units at a particular level of output, the result would be an amount of total costs that are also applicable to a different level of output.

___ 9. In the income statement for a service company, there is no line item for cost of goods sold.

___ 10. In the income statement for a manufacturing company, cost of goods manufactured refers to the goods brought to completion, whether they were started before or during the current accounting period.

___ 11. The concept of inventoriable costs is applicable to both manufacturing companies and merchandising companies.

___ 12. Manufacturing costs incurred minus the decrease in work in process inventory is equal to cost of goods manufactured.

___ 13. Period costs are the portion of capitalized costs expensed this period.

___ 14. Manufacturing overhead costs and indirect manufacturing costs are synonyms.

___ 15. If direct manufacturing labor becomes a small proportion of total manufacturing costs, the company would not necessarily use the traditional three-part classification of manufacturing costs.

___ 16. An argument in favor of including payroll fringe benefit costs of direct manufacturing workers as part of direct manufacturing labor is that these benefits are a fundamental part of acquiring the labor services.

III. Select the best answer for each of the following multiple-choice questions and put the identifying letter in the space provided.

___ 1. Within the relevant range:
   a. total variable costs would remain the same.
   b. per unit fixed costs would change.
   c. per unit total costs would remain the same.
   d. per unit variable costs would change.

___ 2. The classification of the company president's salary, where the cost object is the company itself, would be:
   a. variable cost and direct cost.
   b. variable cost and indirect cost.
   c. fixed cost and direct cost.
   d. fixed cost and indirect cost.

___ 3. Total fixed costs are $64,000 when 8,000 units are produced. When 10,000 units are produced, fixed costs would be:
   a. $80,000 in total.
   b. $8 per unit.
   c. $48,000 in total.
   d. $6.40 per unit.

___ 4. Total variable costs are $120,000 when 15,000 units are produced. When 12,000 units are produced, variable costs would be:
   a. $10 per unit.
   b. $120,000 in total.
   c. $8 per unit.
   d. none of the above.

___ 5. In general, the costs that could usually be most reliably predicted are:
   a. fixed costs per unit.
   b. total costs per unit.
   c. total variable costs.
   d. variable costs per unit.

___ 6. (CPA adapted) Anthony Company has projected its cost of goods sold at $4,000,000, including fixed costs of $800,000. The variable portion of cost of goods sold is expected to be 75% of sales. Projected sales would be:
   a. $4,266,667.
   b. $4,800,000.
   c. $5,333,333.
   d. $6,400,000.

____ 7. (CPA adapted) The monthly cost of renting a manufacturing plant is:
   a. a prime cost and an inventoriable cost.
   b. a prime cost and a period cost.
   c. a conversion cost and an inventoriable cost.
   d. a conversion cost and a period cost.

____ 8. (CPA) The following data pertains to Lam Co.'s manufacturing operations for April 19_5:

Inventories	Beginning	Ending
Direct materials	$18,000	$15,000
Work in process	9,000	6,000
Finished goods	27,000	36,000

Additional cost information for April 19_5:

Direct materials purchased	$42,000
Direct manufacturing labor	30,000
Direct manufacturing labor rate per hour	7.50
Manufacturing overhead rate per direct manufacturing labor-hour	10.00

Lam's cost of goods manufactured for April 19_5 would be:
   a. $115,000.
   b. $118,000.
   c. $109,000.
   d. $112,000.

____ 9. (CPA adapted) The following information was taken from Cody Co.'s accounting records for the year ended December 31, 19_4:

Decrease in direct materials inventory	$ 15,000
Increase in finished goods inventory	35,000
Direct materials purchased	430,000
Direct manufacturing labor	200,000
Manufacturing overhead	300,000

There was no work in process inventory at the beginning or end of the year. Cody's 19_4 cost of goods sold would be:
   a. $895,000.
   b. $910,000.
   c. $950,000.
   d. $955,000.

____ 10. (CPA) For the year 19_5, the gross margin of Dumas Company was $96,000; the cost of goods manufactured was $340,000; the beginning inventories of work in process and finished goods were $28,000 and $45,000, respectively; and the ending inventories of work in process and finished goods were $38,000 and $52,000, respectively. The sales of Dumas Company for 19_5 were:
   a. $419,000.
   b. $429,000.
   c. $434,000.
   d. $436,000.

____ 11. (CPA) If the work in process inventory has increased during the period:
   a. cost of goods sold will be greater than cost of goods manufactured.
   b. cost of goods manufactured will be greater than cost of goods sold.
   c. manufacturing costs incurred during the period will be greater than cost of goods manufactured.
   d. manufacturing costs incurred during the period will be less than cost of goods manufactured.

____ 12. Using the traditional three-part classification of manufacturing costs, prime costs and conversion costs have the common component of:
   a. direct materials costs.
   b. direct manufacturing labor costs.
   c. variable manufacturing overhead costs.
   d. fixed manufacturing overhead costs.

IV. Classify each of the following costs of Menlo Company in two ways: (a) as variable costs (V) or fixed costs (F); (b) as inventoriable costs (I) or period costs (P):

	(a) V or F	(b) I or P
0. Example: Direct manufacturing labor	V	I
1. Salary of company controller	___	___
2. Fire insurance on direct materials inventory	___	___
3. Property taxes on finished goods held for sale	___	___
4. Direct materials used	___	___
5. Plant rent	___	___
6. Sales commissions	___	___
7. Lubricants for plant machines	___	___
8. Straight-line depreciation on plant equipment	___	___
9. Straight-line depreciation on trucks used for sales deliveries	___	___
10. Salary of plant manager	___	___

V. (CMA adapted) Backus Company estimated its unit costs of producing and selling 12,000 units per month as follows:

Direct materials used	$32
Direct manufacturing labor	20
Variable manufacturing overhead	15
Fixed manufacturing overhead	6
Variable nonmanufacturing costs	3
Fixed nonmanufacturing costs	4
Full product costs	$80

The cost driver for manufacturing costs is units produced, and the cost driver for nonmanufacturing costs is units sold.

Compute:
1. Fixed manufacturing overhead per unit for a monthly production level of 10,000 units.
2. Total manufacturing and nonmanufacturing costs during a month when 9,000 units are produced and 8,000 units are sold.

Check figures: (1) $7.20, (2) $747,000

VI. Yardley Corp. incurred the following manufacturing costs in 19_3:

Variable manufacturing costs:		
Direct materials	$	600,000
Direct manufacturing labor		500,000
Manufacturing overhead		40,000
Fixed manufacturing overhead		600,000
Total manufacturing costs		$1,740,000

In 19_3, the costs per unit at production levels of 40,000 units and 60,000 units were $37.80 and $32.80, respectively. How many units were produced in 19_3?

Check figure: 50,000

VII. The income statement of Kingsbury Corporation included these items:

Marketing and distribution costs	$ 80,000
Direct manufacturing labor costs	105,000
Administrative costs	45,000
Direct materials used	85,000
Fixed manufacturing overhead costs	55,000
Variable manufacturing overhead costs	25,000
Interest expense	10,000
Income tax expense	30,000

Compute:
1. Prime costs
2. Conversion costs
3. Inventoriable costs
4. Period costs

Check figures: (1) $190,000 (2) $185,000 (3) $270,000, (4) $165,000

VIII. (CPA) The following information is taken from the records of McMechen & Sons for 19_3:

	Inventories	
	Ending	Beginning
Finished goods	$95,000	$110,000
Work in process	80,000	70,000
Direct materials	95,000	90,000

<u>Costs Incurred During the Period</u>

Total manufacturing costs	$584,000
Manufacturing overhead	167,000
Direct materials used	193,000

Compute:
1. Direct materials purchased
2. Direct manufacturing labor costs
3. Cost of goods sold

Check figures: (1) $198,000 (2) $224,000
(3) $589,000

IX. Pyramid Company's operating data for last year includes $180,000 of conversion costs and $132,000 of prime costs. If manufacturing overhead costs are 50% larger than direct materials costs, compute each of the following:

1. Direct materials costs
2. Direct manufacturing labor costs
3. Manufacturing overhead costs

Check figures: (1) $96,000 (2) $36,000
(3) $144,000

CHAPTER 2 SOLUTIONS TO PRACTICE TEST

I. 1 cost object; 2 traced, allocated; 3 cost driver; 4 relevant range; 5 fixed; 6 gross margin; 7 direct materials, work in process, finished goods; 8 inventoriable costs; 9 perpetual, periodic; 10 conversion costs; 11 product pricing and product emphasis decisions, contracting with government agencies, financial reporting under generally accepted accounting principles.

II.

1 F	5 T	9 T	13 F
2 F	6 T	10 T	14 T
3 F	7 F	11 T	15 T
4 T	8 F	12 F	16 T

Explanations:

1 A cost object is anything for which a separate measurement of costs is desired. Some examples of cost objects are a product, customer, project, and department. (F)

2 Inventory is an example of a cost object; however, the main purpose for choosing cost objects is to help decision making. (F)

3 Cost assignment is a general term that encompasses both tracing and allocating costs to a chosen cost object. Cost accumulation is the collection of cost data in some organized way through an accounting system. (F)

4 Whether a given cost item is a direct cost or an indirect cost depends on the cost object. Consider a store manager's salary. It is a direct cost if the store itself is the cost object. It is an indirect cost if one of the store's product lines is the cost object. (T)

5 Managers have more confidence in the accuracy of direct costs than indirect costs, so they prefer direct costs for decision making. (T)

6 Some other examples of cost drivers are number of parts per product, number of production setups, number of sales personnel, and number of customers. (T)

7 When graphed on a *total basis*, both variable costs and fixed costs are linear (straight lines) within the relevant range. When graphed on a *per unit basis*, only variable costs are linear. Per unit fixed costs decrease as the cost driver increases, and vice versa. (F)

8 The computation described is appropriate for total fixed costs. However, variable costs per unit should be multiplied by the second (different) level of output to obtain the appropriate amount of total variable costs at that output. (F)

9 Service companies do not hold inventory for resale, which means there is no line item in their income statement for cost of goods sold. (T)

10 To compute cost of goods manufactured, the goods not yet brought to completion (ending work in process inventory) is subtracted from total manufacturing costs incurred during the period. Therefore, cost of goods manufactured refers to completed goods, whether they were started before or during the current period. (T)

11 Capitalized costs are costs that are recorded as an asset when incurred and then later become an expense. Inventoriable costs are a specific type of capitalized costs associated with purchase of goods for resale by merchandising companies or associated with purchase of direct materials and their conversion into finished goods by manufacturing companies. (T)

12 When work in process inventory decreases (that is, beginning inventory exceeds ending inventory), cost of goods manufactured exceeds manufacturing costs incurred during the period. Therefore, cost of goods manufactured is equal to manufacturing costs incurred during the period *plus* the decrease in work in process inventory. (F) The opposite case, where work in process inventory increased during the period, is in Exhibit 2-10 (Panel B).

13 Period costs are equal to the portion of capitalized costs expensed this period plus costs expensed as incurred. Exhibit 2-11 describes period costs in service, merchandising, and manufacturing companies. (F)

14 Manufacturing overhead costs consist of all manufacturing costs that are not direct manufacturing costs (that is, all indirect manufacturing costs). Manufacturing overhead also is called factory overhead. (T)

15 Some companies are using the two-part classification when direct manufacturing labor becomes a small proportion of total manufacturing costs. (T)

16 Despite the validity of this argument, some companies include payroll fringe benefit costs of direct manufacturing workers as part of manufacturing overhead. (T)

III.

1 b	4 c	7 c	10 b
2 c	5 d	8 b	11 c
3 d	6 a	9 b	12 b

Explanations:

1 On a *total basis* within the relevant range, variable costs change in proportion to changes in the level of a cost driver, and fixed costs do not change as the level of a cost driver changes. On a *per unit basis* within the relevant range, variable costs do not change as the level of a cost driver changes, and fixed costs change in the opposite direction to changes in the level of a cost driver. (b)

2 The company president's salary is a fixed cost because it would not change within the relevant range and, because the cost object is the company as a whole, this salary would be a direct cost. If the cost object were an individual department such as the customer service department, the salary would be an indirect cost. (c)

3 $64,000 \div 10,000 = $6.40 per unit (d)

4 $120,000 \div 15,000 = $8 per unit, which is also the variable costs per unit when 12,000 units are produced. (c)

5 Variable costs *per unit* and *total* fixed costs can usually be most reliably predicted because a forecast of the level of a cost driver is not required. (d)

6 The variable portion of projected cost of goods sold is $4,000,000 − $800,000 = $3,200,000. Since this amount is 75% of sales, projected sales will be $3,200,000 ÷ .75 = $4,266,667. (a)

7 Plant rent is part of manufacturing overhead costs. Therefore, it is an inventoriable cost and a conversion cost. (c)

8

Direct material used ($18,000 + $42,000 − $15,000)	$ 45,000
Direct manufacturing labor	30,000
Manufacturing overhead ($30,000 ÷ $7.50)($10)	40,000
Manufacturing costs incurred during the period	115,000
Add beginning work in process inventory	9,000
Total manufacturing costs to account for	124,000
Deduct ending work in process inventory	6,000
Cost of goods manufactured	$118,000 (b)

9 The decrease in direct materials inventory should be added to direct materials purchased, and the increase in finished goods inventory should be subtracted from cost of goods manufactured: ($430,000 + $15,000) + $200,000 + $300,000 = $945,000; $945,000 − $35,000 = $910,000 (b)

10 | | |
|---|---|
| Beginning finished goods | $ 45,000 |
| Cost of goods manufactured | 340,000 |
| Cost of goods available for sale | 385,000 |
| Ending finished goods | 52,000 |
| Cost of goods sold | $333,000 |

Sales	$ X
Cost of goods sold	333,000
Gross margin	$ 96,000

X − $333,000 = $96,000; X = $429,000 (b)

Note that the work in process inventories are not explicitly included in these computations because the cost of goods manufactured of $340,000 reflects the changes in work in process inventories.

11 *An effective way to answer this type of question is to use assumed figures that satisfy the situation described.* Accordingly, suppose that work in process inventory increased from $100,000 at the beginning of the period to $150,000 at the end of the period, and that manufacturing costs incurred during the period were $800,000. The following schedule shows that manufacturing costs will be greater than cost of goods manufactured:

Manufacturing costs incurred during the period	$800,000
Beginning work in process	100,000
Manufacturing costs to account for	900,000
Ending work in process	150,000
Cost of goods manufactured	$750,000 (c)

12 Prime costs = Direct materials costs + Direct manufacturing labor costs
Conversion costs = Direct manufacturing labor costs + Manufacturing overhead costs (b)

IV. Menlo Company

1 FP	3 FP	5 FI	7 VI	9 FP
2 FI	4 VI	6 VP	8 FI	10 FI

V. Backus Company

1. 12,000 × $6 = $72,000; $72,000 ÷ 10,000 = $7.20
2. Variable manufacturing costs,

9,000 × ($32 + $20 + $15)	$603,000
Fixed manufacturing costs,	
12,000 × $6	72,000
Variable nonmanufacturing costs,	
8,000 × $3	24,000
Fixed nonmanufacturing costs,	
12,000 × $4	48,000
Total value-chain costs	$747,000

VI. Yardley Corp.

Variable costs per unit:
$37.80 − ($600,000 ÷ 40,000) = $22.80
or
$32.80 − ($600,000 ÷ 60,000) = $22.80
Units produced = ($600,000 + $500,000 + $40,000) ÷ $22.80 = $1,140,000 ÷ $22.80 = 50,000 units

VII. Kingsbury Corporation

1. $105,000 + $85,000 = $190,000
2. $105,000 + $55,000 + $25,000 = $185,000
3. $105,000 + $85,000 + $55,000 + $25,000 = $270,000
4. $80,000 + $45,000 + $10,000 + $30,000 = $165,000

VIII. McMechen & Sons

1. Direct materials costs:

Beginning inventory	$ 90,000
Add purchases	P
Available for use	?
Deduct ending inventory	95,000
Used	$193,000

$90,000 + P − $95,000 = $193,000; P = $198,000

2.

Direct materials used	$193,000
Direct manufacturing labor costs	D
Manufacturing overhead costs	167,000
Manufacturing costs incurred during the period	$584,000

$193,000 + D + $167,000 = $584,000; D = $224,000

3. Two steps are used to obtain the answer. First, compute cost of goods manufactured:

Manufacturing costs incurred during the period	$584,000
Beginning work in process	70,000
Manufacturing costs to account for	654,000
Ending work in process	80,000
Cost of goods manufactured	$574,000

Second, compute cost of goods sold:

Beginning finished goods	$110,000
Cost of goods manufactured	574,000
Cost of goods available for sale	684,000
Ending finished goods	95,000
Cost of goods sold	$589,000

IX. Pyramid Company

Let   DM = Direct materials costs
                DL   = Direct manufacturing labor costs
                MO = Manufacturing overhead costs

Then: Conversion costs − Prime costs = \$180,000 − \$132,000
            (DL + MO) − (DL + DM) = \$48,000
            MO − DM = \$48,000

And: MO = 1.50(DM)

Therefore: 1.50(DM) − DM = \$48,000
            .50(DM) = \$48,000
            DM = \$96,000 (1)
            DL = Prime costs − DM = \$132,000 − \$96,000 = \$36,000 (2)
            MO = 1.50(DM) = 1.50(\$96,000) = \$144,000 (3)

Proof: Prime costs = \$96,000 + \$36,000 = \$132,000
            Conversion costs = \$36,000 + \$144,000 = \$180,000

COST-VOLUME-PROFIT RELATIONSHIPS

MAIN FOCUS AND OBJECTIVES

Cost-volume-profit (CVP) analysis provides a sweeping overview of the planning process. The term CVP analysis is widely used to represent a special case for predicting total revenues and total costs where units of output are the only revenue and cost driver. The overriding concept in this chapter is contribution margin. The dollar amount of contribution margin is highlighted in the contribution income statement. This income statement builds on our knowledge of variable costs and fixed costs from Chapter 2. Your overall objective for this chapter is to develop a confident grasp of CVP computations and applications. Eight learning objectives are stated in the textbook (p. 60).
Give special attention to:

- the three methods for determining the breakeven point
- the impact of target income (both before tax and after tax) on CVP analysis
- the use of sensitivity analysis to cope with uncertainty
- the effect of sales mix on CVP analysis
- the distinction between contribution margin and gross margin

Keep in mind that the intelligent use of CVP analysis depends on knowledge of many underlying assumptions that limit precision and reliability. The chapter Appendix includes an illustration of the additional insights gained in CVP analysis when the expected value decision criterion is used to deal with uncertainty.

REVIEW OF KEY TERMS AND CONCEPTS

A. Costs and revenues are *driven by* (behave in response to) a variety of influences.
  1. **Cost driver**: any factor that affects costs (that is, a change in the cost driver will cause a change in the total costs of a related cost object).
  2. **Revenue driver**: any factor (such as units sold, marketing outlays, product quality) that affects revenues.
  3. Distinguish between two cases for predicting total revenues and total costs:
    a. *General case*: analyzes how combinations of *several* revenue drivers and *several* cost drivers affect total revenues and total costs, respectively.
    b. *Special case*: assumes that *units of output* (such as units manufactured or sold, passenger miles for an airline, patient days for a hospital) is the only revenue and cost driver.
  4. The term **cost-volume-profit (CVP) analysis** is widely used to represent the special case.

5. The simplifying assumptions of CVP are preferable provided that management decisions would not be significantly improved by use of the more complicated and costly general case. (The general case is discussed in Chapter 10.)
6. The special case is valid only for *short-run* decisions because total fixed costs are fixed only in the short run.

B. The **breakeven point** is the quantity of output where total revenues and total costs are equal. At this point there is neither a profit nor a loss.
1. The breakeven point is often of interest in CVP analysis, but the analysis considers a broader question: What is the impact on income of various decisions affecting revenues and costs?

> **Pinpoint the meanings of these key terms:**
> - **Revenues and sales are synonyms.**
> - **Costs and expenses are synonyms.**
> - **Operating income = Revenues − (Variable costs + Fixed costs)**
> - **Net income = Operating income − Income taxes**

2. Three methods for determining the breakeven point—the equation method, the contribution margin method, and the graph method—are merely restatements of each other.
3. The **equation method** is based on the relationships among the following elements in an income statement:
    a. Revenues   xxx
       Deduct costs:
          Variable costs   xxx
          Fixed costs   xxx
          Total costs   xxx
       Operating income   xxx
    b. Equation form of this income statement:
       Revenues − Variable costs − Fixed costs = Operating income
    c. Example: selling price per unit $50, variable costs per unit $20, total fixed costs $6,000 per month, breakeven units N:

$$\$50N - \$20N - \$6,000 = 0$$
$$\$30N = \$6,000$$
$$N = 200 \text{ units}$$

The intuition behind this computation is: How many units must be sold at a unit contribution margin of $30($50 − $20) to cover the monthly fixed costs of $6,000?
    d. The breakeven point in dollars in this example is 200 units × $50 = $10,000. Prove this breakeven point by filling in these blanks:

Revenues, 200 × $50 $10,000
Deduct costs:
    Variable costs, 200 × $20 $ 4000
    Fixed costs   6000
    Total costs   10,000
Operating income $ -0-

e. The income statement used in CVP analysis includes an important subtotal called contribution margin:

Revenues, 200 × $50	$10,000
Variable costs, 200 × $20	4,000
Contribution margin	6,000
Fixed costs	6,000
Operating income	$ -0-

This presentation is called a **contribution income statement**. By remembering the format of this statement, the equation in (b) above can be easily reconstructed—*no memorizing is needed*.

4. The **contribution margin method** is a restated form of the equation method:

$$\text{Breakeven point in units} = \frac{\text{Total fixed costs}}{\text{Unit contribution margin}}$$

a. **Unit contribution margin** (also called **contribution margin per unit**) is equal to selling price minus unit variable costs: $50 − $20 = $30

b. Breakeven point *in units* (denoted by N):

$$N = \frac{\$6,000}{\$50 - \$20} = \frac{\$6,000}{\$30} = 200 \text{ units}$$

c. Another computation is the breakeven point *in dollars*:

$$\text{Breakeven point in dollars} = \frac{\text{Total fixed costs}}{\text{Contribution-margin percentage}}$$

d. **Contribution-margin percentage** (also called contribution-margin ratio) is equal to unit contribution margin divided by selling price: $30 ÷ $50 = 0.60

e. Breakeven point *in dollars* (denoted by S):

$$S = \frac{\$6,000}{(\$50 - \$20) \div \$50} = \frac{\$6,000}{\$30 \div \$50} = \frac{\$6,000}{0.60} = \$10,000$$

f. A related term is *variable-cost percentage*, which is equal to 1 minus contribution-margin percentage.

5. The **graph method** (illustrated in Exhibit 3-1) is useful in visualizing CVP relationships. It is important that such graphs be drawn accurately.

6. The amount of sales in units or in dollars that must be made to attain a particular **target operating income** can be computed either by the equation method or by the contribution margin method. See the textbook examples (pp. 64-65).

7. The CVP model, with slight modification, can be applied to nonprofit situations (see the example in the textbook, p. 72).

Check your understanding of how to use the equation method and the contribution margin method:
- *See Practice Test Question III (items 1-3, 6, and 8-10)*
- *See Practice Test Problems IV, VI, and VIII*

C. Five "special case" CVP assumptions are listed in the textbook (p. 65).
   1. Two key assumptions noted here are:
      a. The behavior of total revenues and total costs is linear (straight line) in relation to output units within the **relevant range**: the range of the revenue and cost driver in which a specific relationship between revenues and costs and the driver is valid.
      b. CVP analysis either covers a *single product* or assumes that a *given sales mix* of products will remain constant, although changes occur in the number of units sold.
   2. In practice, the five assumptions are usually violated to some extent.
      a. CVP analysis should be thought of as a rough tool, "more like an ax than a scalpel."
      b. However, the analysis is a low-cost tool, so there is a cost-benefit tradeoff.
      c. The critical question is, Would more sophisticated and costly analyses yield better management decisions?
   3. As a cost planning tool, CVP analysis can highlight the risks of different cost structures.
      a. Companies can often substitute or tradeoff fixed costs for variable costs, or vice versa.
      b. Trading off fixed costs for higher unit variable costs decreases a manager's downside risk if demand is low, but decreases the potential return if demand is high. Why? Because the higher unit variable costs decrease unit contribution margin.
      c. Exhibit 3-2 illustrates this tradeoff as you move from option 1 to option 2 to option 3.

> *Question*: **How does the time span in a particular decision situation affect total costs?**
> *Answer*: **In the long-run all costs are variable. Total costs are least likely to vary significantly in a decision situation where the time span is quite short and the change in the level of output is quite small.**

D. Costs, volume, and profit are interrelated.
   1. A change in any input data in the CVP model can affect the breakeven point and operating income.
   2. Single-number "best estimates" of input data in the CVP model are subject to varying degrees of **uncertainty**: the possibility that an actual amount will deviate from an expected amount.
   3. A widely used approach to cope with uncertainty is called **sensitivity analysis** (that is, asking "**what-if**" questions):
      a. Make different predictions of selling price, unit variable costs, fixed costs, and output level in a given decision situation.
      b. Compute the effects of these changes on operating income.
      c. Such analysis can help managers focus on the most sensitive aspects of a particular plan of action *before* making cost commitments.
   4. Electronic spreadsheets help managers rapidly conduct sensitivity analysis, both computationally and graphically.

5. A tool of sensitivity analysis is *margin of safety*: the excess of budgeted revenues over breakeven revenues.
6. Further discussion of uncertainty is in the chapter Appendix.
7. A *P/V chart* (Exhibit 3-4) can help managers understand the impact on operating income ("profit") of changes in the output level ("volume").

E. **Sales mix** is the relative combination of quantities of products (or services) that constitutes total sales.
   1. The breakeven point can be computed for any given sales mix.
      a. See the textbook example of a two-product pen company (p. 69).
      b. *Also see Practice Test Question III (item 13) and Problem IX.*
   2. For any given level of sales above breakeven, the higher the proportion of units having relatively high unit contribution margins, the higher the operating income.

F. Income taxes play an important role in CVP analysis.
   1. Fundamental equation ignoring income taxes:

      Revenues − Variable costs − Fixed costs = Target operating net income

   2. Target operating income $(1 -$ Tax rate$) =$ Target net income

      $$\text{Target operating income} = \frac{\text{Target net income}}{1 - \text{Tax rate}}$$

   3. Fundamental equation incorporating income taxes:

      $$\textbf{Revenues} - \textbf{Variable costs} - \textbf{Fixed costs} = \frac{\textbf{Target net income}}{\textbf{1} - \textbf{Tax rate}}$$

   4. The breakeven point is unaffected by the presence of income taxes. Why? Because no income taxes are paid if there is no operating income.
   5. *See Practice Test Question III (item 15) and Problems V and VI.*

G. Do not confuse the terms *contribution margin* and *gross margin* in merchandising and manufacturing companies.

$$\textbf{Contribution margin} = \textbf{Revenues} - \textbf{All variable costs}$$
$$\textbf{Gross margin} = \textbf{Sales} - \textbf{Cost of goods sold}$$

   1. Cost of goods sold in merchandising companies is a variable cost.
   2. Cost of goods sold in manufacturing companies includes fixed manufacturing costs.
   3. Service companies do not have a cost of goods sold line item in their income statements because they have no inventory, so they cannot compute gross margin.
   4. *See Practice Test Question III (items 4 and 5).*

H. **(Appendix)** Decision models, which formally measure the forecasted effects of alternative actions, help managers cope with uncertainty.
   1. A decision model has five elements: (i) choice criterion, (ii) set of actions, (iii) set of events, (iv) probability distribution, and (v) set of outcomes.

a. A *choice criterion* (also called an *objective function*), which is to maximize (minimize) some form of income (cost), provides a basis for selecting the best alternative action.
b. A set of the alternative *actions* (that is, the choices available to managers).
c. A set of *events* (that is, the possible occurrences or states of nature).
   (1) A set of events should be *mutually exclusive* (that is, each event is separate from the others).
   (2) A set of events should be *collectively exhaustive* (that is, it accounts for all of the possible events).
d. A set of probabilities, called a *probability distribution*, quantifies the likelihood of each of the events and always sums to 1.00 because the events are collectively exhaustive.
e. A set of *outcomes* (also called payoffs) that measure the predicted consequences of various possible combinations of actions and events.
f. Exhibit 3-5 presents a helpful overview of the link between a decision model and performance evaluation.

2. When decisions are made under conditions of uncertainty, this means that for each action there are two or more events, each with a probability of occurrence. The proper action to choose is the one with the best expected value.

3. **Expected value**: a weighted average of the outcomes with the probability of each outcome serving as the weights.

4. The textbook example (pp. 79-80) illustrates the five elements of a CVP decision model. Expected value is computed in two formats: decision table (Exhibit 3-7) and decision tree (Exhibit 3-8).

5. *See Practice Test Question III (item 16) and Problem X.*

6. Distinguish between a good decision and a good outcome.
   a. Because of uncertainty, choosing the best action (a good decision) does not necessarily mean that a good outcome will be obtained.
   b. Bad luck could produce unfavorable consequences when a good decision has been made. See the textbook example of tossing a coin (p. 81).

PRACTICE TEST QUESTIONS AND PROBLEMS

I. Complete each of the following statements.

1. The report that highlights the dollar amount of contribution margin is called the _____ _____.

2. The chapter assumes that total revenues and variable costs are driven by a(n) _____ _____ driver.

3. The basic formula to determine the breakeven point under the equation method is _____ _____ equals zero _____.

4. Net income is equal to contribution margin minus the sum of _____ _____.

5. In the CVP chart, the horizontal axis represents _____ and the vertical axis represents _____.

6. The range of output within which variable costs and fixed costs behave according to their respective definitions is called the _____ _____.

7. The possibility that an actual amount will deviate from an expected amount is called _____.

8. _____ is a "what if" technique that examines how a result such as operating income will change if the original predicted data are not achieved or if an underlying assumption changes.

9. The relative combinations of quantities of products or services that constitute total sales is called _____.

10. Sales minus cost of goods sold equals _____ _____.

11. (Appendix) The five elements of a decision model are _____

_____

_____

_____.

12. (Appendix) The set of probabilities in a decision model always sums to _____ because the set of events is _____ _____.

II. Indicate whether each of the following statements is true or false by putting T or F in the space provided.

___ 1. Generally, the breakeven point in dollars can be easily determined by simply totaling all the costs in the company's income statement.

___ 2. At the breakeven point, total fixed costs always will be equal to contribution margin.

___ 3. As sales exceed the breakeven point in a single product company, a high contribution-margin percentage would result in lower operating income than would a low contribution-margin percentage.

___ 4. The breakeven point is often an overemphasized part of CVP analysis.

___ 5. Sensitivity analysis is designed to help determine the effects of proposed plans on managers' behavior.

___ 6. The excess of budgeted revenues over breakeven revenues is called the margin of forecasting error.

___ 7. An increase in the income tax rate would increase the breakeven point.

___ 8. Cost of goods sold in manufacturing companies is a variable cost.

___ 9. Gross margin does not pertain to service companies.

___ 10. (Appendix) A decision model includes a mutually exclusive and collectively exhaustive set of actions.

___ 11. (Appendix) In a particular decision situation, a bad outcome can occur even though a good decision was made.

III. Select the best answer for each of the following multiple-choice questions and put the identifying letter in the space provided.

___ 1. If Castle Corporation has sales of $500,000, variable costs of $350,000 and fixed costs of $135,000, then:
a. contribution margin is $15,000.
b. contribution-margin percentage is 70%.
c. contribution margin is $365,000.
d. contribution-margin percentage is 30%.

___ 2. See item 1. The breakeven sales for Castle Corporation would be:
a. $485,000.
b. $192,587.
c. $450,000.
d. none of the above.

___ 3. See item 1. The sales needed to achieve a target operating income of $45,000 would be:
a. $600,000.
b. $495,000.
c. $530,000.
d. none of the above.

___ 4. Given for Winn Company (in thousands): sales $530, manufacturing costs $220 (one-half fixed), and marketing and administrative costs $270 (two-thirds variable). Ignoring inventories, gross margin would be:
a. $260.
b. $310.
c. $40.
d. none of the above.

___ 5. See item 4. The contribution margin for Winn Company would be:
a. $330.
b. $310.
c. $40.
d. $240.

6. Given for Santori Co. (in thousands): sales $650, fixed costs $330, variable costs $390, number of units sold 130. The breakeven point would be:
   a. 110 units.
   b. $825.
   c. 220 units.
   d. $720.

7. The breakeven point for a given situation would be increased by an increase in the:
   a. total fixed costs.
   b. contribution-margin percentage.
   c. income tax rate.
   d. contribution margin per unit.

8. (CPA) Koby Co. has sales of $200,000 with variable costs of $150,000, fixed costs of $60,000, and an operating loss of $10,000. By how much would Koby need to increase its sales in order to achieve a target operating income of 10% of sales?
   a. $200,000
   b. $251,000
   c. $400,000
   d. $231,000

9. (CPA) The following information pertains to Nova Co.'s CVP relationships:

Breakeven point in units	1,000
Variable costs per unit	$500
Total fixed costs	$150,000

   How much will be contributed to operating income by the 1001st unit sold?
   a. $650
   b. $500
   c. $150
   d. $0

10. (CPA) Tice Company is a medium-sized manufacturer of lamps. During the year a new line called "Horolin" was made available to Tice's customers. The breakeven point for sales of Horolin is $200,000 with a contribution-margin percentage of 40%. Assuming that the operating income for the Horolin line during the year amounted to $100,000, total sales for the year would have been:
    a. $300,000.
    b. $420,000.

c. $450,000.
d. $475,000.

11. (CPA) CVP analysis does not assume that:
    a. selling prices remain constant.
    b. there is a single revenue and cost driver.
    c. total fixed costs vary inversely with units of output.
    d. total costs are linear within the relevant range.

12. The amount of total costs probably will not vary significantly in decision situations where:
    a. the time span is quite short and the change in units of output is quite large.
    b. the time span is quite long and the change in units of output is quite large.
    c. the time span is quite long and the change in units of output is quite small.
    d. the time span is quite short and the change in units of output is quite small.

13. (CPA) The following data pertain to the two products manufactured by Korn Corp.:

	Per Unit	
	Selling price	Variable costs
Product Y	$120	$ 70
Product Z	500	200

    Fixed costs total $300,000 annually. The expected sales mix in units is 60% for product Y and 40% for product Z. How many units of the two products together must Korn sell to break even?
    a. 857
    b. 1,111
    c. 2,000
    d. 2,459

14. In multiple-product companies, a shift in sales mix from products with high contribution-margin percentages to products with low contribution-margin percentages would cause the breakeven point to be:

a. lower.

b. higher.

c. unchanged.

d. different but undeterminable.

15. A company produces a product for sale at $24 per unit. Total fixed costs are $48,000 and variable costs per unit are $16. The number of units to be produced and sold to obtain a $14,400 net income when the income tax rate is 40% would be:

a. 7,500.

b. 3,000.

c. 9,000.

d. 3,750.

16. (Appendix, CMA) The College Honor Society sells large pretzels at the home football games. The following information is available:

Unit Sales	Probability
2,000 pretzels	.10
3,000 pretzels	.15
4,000 pretzels	.20
5,000 pretzels	.35
6,000 pretzels	.20

The pretzels are sold for $1.00 each, and the cost per pretzel is $0.30. Any unsold pretzels are discarded because they will be stale before the next home game. The operating income per game of having 4,000 pretzels available but only selling 3,000 pretzels is:

a. $1,800.

b. $2,100.

c. $2,800.

d. $450.

e. none of the above.

IV. Given for Kitchen Wizard, Inc. (in thousands):

Sales	$450
Total manufacturing costs	240
Total marketing and administrative costs	180

Of the manufacturing costs, 40% are fixed and 70% of the marketing and administrative costs are variable.

Compute the breakeven point.

Check figure: $375

V. (CMA) Donnelly Corporation manufactures

and sells key rings embossed with college names and slogans. Last year, the key rings sold for $7.50 each, and the variable costs to manufacture them were $2.25 per unit. The company needed to sell 20,000 key rings to break even. The net income last year was $5,040. Donnelly's expectations for the coming year include the following:

• The selling price of the key rings will be $9.00.

• Variable manufacturing costs per unit will increase by one third.

• Fixed costs will increase by 10%.

• The income tax rate of 40% will remain unchanged.

1. Sales in the coming year are expected to exceed last year's sales by 1,000 units. If this event occurs, how many key rings will Donnelly sell in the coming year?

2. How many key rings must Donnelly sell in the coming year to break even?

Check figures: (1) 22,600, (2) 19,250

VI. (CMA) The income statement for Davann Co. presented below represents the operating results for the fiscal year just ended. Davann had sales of 1,800 tons of product during the current year. The manufacturing capacity of Davann's facilities is 3,000 tons of product.

Davann Co.
Income Statement
For the Year Ended December 31, 19_3

Sales		$900,000
Variable costs:		
Manufacturing	$315,000	
Nonmanufacturing	180,000	495,000
Contribution margin		405,000
Fixed costs:		
Manufacturing	90,000	
Nonmanufacturing	157,500	247,500
Operating income		157,500
Income taxes (40%)		63,000
Net income		$ 94,500

1. If the sales volume is estimated to be 2,100 tons in the next year, and if the selling price and cost behavior patterns remain the same next year, how much net income would Davann expect to earn in 19_4?

2. Assume that Davann estimates that the per ton selling price will decline 10% next year. Variable costs would increase $40 per ton and the total fixed costs would not change. What amount of sales in dollars would be required to earn net income of $94,500 next year?

Check figures: (1) $135,000, (2) $1,350,000

VII. (CMA adapted) William Company owns and operates a chain of movie theaters. The theaters in the William chain vary from low volume, small town, single-screen theaters to high volume, big city, multi-screen theaters.

Management is considering installing machines that will make popcorn on the premises. These machines would allow the theaters to sell popcorn that would be freshly popped rather than the pre-popped corn that is currently purchased in large bags. This proposed feature would be properly advertised and is intended to increase patronage at the company's theaters.

These machines are available in two different sizes. The machine capacities and costs are as follows:

	Economy Popper	Regular Popper
Annual capacity	50,000 boxes	120,000 boxes
Costs:		
Annual machine rental	$8,000	$11,000
Popcorn cost per box	.13	.13
Cost of each box	.08	.08
Other variable costs per box	.22	.14

Compute the level of output in boxes at which the Economy Popper and Regular Popper would earn the same profit (loss).

Check figure: 37,500

VIII. (CPA) Dallas Corporation wishes to market a new product at a selling price of $1.50 per unit. Fixed costs for this product are $100,000 for less than 500,000 units of output and $150,000 for 500,000 or more units of output. The contribution-margin percentage is 20%. How many units of this product must be sold to earn a target operating income of $100,000?

Check figure: 833,334

IX. Valdosta Manufacturing Co. produces and sells two products as follows:

	T	U
Selling price per unit	$25	$16
Variable costs per unit	20	13

Total fixed costs are $40,500.

Compute the breakeven point in units when the sales mix is five units of U for each unit of T.

Check figures: T = 2,025, U = 10,125

X. (Appendix, CMA) The ARC Radio Company is trying to decide whether to introduce a new product, a wrist "radiowatch" designed for short-wave reception of the exact time as broadcast by the National Bureau of Standards. The "radiowatch" would be priced at $60, which is exactly twice the variable costs per unit to manufacture and sell it. The incremental fixed costs necessitated by introducing this new product would be $240,000 per year. Subjective estimates of the probable demand for the product are shown in the following probability distribution:

Annual Demand	Probability
6,000 units	.20
8,000 units	.20
10,000 units	.20
12,000 units	.20
14,000 units	.10
16,000 units	.10

Compute:
1. The expected value of demand for the new product.
2. The probability that the introduction of the new product will not increase the company's operating income.

Check figures: (1) 10,200 units, (2) 0.40

CHAPTER 3 SOLUTIONS TO PRACTICE TEST

I. 1 contribution income statement; 2 output-related; 3 Revenues − Variable costs − Fixed costs, Operating income; 4 fixed costs and income taxes; 5 units of output, dollars; 6 relevant range; 7 uncertainty; 8 Sensitivity analysis; 9 sales mix; 10 gross margin; 11 choice criterion, set of actions, set of events, set of probabilities, set of outcomes; 12 1.00, collectively exhaustive.

II.

1 F	4 T	7 F	10 F
2 T	5 F	8 F	11 T
3 F	6 F	9 T	

Explanations:

1 The breakeven point in dollars is computed by dividing total fixed costs by the contribution-margin percentage. The computation described in the statement gives breakeven revenues *only if* the company happened to be operating at the breakeven point. (F)

2 If contribution margin is larger than total fixed costs, the difference is operating income. If the opposite is the case, the difference is operating loss. (T) Note that the word "always" *does not necessarily* make cost accounting statements false.

3 As sales exceed the breakeven point, the higher the contribution-margin percentage, the higher the operating income. (F)

4 The breakeven point is often of interest in CVP analysis, but the analysis considers a broader question: What is the impact on income of various decisions affecting revenues and costs? (T)

5 Sensitivity analysis is a tool to help managers cope with the financial consequences of possible prediction errors in a given decision situation. (F)

6 The excess of budgeted revenues over breakeven revenues is called the margin of safety. (F)

7 The breakeven point is unaffected by the presence of income taxes because no income taxes are paid if there is no operating income. (F)

8 Cost of goods sold in manufacturing companies consists of all manufacturing costs, including fixed manufacturing costs. (F)

9 Service companies can compute a contribution margin figure but not a gross margin figure. These companies do not have a cost of goods sold line item in their income statement. (T)

10 A decision model includes a mutually exclusive and collectively exhaustive set of events. (F)

11 The textbook example of tossing a coin (p. 81) illustrates a good decision but a bad outcome. (T)

III.

1 d	4 b	7 a	10 c	13 c	16 a
2 c	5 d	8 a	11 c	14 b	
3 a	6 b	9 c	12 d	15 c	

Explanations:

1 Contribution margin = $500,000 − $350,000 = $150,000; contribution-margin percentage = $150,000 ÷ $500,000 = 30% (d)

2 $135,000 ÷ 0.30 = $450,000 (c)

3 ($135,000 + $45,000) ÷ 0.30 = $600,000 (a)

4 $530 − $220 = $310 (b)

5 $530 − ($220)(½) − ($270)(⅔) = $530 − $110 − $180 = $240 (d)

6 Selling price = $650 ÷ 130 = $5; variable costs per unit = $390 ÷ 130 = $3; unit contribution margin = $5 − $3 = $2; breakeven sales in dollars = ($330 ÷ $2) × $5 = $825 (b). *Alternate solution:* contribution margin percentage = ($650 − $390) ÷ $650 = 40%; breakeven sales in dollars = $330 ÷ 0.40 = $825 (b)

7 The breakeven point would be increased by an increase in total fixed costs. An increase in the contribution-margin percentage would decrease the breakeven point. (a)

8 Let S = Sales needed to earn a target operating income of 10% of sales

$$S - (\$150,000 \div \$200,000)S - \$60,000 = .10S$$
$$S - .75S - .10S = \$60,000$$
$$.15S = \$60,000$$
$$S = \$400,000$$

Since current sales are $200,000, an increase in sales of $200,000 is needed to earn a target operating income of $200,000. (a)

9 Total costs at break even = (1,000 × $500) + $150,000 = $650,000; Selling price = $650,000 ÷ 1,000 units = $650; Unit contribution margin = $650 − $500 = $150 (c)

10 Fixed costs = $200,000(.40) = $80,000; Sales = ($80,000 + $100,000) ÷ .40 = $450,000 (c)

11 One of the five assumptions of CVP analysis is that total fixed costs remain the same within the relevant range. (c)

12 An example is deciding whether to add a passenger to an airline flight that has empty seats and will depart soon. Variable costs for that passenger would be negligible. Virtually all the costs in this decision are fixed. (d)

13 Let 3N = Number of units of product Y to be sold to break even
    Let 2N = Number of units of product Z to be sold to break even

$$\$120 (3N) + \$500(2N) - \$70(3N) - \$200(2N) - \$300,000 = 0$$
$$\$360N + \$1,000N - \$210N - \$400N = \$300,000$$
$$\$750N = \$300,000$$
$$N = 400$$
$$5N = 2,000 \text{ (c)}$$

14 A shift in the sales mix from high contribution-margin percentage products to low ones decreases the overall contribution-margin percentage of the sales mix. This type of change increases the breakeven point. (b)

15 $14,400 ÷ (1 − 40%) = $14,400 ÷ 60% = $24,000 operating income; $24 − $16 = $8 unit contribution margin; ($48,000 + $24,000) ÷ $8 = $72,000 ÷ $8 = 9,000 (c)

16 3,000($1.00) − 4,000($0.30) = $1,800 (a)

IV. Kitchen Wizard, Inc.

Three steps are used to obtain the answer. First, compute total variable costs: ($240 × .60) + ($180 × .70) = $144 + $126 = $270. Second, compute total fixed costs: ($240 × .40) + ($180 × .30) = $96 + $54 = $150. Third, compute the breakeven point (denoted by S):

$$S - (\$270 \div \$450)S - \$150 = 0$$
$$S - .60S = \$150$$
$$.40S = \$150$$
$$S = \$375$$

Proof:		
Sales		$375
Variable costs, $375 × .60		225
Contribution margin		150
Fixed costs		150
Operating income		$ -0-

V. Donnelly Corporation

1. Three steps are used to obtain the answer. First, compute total fixed costs: ($7.50 − $2.25) × 20,000 = $5.25 × 20,000 = $105,000. Second, compute sales in units for last year (denoted by N):

$$\$7.50N - \$2.25N - \$105,000 = \frac{\$5,040}{1 - .40}$$

$$\$5.25N = \$8,400 + \$105,000$$
$$\$5.25N = \$113,400$$
$$N = 21,600 \text{ units}$$

Third, compute sales in units for the coming year: $21,600 + 1,000 = 22,600$.

2. Let N = Number of units to sell to break even in the coming year

$$\$9.00N - \$2.25(4/3)N - \$105,000(1.10) = 0$$
$$\$9.00N - \$3.00N = \$115,500$$
$$\$6.00N = \$115,500$$
$$N = 19,250 \text{ units}$$

VI. Davann Co.

1. Three steps are used to obtain the answer. First, compute selling price: $\$900,000 \div 1,800 = \$500$. Second, compute unit variable costs: $\$495,000 \div 1,800 = \$275$. Third, prepare a contribution income statement at the 2,100-ton level of output:

Sales, $2,100 \times \$500$	$1,050,000
Variable costs, $2,100 \times \$275$	577,500
Contribution margin	472,500
Fixed costs	247,500
Operating income	225,000
Income taxes (40%)	90,000
Net income	$ 135,000

2. Let N = Number of tons to break even next year

$$\$500N(1 - .10) - (\$275N + \$40N) - \$247,500 = \frac{\$94,500}{1 - .40}$$

$$\$450N - \$315N = \$247,500 + \$157,500$$
$$\$135N = \$405,000$$
$$N = 3,000 \text{ tons}$$
$$\text{Sales in dollars} = 3,000 \times \$500(1 - .10)$$
$$\text{Sales in dollars} = \$1,350,000$$

VII. William Company

The total variable costs per unit are $0.43 for the Economy Popper and $0.35 for the Regular Popper. The two models of poppers will earn the same income (loss) when their total operating costs are equal.

Let N = Number of boxes at which Economy Popper and Regular Popper earn the same income (loss)
$$\$0.43N + \$8,000 = \$0.35N + \$11,000$$
$$\$0.08N = \$3,000$$
$$N = 37,500 \text{ boxes}$$

VIII. Dallas Corporation

Two steps are used to obtain the answer. First, determine if fixed costs will be $100,000 or $150,000. When fixed costs are $100,000, the *maximum* operating income would be attained at 499,999 units:

Sales, 499,999 × $1.50	$749,998.50
Variable costs, 80% of sales	599,998.80
Contribution margin, 20% of sales	149,999.70
Fixed costs	100,000.00
Operating income	$ 49,999.70

Since this operating income is below the target of $100,000, the level of output will need to be greater than 499,999 units and hence fixed costs will be $150,000. The second step is to compute the required level of output.

Let N = Number of units to be sold to earn a target operating income of $100,000

$$\$1.50N - (1 - .20)(\$1.50)N - \$150,000 = \$100,000$$
$$\$1.50N - \$1.20N = \$250,000$$
$$\$0.30N = \$250,000$$
$$N = 833,333.33, \text{ rounded to } 833,334 \text{ units}$$

IX. Valdosta Manufacturing Co.

Let T = Number of units of T to be sold to break even
Let 5T = Number of units of U to be sold to break even
$$\$25T + \$16(5T) - \$20T - \$13(5T) - \$40,500 = \$0$$
$$\$25T + \$80T - \$20T - \$65T = \$40,500$$
$$\$20T = \$40,500; \quad T = 2,025; \quad 5T = 2,025 \times 5 = 10,125 \text{ units}$$
Proof: $\$25(2,025) + \$16(10,125) - \$20(2,025) - \$13(10,125) - \$40,500 = \$0$
$\$50,625 + \$162,000 - \$40,500 - \$131,625 - \$40,500 = \$0$

X. ARC Radio Company

1. $6,000(.20) + 8,000(.20) + 10,000(.20) + 12,000(.20) + 14,000(.10) + 16,000(.10) = 1,200 + 1,600 + 2,000 + 2,400 + 1,400 + 1,600 = 10,200$ units

2. If the number of units sold each year is equal to or less than the breakeven point, the new product would not increase the company's operating income. At the breakeven point,

Sales − Variable costs − Fixed costs = Zero operating income
Let N = Number of units to be sold to break even
$$\$60N - (\$60 \div 2)N - \$240,000 = 0$$
$$\$60N - \$30N = \$240,000$$
$$\$30N = \$240,000$$
$$N = 8,000 \text{ units}$$

Since the company's operating income would not increase if 8,000 units or 6,000 units are sold, the probability of *either* of these events occurring is equal to the sum of their individual probabilities: 0.20 + 0.20 = 0.40.

CHAPTER 4

COSTING SYSTEMS IN THE SERVICE AND MERCHANDISING SECTORS

MAIN FOCUS AND OBJECTIVES

This chapter explains different types of costing systems and applies them to service and merchandising companies. Because of today's increasing competition and lower information gathering and processing costs, managers are reevaluating and often upgrading (refining) costing systems. Your overall objective for this chapter is to understand how costing systems help managers make strategic decisions and pursue cost management actions. Eleven learning objectives are stated in the textbook (p. 98).

Give special attention to:

- the building blocks and overview diagrams of costing systems
- the three guidelines for refining costing systems
- product-cost cross-subsidization
- activity-based costing
- customer costing systems

Also, be able to distinguish clearly between:

- job costing systems and process costing systems
- actual cost rates and budgeted cost rates
- actual costing, normal costing, and budgeted costing

Keep in mind that the cost-benefit approach is central to designing and choosing costing systems. Any costing system should be tailored to the underlying operations of an organization, not vice versa.

REVIEW OF KEY TERMS AND CONCEPTS

A. **Costing systems** aim to report cost numbers that reflect the way in which particular cost objects—such as products, services, and customers—use the resources of an organization.
  1. For example, a costing system could report that it cost a law firm $32,500 to conduct a particular case for one of its clients.
  2. *Eight key cost terms are the building blocks of costing systems.*
     a. The relationship among six of these terms is as follows:

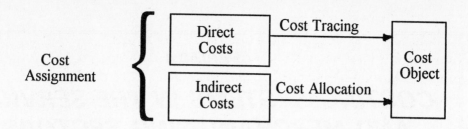

b. These six terms were introduced in section A of Chapter 2's outline (pp. 9-10). Review the definitions there.

c. The other two terms:

(1) **Cost pool**: a grouping of individual cost items such as for an entire organization or for one of its departments.

(2) **Cost allocation base**: a financial or nonfinancial variable that links indirect cost(s) to a cost object; managers often seek to use a *cost driver* of the indirect cost(s) as the cost allocation base.

d. *Overview diagrams of costing systems* present these building blocks in a systematic way. For example, see Exhibit 4-3.

3. Two types of costing systems are polar extremes:

a. **Job costing systems**: they report the cost of a product or service by assigning costs to a distinct, identifiable job; a job is often a *custom-made* product or service for a specific customer.

b. **Process costing systems**: they report the cost of a product or service by assigning costs to masses of *similar* units and then computing costs per unit on an average basis; often the product or service is produced for inventory or general sale and not for any specific customer.

c. Companies using job costing usually produce a relatively small number of units that are *heterogeneous* in nature (such as audit engagements or custom-made machinery), while companies using process costing usually produce a very large number of units that are basically *homogeneous* in nature (such as simple tax returns or soft drinks).

d. Both types of costing systems are found in service, merchandising, and manufacturing companies. See Exhibit 4-1 for specific examples.

e. The costing systems in many companies combine some elements of both job costing and process costing.

4. Job costing in the service sector is covered first in the textbook for two reasons:

a. Services are the largest sector in many of the world economies. For example, in the U.S. more than 60% of all employment is in the service sector.

b. The service sector is less complex in that there is no inventory.

B. The jobs done by service companies differ considerably in terms of time required, resources used, and technical complexity.

1. *Job costing information in service companies has two main uses*:

a. To guide decisions on job pricing and job emphasis.

b. To assist in cost planning and cost management.

2. The general approach to job costing (applicable to service, merchandising, and manufacturing companies) involves five steps:

Step 1: Identify the job that is the chosen cost object.
Step 2: Identify the direct cost categories for the job.
Step 3: Identify the indirect cost pools associated with the job.
Step 4: Select the cost allocation base to use in assigning each indirect cost pool to the job.
Step 5: Develop the cost allocation rate(s) by dividing each indirect cost pool by its cost allocation base.

> **Carefully study this five-step approach in the key textbook example, Lindsay & Associates CPA firm (pp. 102-03). Note the simplicity of Lindsay's costing system:**
> - **a single direct cost category (professional labor)**
> - **a single indirect cost pool (audit support) with professional labor-hours used as the cost allocation base.**
>
> ***See Practice Test Problem IV.***

3. Source documents, such as time records filled out by the professional staff, are used to gather information for job costing systems.
4. Distinguish between two main categories of direct cost items:
    a. *Category 1*: resources are used exclusively on a specific job; therefore, tracing these items to jobs is straightforward.
    b. *Category 2*: resources are used on multiple jobs; therefore, tracing these items to jobs is more difficult.
5. Most direct cost items in service organizations are labor-related and fall into category 2.

C. Two important issues relate to category 2 items: (i) using actual amounts or budgeted amounts and (ii) measuring the capacity of resources used on multiple jobs.
    1. Consider the choice between **actual cost rates** and **budgeted cost rates**.
       Question: Which type of rates is used most frequently? Why?
       Answer: Budgeted cost rates, because (three reasons):
        a. They are timely, given that decisions such as pricing often must be made *before* jobs are started. (Actual cost rates, of course, cannot be computed until the *end* of the period.)
        b. They are unaffected by fluctuations in actual costs due to factors such as overtime.
        c. They are unaffected by changes in the budgeted work done on other jobs during the period.
    2. In developing a budgeted direct labor cost rate, it is preferable to exclude time for vacation, sick leave, and professional development from the denominator. Under this approach, each billable hour is allocated a proportional share of the costs of vacations, sick leave, and professional development.

$$\frac{\text{Budgeted direct}}{\text{labor cost rate}} = \frac{\text{Budgeted total direct labor compensation}}{\text{Budgeted billable hours for clients}}$$

3. Formula to determine a budgeted indirect cost rate:

$$\text{Budgeted indirect cost rate} = \frac{\text{Budgeted total costs in indirect cost pool}}{\text{Budgeted total quantity of cost allocation base}}$$

4. In reference to this formula, budgeted indirect cost rates are developed *annually* rather than more often for three reasons:
   a. *Numerator reason*—to avoid the volatility in rates caused by seasonal fluctuations in costs such as heating.
   b. *Denominator reason*—to avoid the volatility in rates caused by monthly fluctuations in the total quantity of the cost allocation base, when a portion of the budgeted costs are fixed (see the textbook example, p. 108).
   c. *Cost-benefit reason*—to avoid using management time to recompute rates frequently.
5. Actual costs and budgeted costs likely will differ for a reporting period. Alternative ways of dealing with these variances are discussed in Chapter 5.
6. Three combinations of actual and budgeted rates—called actual costing, normal costing, and budgeted costing—are used by companies in either a job costing system or process costing system.

Type of Costing	Direct Costs	Indirect Costs
Actual costing	Actual rate(s)	Actual rate(s)
Normal costing	Actual rate(s)	Budgeted rate(s)
Budgeted costing	Budgeted rate(s)	Budgeted rate(s)

   a. Under all three types of costing, the rates are multiplied by the *actual* quantity of inputs used. Exhibit 4-4 provides a helpful summary.
   b. *See Practice Test Problem V.*

D. **Costing system refinement** occurs when changes made in an existing system result in cost numbers that better measure the way jobs, products, services, and customers use an organization's resources.
   1. Any refinement must pass the cost-benefit test; the benefit is the expectation that managers can make better decisions.
   2. The sources of information for possible refinements include interviews with personnel of the organization and feedback about the experiences of other organizations.
   3. Three guidelines are used for costing system refinement:
      Guideline 1: Classify as many of the total costs as direct costs as is economically feasible.
      Guideline 2: Use the concept of a homogeneous cost pool for determining how many indirect cost pools to form.
      Guideline 3: Identify the driver of the costs in each indirect cost pool and use it as the cost allocation base.
   4. In a **homogeneous cost pool**, all costs have the same or a similar *cause-and-effect relationship* with the cost allocation base.

> **The underlying theme of refining costing systems is: Tracing more costs directly to a particular cost object increases the accuracy of assigned costs because the amount of indirect costs remaining to be allocated has been reduced. Any cost allocation is inherently somewhat arbitrary.**

5. The textbook example (pp. 111-14) illustrates costing system refinements — more direct cost categories and more indirect cost categories.
   a. Before those refinements, the audit cost $76,000 (see Exhibit 4-3).
   b. After those refinements, the audit cost $65,020 (see Exhibit 4-6).
6. A colorful term is **peanut-butter costing**: an approach that uniformly assigns ("spreads") the cost of resources to products, services, or customers, although these individual cost objects in fact use resources nonuniformly.
   Question: Which costing system in Exhibit 4-5 is the best example of peanut-butter costing?
   Answer: Panel A because, while the individual audits (jobs) differ significantly in the use of resources, only one difference is recognized — the use of professional labor-hours.
7. Peanut-butter costing (like Exhibit 4-5, Panel A) overcosts products (services and customers) that consume relatively more of the cost allocation base, and consequently undercosts other products.
   a. This phenomenon is called **product-cost cross-subsidization**.
   b. See the textbook example of splitting a restaurant bill (pp. 114-15). Note that *all* costs are traceable in that example.
8. Exhibit 4-5 (Panel C) can be called *menu-based costing* because individual jobs are costed according to what each of them "orders from the menu."
9. *See Practice Test Problems VI and VII.*

E. Activity-based costing is a specific type of costing system refinement.
   1. **Activity-based costing (ABC)**: focuses on activities as the fundamental cost object and assigns the costs of those activities to products, services, or customers.
   2. ABC was originally developed in the manufacturing sector but is now also used in the merchandise and service sectors.

Sector	ABC Approach	Examples of Activities
Service	Exhibit 4-5 (Panel C)	General audit support, travel
Merchandising	Exhibit 4-8	Goods handling, marketing
Manufacturing	Exhibit 5-7	Parts insertion, testing

   3. ABC is an approach to developing cost numbers used in job costing or process costing systems; *ABC is not an alternative to job costing or process costing*.
   4. Since ABC is expensive to implement and maintain, the cost-benefit test plays a key role.

a. Costs include clerical and computer time as well as user education.

b. Benefits are the expected improvements in collective operating decisions in an organization.

c. Today's less expensive computer technology has made the gathering and processing of activity-based information more practical.

5. ABC has two main benefits:

a. More accurate costing of products, services, and customers.

b. Information for cost management—reducing the consumption of cost drivers can help control costs.

6. In merchandising companies, ABC can be used to help measure the profitability of individual products or product lines.

a. See the textbook example of a supermarket (pp. 116-18).

b. Exhibit 4-8 shows the differences in product-line profitability under the original costing system and the refined (ABC) system.

F. Customer costing is management accounting's response to the management and marketing philosophy that satisfying the customer is priority one.

1. **Customer costing system**: reports cost numbers that reflect the way in which customers differentially use the resources of a company.

2. Managers need to ensure that customers contributing sizably to the profitability of a company receive a comparable level of attention from the company.

3. Exhibits 4-9, 4-10, and 4-11 show three alternative presentations of customer profitability information. In particular, note in Exhibit 4-10 that some of the most profitable customers are *not* the major sources of revenue.

4. The pattern of a low percentage of customers contributing a high percentage of total operating income exists in many companies.

5. Managers desire to maintain *long-run* profitable relationships with customers, so the profit or loss attributed to a customer in a given reporting period should be interpreted carefully.

> **To assist managers in their decisions such as pricing, product emphasis, and customer emphasis, costing systems need the capability to combine costs from all business functions of the value chain.**

PRACTICE TEST QUESTIONS AND PROBLEMS

I. Complete each of the following statements.

1. _____ aim to report cost numbers that reflect the way in which particular cost objects – such as products, services, and customers – use the resources of an organization.

2. The_____approach is central to designing and choosing costing systems.

3. For a given cost object such as a job, direct costs are _____ to it and indirect costs are _____ to it.

4. Companies using _____ costing systems usually produce many units that are like or similar in nature.

5. _____occurs when changes made in an existing system result in cost numbers that will better measure the way jobs, products, services, and customers use an organization's resources.

6. One guideline for costing system refinement is to classify as many of the total costs as _____ costs as is economically feasible.

7. In a homogeneous cost pool, all costs have the same or a similar _____ relationship with the cost allocation base.

8. _____ uniformly assigns the cost of resources to products, services, or customers although these individual cost objects in fact use resources nonuniformly.

9. When a company's costing system overcosts some products and undercosts other products, this phenomenon is called _____ _____.

10. A _____ system reports cost numbers that affect the way in which customers differentially use the resources of a company.

II. Indicate whether each of the following statements is true or false by putting T or F in the space provided.

___ 1. The underlying operations of an organization should be tailored to the organization's costing system.

___ 2. The costing systems in many companies combine some elements of both job costing and process costing.

___ 3. Job costing systems tend to be less complex in service companies than in merchandising or manufacturing companies.

___ 4. The five-step general approach to job costing is applicable to service, merchandising, and manufacturing companies.

___ 5. Actual cost rates are used more frequently than budgeted cost rates.

___ 6. In developing a budgeted direct labor cost rate, it is preferable to exclude the cost of vacation, sick leave, and professional development from the numerator.

___ 7. A main factor driving costing system refinement is increasing competition in the marketplace.

___ 8. One of the guidelines for costing system refinement is to use the concept of a homogeneous cost pool for determining how many indirect cost pools to form.

___ 9. Tracing more costs directly to jobs increases the accuracy of their assigned costs.

___ 10. Activity-based costing focuses on activities as the fundamental cost object and assigns the costs of products, services, and customers to those activities.

___ 11. The pattern of a low percentage of customers contributing a high percentage of total operating income exists in many companies.

III. Select the best answer for each of the following multiple-choice questions and put the identifying letter in the space provided.

___ 1. A cost allocation base can be:
   a. a financial variable but not a nonfinancial variable.
   b. a nonfinancial variable but not a financial variable.
   c. either a financial variable or a nonfinancial variable.
   d. neither a financial variable nor a nonfinancial variable.

___ 2. Companies using job costing systems usually produce:
   a. a relatively small number of heterogeneous units.
   b. a very large number of homogeneous units.
   c. a relatively small number of homogeneous units.
   d. a very large number of heterogeneous units.

___ 3. Most direct cost items in service organizations are labor-related and:
   a. are resources used on multiple jobs, and tracing them to jobs is straightforward.
   b. are resources used on multiple jobs, and tracing them to jobs is not straightforward.
   c. are resources used exclusively on a specific job, and tracing them to jobs is straightforward.
   d. are resources used exclusively on a specific job, and tracing them to jobs is not straightforward.

4. Under a normal costing system:
   a. actual rates are used for direct costs and indirect costs.
   b. budgeted rates are used for direct costs and indirect costs.
   c. budgeted rates are used for direct costs and actual rates are used for indirect costs.
   d. actual rates are used for direct costs and budgeted rates are used for indirect costs.

5. If a costing system uses a single allocation base:
   a. products that use relatively more of this base will tend to be undercosted.
   b. products that use relatively less of this base will tend to be overcosted.
   c. products that use relatively more of this base will tend to be overcosted.
   d. products that use none of this base will tend to be overcosted.

6. Activity-based costing is beneficial to companies because it provides:
   a. information for cost management.
   b. more accurate costing of products, services, and customers.
   c. both of the above.
   d. none of the above.

IV. Riddle, Wimbish & Crain, an advertising agency, uses a simple costing system. The only category of direct cost is direct professional labor. All indirect costs are included in a single cost pool. The budgeted indirect cost rate is 200% of direct professional labor costs. Currently, the agency is preparing a proposal for a prospective client. Direct professional labor for the proposal is budgeted at $24,640. Management has decided to use a markup rate that budgets operating income at 12% of revenue.

Prepare the budgeted income statement for the proposal.

Check figure: Operating income = $10,080

V. Springer Clinic employs five doctors at budgeted annual total compensation of $142,400 each and nine nurses at budgeted annual total compensation of $37,000 each. For the current year, actual total compensation was $138,300 for the doctors and $37,500 for the nurses. Indirect

costs such as supplies, utilities, postage, rent, and depreciation on equipment were budgeted at $513,000 for the current year, but actually amounted to $521,500. Both direct and indirect costs are assigned to patients based on patient-hours (PH). In the current year, Springer budgeted for 19,000 PH but actually provided 17,950 PH.

For a patient who uses 1.5 hours of the clinic's services, compute the cost of these services:
1. Under actual costing
2. Under normal costing
3. Under budgeted costing

Check figures: (1) $129.58 (2) $126.50 (3) $123.00

VI. Jay & Associates, a CPA firm, has many audit clients. The following information is available on two recent audit engagements:

	Fuentes Footwear	Detrick Properties
Partner time used	30 hours	75 hours
Staff time used	150 hours	105 hours
Travel time	.5 hours	3.0 hours
Phone calls and faxes (estimated hours, detailed records are not kept)	Under 20	Over 100

The current costing system uses (i) a single direct cost category, direct professional labor-hours (DPLH), budgeted at $120/DPLH and (ii) a single indirect cost pool allocated at a budgeted rate of $80/DPLH.

1. Intuitively, which audit engagement do you think costs Jay more? Explain.
2. Compute the costs assigned to each audit engagement under the current costing system.
3. Explain what is wrong with the current costing system.
4. What is a likely outcome of using the current system?
5. In general, how could the current costing system be improved?

Check figure: (2) $36,000 in both cases

VII. Four managers of Torchlight Company had dinner to celebrate their recent promotions. Details of the restaurant bill are as follows:

Diner	Entree	Dessert	Drinks	Total
Jason	$17	$8	$19	$ 44
Kent	24	3	10	37
Lynne	15	4	6	25
Marci	31	6	5	42
				$148

Kent put the entire bill on one of his credit cards. A few days later, he billed each of the other diners for the average cost per diner.

1. Compute the amount of diner-cost cross-subsidization for each diner.
2. What are the likely negative aspects of the average costing approach, assuming that the four managers dine together on a monthly basis?

Check figure: (1) Lynne's meal is over-costed by $12

CHAPTER 4 SOLUTIONS TO PRACTICE TEST

I. 1 Costing systems; 2 cost-benefit; 3 traced, allocated; 4 process; 5 Costing system refinement; 6 direct; 7 cause-and-effect; 8 Peanut-butter costing; 9 product-cost cross-subsidization; 10 customer costing.

II.

1 F	4 T	7 T	10 F
2 T	5 F	8 T	11 T
3 T	6 F	9 T	

Explanations:

1 Costing systems should be tailored to the underlying operations of an organization, not vice versa. (F)
2 These costing systems are hybrids; they are neither purely job costing nor purely process costing. (T)
3 The costing systems in service companies tend to be less complex because there is no inventory. Merchandising companies have merchandise inventory and manufacturing companies have direct materials, work in process, and finished goods inventories. (T)
4 The five steps are listed in section B of the chapter outline. (T)
5 Budgeted cost rates are used more frequently than actual cost rates. The three reasons are listed in section C of the chapter outline. (F)
6 In developing a budgeted direct labor cost rate, *total* direct labor compensation is the numerator. However, it is preferable to *exclude* time for vacation, sick leave, and professional development from the denominator. This practice, in effect, treats the cost of this non-billable time as direct labor compensation. (F)
7 Another main factor driving costing system refinement is lower information gathering and processing costs. (T)
8 This statement refers to the second of three guidelines. Guideline 1 is to classify as many of the total costs as direct costs as is economically feasible. Guideline 3 is to identify the driver of the costs in each indirect cost pool and use it as the cost allocation base. (T)
9 The statement is true because the amount of indirect costs remaining to be allocated have been reduced, and any allocation is inherently somewhat arbitrary. (T)
10 ABC focuses on activities as the fundamental cost object and assigns the costs of these activities to products, services, or customers. (F)
11 This pattern is but one of the insights that can be gained from customer costing systems. Another common insight is that some of the most profitable customers are *not* the major sources of revenue. (T)

III. 1 c   3 b   5 c
  2 a   4 d   6 c

Explanations:

1 A cost allocation base is a financial or nonfinancial variable that links indirect cost(s) to a cost object. Managers often seek to use the cost driver of the indirect cost(s) as the cost allocation base. (c)

2 The "units" in a job costing system are jobs, which are often custom-made products or services for a specific customer. Examples include audit engagements, law cases, and printing of brochures. (a)

3 The textbook distinguishes between two main categories of direct cost items: category 1 is described in (c) and category 2 is described in (b). Most direct cost items in service organizations are labor-related and fall into category 2. (b)

4 Choice (a) refers to actual costing, (d) refers to normal costing and (b) refers to budgeted costing. All three types of costing use *actual* quantities of direct cost inputs and *actual* quantities of the allocation base(s) for indirect costs. (d)

5 If a costing system uses a single allocation base, products (services and customers) that consume relatively more (less) of that base will be overcosted (undercosted). The reason is that all indirect costs are allocated via that base. The costing system described in the question is called peanut-butter costing. (c)

6 Choices (a) and (b) are the two main benefits of ABC. With regard to the cost management benefit, reducing the consumption of cost drivers can help control costs. (c)

IV. Riddle, Wimbish & Crain

Budgeted total costs = $24,640 + $24,640(200\%) = $73,920$
    Budgeted revenue = $73,920 \div (1 - .12) = $84,000$

Budgeted income statement:

Revenue		$84,000
Direct costs	$24,640	
Indirect costs, $24,640 \times 200\%$	49,280	73,920
Operating income, $84,000 \times 12\%$		y$10,080

V. Springer Clinic

Three steps are used to obtain the answer. First, compute the actual cost rates for direct and indirect costs:

$$\frac{\text{Actual direct}}{\text{cost rate}} = \frac{(\$138,300 \times 5) + (\$37,500 \times 9)}{17,950 \text{ PH}} = \frac{\$1,029,000}{17,950 \text{ PH}} = \$57.33/\text{PH}$$

$$\frac{\text{Actual indirect}}{\text{cost rate}} = \frac{\$521,500}{17,950 \text{ PH}} = \$29.05/\text{PH}$$

Second, compute the budgeted cost rates for direct and indirect costs:

$$\frac{\text{Budgeted direct}}{\text{cost rate}} = \frac{(\$142,400 \times 5) + (\$37,000 \times 9)}{19,000 \text{ PH}} = \frac{\$1,045,000}{19,000 \text{ PH}} = \$55/\text{PH}$$

$$\frac{\text{Budgeted indirect}}{\text{cost rate}} = \frac{\$513,000}{19,000 \text{ PH}} = \$27/\text{PH}$$

The third step is to compute the cost of 1.5 PH under each type of costing:

Actual costing = Actual direct costs + Actual indirect costs
Actual costing = $(1.5 \times \$57.33) + (1.5 \times \$29.05) = \$86.00 + \$43.58 = \$129.58$

Normal costing = Actual direct costs + Budgeted indirect costs
Normal costing = $(1.5 \times \$57.33) + (1.5 \times \$27) = \$86.00 + \$40.50 = \$126.50$

Budgeted costing = Budgeted direct costs + Budgeted indirect costs
Budgeted costing = $(1.5 \times \$55) + (1.5 \times \$27) = \$82.50 + \$40.50 = \$123.00$

VI. Jay & Associates

1. The audit of Detrick Properties costs Jay more. Although both audits use 180 DPLH, a much higher proportion of partner hours is used for Detrick: 75/180 versus 30/180. Also, Detrick uses much more of the travel and communication resources. When the mix of labor and other resources differs between audits, the audits should be costed differently.
2. Fuentes audit = $(180 \times \$120) + (180 \times \$80) = \$21,600 + \$14,400 = \$36,000$
   Detrick audit = $(180 \times \$120) + (180 \times \$80) = \$21,600 + \$14,400 = \$36,000$
3. With only one direct cost category and only one indirect cost pool, the current costing system does not capture the cost of resources used by each audit. The Fuentes audit is overcosted because it used a lower proportion of the more expensive partner hours as well as relatively less travel and communication. For the opposite reasons, the Detrick audit is undercosted.
4. By misstating or distorting the cost of the audits, Jay could easily lose Fuentes as a client. A competing CPA firm with a better costing system would likely make a lower bid for the Fuentes audit.
5. The costing system could be refined in two basic ways: (a) increase the number of direct cost categories and (b) increase the number of indirect cost pools/cost allocation bases.

VII. Torchlight Company

1. Average cost per diner = $\$148 \div 4 = \$37$
   Diner-cost cross-subsidization:
   Jason: $\$44 - \$37 = \$7$ undercosted
   Kent: $\$37 - \$37 = \$0$ (accurately costed)
   Lynne: $\$25 - \$37 = \$12$ overcosted
   Marci: $\$42 - \$37 = \$5$ undercosted
2. The average costing approach likely would induce some diners to order the most expensive items on the menu because other diners will "subsidize" their extravagance. Obviously, ill feelings would develop. Note that when direct cost figures are readily available (as in this case), they should be used.

CHAPTER 5

COSTING SYSTEMS IN THE MANUFACTURING SECTOR

MAIN FOCUS AND OBJECTIVES

This chapter builds on the coverage of costing systems from Chapter 4 but shifts the focus to manufacturing companies. The concepts introduced here provide a foundation for many subsequent chapters. The chapter is divided into three major parts: (1) job costing systems in manufacturing, (2) process costing systems in manufacturing, and (3) activity-based costing in manufacturing. Costing systems in the manufacturing sector tend to be more complex than those in the service and merchandising sectors because of the additional procedures required by the existence of work in process and finished goods inventories. Your overall objective for this chapter is to gain a working knowledge of the terms and procedures involved in manufacturing costing systems. Nine learning objectives are stated in the textbook (p. 140).

Carefully study the key textbook Exhibit 5-3. This diagram provides the framework for understanding the flow of costs through the accounts in the general and subsidiary ledgers.

Also give special attention to:

- the two approaches and related alternatives for disposing of underallocated or overallocated manufacturing overhead at the end of an accounting period
- the five-step approach used in process costing
- how activity-based costing can be incorporated into job costing or process costing systems in manufacturing

REVIEW OF KEY TERMS AND CONCEPTS

> Before studying any of the parts of this chapter, be sure you understand the building block concepts of costing systems in section A(2) of Chapter 4's outline (pp. 37-38).

Part One: Job Costing Systems in Manufacturing

A. The jobs done by manufacturing companies differ considerably in terms of time required, resources used, routing in the plant, and technical complexity.

    1. To cost those jobs, follow a five-step general approach (the same approach used in service and merchandising companies):

Step 1: Identify the job that is the chosen cost object.

Step 2: Identify the direct cost categories for the job.

Step 3: Identify the indirect cost pools associated with the job.

Step 4: Select the cost allocation base to use in assigning each indirect cost pool to the job.

Step 5: Develop the cost allocation rate(s) by dividing each indirect cost pool by its cost allocation base.

2. An overview of a manufacturer's job costing system is diagrammed in Exhibit 5-1.

3. Job costing systems in manufacturing accumulate the costs of individual *departments* and determine the cost of individual *jobs* (and then individual *products*).

   a. That is, the main cost objects of these systems are departments, jobs, and products.

   b. The relationship between these cost objects is shown in the textbook (p. 142). *That diagram gives you the big picture*.

Question: **What is the respective cost accounting purpose of using departments and products as cost objects?**

Answer:

- **Departments—cost planning and cost management (reducing and controlling costs)**
- **Products—decisions on pricing and product emphasis, and inventoriable costs for financial statements under generally accepted accounting principles**

---

   c. As indicated by this answer, *different product costs are used for different purposes*.

   (1) Review textbook Exhibit 2-14 (p. 45).

   (2) Note that the focus of Parts One and Two of Chapter 5 is on the product costs that appear as *inventories* and *cost of goods sold* in the financial statements.

4. Standardized *source documents* are used to gather information for job costing systems in manufacturing.

   a. **Job cost records:** used to accumulate product costs of individual units or small batches of identical units for both product costing and control purposes.

   b. **Materials requisition records:** used to charge departments and job cost records for the cost of the materials used on a specific job.

   c. **Labor time records:** used to charge departments and job cost records for labor time used on a specific job.

   d. Materials requisition records and labor time records help management fix the responsibility for the control and usage of the resources.

   e. Job cost records use information from materials requisition records and labor time records. Exhibit 5-2 illustrates these source documents.

5. The Robinson Company example in the textbook (pp. 141-46) illustrates a **normal costing system**.

a. For computing the direct manufacturing costs of jobs under normal costing, actual cost rates are multiplied by the actual quantities of direct materials and direct labor used.

b. For computing the indirect manufacturing costs of jobs under normal costing, the budgeted overhead rate is multiplied by the actual quantity of its allocation base (machine-hours).

6. As discussed in Chapter 4, budgeted indirect cost rates are used more frequently than actual indirect cost rates for three reasons:

a. They are timely, given that (i) job costs must be computed *during* the period for financial accounting purposes and (ii) decisions such as pricing often must be made *before* jobs are started. (Actual indirect cost rates, of course, cannot be computed until the *end* of the period.)

b. They are unaffected by fluctuations in actual costs due to factors such as overtime.

c. They are unaffected by changes in the budgeted work on other jobs during the period.

7. Formula to determine a budgeted indirect cost rate (such as for manufacturing overhead costs):

$$\frac{\text{Budgeted indirect}}{\text{cost rate}} = \frac{\text{Budgeted total costs in indirect cost pool}}{\text{Budgeted total quantity of cost allocation base}}$$

8. In reference to this formula, budgeted indirect cost rates are developed *annually* rather than more often for three reasons, which are set forth in section C(4) of the Chapter 4 outline (p. 40).

B. Under job costing systems in manufacturing, costs flow through the accounts in the general and subsidiary ledgers.

1. **Exhibit 5-3 (Panel A)** shows T-account relationships for summary information in the **general ledger**. The debits and credits are keyed to the eight summary transactions in the textbook illustration.

a. The sequence of these transactions is that materials and other manufacturing inputs are purchased, placed in process, and converted into finished goods. Then the finished goods are sold.

b. Note in the general ledger that actual direct manufacturing costs are debited to Work in Process Control and actual indirect manufacturing costs are debited to Manufacturing Department Overhead Control.

c. Also note Transaction 6: Work in Process Control is debited and Manufacturing Overhead Allocated is credited for the amount of the budgeted overhead rate times actual machine-hours.

2. **Exhibit 5-3 (Panel B)** shows the various cost records in the underlying **subsidiary ledgers**.

a. Materials records are the perpetual inventory of individual types of direct and indirect materials supporting Materials Control.

b. Job cost records for unfinished jobs are the perpetual inventory supporting Work in Process Control.

c. Finished goods records are the perpetual inventory supporting Finished Goods Control.

d. Manufacturing department overhead records are the detailed costs supporting Manufacturing Department Overhead Control.

> **Be sure you are thoroughly familiar with the journal entries and ledger relationships in the textbook illustration. To check your understanding, see Practice Test Question III (items 1-3) and Problem V.**

C. At the end of an accounting period, actual manufacturing overhead incurred will almost always differ from manufacturing overhead allocated.

1. **Underallocated overhead** (also called *underapplied overhead* or *underabsorbed overhead)* arises when the allocated amount is less than the actual costs incurred; **overallocated overhead** arises when the allocated amount is more than the actual costs incurred.

2. Underallocated or overallocated overhead is the difference between the balances of Manufacturing Department Overhead Control and Manufacturing Overhead Allocated.

3. *See Practice Test Question III (item 5) and Problem IV.*

4. Two approaches to dispose of underallocated or overallocated overhead:

   a. **Restated Allocation Rate Approach**, in effect, restates all entries in the general and subsidiary ledgers by using actual cost rates rather than budgeted cost rates. This approach is perfectly accurate and is more likely to pass the cost-benefit test as information processing costs decline.

   b. **End-of-Period Accounts Approach** disposes of underallocated or overallocated overhead by (three alternatives):

      (1) Immediate writeoff to Cost of Goods Sold (an unacceptable alternative under GAAP when underallocated or overallocated overhead is material in amount).

      (2) Proration on the basis of the total ending balances (before proration) of Work in Process, Finished Goods, and Cost of Goods Sold (an acceptable alternative when underallocated or overallocated overhead is material in amount).

      (3) Proration on the basis of the total amount of allocated overhead (before proration) in the ending balances of Work in Process, Finished Goods, and Cost of Goods Sold (the theoretically preferred alternative).

5. Note that *the results under 4a and 4b(3) are identical in terms of financial statement effects.*

6. Also note in the textbook example (p. 154) that none of the underallocated or overallocated overhead is assigned to Materials Control in any case. Why? Because no overhead is allocated to materials inventory.

7. Depending on the approach used, a journal entry must be made to close Manufacturing Department Overhead Control and Manufacturing Overhead Allocated. In the case of underallocated overhead, Work in Process, Finished Goods, and Cost of Goods Sold are understated—so prorated amounts would be *debited* to these accounts.

8. *See Practice Test Question III (item 6) and Problem VI.*

Part Two: Process Costing Systems in Manufacturing

D. The principle difference between process costing and job costing is the extent of averaging used to compute *unit* costs of products or services.

1. Under both types of systems, unit costs are averages that result from taking some amount of total costs and dividing it by units produced.

    a. In process costing, the numerator is the costs of a process and the denominator is often a large number of units.

    b. In job costing, the numerator is the costs of a job and the denominator is usually one unit or a small number of units.

2. Two cases of process costing are illustrated:

    Case 1:   All units fully complete at end of reporting period.

    Case 2:   Some units incomplete at end of reporting period.

3. Both cases are illustrated in the textbook with one direct cost category (direct materials), one indirect cost pool (conversion costs—all manufacturing costs other than direct materials costs), and no beginning work in process inventory.

4. Case 1 allows you to grasp the basic concept of process costing without the complication of work in process inventory.

5. Case 2 requires that the total costs of a process be allocated to units completed (and transferred out) and units in ending work in process inventory.

6. Case 2 requires that physical units be distinguished from equivalent units.

    a. **Physical units** measure the output by ignoring the percentage of completion.

    b. **Equivalent units** measure the output in terms of the quantities used of each of the factors of production.

    c. Example: Suppose a total of 400 physical units are started in a process. Of these units, 300 are fully complete with respect to conversion costs and 100 (the ending inventory) are 40% complete with respect to conversion costs.

    Question: How many of the 400 physical units are equivalent units of conversion costs?

    Answer: $300 + 100(.40) = 340$

7. To effectively and efficiently solve Case 2 problems, follow a **five-step approach**:

    Step 1:   Summarize the flow of physical units of a product (output).

    Step 2:   Compute output in terms of equivalent units.

    Step 3:   Compute the total costs to account for, which are all the costs debited to Work in Process.

    Step 4:   Compute equivalent unit costs.

    Step 5:   Assign total costs to units completed and to units in ending work in process.

8. Steps 1 and 2 are illustrated in Exhibit 5-4. Steps 3, 4, and 5 constitute a *production-cost worksheet* illustrated in Exhibit 5-5.

- **To see the big picture, tie the numbers in Exhibit 5-5 to the T-account for Work in Process in the textbook (p. 159).**
- *See Practice Test Question III (items 8-11) and Problems VII and VIII.*

Part Three: Activity-Based Costing in Manufacturing

E. **Activity-based costing (ABC)** is a specific type of costing system refinement that focuses on activities (also called activity areas) as the fundamental cost object.

1. In a manufacturing context, ABC assigns the costs of activities to jobs, products, or customers.

2. Manufacturing is where most of the ABC implementation has occurred.

3. ABC is an approach to developing cost numbers used *in* job costing or process costing systems; *ABC is not an alternative to job costing or process costing*.

4. The textbook provides an important illustration of an actual activity-based job costing system of a manufacturer of printed-circuit boards (p. 159).

   a. Compared to the prior costing system, this system better measures the way jobs and products differently use the resources of the company.

   b. Six activity areas (indirect cost pools) were identified by a cross-functional team of managers.

   c. The six cost-allocation bases were selected to accurately reflect the causes of the manufacturing overhead costs, so that product cost information would be more accurate.

   d. Exhibit 5-7 is an overview diagram of the costing system.

   e. Exhibit 5-8 illustrates the costing of two different products.

   f. *See Practice Test Problem IX.*

5. Helpful summary of major differences in the design of costing systems:

Traditional Approach	*ABC Approach*
• One or a few indirect cost pools are used for each department or entire plant, usually with little *homogeneity* (that is, the cause-and-effect relationship between the cost allocation bases and indirect cost pools has not been captured).	• Many homogeneous indirect cost pools because many activity areas are used. Operating personnel play a key role in designating which activity areas need to be considered.
• Indirect cost allocation bases may or may not be cost drivers.	• Indirect cost allocation bases are highly likely to be cost drivers.
• Indirect cost allocation bases are often financial variables, such as direct labor costs or direct materials costs.	• Indirect cost allocation bases are often nonfinancial variables, such as number of parts in a product or hours of test time.

6. The traditional approach tends to allocate indirect manufacturing costs too heavily to high-volume products and too lightly to low-volume products.

   a. When such allocations occur, *high-volume products are overcosted* and *low-volume products are undercosted*.

   b. This overcosting/undercosting phenomenon is called **product-cost cross-subsidization**.

7. Although ABC provides more accurate product costs, some companies believe its most important benefit is providing information for cost management (that is, reducing the usage of cost drivers can help control costs).
   a. If the allocation bases really cause the indirect costs (that is, they really are the cost drivers), using less of them can ultimately reduce costs — such as when products are designed with fewer parts or less soldering.
   b. Stating the same point differently: *managers cannot control costs per se, but they can control the variables (drivers) that cause costs.*
8. ABC should be used only if it passes the *cost-benefit test.*
   a. The costs include clerical and computer time as well as user education.
   b. The benefits are the expected improvements in collective operating decisions in an organization.
   c. Today's less expensive computer technology has made the gathering and processing of ABC information more practical.
9. ABC most likely would be beneficial to companies with:
   a. Many products that use different amounts of resources.
   b. Operations that are varied and complex.
   c. A highly competitive environment where knowledge of costs and cost control are critical.
   d. Access to accounting and information systems expertise to implement and maintain refined costing systems.

> **Exhibit 5-9 explains the distinction between business functions, departments, and activities. The exhibit also highlights the fact that only manufacturing costs are inventoriable costs for financial statement purposes under generally accepted accounting principles.**

PRACTICE TEST QUESTIONS AND PROBLEMS

I. Complete each of the following statements.

Part One

1. When the cost object is a manufacturing job, direct costs are _____ to this job and indirect costs are _____ to it.
2. Besides jobs, the two main cost objects of costing systems in manufacturing are _____ and _____.
3. A source document that helps management fix the responsibility for the control and usage of materials is called the _____ _____.
4. Under _____ costing, a manufacturing company debits Work in Process Control with direct manufacturing costs incurred and indirect manufacturing costs allocated.
5. The supporting detail for a general ledger control account is called a _____ _____.

Part Two

6. In process costing, _____ units measure the output by ignoring the percentage of completion.
7. In process costing, _____ units measure the output in terms of the quantities used of each of the factors of production.
8. Conversion costs are defined as _____ _____.

Part Three

9. Although activity-based costing provides more accurate product costs, some companies believe its most important benefit is providing information for _____ _____.
10. In a homogeneous cost pool, all costs have the same or a similar _____ relationship with the cost allocation base.

11. When a company's costing system overcosts some products and undercosts other products, this phenomenon is called _____ _____.

II. Indicate whether each of the following statements is true or false by putting T or F in the space provided.

Part One

___ 1. Costing systems in the manufacturing sector tend to be more complex than those in the service and merchandising sectors.

___ 2. In general, the same product costs should be used for financial statements and pricing decisions.

___ 3. In manufacturing, job costing systems use budgeted cost rates more often than actual cost rates.

___ 4. A perpetual inventory of Materials Control is the file of job cost records for uncompleted jobs.

___ 5. The subsidiary ledger for Manufacturing Department Overhead Control contains entries for allocated overhead.

___ 6. Overallocated overhead arises when the balance of Manufacturing Department Overhead Control exceeds the balance of Manufacturing Overhead Allocated.

___ 7. The amount of underallocated or overallocated manufacturing overhead would usually be larger at year-end than at the end of a month or quarter.

___ 8. In disposing of underallocated or overallocated overhead, it is theoretically preferred to prorate based on the total amount of allocated overhead (before proration) in the ending balances of Work in Process, Finished Goods, and Cost of Goods Sold than to prorate based on the ending balances of these accounts.

___ 9. In disposing of overallocated overhead, Materials Control should never be credited.

Part Two

___ 10. In comparison to job costing systems, process costing systems are usually more complicated and more expensive.

___ 11. In terms of the five-step approach used in process costing systems, it is necessary to compute output in terms of equivalent units before costs are allocated to units completed and to units in ending work in process inventory.

___ 12. In a particular process, physical units will always be equal to or greater than equivalent units.

Part Three

___ 13. Activity-based costing focuses on activities as the fundamental cost object and assigns the costs of products to those activities.

___ 14. Activities is a synonym for departments.

___ 15. Activity-based costing is properly viewed as an alternative costing system to job costing or process costing.

___ 16. The benefits of activity-based costing are the expected improvements in collective operating decisions in an organization.

III. Select the best answer for each of the following multiple-choice questions and put the identifying letter in the space provided.

Part One

___ 1. Under a manufacturing company's job costing system, issuances of direct materials are debited to:
   a. Manufacturing Department Overhead Control.
   b. Work in Process Control.
   c. Materials Control.
   d. none of the above.

___ 2. In a job costing system, indirect manufacturing labor is debited to:
   a. Wages Payable Control.
   b. Work in Process Control.
   c. Finished Goods Control.
   d. none of the above.

___ 3. (CPA) Under a job costing system, the dollar amount of the entry transferring inventory from Work in Process to Finished Goods is the sum of the costs charged to all jobs:
   a. started in process during the period.
   b. in process during the period.
   c. completed and sold during the period.
   d. completed during the period.

4. A budgeted rate for applying manufacturing overhead costs to products would be preferred to an actual rate if the objective is:
   a. timeliness but not accuracy.
   b. accuracy but not timeliness.
   c. both accuracy and timeliness.
   d. neither timeliness nor accuracy.

5. (CPA adapted) Avery Co. uses a budgeted manufacturing overhead rate based on machine-hours. For the month of October, Avery's budgeted overhead was $300,000 based on a budgeted allocation base of 10,000 machine-hours. Actual overhead incurred amounted to $325,000 and 11,000 actual machine-hours were used. How much was the overallocated or underallocated overhead?
   a. $30,000 overallocated
   b. $30,000 underallocated
   c. $5,000 overallocated
   d. $5,000 underallocated

6. (CPA) Worley Company has overallocated overhead of $45,000 for the year ended December 31, 19_5. Before disposition of the overallocated overhead, selected December 31, 19_5, balances from Worley's accounting records are as follows:

Sales	$1,200,000
Cost of Goods Sold	720,000.
Inventories:	
Direct Materials Control	36,000
Work in Process Control	54,000
Finished Goods Control	90,000

Under Worley's cost accounting system, overallocated or underallocated overhead is allocated to applicable inventories and cost of goods sold based on year-end balances (before proration). In its 19_5 income statement, Worley should report cost of goods sold of:
   a. $682,500.
   b. $684,000.
   c. $756,000.
   d. $757,500.

Part Two

*7. (CPA) Assuming that there was no beginning work in process inventory, and the ending work in process inventory is 60% complete as to conversion costs, the number of equivalent units of conversion costs would be:
   a. the same as the units completed.
   b. the same as the units started in process.
   c. less than the units completed.
   d. less than the units started in process.

8. (CPA adapted) During March 19_5, Bly Co.'s Department Y equivalent unit costs were computed as follows:

Materials	$1
Conversion costs	3

Materials are introduced at the end of the process in Department Y. There were 4,000 units (40% complete as to conversion costs) in work in process at March 31, 19_5. The total costs assigned to the March 31, 19_5, work in process inventory should be:
   a. $4,800.
   b. $7,200.
   c. $8,800.
   d. none of the above.

9. The Molding Process started and completed 550 units in May and showed an ending inventory of 150 units, which were 60% completed as to conversion costs and 100% completed as to materials costs. Materials costs were $2,450, and conversion costs were $3,200. Conversion costs per equivalent unit would be:
   a. $4.57.
   b. $5.00.
   c. $3.83.
   d. none of the above.

10. See item 9. Materials costs per equivalent unit would be:
   a. $3.83.
   b. $4.00.
   c. $3.50.
   d. none of the above.

___ 11. See items 9 and 10. What is the cost of the ending work in process inventory?
   a. $765
   b. $975
   c. $1,275
   d. none of the above

Part Three

___ 12. When there are multiple drivers of a company's indirect costs but a single allocation base is used in the costing system:
   a. products that use relatively more of this base will be undercosted.
   b. products that use relatively less of this base will be overcosted.
   c. products that use relatively less of this base will be undercosted.
   d. products that use none of this base will be overcosted.

___ 13. Under the activity-based costing approach:
   a. managers can control costs per se, and they can control the related cost driver.
   b. managers can control costs per se, but they cannot control the related cost drivers.
   c. managers cannot control costs per se, but they can control the related cost drivers.
   d. managers cannot control costs per se, and they cannot control the related cost drivers.

___ 14. Which of the following is *not* a characteristic of the activity-based costing approach?
   a. Operating personnel play a key role in designating which activity areas need to be considered.
   b. Allocation bases of indirect cost pools are highly likely to be cost drivers.
   c. There are many homogeneous indirect cost pools.
   d. Allocation bases of indirect cost pools are usually financial variables.

___ 15. Activity-based costing most likely would be beneficial to companies with:
   a. operations that are relatively simple.
   b. many products that use different amounts of resources.
   c. many products that use about the same amount of resources.
   d. few products that use about the same amount of resources.

Part One

IV. Given for Glenrose Products, Inc.:

Budgeted manufacturing overhead costs	$660,000
Budgeted machine-hours	440,000
Actual manufacturing overhead costs	$662,000
Actual machine-hours	450,000

Compute:
1. Budgeted overhead rate
2. Manufacturing overhead allocated
3. Underallocated or overallocated overhead

Check figures: (1) $1.50 (2) $675,000 (3) $13,000 overallocated

V. (CPA) Worrell Corporation has a job costing system. The following debits (credits) appeared in the general ledger account Work in Process Control for the month of March 19_5:

March 1, balance	$ 12,000
March 31, direct materials	40,000
March 31, direct manufacturing labor	30,000
March 31, manufacturing overhead	27,000
March 31, to finished goods	(100,000)

Worrell allocates overhead to production at a budgeted rate of 90% based on the direct manufacturing labor costs. Job 232, the only job still in process at the end of March 19_5, has been charged with manufacturing overhead of $2,250. Compute the amount of direct materials charged to Job 232.

Check figure: $4,250

VI. (CMA adapted) Given for Sanger Company:

Department 203 Costs Incurred for Current Year

Incurred By Jobs	Materials	Labor	Other	Total
1376	$ 1,000	$ 7,000		$ 8,000
1377	26,000	53,000		79,000
1378	12,000	9,000		21,000
1379	4,000	1,000		5,000
Not Incurred by Jobs				
Indirect materials and supplies	15,000			15,000
Indirect labor		53,000		53,000
Employee fringe benefits			$23,000	23,000
Depreciation			12,000	12,000
Supervision		20,000		20,000
Total	$58,000	$143,000	$35,000	$236,000

Department 203 Budgeted Overhead Rate for Current Year

Budgeted overhead:

Variable

Indirect materials and supplies	$ 16,000
Indirect labor	56,000
Employee fringe benefits	24,000

Fixed

Depreciation	12,000
Supervision	20,000
Total	$128,000

Budgeted direct manufacturing labor costs	$80,000
Budgeted overhead rate, $128,000 ÷ $80,000	160%

Department 203 Work in Process at Beginning of Current Year

Job. No.	Direct Materials	Direct Labor	Overhead	Total
1376	$17,500	$22,000	$33,000	$72,500

Assume that Job 1376 was the only job completed during the current year. It was sold upon completion.

1. Compute underallocated or overallocated overhead for Department 203 for the current year.
2. Compute cost of goods sold.
3. Compute cost of work in process inventory at the end of the current year.
4. Ignoring your answer in requirement 1, assume that overhead is underallocated by $14,000 in Department 203. If underallocated overhead is prorated to cost of goods sold and applicable inventories based on the current year's allocated overhead component in the ending balances of these accounts, compute the underallocated overhead that should be charged to work in process inventory at year-end.

Check figures: (1) $11,000 underallocated (2) $91,700 (3) $205,800 (4) $12,600

Part Two

VII. General Plastics Co. presented the following data for the June operations of its Laminating Process:

Materials added	$15,000
Conversion costs	$16,920
Work in process	
Beginning inventory	none
Ending inventory	1,200 units
Units started	6,000 units
Units completed and transferred out	4,800 units

The ending inventory is 70% completed as to conversion costs and 100% completed as to materials.

Compute:
1. Equivalent units of materials.
2. Equivalent units of conversion costs.
3. Materials costs per equivalent unit.
4. Conversion costs per equivalent unit.
5. Cost of units completed and transferred out.
6. Cost of ending work in process inventory.

Prepare the journal entries to record:
7. Materials added to the Laminating Process.
8. Conversion costs added to the Laminating Process.
9. Cost of units completed in the Laminating Process and transferred to the Cutting Process.

Check figures: (1) 6,000 (2) 5,640 (3) $2.50 (4) $3.00 (5) $26,400 (6) $5,520

VIII. During October, Utica Corporation completed and transferred out units from its Forming Process at a total cost of $69,600. The ending inventory of work in process consisted of 1,000 units, which were 100% completed as to materials and 40% complete as to conversion costs. The materials costs per equivalent unit were $5. Materials costs charged to the process were $35,000. There was no beginning inventory.

Compute:
1. Number of units completed and transferred out.
2. Materials costs portion of costs transferred out.
3. Conversion costs per equivalent unit.
4. Cost of ending work in process inventory.

Check figures: (1) 6,000 (2) $30,000 (3) $6.60 (4) $7,640

Part Three

IX. A. H. Church, Inc., manufactures a variety of children's wooden toys. Activity-based costing is used. The manufacturing activity areas and related data are:

Activity Area	Cost Driver Used as Allocation Base	Conversion Costs per Unit of Allocation Base
Materials handling	Board feet of lumber	$ 0.10
Forming and sanding	Direct labor-hours	10.00
Painting	Number of painted sets	0.30
Inspection	Number of finished sets	0.04
Packaging	Number of finished sets	0.20

Two types of wooden blocks were manufactured in September, alphabet cubes and assorted shapes. Their quantities and per set data are:

	Alphabet Cubes	Assorted Shapes
Sets produced	12,000	2,000
Direct materials costs per set	$1.20	$2.00
Board feet of lumber per set	1.5	2.0
Direct labor-hours per set	.05	.10
Sets painted	12,000	none

Nonmanufacturing costs per set:

	Alphabet Cubes	Assorted Shapes
Business functions upstream from manufacturing (such as product design)	$0.10	$0.20
Business functions downstream from manufacturing (such as marketing and distribution)	$0.25	$0.25

For each type of blocks:
1. Compute the manufacturing costs per set.
2. Compute the full product costs per set.

Check figures: Alphabet cubes (1) $2.39 (2) $2.74

CHAPTER 5 SOLUTIONS TO PRACTICE TEST

I. 1 traced, allocated; 2 departments, products; 3 materials requisition record; 4 normal; 5 subsidiary ledger; 6 physical; 7 equivalent; 8 all manufacturing costs other than direct materials costs; 9 cost management; 10 cause-and-effect; 11 product-cost cross-subsidization.

II.
1 T	5 F	9 T	13 F
2 F	6 F	10 F	14 F
3 T	7 F	11 T	15 F
4 F	8 T	12 T	16 T

Explanations:
1 The additional procedures required by the existence of work in process and finished goods inventories tend to make costing systems more complex in the manufacturing sector. (T)
2 Product costs for financial statements are called inventoriable costs and include only manufacturing costs. Product costs in pricing decisions can include costs of all business functions in the value chain. See Exhibit 2-14. (F)
3 Three reasons that budgeted cost rates are used more often are listed in section A(5) of the chapter outline. (T)
4 The file of materials records of unused materials is a perpetual inventory of Materials Control. The file of job cost records for uncompleted jobs is a perpetual inventory of Work in Process Control. (F)
5 This subsidiary ledger contains entries for actual overhead incurred. (F)
6 The statement refers to underallocated overhead. Overallocated overhead arises when the balance of Manufacturing Department Overhead Control is less than the balance of Manufacturing Overhead Allocated. (F)
7 The amount of underallocated or overallocated overhead would tend to be larger for a month or quarter than for a year, because of seasonal influences. (F)
8 The statement is true because the results obtained by prorating based on the total amount of allocated overhead (before proration) in the ending balances of the named accounts would be identical to the results obtained under the restated allocation rate approach. This approach, in

effect, restates all entries in the general and subsidiary ledgers using actual cost rates rather than budgeted cost rates. (T)

9 None of the overallocated (or underallocated) overhead is assigned to Materials Control because no overhead is allocated to materials inventory. (T)

10 Process costing systems are usually simpler and less expensive than job costing systems because there are no individual job cost records to be maintained. (F)

11 Equivalent units are computed in step 2 of the five-step approach. Costs are allocated to units completed and to ending work in process inventory in step 5. (T)

12 Physical units measure output by ignoring the percentage of completion, while equivalent units incorporate the percentage of completion by measuring output in terms of the quantities used of each of the factors of production. At the extreme, then, equivalent units would be equal to physical units. Otherwise, equivalent units would be less than physical units. (T)

13 The last part of the statement is reversed. ABC focuses on activities as the fundamental cost object and assigns the costs of activities to products as well as other cost objects such as customers. (F)

14 A department can be an activity, but usually a department consists of more than one activity. In Exhibit 5-9, for example, the assembly department is divided into four activities: start station, machine insertion, manual insertion, and wave soldering. (F)

15 ABC is an approach to developing cost numbers used in job costing or process costing systems. ABC is *not* an alternative to job costing or process costing. (F)

16 These benefits must be weighed against the costs of ABC, which include clerical and computer time as well as user education. Today's less expensive computer technology has made the gathering and processing of ABC information more practical. ABC should not be used unless it passes the cost-benefit test. (T)

III.

1 b	5 c	9 b	13 c
2 d	6 a	10 c	14 d
3 d	7 d	11 b	15 b
4 a	8 a	12 c	

Explanations:

1 The debit is to Work in Process Control and the credit is to Materials Control. Issuances of indirect materials are debited to Manufacturing Department Overhead Control and credited to Materials Control. (b)

2 Indirect manufacturing labor is debited to Manufacturing Department Overhead Control and credited to Wages Payable Control. (d)

3 The entry described is triggered by the completion of jobs. (d)

4 A budgeted overhead rate is more timely but an actual overhead rate is more accurate. (a)

5 Budgeted overhead rate = $300,000 \div 10,000$ hours = $30 per hour; $325,000 - (11,000 \times $30) = $325,000 - $330,000 = $5,000$ overallocated (c)

6 $720,000 \div ($54,000 + $90,000 + $720,000) = $720,000 \div $864,000 = 5/6; $720,000 - 5/6($45,000) = $682,500$ (a)

7 Given that there is an ending work in process inventory but no beginning work in process, the number of equivalent units of conversion costs would be less than the number of units started in process (that is, all units started in the process were not completed). (d)

8 No material costs are included in the ending work in process inventory because materials are added at the *end* of the process in Department Y: $4,000(40\%)($3) = $4,800$ (a)

9 $550 + 150(60\%) = 640; $3,200 \div 640 = 5.00 (b)

10 $550 + 150(100\%) = 700; $2,450 \div 700 = 3.50 (c)

11 $150($3.50) + 150(60\%)($5.00) = $525 + $450 = 975 (b)

12 If a costing system uses a single allocation base, products that use relatively more (less) of that base will be overcosted (undercosted). The reason is that all *indirect* costs are allocated via that base. (c)

13 Although managers cannot control costs per se, they can control the variables that cause costs. That is, managers can control cost drivers. Using less of cost drivers can ultimately reduce costs, such as when products are designed with less parts or less soldering. (c)

14 Under the ABC approach, allocation bases of indirect cost pools are often nonfinancial variables, such as number of parts in a product or hours of test time. (d)

15 ABC most likely would be beneficial to companies with the four characteristics listed in section E(9) of the chapter outline. (b)

IV. Glenrose Products, Inc.

1. $660,000 \div 440,000 = \$1.50$ per machine-hour
2. $450,000 \times \$1.50 = \$675,000$
3. $\$675,000 - \$662,000 = \$13,000$ overallocated

V. Worrell Corporation

Ending balance of work in process: $\$12,000 + \$40,000 + \$30,000 + \$27,000 - \$100,000 = \$9,000$; this amount is also the balance of Job 232, the only uncompleted job: direct materials charged to this job $= \$9,000 - \$2,250 - (\$2,250 \div .90) = \$6,750 - \$2,500 = \$4,250$

VI. Sanger Company

1. Actual overhead for the current year:

Indirect materials and supplies	$ 15,000
Indirect labor	53,000
Employee fringe benefits	23,000
Depreciation	12,000
Supervision	20,000
Total	$123,000

Total direct manufacturing labor costs for the current year:

Job 1376	$ 7,000
Job 1377	53,000
Job 1378	9,000
Job 1379	1,000
Total	$70,000

$\$123,000 - (\$70,000 \times 160\%) = \$123,000 - \$112,000 = \$11,000$ underallocated overhead

2. $\$72,500 + \$1,000 + \$7,000 + (\$7,000 \times 160\%) = \$80,500 + \$11,200 = \$91,700$. Note that, for use in requirement 4 below, overhead allocated to cost of goods sold during the current year $= \$7,000 \times 160\% = \$11,200$.

3.

	Job 1377	Job 1378	Job 1379	Total
Direct materials	$ 26,000	$12,000	$4,000	$ 42,000
Direct manufacturing labor	53,000	9,000	1,000	63,000
Overhead allocated (direct labor costs × 160%)	84,800	14,400	1,600	100,800
Work in process, year-end	$163,800	$35,400	$6,600	$205,800

4. Overhead allocated during the current year:

Cost of goods sold portion (from part 2)	$ 11,200
Work in process portion (from part 3)	100,800
Total overhead allocated	$112,000

Underallocated overhead charged (debited) to ending Work in Process $= (\$100,800 \div \$112,000) \times \$14,000 = .90 \times \$14,000 = \$12,600$

VII. General Plastics Co.

1. 4,800 + 100%(1,200) = 6,000
2. 4,800 + 70%(1,200) = 5,640
3. $15,000 ÷ 6,000 = $2.50
4. $16,920 ÷ 5,640 = $3.00
5. 4,800($2.50 + $3.00) = $26,400
6. 1,200($2.50) + 1,200(70%)($3.00) = $3,000 + $2,520 = $5,520

   Proof: Total costs to account for = Total costs allocated

   $$\$15,000 + \$16,920 = \$26,400 + \$5,520$$
   $$\$31,920 = \$31,920$$

7. Work in Process—Laminating $15,000
      Materials Inventory $15,000

8. Work in Process—Laminating $16,920
      Wages Payable Control, Accumulated
        Depreciation on Manufacturing
        Equipment, etc. $16,920

9. Work in Process—Cutting $26,400
      Work in Process—Laminating $26,400

VIII. Utica Corporation

1. Equivalent units of materials = $35,000 ÷ $5 = 7,000;
   Units completed and transferred out = 7,000 − 1,000 = 6,000
2. 6,000 × $5 = $30,000
3. Conversion costs portion of costs transferred out = $69,600 − $30,000 = $39,600
   Conversion cost per equivalent unit = $39,600 ÷ 6,000 = $6.60
4. Ending inventory:

Materials, 1,000 × $5	$5,000
Conversion costs, 1,000(40%) × $6.60	2,640
Total costs	$7,640

IX. A. H. Church, Inc.

1.

	Alphabet Cubes	Assorted Shapes
Direct material costs,		
12,000 × $1.20 and 2,000 × $2.00	$14,400	$4,000
Conversion costs:		
Materials handling, 12,000 × 1.5 × $0.10 and		
2,000 × 2.0 × $0.10	1,800	400
Forming and sanding, 12,000 × .05 × $10 and		
2,000 × .10 × $10	6,000	2,000
Painting, 12,000 × $0.30	3,600	
Inspection, 12,000 × $0.04 and 2,000 × $0.04	480	80
Packaging, 12,000 × $0.20 and 2,000 × $0.20	2,400	400
Total manufacturing costs	$28,680	$6,880
Divide by number of sets produced	÷12,000	÷2,000
Manufacturing costs per set	$ 2.39	$ 3.44

2.

	Alphabet Cubes	Assorted Shapes
Upstream costs per set	$0.10	$0.20
Manufacturing costs per set	2.39	3.44
Downstream costs per set	0.25	0.25
Full product costs per set	$2.74	$3.89

CHAPTER 6

MASTER BUDGET
AND RESPONSIBILITY ACCOUNTING

MAIN FOCUS AND OBJECTIVES

Budgets are a key tool in management control systems. In this chapter, we focus on the master budget, a coordinated set of detailed operating and financing plans for all parts of an organization – usually covering a year. Your overall objective for this chapter is to understand the importance of two intertwining aspects of budgeting, the preparation procedures and human behavior. Seven learning objectives are stated in the textbook (p. 182).

Give special attention to:

- the steps in preparing the operating budget
- "what-if" scenarios used in budgeting
- responsibility accounting and the concept of controllability

Carefully study two key textbook exhibits. Exhibit 6-3 is a diagram of the master budget showing the supporting budgets that constitute the operating budget and the financial budget. Exhibit 6-7 illustrates responsibility accounting at three management levels of an actual organization.

The chapter Appendix is particularly important. It explains the cash budget and budgeted balance sheet, which are parts of the financial budget.

REVIEW OF KEY TERMS AND CONCEPTS

A. Budgeting systems are widely used in profit-seeking and nonprofit organizations.
   1. These systems report *both* historical (actual) results and expected amounts.
   2. These systems must pass the *cost-benefit test*.
      a. The costs include personnel and computer time as well as user education.
      b. The benefits are changing human behavior and decisions in ways sought by top management.

B. A **budget** is a quantitative expression of a plan of action and an aid to the coordination and implementation of the plan.
   1. Budgets may be formulated for the organization as a whole or any of its parts.
   2. *Budgets serve a variety of functions*:
      a. Planning of operating activities (the focus of this chapter)
      b. Planning of financing activities
      c. Coordinating of operating and financing activities
      d. Implementing plans

e. Communicating performance criteria
f. Authorizing actions
g. Motivating
h. Controlling
i. Evaluating performance

3. In Japan, budgetary planning and control is the most important cost management technique for continuously reducing product costs.

4. Well-managed organizations usually have the following elements in the *budgetary cycle*:
   a. Planning the performance of the organization as a whole and its parts.
   b. Providing specific expectations against which actual results can be compared.
   c. Investigating significant variances from plans and taking corrective action if desirable.
   d. Planning again, taking into account feedback and changed conditions.

5. Forced planning for changing conditions is by far the main benefit of budgeting.

6. Developing a budget is an iterative process; each draft of a budget almost always leads to further revisions before a final budget is chosen.

7. Budgets should not be administered too rigidly.
   a. Changing conditions call for changes in plans.
   b. Budgets should be adaptable (a means to an end) to help management achieve its strategic goals.

8. Budgeting is an integral part of strategy and tactics.
   a. *Strategy*: selection of overall objectives (goals) of an organization.
   b. *Tactics*: general means for attaining strategic objectives.

9. Strategy analysis underlies both long-run and short-run planning, as shown in Exhibit 6-2.

Question: As a basis for judging actual results, why is budgeted performance generally a better criterion than past performance?
Answer: Because when historical performance is the criterion (i) inefficiencies can be buried in past actions and (ii) opportunities in the future, which did not exist in the past, may be ignored.

---

10. Top management must understand and enthusiastically support the budget and all aspects of the management control system.

11. Budgets often span a year or less but they sometimes cover longer periods.
    a. The usual budget period is one year.
    b. The annual budget is often broken down by months for the first quarter and by quarters for the remainder of the year.
    c. *Rolling budget*: a plan that is always available for a specified future period by adding a period such as a month as the month just ended is dropped.

12. Exhibit 6-1 shows how budgets and performance reports help managers.

C. The master budget is basically the preparation of familiar financial statements using expected future amounts instead of actual results.
   1. **Master budget**: summarizes the financial plans for all business functions in the value chain and quantifies management's expectations regarding future income, cash flows, and financial position.
   2. The master budget itself is not a strategic plan, but it helps managers implement their strategic plans.
   3. Management accountants usually coordinate the master budget process.
   4. The master budget embraces both operating decisions and financing decisions.
      a. *Operating decisions*: acquiring and using resources.
      b. *Financing decisions*: obtaining money to acquire resources.
   5. The master budget consists of two main budgets.
      a. **Operating budget**: budgeted income statement, supported by the sales budget, production budget, inventory budget, and budgets of the other value chain costs.
      b. **Financial budget**: capital expenditures budget, cash budget, budgeted balance sheet, and budgeted statement of cash flows.
   6. Budgeted financial statements are sometimes called *pro forma statements*.
   7. Top management's strategies for achieving sales and operating income goals influence the costs budgeted for the different business functions in the value chain.

> **See important textbook Exhibit 6-3. Follow the arrows in the master budget to study the sequence of preparing the individual budgets that constitute the operating budget and financial budget in this manufacturing company.**

   8. Carefully trace the 13 steps (!) in the textbook illustration of **preparing the operating budget** (beginning p. 191):
      a. Sales budget (the cornerstone of the master budget)
      b. Production budget
      c. Direct materials usage and purchases budgets
      d. Direct manufacturing labor budget
      e. Manufacturing overhead budget
      f. Ending inventory budget
      g. Cost of goods sold budget
      h. Research and development/design costs budget
      i. Marketing costs budget
      j. Distribution costs budget
      k. Customer-service costs budget
      l. Administration costs budget
      m. Budgeted income statement (shown in Exhibit 6-4)
   9. It is *not* necessary to memorize the formats of all these schedules if you understand the logical flow within each schedule.

> *See Practice Test Question III (items 4-6) and Problems IV and V.*

D. Forecasting sales is a difficult task because some important factors are beyond management's control.
  1. Distinguish between a *sales forecast* and a *sales budget*: the forecast is the predicted or estimated sales that may or may not become the sales budget.
  2. Many factors influence the sales forecast, including:
     a. Past sales volume
     b. General economic and industry conditions
     c. Market research studies
     d. Pricing policies
     e. Advertising and other promotion
     f. Competition
  3. In forecasting sales, use a suitable combination of methods:
     a. Views of sales personnel on customer needs and competitors' products.
     b. Statistical approaches such as regression analysis.
     c. Group sales prediction based on the collective experience and knowledge of top executives and administrators.
  4. A key concept related to sales forecasts is budgetary slack.
     a. **Budgetary slack** (also called *padding the budget*): the practice of underestimating budgeted revenues (sales) or overestimating budgeted costs in order to make budgeted targets more easily achievable.
     b. From the sales staff's standpoint, budgetary slack hedges against unexpected adverse circumstances.
     c. The sales staff's incentive to develop budget numbers truthfully is linked to the way sales performance is evaluated.

E. Two relatively new types of budgeting are activity-based budgeting and *kaizen* budgeting.
  1. Activity-based budgeting is a natural complement to the activity-based costing material covered in Chapters 4 and 5.
  2. *Activity-based budgeting* focuses on activities as the fundamental cost object and assigns the budgeted costs of those activities to products and services.
  3. Activity-based budgeting is especially valuable in the case of indirect costs.
     a. The cause-and-effect criterion guides separating indirect costs into homogeneous cost pools.
     b. To build budgets, the budgeted indirect cost rates are multiplied by expected usage of the various activities.
  4. *Kaizen budgeting* projects costs on the basis of *future* improvements in products and processes rather than current practices and methods. (*Kaizen* is the Japanese word for a process of continuous improvement.)
     a. Suggestions for improvements can come from employees in all parts of the organization.
     b. The success of *kaizen* budgeting depends on the quantity and quality of these suggestions.
     c. The key point regarding *kaizen* budgeting is that budgets cannot be achieved *unless* improvements are made.

F. Master budgets are often developed by means of computer-based **financial planning models**.

1. Those models are mathematical statements of the relationships among an organization's activities and related internal and external factors.
2. Those models are used not only for preparing and revising budgets, but also for quickly estimating the effects of various "*what-if*" scenarios on operating income and other items (a technique called *sensitivity analysis*).

> **Exhibit 6-5 illustrates three "what-if" scenarios.**

G. Coordinating an organization's efforts means assigning responsibility to managers who are accountable for their actions in planning and controlling human and physical resources.
  1. *Organization structure*: an arrangement of the lines of responsibility within the organization.
  2. The organization structure that results when operations are divided into increasingly smaller areas of responsibility is shaped like a pyramid, with top management at the peak.
  3. *Responsibility center*: a subunit of an organization with a manager accountable for its activities.
     a. A "subunit" refers to any part of an organization, ranging from a large division to a small department.
     b. The higher the level of the manager, the broader the responsibility center he or she manages.
  4. Types of responsibility centers:
     a. *Cost center*: manager is accountable for costs (expenses) only.
     b. *Revenue center*: manager is accountable for revenues (sales) only.
     c. *Profit center*: manager is accountable for revenues and costs.
     d. *Investment center*: manager is accountable for capital investments, revenues, and costs.
  5. **Responsibility accounting**: a system for measuring plans (by budgets) and measuring actions (by actual results) of each responsibility center within an organization.
     a. For each responsibility center, the responsibility accounting system traces the costs either (i) to the individual who has the best knowledge about why the costs arose or (ii) to the activity that caused the costs.
     b. For each responsibility center, a **performance report** shows by line item, *actual results, budgeted amounts, and variances*.
     c. Performance reports prepared for higher management levels aggregate lower level reports; therefore, reports to higher level managers include larger dollar amounts but less detail than lower level reports.
     d. Managers are practicing *management by exception* when they concentrate on areas that deserve attention and place less attention on areas that are operating as expected.

> **Carefully study Exhibits 6-6 and 6-7. (In the latter exhibit, start at the bottom and move upward.) They illustrate how responsibility accounting can be used to evaluate profit centers and their managers.**

6. **Controllability**: the degree of influence that a given manager has over costs, revenues, or other items in question.
7. In practice, controllability is difficult to pinpoint: see the two helpful examples in the textbook (p. 206).
8. **Controllable:** any cost that is primarily subject to the influence of a given responsibility center manager for a specified time period.
9. Preferably, responsibility accounting systems should either (i) exclude all uncontrollable costs from a manager's performance report or (ii) segregate such costs from the controllable costs.
10. Variances should be used to raise questions and direct attention to employees who should have answers; *initially, variances should not be used to "fix the blame."*

> **Question**: Why is responsibility assigned to managers even though their controllability may be limited?
>
> **Answer**: Because this approach tends to influence their behavior in the directions top management desires.

H. Many organizations have successfully used some form of management by objectives (MBO).
   1. MBO is perfectly compatible with responsibility accounting.
   2. Under MBO, a manager and his or her subordinate jointly specify objectives and plans of action.
   3. The manager evaluates the subordinate's performance accordingly.

I. (**Appendix**) The cash budget and the budgeted balance sheet are two main parts of the financial budget.
   1. The **cash budget** is a schedule of expected cash receipts and disbursements. Exhibit 6-8 illustrates a cash budget.
      a. It is *not* necessary to memorize the format of the cash budget if you remember the way a bank statement works:

      Beginning balance + Receipts − Disbursements = Ending balance (before financing)

      b. Seasonal peaks of production or sales often result in heavy cash disbursements for purchases, payroll, and other operating outlays as products are produced and sold. Cash receipts from customers typically lag behind sales.
      c. *Depreciation does not require a cash disbursement.*
      d. Computer-based financial planning models help to examine the impact on budgeted cash flows of various "what-if" scenarios.
   2. The **budgeted balance sheet** is presented in Exhibit 6-9.
   3. *See Practice Test Question III (items 9-12) and Problem VI.*

PRACTICE TEST QUESTIONS AND PROBLEMS

I. Complete each of the following statements.

1. A _____ is a plan that is always available for a specified future period by adding a period such as a month as the month just ended is dropped.

2. The master budget consists of two main budgets: _____ and _____.

3. _____ is the practice of underestimating budgeted revenues (sales) or overstating budgeted costs in order to make budgeted targets more easily achievable.

4. _____ projects costs on the basis of future improvements in products and processes rather than current practices and methods.

5. _____ are used not only for preparing and revising budgets, but also for quickly estimating the effect of various "what-if" scenarios on operating income and other items.

6. A _____ is a subunit of an organization with a manager accountable for its activities.

7. A _____ cost is any cost that is primarily subject to the influence of a given responsibility center manager for a specified time period.

8. For each responsibility center, a _____ shows by line item, actual results, budgeted amounts, and variances.

9. Managers are practicing _____ when they concentrate on areas that deserve attention and place less attention on areas that are operating as expected.

10. Preferably, _____ systems should either exclude all uncontrollable costs from a manager's performance report or segregate such costs from the controllable costs.

11. Under _____, a manager and his or her subordinate jointly specify objectives and plans of action.

II. Indicate whether each of the following statements is true or false by putting T or F in the space provided.

____ 1. The primary purpose of a budget is to set official limits on spending for various costs.

____ 2. The final step in the budgetary cycle is providing specific expectations against which actual results can be compared.

____ 3. The preferable basis for evaluating a month's operating results is the actual results for the same month in the preceding year.

____ 4. The usual budget period is one year.

____ 5. The master budget consists of two main budgets, the operating budget and the cash budget.

____ 6. The most common constraint on the budgeted level of operations is production capacity.

____ 7. Generally, the most effective way of forecasting sales is to use last year's sales and add a conservatively estimated increase.

____ 8. From the sales staff's standpoint, budgetary slack hedges against unexpected adverse circumstances.

____ 9. The organization structure that results when operations are divided into increasingly smaller areas of responsibility is shaped like a pyramid.

____ 10. Controllable costs are defined as costs that can vary considerably within a short time span.

____ 11. Variances, the differences between actual results and budgeted amounts, should be used to raise questions and direct attention to employees who should have answers.

____ 12. Management by objectives (MBO) focuses on the ability of a manager to achieve the goals specified by the manager's superior.

____ 13. (Appendix) Depreciation is excluded from the cash budget.

III. Select the best answer for each of the following multiple-choice questions and put the identifying letter in the space provided.

____ 1. Budgeting systems:
   a. report actual results and should be subjected to the cost-benefit test.
   b. do not report actual results but should be subjected to the cost-benefit test.
   c. report actual results but need not be subjected to the cost-benefit test.
   d. do not report actual results and need not be subjected to the cost-benefit test.

____ 2. Decisions concerning the acquisition and utilization of resources are:
   a. activity-based costing decisions.
   b. performance decisions.
   c. operating decisions.
   d. financing decisions.

____ 3. In the construction of an operating budget, the last step is usually the preparation of the:
   a. budgeted income statement.
   b. budgeted balance sheet.
   c. budgeted statement of cash flows.
   d. cash budget.

____ 4. Packer Plastic, Inc. has a target inventory of 14,500 units of a particular product at the end of the budget period, a beginning inventory of 20,000 units, and budgeted production of 59,000 units. Budgeted sales would be:
   a. 53,500 units.
   b. 64,500 units.
   c. 59,000 units.
   d. none of the above.

____ 5. Sawyer, Inc. desires to reduce its inventory of a particular direct material by 40%. The inventory at the beginning of the budget period is 120,000 gallons, and the company plans to manufacture 84,000 units of output. Each of these units requires 2.5 gallons of the direct material. How much of the direct material should be purchased during the budget period?
   a. 138,000 gallons
   b. 258,000 gallons
   c. 64,800 gallons
   d. none of the above

____ 6. (CPA adapted) The Zel Company, a wholesaler, budgeted $150,000 of credit sales and $20,000 of cash sales for June 19_5. All merchandise is marked up to sell at 125% of its invoice cost. What is the budgeted cost of goods sold for June 19_5?
   a. $127,500
   b. $140,000
   c. $136,000
   d. $132,500

____ 7. Financial planning models are useful mainly in:
   a. management by objectives.
   b. responsibility accounting.
   c. management by exception.
   d. sensitivity analysis.

____ 8. (CPA) When used for performance evaluation, periodic reports in a responsibility accounting system should not:
   a. be related to the organization structure.
   b. include allocated fixed manufacturing overhead.
   c. include variances between actual results and budgeted amounts of controllable costs.
   d. distinguish between controllable and uncontrollable costs.

____ 9. (Appendix, CMA) Information pertaining to Noskey Corporation's sales revenue is presented in the following table.

	November 19_4 (Actual)	December 19_4 (Budget)	January 19_5 (Budget)
Cash sales	$ 80,000	$100,000	$ 60,000
Credit sales	240,000	360,000	180,000
Total sales	$320,000	$460,000	$240,000

Management estimates that 5% of credit sales are uncollectible. Of the credit sales that are collectible, 60% are collected in the month of sale and the remainder in the month following the sale. Purchases of inventory are equal to next month's sales, and gross margin is 30%. All purchases of inventory are on account; 25% are paid in the month of purchase, and the remainder are paid in the month following purchase. Noskey Corporation's budgeted total cash receipts in January 19_5 are:

a. $240,000.
b. $294,000.
c. $299,400.
d. $239,400.
e. $312,000.

___ 10. See item 9. Noskey Corporation's budgeted total cash payments in December 19_4 for inventory purchases are:
a. $405,000.
b. $283,500.
c. $240,000.
d. $168,000.
e. $295,000.

___ 11. (Appendix) During the budget period, Bama Manufacturing Company expects to make $219,000 of sales on account and to collect $143,500 of cash on account. Assume that no other cash inflows are expected, that total cash payments during the budget period are expected to be $179,000, and that the minimum increase desired in the cash balance is $10,000. How much cash needs to be borrowed?
a. $45,500
b. $44,500
c. $24,500
d. none of the above

___ 12. (Appendix, CPA) Steven Corporation began operations in 19_4. Steven made available the following information:

Total merchandise pur-	
chases for the year	$350,000
Merchandise inventory	
at December 31, 19_4	70,000
Collections from cus-	
tomers	200,000

All merchandise was marked to sell at 40% above cost. Assuming that all sales are on a credit basis and all receivables are collectible, what should be the balance in accounts receivable at December 31, 19_4?
a. $50,000
b. $192,000
c. $250,000
d. $290,000

IV. (CPA) Eriksen Company has budgeted its activity for October 19_5 based on the following information:

- Sales are budgeted at $300,000. All sales are credit sales and a provision for uncollectible accounts is made monthly at the rate of 3% of sales.
- Merchandise inventory was $70,000 at September 30, 19_5, and an increase of $10,000 is planned for the next month.
- All merchandise is marked up to sell at invoice cost plus 50%.
- Estimated cash disbursements for marketing and administrative costs for the month are $40,000.
- Depreciation for the month is projected at $5,000.

Compute:
1. The budgeted net cost of purchases for October, 19_5.
2. The budgeted operating income for October, 19_5.

Check figures: (1) $210,000 (2) $46,000

V. (CMA) Berol Company plans to sell 200,000 units of finished product in July of 19_5 and anticipates a growth rate in sales of 5% per month. The target monthly ending inventory in units of finished product is 80% of the next month's estimated sales. There are 150,000 finished units in inventory on June 30, 19_5.

Each unit of finished product requires four pounds of direct materials at a cost of $1.20 per pound. There are 800,000 pounds of direct materials in inventory on June 30, 19_5.

Compute:
1. The production requirement in units of finished product for the quarter ending September 30, 19_5.
2. The estimated cost of direct materials purchases for the quarter ending September 30, 19_5, assuming that direct materials inventory on hand at the end of the quarter is to equal 25% of the usage during this period.

Check figures: (1) 665,720 (2) $3,034,320

VI. (Appendix) Given for Venice Frames, Inc.

Beginning cash balance	$ 4,200
Expected cash receipts	98,000
Expected cash disbursements	89,000
Minimum ending cash balance desired	8,000

Compute the estimated amount that needs to be borrowed or is available for repayment of loans and interest.

Check figure: $5,200 available

CHAPTER 6 SOLUTIONS TO PRACTICE TEST

I. 1 rolling budget; 2 operating budget, financial budget; 3 Budgetary slack; 4 Kaizen budgeting; 5 Financial planning models; 6 responsibility center; 7 controllable; 8 performance report; 9 management by exception; 10 responsibility accounting; 11 management by objectives (MBO).

II.

1 F	5 F	9 T	13 T
2 F	6 F	10 F	
3 F	7 F	11 T	
4 T	8 T	12 F	

Explanations:

1 The primary purpose of a budget is to establish a plan of action and to aid in coordinating and implementing that plan. Budgets should not be administered too rigidly. (F)
2 The step referred to in the statement is followed by two steps: (i) investigating significant variances from plans and taking corrective action if desirable and (ii) planning again, taking into account feedback and changed conditions. (F)
3 As a basis for judging actual results, budgeted performance generally is a better criterion than past performance, because when historical performance is the criterion (i) inefficiencies can be buried in past actions and (ii) opportunities in the future, which did not exist in the past, may be ignored. (F)
4 The annual budget is often broken down by months for the first quarter and by quarters for the remainder of the year. (T)
5 The master budget consists of two main budgets, the operating budget and the financial budget. The cash budget is one of four budgets that constitute the financial budget, as shown in Exhibit 6-3. (F)
6 Most companies are limited by their ability to sell, not their ability to produce. Therefore, the most common constraint on the operating budget is units of output sold. (F)
7 Sales forecasting should be based on a suitable combination of statistical approaches and input from sales personnel and top executives. Factors to be considered in forecasting sales include past sales volume, general economic and industry conditions, market research studies, and competition. (F)
8 The sales staff's incentive to develop budget numbers truthfully is linked to the way sales performance is evaluated. (T)
9 For example, see Exhibit 6-6. (T)
10 Controllable costs are costs that are primarily subject to the influence of the responsibility center manager for a specified time span. (F)
11 Initially, variances should not be used to "fix the blame." (T)
12 The subordinate manager and his or her superior *jointly* specify the goals and plans for attaining them. (F)
13 Depreciation does not require a cash disbursement, so it is not a part of the cash budget. (T)

III.

1 a	4 b	7 d	10 b
2 c	5 d	8 b	11 a
3 a	6 c	9 c	12 b

Explanations:

1 Budgeting systems report both actual results and expected amounts, so that variances can be determined. Like all internal systems, budgeting must pass the cost-benefit test. (a)

2 Operating decisions concern acquisition and utilization of resources. Financing decisions concern obtaining money to acquire resources. (c)

3 As shown in Exhibit 6-3, the budgeted income statement is the last step in preparing the operating budget. The budgeted balance sheet and budgeted statement of cash flows are components of the financial budget. (a)

4 Budgeted sales $+ 14,500 - 20,000 = 59,000$; Budgeted sales $= 64,500$ (b)

5 $84,000(2.5) + 120,000(1 - .40) - 120,000 = 162,000$ (d)

6 Let X $=$ Budgeted cost of goods sold for June 19_5; $1.25X = \$170,000$; X $= \$136,000$ (c) Note that the amount of the markup (that is, gross margin) is $\$170,000 - \$136,000 = \$34,000$, and the markup as a percentage of sales is $\$34,000 \div \$170,000 = 20\%$.

7 Financial planning models are used for preparing and revising budgets, as well as for quickly estimating the effect on operating income and other items of various "what if" scenarios. (d)

8 Many advocates of responsibility accounting favor including only controllable costs in reports used for performance evaluation. Allocated fixed overhead is not a controllable cost because it cannot be directly influenced by the manager who is being evaluated. (b)

9 Cash collection in January 19_5:

From credit sales in December 19_4,	
$\$360,000(1 - .05)(1 - .60)$	$\$136,800$
From credit sales in January 19_5,	
$\$180,000(1 - .05)(.60)$	102,600
Cash sales in January 19_5	60,000
Total	$\underline{\$299,400}$ (c)

10 Cash payments in December 19_4:

From purchases in November 19_4,	
$\$460,000(1 - .30)(1 - .25)$	$\$241,500$
From purchases in December 19_4,	
$\$240,000(1 - .30)(.25)$	42,000
Total	$\underline{\$283,500}$ (b)

11 $\$179,000 + \$10,000 - \$143,500 = \$45,500$ (a)

12 Costs of goods sold $= \$350,000 - \$70,000 = \$280,000$; Sales $= \$280,000(1.40) = \$392,000$; Accounts receivable balance at December 31, 19_4 $= \$392,000 - \$200,000 = \$192,000$ (b)

IV. Eriksen Company

1. (All figures are budgeted amounts.)
   Cost of goods sold $= \$300,000 \div 1.50 = \$200,000$

Beginning finished goods	$\$ 70,000$
Net cost of purchases	P
Cost of goods available for sale	?
Ending finished goods ($\$70,000 + \$10,000$)	80,000
Cost of goods sold	$\underline{\$200,000}$

   $\$70,000 + P - \$80,000 = \$200,000$; P $= \$210,000$

2. Sales $300,000

   Cost of goods sold $\underline{200,000}$

   Gross margin $100,000$

   Operating costs

     Cash disbursed for marketing

     and administrative costs $40,000

     Depreciation 5,000

     Uncollectible accounts,

       $300,000 \times .03$ $\underline{9,000}$ $\underline{54,000}$

   Operating income $\underline{\underline{\$ 46,000}}$

V. Berol Company

1. $$\begin{array}{c}\text{Production requirement}\\\text{in units of}\\\text{finished goods}\end{array} = \begin{array}{c}\text{Expected}\\\text{sales}\end{array} + \begin{array}{c}\text{Target ending finished}\\\text{goods inventory}\end{array} - \begin{array}{c}\text{Beginning finished}\\\text{goods inventory}\end{array}$$

Expected sales: July = 200,000; August = 200,000 (1.05) = 210,000; September = 210,000(1.05) = 220,500; October = 220,500(1.05) = 231,525

Production requirement in units of
finished goods for the quarter:

July,	200,000 + 210,000(.80) − 150,000	218,000
August,	210,000 + 220,500(.80) − 210,000(.80)	218,400
September,	220,500 + 231,525(.80) − 220,500(.80)	$\underline{229,320}$
Total		$\underline{665,720}$

$$\begin{array}{c}\text{Purchases}\\\text{in}\\\text{pounds}\end{array} = \begin{array}{c}\text{Production}\\\text{requirement}\\\text{in pounds}\end{array} + \begin{array}{c}\text{Target ending}\\\text{materials inventory}\end{array} - \begin{array}{c}\text{Beginning materials}\\\text{inventory}\end{array}$$

Purchases in pounds = 665,720(4) + 665,720(4)(.25) − 800,000

Purchases in pounds = 2,662,880 + 665,720 − 800,000 = 2,528,600

Cost of purchases = 2,528,600 × $1.20 = $3,034,320

VI. Venice Frames, Inc.

Beginning cash balance	$ 4,200
Add expected cash receipts	$\underline{98,000}$
Total available before financing, (a)	102,200
Expected cash disbursements	89,000
Add minimum ending cash balance desired	$\underline{8,000}$
Total cash needed, (b)	$\underline{97,000}$
Available for repayment of loans and interest, (a) − (b)	$\underline{\underline{\$ 5,200}}$

FLEXIBLE BUDGETS, VARIANCES, AND MANAGEMENT CONTROL: I

MAIN FOCUS AND OBJECTIVES

We have learned that managers quantify their plans in the form of budgets. This chapter and the next focus on how flexible budgets and variances can play a key role in planning, control, and cost management. Four different levels of detail are illustrated for analyzing variances. Your overall objective for this chapter is to understand how flexible budgets and variances help managers gain insights into why actual results differ from budgeted amounts. Nine learning objectives are stated in the textbook (p. 226).

Give special attention to:

- the distinction between performance gaps and variances
- the distinction between static budgets and flexible budgets
- computing and interpreting five types of variances: static-budget variances, flexible-budget variances, sales-volume variances, and price and efficiency variances for direct cost categories
- perfection standards, currently-attainable standards, and benchmarking
- journal entries to record price and efficiency variances

Be aware that the newly evolving management themes of total value-chain analysis, continuous improvement, and dual internal/external focus have implications for the topics in this chapter. The chapter Appendix explains variance investigation decisions under conditions of uncertainty.

REVIEW OF KEY TERMS AND CONCEPTS

A. A key to understanding the material in this chapter and the next is learning some basic terms.
   1. Distinguish between budgeted amounts and standard amounts.
       a. All figures in a budget are budgeted amounts, but not all budgeted amounts are standard amounts.
       b. *Standard amounts are a specific type of budgeted amounts.*
       c. Standards represent good levels or best levels of performance. They are usually developed from a careful study of specific operations and are expressed on a *per-unit-of-output basis*.
       d. *Standard input*: the allowed quantity of input (such as pounds of materials or hours of labor time) for any quantity of output achieved, given good or best levels of performance.
       e. **Standard cost**: the cost per unit of output for standard input.

f. Standard costs are most frequently found in the manufacturing and distribution parts of the value chain.

> **Question**: Why are budgeted costs not necessarily the same as standard costs?
>
> **Answer**: Because many budgeted costs are based on past cost relationships, but without a careful study of the specific operations to determine good or best levels of performance.

2. Distinguish between a performance gap and a variance.
   a. **Performance gap**: the difference between an actual result and a benchmark amount.
   b. *Benchmark amount*: the best levels of performance that can be found inside or outside the organization.
      (1) Benchmark amounts can be financial or nonfinancial variables.
      (2) Benchmark amounts may or may not be reported in the accounting system.
   c. **Variance**: the difference between an actual result and a budgeted amount, when that budgeted amount is (i) a financial variable reported in the accounting system and (ii) may or may not be a benchmark amount.
   d. Therefore, *a variance is a special case of a performance gap*.
   e. See the helpful diagram in the textbook (p. 227).

B. Variances can be computed on the basis of a static budget or flexible budget.
   1. **Static budget** (also called a *master budget* in Chapter 6): a budget that is based on one level of output and is *not* adjusted after it is finalized, regardless of changes in output or input prices, quantities, or costs.
   2. **Flexible budget**: a budget that can be adjusted (flexed) to the actual level of output achieved or expected to be achieved during the budget period.
   3. Flexible budgets help managers gain more insight into the causes of variances than do static budgets.
   4. Flexible budgets can use any budgeted amounts for individual cost items, *regardless of whether or not these amounts are based on standard costs*.
   5. Static budgets and flexible budgets can differ in terms of the *level of detail* they report:

> - **Level 0 analysis is based on the static budget.**
> - **Level 1 analysis is based on the static budget with more detail than in Level 0.**
> - **Level 2 analysis is based on the flexible budget.**
> - **Level 3 analysis is based on the flexible budget with more detail than in Level 2.**

6. Level 0 analysis reports the least detail, Level 1 analysis offers more detail, and so on.

7. **Favorable variances** (denoted by F) increase operating income compared to the budgeted amount.
8. **Unfavorable variances** (denoted by U) decrease operating income compared to the budgeted amount.
9. The static budget is used to compute **static-budget variances** under Level 0 and Level 1 analyses. See Exhibit 7-1 for an illustration.
10. *See Practice Test Question III (items 1 and 3).*

C. Level 2 analysis is based on the flexible budget and can be used either *with or without standard costs.*

> **Question:** Since the flexible budget often is based on actual output, which is not known until the end of the budget period, how can it be a budget?
> **Answer:** The flexible budget shows the budgeted costs that *should have been incurred* to achieve the *actual* output—a useful control tool.

1. With or without standard costs, the flexible budget can help managers in two ways.
   a. **Planning tool:** *Before* the budget period, the flexible budget is used to predict costs at different output levels (as shown in Exhibit 7-2, columns 3, 4, and 5).
   b. **Control tool:** *After* the budget period, the flexible budget is used to determine what costs *should have been* incurred at the output level *actually* achieved (as shown in Exhibit 7-3, column 3).
2. The **building blocks of flexible budgets** are budgeted selling price, budgeted variable costs per unit of output (developed with or without standard costs) and budgeted total fixed costs.
3. Note that only revenues and variable costs put the "flex" in the flexible budget.
4. The textbook example of Goodride Company (beginning p. 228) illustrates the flexible budget *without standard costs.*

> **Carefully study Level 2 analysis in Exhibit 7-3. The static-budget variance of operating income (from Level 1) is divided into two parts:**
> • **the flexible-budget variance**
> • **the sales-volume variance**

5. **Flexible-budget variance:** the difference between an actual result and the flexible budget amount for actual output achieved.
6. **Sales-volume variance:** the difference between the flexible budget amount and the static budget amount; unit selling prices, unit variable costs, and fixed costs are held constant.
   a. This variance arises solely because the actual units sold differ from the budgeted units sold.

b. This variance is usually the responsibility of the senior marketing manager because he or she is in the best position to explain why the actual units sold differ from the static budget units sold.

c. By formula:

$$\text{A} \quad \begin{array}{c}\textbf{Sales–volume}\\ \textbf{variance of}\\ \textbf{operating income}\end{array} = \left(\begin{array}{c}\textbf{Flexible budget}\\ \textbf{output units}\end{array} - \begin{array}{c}\textbf{Static budget}\\ \textbf{output units}\end{array}\right) \times \begin{array}{c}\textbf{Budgeted unit}\\ \textbf{contribution margin}\end{array}$$

7. The insights provided by Level 2 analysis in Exhibit 7-3 are explained in the textbook (p. 233).

8. The textbook example of Webb Company (beginning p. 233) illustrates the flexible budget *with standard costs*.

9. *See Practice Test Question III (item 2) and Problem IV.*

10. Standards represent good or best levels of performance.

a. **Perfection standard**: the best level of performance under the best conceivable conditions, with no provision for normal spoilage and the like.

b. **Currently attainable standard**: a good level of performance taking into account normal spoilage and the like.

c. Currently attainable standards are more frequently used in accounting systems, but a growing number of organizations now use perfection standards. Why? Because perfection standards harmonize with the notion of continuous improvement of quality and operating efficiency.

d. Note that there is a tradeoff between using perfection standards and the motivation problems associated with judging performance against a goal workers perceive to be unattainable.

11. Exhibit 7-4 presents Webb's Level 0 and Level 1 analysis.

12. Exhibit 7-5 provides the numbers used to develop the Level 2 analysis in Exhibit 7-6.

> **Exhibits 7-4 through 7-6 exactly parallel Exhibits 7-1 through 7-3, except the latter set is based on standard costs.**

13. In the Webb example, standard costs are determined for five variable cost items—including both manufacturing *and* marketing costs—and the total standard cost per unit of output ($99) is used in the flexible budget.

14. Note that standard costs add a layer of complexity to variance analysis; it is necessary to first compute the standard costs per unit of output.

15. Distinguish between two attributes of performance measurement.

a. *Effectiveness*: the degree to which a predetermined objective or target is met.

b. *Efficiency*: the relative amount of inputs used to achieve a given level of output. (The fewer the inputs used to obtain a given output, the greater the efficiency.)

c. The sales-volume variance of operating income is a measure of effectiveness.

d. The flexible-budget variance of operating income is often a measure of efficiency.

D. Level 3 analysis requires information on prices and quantities of *inputs* to isolate price variances and efficiency variances.
  1. The price variance and efficiency variance are subdivisions of the Level 2 flexible-budget variance.
  2. **Price variance**: the difference between actual price and budgeted price multiplied by the actual quantity of input in question.

$$\begin{array}{c} \text{Price} \\ \text{variance} \end{array} = \left(\begin{array}{c} \text{Actual price} \\ \text{of input} \end{array} - \begin{array}{c} \text{Budgeted price} \\ \text{of input} \end{array} \right) \times \begin{array}{c} \text{Actual quantity of} \\ \text{input purchased} \end{array}$$

  3. **Efficiency variance**: the difference between the actual quantity of input used and the budgeted quantity of input that should have been used, multiplied by the budgeted price.

$$\begin{array}{c} \text{Efficiency} \\ \text{variance} \end{array} = \left(\begin{array}{c} \text{Actual} \\ \text{quantity of} \\ \text{input used} \end{array} - \begin{array}{c} \text{Budgeted quantity of} \\ \text{input allowed for actual} \\ \text{output units achieved} \end{array} \right) \times \begin{array}{c} \text{Budgeted} \\ \text{price of} \\ \text{input} \end{array}$$

  4. Note that to facilitate control, price variances are usually based on actual quantities of inputs *purchased* rather than *used*. (In the Webb example, inputs purchased equal inputs used.)
     a. For direct materials, actual quantity purchased *often does not equal* actual quantity used. Exhibit 7-10 illustrates this point.
     b. For direct labor, actual hours purchased always equals actual hours worked.

Problem: **Compute the price and efficiency variances for direct materials cost for the Webb Company illustration in the textbook (pp. 238–39).**
Solution: **See Exhibit 7-7.**

---

  5. The advantage of computing price and efficiency variances separately is that they are often the responsibility of *different* managers. For example, a purchasing manager is responsible for the materials price variance, and a production manager is responsible for the materials efficiency variance.
  6. Some possible reasons why price variances arise are given in the textbook (p. 240).
  7. Some possible reasons why efficiency variances arise are given in the textbook (p. 240).
  8. *Question*: Why do managers generally have more control over efficiency variances than price variances?
     Answer: Because the quantity of inputs used is primarily affected by factors inside the company, while price changes arise primarily from factors outside the company.
  9. **Caution**: Do not interpret the price (efficiency) variance individually as the sole performance measure for a purchasing (production) manager.
     a. Why? Because the causes of price and efficiency variances can be interrelated.
     b. See the textbook example (p. 245) and the Concepts in Action Box (p. 243).

Key Exhibit 7-9 provides a very useful framework for understanding Levels 0 through 3 of variance analysis. This framework will help you solve *Practice Test Question III* (items 5-9).

---

10. The formula for the price variance on the preceding page includes some inefficiencies in the usage of input.
    a. Some companies refine the price variance into a *pure price variance* component and a *joint price-efficiency variance* component.
    b. See the formulas in the textbook (p. 241).
    c. Exhibit 7-8 is a diagram of the refined variance analysis of materials.
11. Note that to compute price and efficiency variances, it is necessary to have budgeted and actual input prices and input quantities.
    a. A standard-costing system is one source of those budgeted amounts.
    b. Another source of budgeted amounts, say, for the current month is actual input prices and quantities from the previous month.
12. Also note that the labels favorable or unfavorable denote a variance's effect on operating income, but they *do not necessarily* mean "good" or "bad" performance. For example, a favorable materials price variance could harm the company if the materials are of such poor quality that they increase spoilage costs or customer service costs.

Variance analysis should not be used to "play the blame game." Instead it should help managers to understand why variances arise, and then apply that knowledge to promote learning and continuous improvement.

E. Managers are regularly faced with a difficult decision: *When should variances be investigated?*
    1. Investigating variances entails activities ranging from phone calls to engineering analyses of the production process, and can be expensive.
    2. Apply the *cost-benefit test*: Investigation of a variance is warranted only when the expected benefits (such as reduced costs or better decisions due to having more detailed information) exceed the expected costs.
    3. Subjective rules of thumb are often used to make the decision, such as "Investigate all variances exceeding $5,000 or 25% of budgeted cost, whichever is lower."
    4. Statistical tools can add objectivity to the decision by helping to separate variances caused by *random events* from variances that are *controllable*.
    5. Further discussion of the decision to investigate variances is in the chapter Appendix.

F. When standard costs are recorded in general ledger accounts, the journal entries should isolate variances at the earliest feasible time.
    1. Materials price variances are recognized when materials are *purchased*.
        a. Materials Control is debited for actual quantities purchased at *standard* prices.
        b. Accounts Payable Control is credited for actual quantities purchased at actual prices.
        c. Using the textbook figures:

Materials Control	$750,000	
Direct Materials Price Variance	25,000	
Accounts Payable Control		$775,000

2. Materials efficiency variances are recognized when materials are *used*.
   a. Work in Process Control is debited for *standard* quantities allowed for *actual* output units achieved at *standard* prices.
   b. Materials Control is credited for actual quantities used at standard prices.
   c. Using the textbook figures:

Work in Process Control	$600,000	
Direct Materials Efficiency Variance	66,000	
Materials Control		$666,000

3. Direct labor variances are recognized when wages are *incurred*. Unlike materials, labor cannot be stored for future use, so purchase and use are in the same journal entry.
   a. Work in Process Control is debited for standard hours allowed for actual output units achieved at standard wage rates.
   b. Wages Payable Control is credited for actual hours worked at actual wage rates.
   c. Using the textbook figures:

Work in Process Control	$160,000	
Direct Manufacturing Labor Price Variance	18,000	
Direct Manufacturing Labor Efficiency Variance	20,000	
Wages Payable Control		$198,000

4. In these entries, *unfavorable variances are always debits and favorable variances are always credits*.
   a. These procedures are intuitive.
   b. Unfavorable variances decrease operating income and favorable variances increase operating income.
5. *See Practice Test Problems V and VI.*

G. Three themes in the newly evolving management approach—total value-chain analysis, continuous improvement, and dual internal/external focus—have implications for the topics covered in this chapter.
   1. Top management should recognize potential tradeoffs among business function costs in the value chain. See the textbook example (pp. 245-46).
   2. An organization's never-ending search for higher levels of performance is signaled by a commitment to continuous improvement.
      a. **Continuous improvement standard**: a standard that is successively reduced over succeeding time periods.
      b. Example: One way managers can avoid unfavorable materials efficiency variances under this type of standard cost is to continually reduce materials waste.
   3. Internal or external benchmarks can be used to evaluate managers' performance.
      a. Either type of benchmark is compatible with the analytical framework presented in this chapter.
      b. **Benchmarking**: the continuous process of measuring products, services, or activities against the best levels of performance that can be found either inside or outside the organization.

c. See the examples of benchmarks in the textbook (p. 249) and the Concepts in Action Box (p. 250).
d. Most organizations use a combination of financial and nonfinancial benchmarks.
   (1) Managers of production lines generally use personal observation and variances expressed in nonfinancial terms (such as labor-hours and spoilage rates) for control purposes.
   (2) Top management uses variances expressed in financial terms to analyze and evaluate the performance of different business functions in the value chain.

H. (**Appendix**) The approach to decision making under uncertainty, which is explained in Chapter 3's Appendix, can be used in variance investigation decisions.
   1. The decision table in Exhibit 7-11 has two actions and two events.
      a. The *actions* are (i) investigate the variance (that is, investigate the process) and (ii) do not investigate the process.
      b. The *events* are (i) an in-control process and (ii) an out-of-control process.
   2. The decision model uses probabilities to compute the *expected value (costs)* of each action.
   3. Prior experience and the magnitude of the variance can be used to estimate the probability of a given process being out of control.
   4. To compute the expected costs of each action, four categories of predicted costs (denoted by letters) are used:
      C = Cost of investigating
      D = Cost per period of being out of control
      M = Cost of correcting, if an out-of-control process is discovered
      L = Cost of a process being out of control this period and not corrected this period
   5. In the textbook example, the expected costs of "investigate" are $4,400 and the expected costs of "do not investigate" are $7,400. Therefore, the optimal action is to investigate the process, the lesser cost alternative.
   6. In this decision model it is helpful to know the probability at which a manager would be indifferent between investigating and not investigating to learn if a process is out of control.
      a. This "indifference probability" is computed as follows: $C \div [L - (D + M)]$.
      b. Investigating the process is desirable when the probability of the process being out of control exceeds the indifference probability.
   7. The textbook example of bottling soft drinks (p. 255) illustrates how the timing of accounting variance reports can affect their usefulness.
   8. *See Practice Test Question III (item 11) and Problem VII.*

PRACTICE TEST QUESTIONS AND PROBLEMS

I. Complete each of the following statements.

1. _____ is the allowed quantity of input for any quantity of output achieved, given good or best levels of performance.

2. The continuous process of measuring products, services, or activities against the best levels of performance that can be found either inside or outside the organization is called _____.

3. The difference between an actual result and a benchmark amount is called a _____ _____.

4. A _____ is the difference between an actual result and a budgeted amount, when that budgeted amount is a financial variable reported in the accounting system and may or may not be a benchmark amount.

5. A budget that can be adjusted to the actual level of output achieved or expected to be achieved during the budget period is called a _____.

6. A _____ is the difference between the flexible budget amount and the static budget amount, holding constant unit selling prices, unit variable costs, and total fixed costs.

7. A good level of performance that takes into account normal spoilage and the like is called a _____.

8. Efficiency is the relative amount of _____ used to achieve a given level of _____.

9. A _____ is a standard that is successively reduced over succeeding time periods.

10. (Appendix) In the model for variance investigation decisions, the two actions are _____ _____ and _____.

11. (Appendix) In the model for variance investigation decisions, the two events are a(an) _____ and a(an) _____.

II. Indicate whether each of the following statements is true or false by putting T or F in the space provided.

____ 1. All figures in a budget are budgeted amounts, but not all budgeted amounts are standard amounts.

____ 2. A performance gap is a special case of a variance.

____ 3. Flexible budgets can differ in terms of the level of detail they report.

____ 4. Favorable variances for both revenue items and cost items increase operating income compared to the budgeted amount.

____ 5. The flexible budget serves as a planning tool and a control tool.

____ 6. Fixed costs "flex" in the flexible budget.

____ 7. The flexible-budget variance of operating income is divided into two parts, the static-budget variance and the sales-volume variance.

____ 8. In computing the sales-volume variance of operating income, fixed costs can be ignored.

____ 9. Currently attainable standards are more frequently used in accounting systems, but a growing number of organizations now use perfection standards.

____ 10. Effectiveness is defined in terms of the relationship between inputs used and the level of output achieved.

____ 11. To facilitate control, direct materials price variances are usually based on actual quantities of inputs used.

____ 12. Generally the same manager is primarily responsible for the materials price variance and the materials efficiency variance.

____ 13. Managers usually have more control over efficiency variances than price variances.

____ 14. As performance measures, price and efficiency variances should be interpreted individually.

____ 15. Price and efficiency variances can be computed without using standard costs.

____ 16. The cost-benefit test should be used to decide whether or not to investigate a particular variance.

____ 17. Under a standard-costing system, direct manufacturing labor costs are credited to Wages Payable Control at standard costs.

____ 18. Under a standard-costing system, unfavorable variances are always debits.

____ 19. Managers of production lines generally use variances expressed in financial terms for control purposes.

____ 20. (Appendix) If a variance is investigated, corrective action would undoubtedly be taken.

____ 21. (Appendix) If the expected probability of being out of control exceeds the probability of being out of control at the point of being indifferent about investigating the variance, investigation is desirable.

III. Select the best answer for each of the following multiple-choice questions and put the identifying letter in the space provided.

_d_ 1. (CPA adapted) The basic difference between the static budget and the flexible budget is that:
   a. the flexible budget includes only variable costs, whereas the static budget includes all costs.
   b. the flexible budget allows management latitude in meeting goals, whereas the static budget is based on rigid goals.
   c. the static budget is for an entire organization, whereas the flexible budget is applicable to individual departments.
   d. the static budget is based on one level of output, whereas the flexible budget can be adjusted for any level of output within the relevant range.

___ 2. (CPA adapted) The static budget for a given cost during a given period was $80,000. The actual cost for the period was $72,000. Assuming this cost is controllable by the production manager, it can be concluded that the manager did a better-than-expected job in controlling the cost if the:
   a. cost is variable and actual production was 90% of budgeted production.
   b. cost is variable and actual production equaled budgeted production.
   c. cost is variable and actual production was 80% of budgeted production.
   d. cost is fixed and actual production equaled budgeted production.

___ 3. (CPA) When a flexible budget is used, a decrease in the output level within the relevant range would:
   a. decrease total costs.
   b. not change fixed costs per unit.
   c. decrease total fixed costs.
   d. increase variable costs per unit.

___ 4. (CMA) Each finished unit of Product DX-25 consists of 60 pounds of direct material. The manufacturing process must provide for a 20% waste allowance. The direct material can be purchased for $2.50 a pound under terms of 2/10, n/30. The company takes all cash discounts. The standard direct material cost for each unit of Product DX-25 is:
   a. $180.00.
   b. $187.50.
   c. $183.75.
   d. $176.40.

___ 5. Courtney Corporation's standards for producing a particular product included 10 pounds of materials at $4 per pound for each unit of output. Planned production for the period was 2,000 units of output. Actually, 1,800 units were produced, each using 11 pounds of materials purchased at $5 per pound. Twenty-thousand pounds of materials were purchased during the period. The standard cost allowed for actual output achieved is:
   a. $80,000.
   b. $72,000.
   c. $90,000.
   d. none of the above.

___ 6. See item 5. The materials price variance is:
   a. $20,000 unfavorable.
   b. $18,000 unfavorable.
   c. $27,000 unfavorable.
   d. none of the above.

___ 7. See item 5. The materials efficiency variance is:
   a. $7,200 favorable.
   b. $27,000 unfavorable.
   c. $8,000 unfavorable.
   d. none of the above.

___ 8. (CPA) Lab Corp. uses a standard-costing system. Direct manufacturing labor information for Product CER for the month of October is as follows:

Standard price	$6.00 per hour
Actual price paid	$6.10 per hour
Standard hours allowed for actual production	1,500 hours
Direct manufacturing labor efficiency variance—unfavorable	$600

What are the actual hours worked?
a. 1,400
b. 1,402
c. 1,598
d. 1,600

___ 9. (CPA) Information on Rex Co.'s direct materials costs for the current month is as follows:

Actual quantity of direct materials purchased and used	30,000 lbs.
Actual cost of direct materials	$84,000
Unfavorable direct materials efficiency variance	$3,000
Standard quantity of direct materials allowed for July production	29,000 lbs.

For July, what was Rex's direct materials price variance?
a. $2,800 favorable
b. $2,800 unfavorable
c. $6,000 unfavorable
d. $6,000 favorable

___ 10. In practice, the joint price-efficiency variance for materials is usually:
a. isolated separately.
b. excluded from variance calculations.
c. included as part of the efficiency variance.
d. included as part of the price variance.

___ 11. (Appendix, CMA) Ron Bagley is contemplating whether or not to investigate a labor efficiency variance in the Assembly Department. It will cost $6,000 to undertake the investigation and another $7,000 to correct operations if the process is found to be out of control. The cost per period of the process being out of control is $11,000. If the process is out of control this period and Bagley fails to make the investigation, operating costs from the various inefficiencies are expected to amount to $33,000. Bagley would be indifferent between investigating and not investigating if the probability of the process being out of control is:
a. 0.29.
b. 0.40.
c. 0.60.
d. 0.71.
e. 0.73.

IV. (CMA adapted) Folsom Fashions sells a line of women's dresses. Folsom's actual results and static budget for November 19_4 are as follows:

	Actual Results	Static Budget
Dresses sold	5,000	6,000
Sales	$235,000	$300,000
Variable costs	145,000	180,000
Contribution margin	90,000	120,000
Fixed costs	84,000	80,000
Operating income	$ 6,000	$ 40,000

The company uses a flexible budget to analyze performance.

Compute for November 19_4:
1. Sales-volume variance of operating income.
2. Flexible-budget variance of operating income.

Check figures: (1) $20,000 U (2) $14,000 U

V. Cyrus Medicinal Products, Inc. uses a standard-costing system and provides the following data concerning its operations during last month for one of its products:

Finished units produced	300 units
Standard pounds of materials allowed per unit of output	10 pounds
Standard materials price per pound	$2.00
Actual materials purchase price per pound	$1.80
Actual quantity of materials purchased	4,000 pounds
Actual quantity of materials used in production	3,500 pounds

1. Show computations of direct materials variances, assuming that the price variance is isolated when materials are purchased. Use F for favorable variances and U for unfavorable variances.
2. Prepare journal entries to record:
   a. Purchase of direct materials.
   b. Usage of direct materials.

   Check figures: (1) Price variance $800 F, Efficiency variance $1,000 U

VI. Tate Corporation uses a standard-costing system and provides the following data concerning its operations during last month for one of its products:

Finished units produced	200 units
Standard labor-hours allowed per unit of output	2.5 hours
Standard wage rate per hour	$12.00
Actual wage rate per hour	$11.00
Total direct labor-hours actually used	550 hours

1. Show computations of direct labor variances. Use F for favorable variances and U for unfavorable variances.
2. Prepare a journal entry to record direct labor costs and variances for the month.

   Check figures: (1) Price variance $550 F, Efficiency variance $600 U

VII. (Appendix) Given for the Balancing Process of Prescott Scales Company:

Cost of investigating (C)	$2,400
Cost per period of the process being out of control (D)	$7,000
Cost of correcting, if an out-of-control process is discovered (M)	$3,000
Cost of the process being out of control this period and not corrected this period (L)	$40,000
Probability of the process being out of control	.05

1. Summarize this information in a decision table.
2. Compute the expected costs of "investigate."
3. Compute the expected costs of "do not investigate."
4. Compute the out-of-control probability at which the manager would be indifferent between the two courses of action.

   Check figures: (2) $2,900 (3) $2,000 (4) .08

CHAPTER 7 SOLUTIONS TO PRACTICE TEST

I. 1 Standard input; 2 benchmarking; 3 performance gap; 4 variance; 5 flexible budget; 6 sales-volume variance; 7 currently attainable standard; 8 inputs, output; 9 continuous improvement standard; 10 investigate, do not investigate; 11 in-control process, out-of-control process.

II.

1 T	6 F	11 F	16 T	21 T
2 F	7 F	12 F	17 F	
3 T	8 T	13 T	18 T	
4 T	9 T	14 F	19 F	
5 T	10 F	15 T	20 F	

Explanations:

1 Standard amounts are a specific type of budgeted amounts. Standards represent good or best levels of performance. They are usually developed from a careful study of the specific operations and are expressed on a *per-unit-of-output basis*. Many budgeted amounts are based on past cost relationships, but without a careful study of the specific operations to determine good or best levels of performance. (T)

2 The statement is reversed. A variance is a special case of a performance gap. A performance gap is the difference between an actual result and a benchmark amount. A variance is the difference between an actual result and a budgeted amount, when that budgeted amount is a financial variable reported in the accounting system and may or may not be a benchmark amount. (F)

3 Level 2 analysis is based on the flexible budget, and Level 3 analysis is based on the flexible budget with more detail than in Level 2. (T) Note that static budgets also can differ in terms of the level of detail they report. Level 0 analysis is based on the static budget, and Level 1 analysis is based on the static budget with more detail than in Level 0.

4 While the statement is true, be aware that favorable variances *do not necessarily* mean "good" performance. For example, a favorable materials price variance could harm the company if the materials are of such poor quality that they increase spoilage costs or customer service costs. (T)

5 For planning purposes, the flexible budget is used to predict revenues and costs at different output levels (as shown in Exhibit 7-2, columns 3, 4, and 5). For control purposes, the flexible budget is used to determine what costs should have been incurred at the output level actually achieved (as shown in Exhibit 7-3, column 3). (T)

6 Only revenues and variable costs put the "flex" in the flexible budget. Fixed costs are held constant within the relevant range. (F)

7 The flexible-budget variance and the sales-volume variance are the two parts of the static-budget variance of operating income, as shown in Exhibit 7-3. (F)

8 The sales-volume variance of operating income is not affected by fixed costs. Why? Because fixed costs are the same in the flexible budget and the static budget. (T)

9 This trend has developed because perfection standards harmonize with the notion of continuous improvement of quality and operating efficiency. However, note that there is a tradeoff between using perfection standards and the motivation problems associated with judging performance against a goal workers perceive to be unattainable. (T)

10 Effectiveness is the degree to which a predetermined objective or target is met. The sales-volume variance of operating income measures effectiveness. Efficiency is the relative amount of inputs used to achieve a given level of output. The flexible-budget variance of operating income is often a measure of efficiency. (F)

11 To facilitate control, direct materials price variances are usually based on actual quantities of inputs *purchased* rather than *used*. This approach isolates the price variance at the earlier time. (F)

12 A purchasing manager is responsible for acquisition of materials and a production manager is responsible for usage of materials. (F)

13 This statement is true because the quantity of inputs used is primarily affected by factors inside the company, while price changes arise primarily from factors outside the company. (T)

14 As performance measures, price and efficiency variances should not be interpreted individually because their causes can be interrelated. See the textbook example (p. 245). (F)

15 To compute price and efficiency variances, it is necessary to have budgeted and actual input prices and input quantities. A standard-costing system is one source of these budgeted amounts. Another source of budgeted amounts, say, for the current month is actual input prices and quantities for the previous month. (T)

16 Investigating a variance is warranted only when the expected benefits (such as reduced costs or better decisions due to having more detailed information) exceed the expected costs (ranging from phone calls to engineering analysis of the production process). (T)

17 Under a standard-costing system, direct manufacturing labor costs are debited to Work in Process Control at standard costs and are credited to Wages Payable Control at actual costs. Any difference between standard costs and actual costs is recorded as a price variance and/or an efficiency variance. (F)

18 Unfavorable variances are always debits because they decrease operating income. (T)

19 Managers of production lines generally use personal observation and variances expressed in nonfinancial terms (such as labor-hours and spoilage rates) for control purposes. On the other hand, top management uses variances expressed in financial terms to analyze and evaluate the performance of business functions in the value chain. (F)

20 If a variance is investigated, the process may be found to be in control. That is, the variance was caused by randomness of the operating process and no corrective action would be required. (F)

21 The situation described in this question coincides with the textbook example (p. 253) and related Exhibit 7-11. The expected probability of being out of control (.20) exceeds the probability of being out of control at the point of indifference (.10), and investigation of the variance is desirable. The expected costs to investigate are $4,400 and the expected costs not to investigate are $7,400. (T)

III.

1	d	4	c	7	d	10	d
2	b	5	b	8	d	11	b
3	a	6	a	9	d		

Explanations:

1 The static budget is based on one level of output and is *not* adjusted after it is finalized, regardless of changes in output or input prices, quantities, or costs. The flexible budget can be adjusted (flexed) to the actual level of output achieved or expected to be achieved during the budget period. Both types of budgets can include variable costs and fixed costs. Both types of budgets can be applied to an entire organization and its subunits. (d)

2 The production manager's performance would be properly evaluated by means of the flexible-budget variance. A performance report for each of the four answers is as follows:

	Actual Cost Incurred	Flexible Budget Based on Actual Output Produced	Flexible-Budget Variance
a.	$72,000	$72,000 (90% of $80,000)	$ -0-
b.	$72,000	$80,000 (100% of $80,000)	$8,000 F
c.	$72,000	$64,000 (80% of $80,000)	$8,000 U
d.	$72,000	$80,000 (100% of $80,000)	$8,000 F

While answers (b) and (d) give the same favorable variance of $8,000, the latter is misleading. Incurring less than the amount budgeted for a fixed cost (such as an employee training program) could result from failure to carry out a plan as budgeted or a poor estimate of the amount of the cost to be incurred. Answer (a) refers to a situation where the manager did exactly *as well as* expected in controlling cost. (b)

3 A decrease in the output level within the relevant range would decrease total costs because total variable costs would decrease and total fixed costs would remain the same. (a)

4   The 20% waste allowance makes the ratio of original pounds of materials to surviving pounds of materials 1.00 to .80. Since each finished unit consists of 60 pounds of surviving materials, the original materials input = $60 \div .80 = 75$ pounds. Thus, $75 \times \$2.50 \times (1 - .02) = \$183.75$. (c)

5   $1,800 \times 10 \times \$4 = \$72,000$ (b)

6   $(2,000 \times 10)(\$5 - \$4) = \$20,000$ U (a)

7   $(1,800 \times 11 \times \$4) - (1,800 \times 10 \times \$4) = \$79,200 - \$72,000 = \$7,200$ U (d)

8   A diagram is helpful in answering this question. Let X = Actual hours worked:

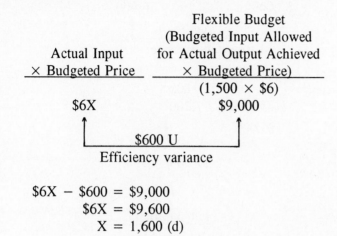

$$\$6X - \$600 = \$9,000$$
$$\$6X = \$9,600$$
$$X = 1,600 \text{ (d)}$$

Note that, since the company in question uses a standard-costing system, you may prefer putting "standard" instead of "budgeted" in the diagram above.

9   Standard cost per lb. = $\$3,000 \div (30,000 - 29,000) = \$3$
    Direct materials price variance = $\$84,000 - (30,000 \times \$3) = \$6,000$ favorable (d)

10 By formula:

$$\text{Price variance} = \left(\begin{array}{c} \text{Actual price} \\ \text{of input} \end{array} - \begin{array}{c} \text{Budgeted price} \\ \text{of input} \end{array} \right) \times \begin{array}{c} \text{Actual quantity of} \\ \text{input purchased} \end{array}$$

This computation includes some inefficiencies in the usage of input. Some companies refine the price variance into a pure price variance component and a joint price-efficiency variance component. The formulas for the refined analysis are in the textbook (p. 241); Exhibit 7-8 is a related diagram. (d)

11
$$\frac{C}{L - (D + M)} = \frac{\$6,000}{\$33,000 - (\$7,000 + \$11,000)} = \frac{\$6,000}{\$15,000} = .40 \text{ (b)}$$

IV. Folsom Fashions

1. Budgeted unit contribution margin = $\$120,000 \div 6,000 = \$20$
   Sales-volume variance of
   operating income = $(5,000 \times \$20) - \$120,000 = \$100,000 - \$120,000 = \$20,000$ U

2. Flexible-budget amount
   of operating income = $(5,000 \times \$20) - \$80,000 = \$100,000 - \$80,000 = \$20,000$
   Flexible-budget variance of operating income = $\$6,000 - \$20,000 = \$14,000$ U
   Note that the sum of these two variances ($\$20,000$ U + $\$14,000$ U = $\$34,000$ U) is equal to the static-budget variance of operating income ($\$6,000 - \$40,000 = \$34,000$ U).

V. Cyrus Medicinal Products, Inc.

1.

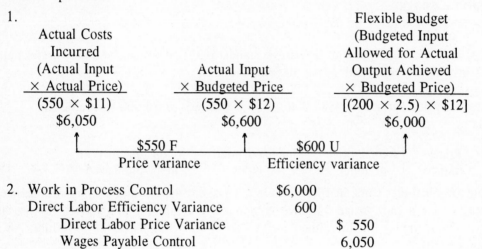

Actual Costs Incurred (Actual Input × Actual Price)	Actual Input × Budgeted Price		Flexible Budget (Budgeted Input Allowed for Actual Output Achieved × Budgeted Price)
(4,000 × $1.80)	(4,000 × $2.00)	(3,500 × $2.00)	[(300 × 10) × $2.00]
$7,200	$8,000	$7,000	$6,000

$800 F ↕ Price variance $1,000 U ↕ Efficiency variance

2. (a) Materials Control $8,000

       Direct Materials Price Variance .... $ 800

       Accounts Payable Control 7,200

  (b) Work in Process Control $6,000

      Direct Materials Efficiency Variance 1,000

       Materials Control $7,000

VI. Tate Corporation

1.

Actual Costs Incurred (Actual Input × Actual Price)	Actual Input × Budgeted Price	Flexible Budget (Budgeted Input Allowed for Actual Output Achieved × Budgeted Price)
(550 × $11)	(550 × $12)	[(200 × 2.5) × $12]
$6,050	$6,600	$6,000

$550 F ↕ Price variance $600 U ↕ Efficiency variance

2. Work in Process Control $6,000

  Direct Labor Efficiency Variance 600

      Direct Labor Price Variance .... $ 550

      Wages Payable Control 6,050

VII. Prescott Scales Company

1. Decision table:

	Events	
	In-Control Process	Out-of-Control Process
Action	(Prob. = .95)	(Prob. = .05)
Investigate	C = $2,400	C + D + M = $12,400
Do not investigate	$0	L = $40,000

2. Expected costs of "investigate":

($2,400 × .95) + ($12,400 × .05) = $2,280 + $620 = $2,900

3. Expected costs of "do not investigate": $0 + ($40,000 × .05) = $2,000

4. Out-of-control probability at the point of indifference:

$$\frac{C}{L - (D + M)} = \frac{\$2,400}{\$40,000 - (\$7,000 + \$3,000)} = \frac{\$2,400}{\$30,000} = .08$$

CHAPTER 8

FLEXIBLE BUDGETS, VARIANCES, AND MANAGEMENT CONTROL: II

MAIN FOCUS AND OBJECTIVES

This chapter builds on the concepts introduced in Chapter 7. We deal with overhead costs, which are a major component of total costs in most organizations. Your overall objective for this chapter is to understand planning and control of variable and fixed overhead costs, allocating those costs to products, and analyzing overhead variances. Nine learning objectives are stated in the textbook (p. 268).
Give special attention to:

- how cost management applies to variable and fixed overhead costs
- computing and interpreting variable overhead spending and efficiency variances
- using the denominator level to compute the budgeted fixed overhead rate
- computing and interpreting fixed overhead spending and output level variances
- the computations under 4-variance, 3-variance, 2-variance, and 1-variance analyses
- the role of the inventory costing purpose for manufacturing overhead costs
- the journal entries to record overhead variances

Carefully study key Exhibit 8-4. It presents a helpful columnar format for analyzing overhead variances. Be aware that accounting for fixed manufacturing overhead costs is usually the most challenging aspect of the study of flexible budgets and variances.
The chapter Appendix explores the proration of variances in a standard-costing system. In particular, the Appendix explains the added complexity of proration when a direct material price variance exists.

REVIEW OF KEY TERMS AND CONCEPTS

A. Organizations can significantly improve their profitability by effectively planning and controlling variable and fixed overhead costs.
1. Overhead costs, which are the indirect costs of products, often account for 20% to 50% of total value-chain costs.
2. Factors that tend to increase overhead costs as a proportion of total value-chain costs include automation, complexity of production and distribution processes, and product proliferation.

3. Effective planning and control of *variable overhead costs* emphasize (i) undertaking only value-added activities, (ii) managing the use of the cost drivers of those activities in the most efficient way, and (iii) then analyzing and understanding the causes of variances.

    a. *Value-added activities*: those activities that customers perceive as increasing the utility (usefulness) of the products or services they purchase.

    b. *Cost driver*: any factor that affects costs.

    c. A three-step approach is used to develop variable overhead rate(s).

       (1) See the textbook example (pp. 270-71).

       (2) Be sure to distinguish between the budgeted rate *per unit of output* ($12 per jacket) and the budgeted rate *per unit of input* ($30 per machine-hour).

Question: What is the fundamental difference between the budgeted variable overhead rate per unit of input and the budgeted price of direct materials or direct labor?

Answer: The budgeted variable overhead rate includes the costs of *many diverse* overhead items, whereas the budgeted prices are for *individual* direct materials and direct labor items.

---

4. Effective planning and control of *fixed overhead costs* emphasize (i) undertaking only value-added activities, (ii) choosing the appropriate capacity level for these activities, and (iii) then analyzing and understanding the causes of variances.

    a. *Choosing the capacity level is one of the most challenging decisions facing managers.*

    b. The capacity level is chosen on the basis of the expected demand and the level of uncertainty pertaining to that demand.

    c. If there is too little capacity, sales and operating income are lost or forgone. If there is too much capacity, costly resources are unused.

Cost Management of Variable Overhead Costs	*Cost Management of Fixed Overhead Costs*
• Eliminate nonvalue-added costs	• Eliminate nonvalue-added costs
• Reduce consumption of the cost drivers	• Plan for appropriate capacity levels of value-added activities

B. Variance analysis for **variable overhead costs** is somewhat similar to the analysis of direct labor variances explained in Chapter 7.

    1. However, there are two main differences:

       a. *For variable overhead, the term spending variance is used instead of price variance.*

       b. Variable overhead consists of many diverse cost items, such as energy, engineering support, indirect materials, and indirect labor.

2. *Exhibit 8-2 illustrates Level 1 and Level 2 analysis of variable manufacturing overhead costs.*
   a. Level 1 analysis isolates the static-budget variance.
   b. Level 2 analysis divides the static-budget variance into the flexible-budget variance and sales-volume variance.
3. Level 3 analysis divides the flexible-budget variance of variable overhead into the spending variance and efficiency variance.

$$\begin{array}{l}\text{Variable overhead} \\ \text{spending variance}\end{array} = \left(\begin{array}{c}\text{Actual VOH costs} \\ \text{per unit of cost} \\ \text{allocation base}\end{array} - \begin{array}{c}\text{Budgeted VOH costs} \\ \text{per unit of cost} \\ \text{allocation base}\end{array}\right) \times \begin{array}{c}\text{Actual quantity} \\ \text{of VOH cost} \\ \text{allocation base} \\ \text{for actual} \\ \text{output achieved}\end{array}$$

$$\begin{array}{l}\text{Variable overhead} \\ \text{efficiency variance}\end{array} = \left(\begin{array}{c}\text{Actual quantity of} \\ \text{VOH cost allocation} \\ \text{base for actual} \\ \text{output achieved}\end{array} - \begin{array}{c}\text{Budgeted quantity of} \\ \text{VOH cost allocation} \\ \text{base allowed for} \\ \text{actual output achieved}\end{array}\right) \times \begin{array}{c}\text{Budgeted} \\ \text{VOH rate}\end{array}$$

4. Although variable overhead spending and efficiency variances are computed similarly to direct cost price and efficiency variances in Chapter 7, the meanings and interpretations are different.
   a. For example, an unfavorable variable overhead efficiency variance arises from inefficient usage of the cost allocation base, not from inefficient usage of the variable overhead items themselves. The latter would result in an unfavorable variable overhead spending variance.
   b. A favorable variable overhead spending variance means less costs were incurred than expected because (i) the price of variable overhead items decreased and/or (ii) less of the variable overhead items were used per unit of the cost allocation base.

Exhibit 8-3 provides a helpful format for Level 3 analysis of variable overhead variances.

---

5. Exhibit 8-5 (Panel A) shows that graphs of variable overhead are *identical* (i) for the planning and control purpose and (ii) for the inventory costing purpose.
6. A pair of general ledger accounts is maintained for variable manufacturing overhead, as shown in these summary journal entries for costs incurred and costs allocated, respectively. Using the textbook figures:

Entry 1: Variable Manufacturing Overhead Control $130,500
        Accounts Payable Control and other accounts $130,500

Entry 2: Work in Process Control $120,000
        Variable Manufacturing Overhead Allocated $120,000

7. The difference between the balances of these two overhead accounts is the under-allocated or overallocated variable overhead, which is equal to the flexible-budget variance for variable overhead.
8. At the end of the period, Variable Manufacturing Overhead Control and Variable Manufacturing Overhead Allocated are closed, and the variable overhead variances are recorded in general ledger accounts. Using the textbook figures:

Entry 3: Variable Manufacturing Overhead Allocated	$120,000	
Variable Manufacturing Overhead Efficiency Variance	15,000	
Variable Manufacturing Overhead Control		$130,500
Variable Manufacturing Overhead Spending Variance		4,500

> **The structure of these entries is simple:**
> - *Entry 1*: **Debit the Overhead Control account for *actual* costs.**
> - *Entry 2*: **Credit the Overhead Allocated account for *budgeted* or *standard* costs allowed for actual output achieved.**
> - *Entry 3*: **Close the Overhead accounts and record the variances —unfavorable variances are debits and favorable variances are credits.**

9. When the balance of Variable Manufacturing Overhead Control is greater (less) than the balance of Variable Manufacturing Overhead Allocated, variable overhead is underallocated (overallocated).
   a. Two approaches to dispose of underallocated or overallocated overhead:
      (1) Restated Allocation Rate Approach
      (2) End-of-Period Account(s) Approach
   b. These approaches are discussed in section C(4) of Chapter 5's outline (p. 52).
   c. This chapter's Appendix explains the proration of variances in a standard-costing system.
10. *See Practice Test Question III (items 1, 4, and 5) and Problem IV.*

C. The variance analysis of **fixed overhead costs** is much different than that of variable overhead costs.
   1. The pair of graphs in Exhibit 8-5 (Panel B) helps explain the difference.
      a. *For planning and control*, fixed overhead is a *lump-sum budget* that does not change in total within the relevant range. For example:
         (1) Managers control a fixed leasing cost *at the time the lease is signed.*
         (2) Subsequently, little can be done to change the monthly lump-sum payment.
      b. *For inventory costing*, fixed *manufacturing* overhead is treated *as if* it were a variable cost.
   2. Fixed manufacturing overhead is "transformed" into a variable cost for inventory costing by means of the budgeted fixed overhead rate.

$$\textbf{Budgeted fixed overhead rate} = \frac{\textbf{Budgeted fixed overhead costs}}{\textbf{Denominator level}}$$

3. **Denominator level**: the preselected level of the cost allocation base used to set a budgeted fixed overhead rate for allocating fixed overhead costs to a cost object.
   a. The denominator level can be expressed either in terms of output or input.
   b. In manufacturing companies, the denominator level is often called the production denominator level or production denominator volume.
   c. In the textbook example (p. 276), the denominator level is *12,000 output units* or *4,800 machine-hours*.
   d. Budgeted fixed overhead costs are *not* affected by the denominator level chosen.
   e. The higher the denominator level, the lower the budgeted fixed manufacturing overhead rate per unit of output, and vice versa.
   f. The denominator level is discussed further in Part Two of the next chapter.
4. For fixed overhead, three variances are always the same: **static-budget variance** (Level 1), **flexible-budget variance** (Level 2), and **spending variance** (Level 3).

$$\begin{array}{c}\text{Each of these}\\\text{three variances}\end{array} = \begin{array}{c}\text{Actual costs}\\\text{incurred}\end{array} - \begin{array}{c}\text{Lump--sum}\\\text{budgeted amount}\end{array}$$

> *Question*: **Why are these three fixed overhead variances always the same?**
> *Answer*: **Because for fixed overhead there is never a sales-volume variance (Level 2) and never an efficiency variance (Level 3).**

5. The other variance for fixed overhead is the **output level variance**.

$$\begin{array}{c}\text{Output level}\\\text{variance}\end{array} = \left(\begin{array}{c}\text{Denominator}\\\text{level in}\\\text{output units}\end{array} - \begin{array}{c}\text{Actual}\\\text{output units}\\\text{achieved}\end{array}\right) \times \begin{array}{c}\text{Budgeted fixed}\\\text{overhead rate}\\\text{per output unit}\end{array}$$

   a. In manufacturing companies, *this variance is often called the production volume variance* or *production level variance*.
   b. The output level variance is unfavorable when actual output units achieved are less than the denominator level, and vice versa.
   c. An unfavorable output level variance indicates that the fixed facilities were not utilized as much as had been specified by the denominator level, and vice versa.
   d. Two reasons explain why the output level variance is *not* a good measure of the income forgone by having unused capacity:
      (1) The denominator level may be less than the plant capacity.
      (2) The economic costs of not fully utilizing capacity should reflect both cost *and* revenue factors. For example, selling price changes may be necessary to spur more demand that would in turn make use of idle capacity.
   e. Exhibit 8-4 (Panel B) illustrates a useful columnar format for computing fixed overhead variances.
6. The summary journal entries for fixed manufacturing overhead are like those for variable manufacturing overhead.
   a. Return to section B (6 through 9) of the outline above, and simply substitute "Fixed" in place of "Variable" throughout.

b. The only other change needed is that the Fixed Manufacturing Output Level (Production Volume) Variance account is used instead of the Variable Manufacturing Overhead Efficiency Variance account.

7. *See Practice Test Problem V.*

D. Variances for overhead costs can be presented in four different levels of detail.
   1. The most detail is called 4-variance analysis.

4-variance analysis isolates four (!) variances:
1. **Variable overhead spending variance**
2. **Fixed overhead spending variance**
3. **Variable overhead efficiency variance**
4. **Output level overhead variance**

---

   2. *Exhibit 8-4 illustrates 4-variance analysis.*
   3. *3-variance analysis* (less detail):
      a. Total overhead spending variances (variable and fixed overhead combined)
      b. Variable overhead efficiency variance
      c. Output level variance
   4. *2-variance analysis* (even less detail):
      a. Total overhead flexible-budget variance
      b. Output level variance
   5. *1-variance analysis* (the least detail).
      a. This variance is called the *total overhead variance*.
      b. The total overhead variance is the difference between actual total overhead incurred and total overhead allocated, often referred to as *underallocated or overallocated overhead* (first introduced in Chapter 4).
      c. When total overhead is underallocated, the total overhead variance is unfavorable, and vice versa.
   6. When 3-variance or 4-variance analysis is used, the variances are not always independent of each other; see the textbook discussion (p. 281).

Carefully study key Exhibit 8-4. In contrast to the 3-column format of Exhibit 8-3, it has a column 4 to accommodate fixed overhead. Special notes on Exhibit 8-4:
- **In both panels, column 4 is allocated overhead.**
- **In both panels, the amount in column 1 minus the amount in column 4 is equal to underallocated or overallocated overhead.**
- **For variable overhead (Panel A), the amounts in columns 3 and 4 are always equal.**
- **For fixed overhead (Panel B), the amounts in columns 2 and 3 are always equal.**

See Practice Test Question III (items 6-11) and Problem VI.

E. Keep in mind the distinction between *manufacturing* overhead costs and *nonmanufacturing* overhead costs.

    1. Both variable and fixed manufacturing overhead costs are capitalized as inventoriable costs for financial reporting purposes under generally accepted accounting principles.

    2. Nonmanufacturing overhead costs are period costs, not inventoriable costs.

    3. Variance analysis of variable overhead costs in all areas of the value chain provides useful information to managers for decisions on pricing and product emphasis.

    4. Variance analysis of fixed nonmanufacturing overhead costs is mainly useful for reimbursement purposes under "full-cost-plus" contracts.

F. The other topics discussed in the chapter are (i) performance gaps and (ii) actual, normal, budgeted, and standard costing.

    1. Chapter 7 explained that variances are one type of performance gap.

        a. *Performance gap*: the difference between an actual result and a benchmark amount.

        b. *Benchmark amount*: the best levels of performance that can be found inside or outside the organization.

            (1) Benchmark amounts may be financial or nonfinancial variables.

            (2) Benchmark amounts may or may not be reported in the accounting system.

        c. *Variance*: the difference between an actual result and a budgeted amount, when that budgeted amount (i) is a financial variable reported in the accounting system and (ii) may or may not be a benchmark amount.

    2. Managers find that many performance gaps based on *nonfinancial benchmarks* provide useful information in their planning and control decisions.

        a. For example, energy usage per machine-hour compared to budgeted energy usage per machine-hour.

        b. This type of performance gap probably would be reported on the manufacturing floor on a daily, or even hourly, basis.

    3. Expressing performance gaps in financial terms (as variances) can highlight their relative importance to managers at all levels in the organization.

    4. Performance gaps, like the variances discussed in this chapter, are best viewed as attention directors, not problem solvers.

    5. Actual costing, normal costing, and budgeted costing are discussed in section C(6) of Chapter 4's outline (p. 40).

    6. These three costing systems along with standard costing (discussed in the Webb Company example in Chapters 7 and 8) are compared in Exhibit 8-6.

G. (**Appendix**) When a standard-costing system is used, it is necessary to know which variances (if any) to prorate, how to make the computations, and the effect of proration on the financial statements.

    1. Generally accepted accounting principles and income tax laws typically require that financial statements show actual costs, *not* standard costs, of inventories and cost of goods sold.

    2. Proration of variances at the end of the accounting period is a means of approximating the *actual costs*.

        a. Some accountants, however, advocate that *standard costs* (based on currently attainable standards) better represent the appropriate inventory costs in the balance sheet.

b. Under this view, variances are immediately written off to cost of goods sold rather than prorated.

3. Three questions are pertinent regarding the proration of variances in a standard-costing system.

   a. *Question 1*: Which variances are subject to proration?
      Answer: Only *manufacturing* variances recorded in the general ledger, namely flexible-budget variances (price, spending, and efficiency) and the output level (production volume) variance.

   b. *Question 2*: Which manufacturing variances should be prorated?
      Answer: It depends on the magnitude of the impact on operating income, which depends on the magnitude of (i) the ending inventory balances and (ii) the variances. If inventories are minimal (as in just-in-time), then proration will not materially affect operating income.

   c. *Question 3*: If proration is called for, which method should be used?
      Answer:
      (1) The theoretically preferred method is to prorate on the basis of the total amount of standard costs (related to each type of variance) lodged in the ending balances of the applicable general ledger accounts.
      (2) The other method is to prorate on the basis of the total of the ending balances of the applicable general ledger accounts (a simpler method but not as accurate).
      (3) "Applicable general ledger accounts" under both methods refers to Work in Process, Finished Goods, and Cost of Goods Sold in the case of all manufacturing variances except direct materials price variance, which is discussed below.

4. The two proration methods would provide the same results in the textbook example (pp. 291-92). Why? Because there is no work in process inventory and the individual standard cost components lodged in Finished Goods and Cost of Goods Sold are proportional to their ending balances (40% and 60%, respectively).

5. *Proration becomes more complex when a direct materials price variance exists.* Why? Because direct materials are inventoried when *purchased*, but all other manufacturing costs are not inventoried until *usage* occurs.

   a. This difference requires an *extra step* to prorate direct materials variances.

   b. Exhibit 8-8 shows that the direct materials price variance is prorated *not only* to Finished Goods and Cost of Goods Sold, *but also* to Direct Materials Inventory and Direct Materials Efficiency Variance.

   c. *The effect of the computations in Exhibit 8-8 is to show identical amounts in the financial statements as would appear under actual costing.*

6. When unfavorable manufacturing variances are prorated, applicable inventories and operating income are increased, and vice versa. Exhibit 8-9 shows that operating income is less if unfavorable variances are immediately written off to Cost of Goods Sold rather than prorated.

7. *See Practice Test Question III (items 12 and 13) and Problem VII.*

PRACTICE TEST QUESTIONS AND PROBLEMS

I. Complete each of the following statements.

1. Budgeted overhead rates can be expressed as an amount per unit of _____ or per unit of _____.

2. An overhead _____ is the difference between an actual result and a budgeted amount, when that budgeted amount (i) is a financial variable reported in the accounting system and (ii) may or may not be a _____ _____ amount.

3. Cost management of _____ costs involves eliminating nonvalue-added costs and planning for appropriate capacity levels of value-added activities.

4. If the balance of the Variable Manufacturing Overhead Control account is greater than the balance of the _____ _____ account variable overhead would be _____.

5. For inventory costing purposes, _____ _____ is treated as if it were a variable cost.

6. _____ is the preselected level of the cost allocation base used to set a budgeted fixed overhead rate for allocating fixed overhead costs to a cost object.

7. Two fixed overhead variances can be isolated: the fixed overhead spending (flexible-budget, static-budget) variance and the _____ _____ variance. In manufacturing companies, the variance in the preceding blank is often called the _____ _____ variance.

8. The _____ is the amount of underallocated or overallocated overhead.

9. Both fixed and variable _____ overhead costs are capitalized as _____ _____ costs for financial reporting purposes under generally accepted accounting principles.

10. (Appendix) Generally accepted accounting principles and income tax laws typically require that financial statements show _____ costs of inventories and cost of goods sold.

11. (Appendix) When the direct materials price variance is isolated at the time materials are purchased, proration of this variance could include a maximum of five general ledger accounts: _____ _____, _____ _____, Work in Process Control, Finished Goods Control, and Cost of Goods Sold.

II. Indicate whether each of the following statements is true or false by putting T or F in the space provided.

___ 1. A factor that tends to increase overhead costs as a proportion of total value-chain costs is product proliferation.

___ 2. Budgeted overhead rates can be expressed as an amount per unit of output or per unit of input.

___ 3. There is no fundamental difference between the budgeted variable overhead rate per unit of input and the budgeted price of direct materials or direct labor.

___ 4. Cost management can be applied to variable overhead costs but not to fixed overhead costs.

___ 5. The variable overhead efficiency variance is computed similarly to the direct labor efficiency variance, and the meaning and interpretation of these variances are basically alike.

___ 6. For a given company, a graph of variable manufacturing overhead costs for the planning and control purpose would look the same as for the inventory costing purpose.

___ 7. Underallocated variable overhead means that the flexible-budget variance for variable overhead would be favorable.

___ 8. There is never an output level variance for variable overhead costs.

___ 9. Fixed manufacturing overhead inventoriable cost per unit is inversely related to the denominator level.

___ 10. The amount of budgeted fixed overhead costs is affected by the denominator level chosen.

11. For fixed overhead, the spending variance is always equal to the flexible-budget variance.

___ 12. The output level variance would be zero if actual output achieved is equal to the denominator level.

___ 13. The output level variance is generally a good measure of the income forgone by having unused capacity.

___ 14. In 2-variance analysis of overhead costs, there is only one spending variance.

___ 15. Variable manufacturing overhead efficiency variances usually are first reported in financial terms by the accounting department, and then they are expressed in nonfinancial terms by personnel on the manufacturing floor.

___ 16. Normal costing and standard costing are different in terms of how they each account for direct costs and overhead (indirect) costs.

___ 17. (Appendix) Only manufacturing variances recorded in the general ledger are subject to proration.

___ 18. (Appendix) For external financial reporting, it is acceptable to deduct from cost of goods sold unfavorable manufacturing variances that are not material in amount.

___ 19. (Appendix) Assuming there were ending inventories of work in process and finished goods, prorating a favorable output level variance would decrease these inventories.

___ 20. Proration becomes more complex when a direct materials price variance exists.

III. Select the best answer for each of the following multiple-choice questions and put the identifying letter in the space provided.

___ 1. (CMA adapted) Variable overhead is allocated on the basis of budgeted direct manufacturing labor-hours. If for a given period, the direct labor efficiency variance is unfavorable, the variable overhead efficiency variance will be:
   a. favorable.
   b. unfavorable.
   c. zero.
   d. the same amount as the labor efficiency variance.

   e. indeterminable since it is not related to the labor efficiency variance.

___ 2. (CPA) Information on Fire Company's overhead costs is as follows:

Actual variable overhead	$73,000
Actual fixed overhead	$17,000
Budgeted hours allowed for actual output achieved	32,000
Budgeted variable overhead rate per direct manufacturing labor-hour	$2.50
Budgeted fixed overhead rate per direct manufacturing labor-hour	$0.50

What is the total overhead variance?
   a. $1,000 unfavorable
   b. $6,000 favorable
   c. $6,000 unfavorable
   d. $7,000 favorable

___ 3. (CPA adapted) Geyer Company uses a standard-costing system. For the month of April 19_5, total overhead is budgeted at $80,000 based on the output of 20,000 machine-hours. At standard, each finished unit of output requires 2 machine-hours. The following data are available for April 19_5 production:

Units of output	9,500
Machine-hours used	19,500
Actual total overhead incurred	$79,500

What amount should Geyer credit to Manufacturing Overhead Allocated for the month of April 19_5?
   a. $76,000
   b. $78,000
   c. $79,500
   d. $80,000

___ 4. Given for Pappillon Corporation's variable manufacturing overhead costs: $2,500 favorable flexible-budget variance, $2,500 unfavorable efficiency variance. The spending variance would be:
   a. $0.
   b. $5,000 unfavorable.
   c. $5,000 favorable.
   d. none of the above.

___ 5. (CMA) Baxter Corporation's master budget calls for the production of 5,000 units of product monthly. The master budget includes indirect marketing labor of $144,000 annually; Baxter considers this indirect labor to be a variable cost. During the month of April, 4,500 units of output were produced, and indirect marketing labor costs of $10,100 were incurred. A performance report would show a flexible-budget variance for indirect marketing labor of:
   a. $1,900 unfavorable.
   b. $700 favorable.
   c. $1,900 favorable.
   d. $700 unfavorable.
   e. none of the above.

___ 6. (CPA) Fawcett Company uses flexible budgeting and prepared the following information for 19_4:

	Budgeted Capacity	Maximum Capacity
Percent of capacity	80%	100%
Direct manufacturing labor-hours	32,000	40,000
Variable manufacturing overhead	$64,000	$80,000
Fixed manufacturing overhead	$160,000	$160,000

Fawcett operated at 90% of maximum capacity during 19_4. Actual manufacturing overhead for 19_4 was $252,000. Fawcett uses the 2-variance analysis of manufacturing overhead. What is the flexible-budget variance for the year?
   a. $36,000 unfavorable
   b. $0
   c. $18,000 unfavorable
   d. $20,000 unfavorable

___ 7. (CMA) Franklin Glass Works uses a standard-costing system. The production budget for the year ended November 30, 19_3 was based on 200,000 units of output. Each unit requires two standard hours of manufacturing labor for completion. Total overhead was budgeted at $900,000 for the year, and the budgeted fixed overhead rate was $3 per unit of output. Both fixed and variable overhead are allocated to the product on the basis of direct manufacturing labor-hours. The actual data for the year ended November 30, 19_3 are as follows:

Actual production in units	198,000
Actual direct manufacturing labor-hours	440,000
Actual variable overhead	$352,000
Actual fixed overhead	$575,000

The fixed overhead spending variance for 19_3 is:
   a. $19,000 favorable.
   b. $25,000 favorable.
   c. $5,750 favorable.
   d. $19,000 unfavorable.
   e. $25,000 unfavorable.

___ 8. See item 7. The output level variance for 19_3 is:
   a. $6,000 unfavorable.
   b. $19,000 favorable.
   c. $25,000 favorable.
   d. $55,000 unfavorable.
   e. $90,800 unfavorable.

___ 9. See item 7. The variable overhead spending variance for 19_3 is:
   a. $20,000 unfavorable.
   b. $19,800 favorable.
   c. $22,000 unfavorable.
   d. $20,000 favorable.
   e. $22,000 favorable.

___ 10. See item 7. The variable overhead efficiency variance for 19_3 is:
   a. $33,000 unfavorable.
   b. $35,520 favorable.
   c. $66,000 unfavorable.
   d. $132,000 unfavorable.
   e. $35,200 unfavorable.

___ 11. See items 7 through 10. Which method of variance analysis is Franklin Glass Works using?
   a. 1-variance analysis
   b. 2-variance analysis
   c. 3-variance analysis
   d. 4-variance analysis

___ 12. (Appendix, CMA adapted) Dori Castings uses a standard-costing system to account for manufacturing costs. Manufacturing overhead is allocated on the basis of machine-hours. If the year-end balances in the manufacturing overhead variance accounts are prorated, what general ledger accounts would be involved in the proration?

a. Direct Materials Control, Work in Process Control, Finished Goods Control, and Cost of Goods Sold.
b. Direct Materials Control, Direct Materials Price Variance, Direct Materials Efficiency Variance, Work in Process Control, Finished Goods Control, and Cost of Goods Sold.
c. All accounts in (b) except Direct Materials Price Variance.
d. Work in Process Control, Finished Goods Control, and Cost of Goods Sold.

___ 13. (Appendix) The most accurate proration of variances would be accomplished by first prorating the:
a. direct labor efficiency variance.
b. direct materials efficiency variance.
c. direct materials price variance.
d. direct labor price variance.

IV. You are given the following data for the manufacturing operations of Regal, Inc.:

Production in output units	400
Budgeted variable manufacturing overhead costs per output unit	$3
Actual direct manufacturing labor-hours used	700
Actual variable manufacturing overhead costs incurred	$1,350
Budgeted labor-hours allowed per output unit	1.50

1. Compute the following amounts. For each variance indicate whether it is favorable (F) or unfavorable (U).
   a. Budgeted variable manufacturing overhead rate per direct manufacturing labor-hour
   b. Budgeted labor-hours allowed for actual output achieved
   c. Underallocated or overallocated variable manufacturing overhead
   d. Flexible-budget variance for variable manufacturing overhead
   e. Variable manufacturing overhead spending variance
   f. Variable manufacturing overhead efficiency variance

2. Prepare the journal entries to record:
   a. Variable manufacturing overhead incurred
   b. Variable manufacturing overhead allocated
   c. Variable manufacturing overhead spending and efficiency variances

   Check figures: (1a) $2 (1b) 600 (1c) $150 underallocated (1d) $150 U (1e) $50 F (1f) $200 U

V. The following information pertains to the manufacturing operations of Payton Corporation:

Budgeted fixed overhead	$1,800
Actual fixed overhead	$1,750
Denominator level in machine-hours	300
Budgeted machine-hours allowed for actual output achieved	280

Compute the following amounts. For each variance, indicate whether it is favorable (F) or unfavorable (U).
1. Budgeted fixed overhead rate per machine-hour
2. Underallocated or overallocated fixed overhead
3. Flexible-budget (spending) variance for fixed overhead
4. Output level variance

   Check figures: (1) $6 (2) $70 underallocated (3) $50 F (4) $120 U

VI. (CPA) The following information relates to a given manufacturing department of Herman Company for the first quarter of 19_5:

Actual total overhead	$178,500
Flexible-budget formula based on direct manufacturing labor-hours (DMLH)	$110,000 plus $0.50 per DMLH
Budgeted total overhead rate per DMLH	$1.50 per DMLH
Total overhead spending variance	$8,000 unfavorable
Output level variance	$5,000 favorable

Herman uses the 3-variance analysis of overhead costs.

Compute for the first quarter of 19_5:
1. Actual direct manufacturing labor-hours worked
2. Budgeted hours allowed for actual output achieved

   Check figures: (1) 121,000 (2) 115,000

VII. (Appendix) Given for Collier Corporation:

Sales	$205,000
Standard cost of goods manufactured	$180,000
Marketing and administrative costs	$41,000
Direct manufacturing labor price variance (unfavorable)	$16,000
Direct manufacturing labor efficiency variance (favorable)	$10,000
Other manufacturing variances	none
Units produced	4,000
Work in process inventories (in units)	none
Beginning finished goods inventory (in units)	none
Ending finished goods inventory (in units)	600

Compute:

1. Cost of goods sold before considering variances
2. The amount of net variances
3. Operating income, assuming the net variances are immediately written off to cost of goods sold
4. Cost of ending finished goods inventory, assuming the net variances are immediately written off to cost of goods sold
5. Operating income, assuming the net variances are prorated on the basis of the related standard costs in the accounts
6. Cost of ending finished goods inventory, assuming the net variances are prorated on the basis of the related standard costs in the accounts
7. Operating income that is logically consistent with the view that the standards are currently attainable
8. Cost of ending finished goods inventory under actual costing

Check figures: (1) $153,000 (2) $6,000 U (3) $5,000 (4) $27,000 (5) $5,900 (6) $27,900 (7) $5,000 (8) $27,900

CHAPTER 8 SOLUTIONS TO PRACTICE TEST

I. 1 output, input; 2 variance, benchmark; 3 fixed overhead; 4 Variable Manufacturing Overhead Allocated, underallocated; 5 fixed manufacturing overhead; 6 Denominator level; 7 output level, production volume (production level); 8 total overhead variance; 9 manufacturing, inventoriable; 10 actual; 11 Direct Materials Control, Direct Materials Efficiency Variance.

II.

1 T	6 T	11 T	16 T
2 T	7 F	12 T	17 T
3 F	8 T	13 F	18 F
4 F	9 T	14 F	19 T
5 F	10 F	15 F	20 T

Explanations:

1 Other factors that tend to increase overhead costs as a proportion of total value-chain costs include automation and complexity of production and distribution processes. (T)

2 In the chapter example, the budgeted variable manufacturing overhead rate is $12 per jacket or $30 per machine-hour; the budgeted fixed manufacturing overhead rate is $23 per jacket or $57.50 per machine-hour. (T)

3 The budgeted variable overhead rate includes the cost of *many diverse* overhead items, whereas the budgeted prices are for *individual* direct materials and direct labor items. (F)

4 Cost management can be applied to both variable and fixed overhead costs. For both types of overhead, cost management involves eliminating nonvalue-added activities. Also cost

management aims to reduce consumption of the variable overhead cost drivers and entails planning for appropriate capacity levels of fixed overhead value-added activities. (F)

5 As an example, an unfavorable variable overhead efficiency variance arises from inefficient usage of the cost allocation base, not from inefficient usage of the variable overhead items themselves. The latter would result in an unfavorable variable overhead spending variance. (F)

6 These graphs are presented in Exhibit 8-5 (Panel A). Panel B of this exhibit shows that for *fixed* manufacturing overhead costs there is a sharp contrast between the planning and control purpose and the inventory costing purpose. (T)

7 Underallocated (overallocated) variable overhead would be an unfavorable (favorable) flexible-budget variance for variable overhead. For example, see Exhibit 8-4 (Panel A). (F)

8 The flexible-budget amount of variable overhead costs is always equal to the variable overhead costs allocated. For example, in Exhibit 8-4 (Panel A) column 3 equals column 4. (T)

9 As the denominator level increases, fixed manufacturing overhead inventoriable cost per unit decreases, and vice versa. (T)

10 Budgeted fixed overhead is a lump-sum amount that does not change in total within the relevant range, and the choice of the denominator level does not affect budgeted fixed overhead. (F)

11 See exhibit 8-4 (Panel B). (T)

12 The output level variance is unfavorable when actual output units achieved are less than the denominator level, and vice versa. This variance is zero when actual output units achieved are equal to the denominator level. (T)

13 Two reasons explain why the output level variance is *not* a good measure of the income forgone by having unused capacity: (i) the denominator level may be less than the plant capacity and (ii) the economic costs of not fully utilizing capacity should reflect both cost *and* revenue factors (for example, selling price changes may be necessary to spur more demand that would in turn make use of idle capacity). (F)

14 In 2-variance analysis of overhead costs, there is no spending variance. The two variances are the flexible-budget variance and the output level variance. (F)

15 This statement has reversed the sequence of events. Variable manufacturing overhead efficiency variances usually first appear on the manufacturing floor on a daily, or even hourly, basis expressed in nonfinancial terms (such as kilowatts used or repair hours); then they are reported in financial terms by the accounting department. (F)

16 See Exhibit 8-6. (T)

17 Direct materials variances, direct manufacturing labor variances, and manufacturing overhead variances—price, spending, efficiency, and output level—are all subject to proration. (T)

18 For external financial reporting, it is acceptable to *add* to cost of goods sold unfavorable variances that are not material in amount. Such variances generally are not prorated between inventories and cost of goods sold. (F)

19 The Output Level Overhead Variance account would have a credit balance because it is favorable. Therefore, the journal entry to prorate it would be:

Output Level Overhead Variance	× × ×	
Work in Process Control		× × ×
Finished Goods Control		× × ×
Cost of Goods Sold		× × × (T)

20 The statement is true because direct materials are inventoried when *purchased*, but all other manufacturing costs are not inventoried until *usage* occurs. This difference requires an *extra step* to prorate direct materials variances. The extra step is illustrated in Exhibit 8-8. (T)

III.

1 b	5 b	9 c	13 c
2 b	6 d	10 a	
3 a	7 b	11 d	
4 c	8 a	12 d	

Explanations:

1   Since variable overhead is allocated on the basis of budgeted direct manufacturing labor-hours, an unfavorable variable overhead efficiency variance and an unfavorable direct labor efficiency variance arise when budgeted direct manufacturing labor-hours allowed for actual output achieved are less than actual direct manufacturing labor-hours worked. These variances would be equal in amount only if the budgeted price of direct manufacturing labor were equal to the budgeted variable overhead rate. (b)

2   Total overhead variance = Actual total overhead incurred − Total overhead allocated
Total overhead variance = ($73,000 + $17,000) − 32,000($2.50 + $0.50)
Total overhead variance = $90,000 − $96,000 = $6,000 F (b)

3   Budgeted total overhead rate = $80,000 ÷ 20,000 = $4 per machine-hour
Budgeted hours allowed for actual output achieved = 9,500 × 2 = 19,000 machine-hours
Manufacturing overhead allocated = 19,000 × $4 = $76,000 (a)

4   Flexible-budget variance = Spending variance + Efficiency variance
$2,500 F = Spending variance + $2,500 U
Spending variance = $2,500 F −($2,500 U) = $2,500 F + $2,500 F = $5,000 F (c)

5
$$\text{Indirect marketing labor cost rate} = \frac{\$144,000}{5,000 \times 12} = \$2.40 \text{ per unit of output}$$

Actual Cost Incurred	Flexible Budget	Flexible-Budget Variance
	(4,500 × $2.40)	
$10,100	$10,800	$700 F (b)

6   Budgeted variable overhead rate = $64,000 ÷ 32,000 = $2 per DMLH (or $80,000 ÷ 40,000 = $2 per DMLH)
Flexible-budget variance = $252,000 − [$160,000 + (40,000 × .90)($2)] = $252,000 − [$160,000 + $72,000] = $252,000 − $232,000 = $20,000 U (d)

7   A diagram is helpful in answering this question and the next:

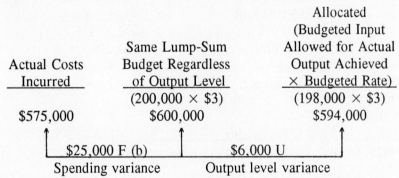

8   See the preceding answer. The output level variance is $6,000 U. (a)

9   A diagram is helpful in answering this question and the next:

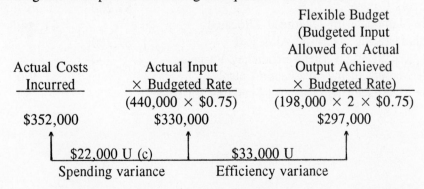

The budgeted variable overhead rate is computed as follows:

Budgeted total overhead $900,000
Deduct budgeted fixed overhead, 200,000 × $3   600,000
Budgeted variable overhead $300,000

$$\text{Budgeted variable overhead rate} = \frac{\$300,000}{200,000 \times 2} = \$0.75 \text{ per DMLH}$$

10 See the preceding answer. The efficiency variance is $33,000 U. (a)
11 4-variance analysis is being used because four overhead variances are isolated:

Variable overhead spending variance $22,000 U
Variable overhead efficiency variance   33,000 U
Fixed overhead spending variance   25,000 F
Output level variance   6,000 U
Total overhead variance (underallocated overhead) $36,000 U (d)

12 Direct materials accounts are involved in the proration only when the direct materials price variance is prorated. See Exhibit 8-8. (d)
13 See Exhibit 8-8. (c)

IV. Regal, Inc.

1. (a) $3 ÷ 1.50 = $2
   (b) 400 × 1.50 = 600
   (c) through (f) are shown below in the same format as Exhibit 8-3:

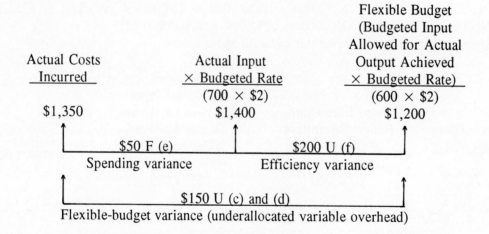

2. (a) Variable Manufacturing Overhead Control $1,350
         Accounts Payable Control and other accounts $1,350
   (b) Work in Process Control $1,200
         Variable Manufacturing Overhead Allocated $1,200
   (c) Variable Manufacturing Overhead Allocated $1,200
         Variable Manufacturing Overhead Efficiency Variance   200
            Variable Manufacturing Overhead Control $1,350
            Variable Manufacturing Overhead Spending Variance   50

V. Payton Corporation

1. $1,800 \div 300 = $6
2 through 4 are shown below in the same format as Exhibit 8-4 (Panel B):

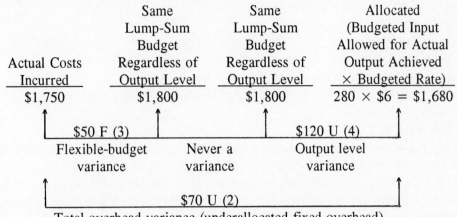

Actual Costs Incurred	Same Lump-Sum Budget Regardless of Output Level	Same Lump-Sum Budget Regardless of Output Level	Allocated (Budgeted Input Allowed for Actual Output Achieved × Budgeted Rate)
$1,750	$1,800	$1,800	280 × $6 = $1,680

$50 F (3) $120 U (4)

Flexible-budget variance   Never a variance   Output level variance

$70 U (2)

Total overhead variance (underallocated fixed overhead)

VI. Herman Company

1. A diagram is helpful in solving this problem. Let X = Actual direct manufacturing labor-hours worked for the first quarter of 19_5:

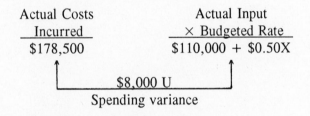

Actual Costs Incurred	Actual Input × Budgeted Rate
$178,500	$110,000 + $0.50X

$8,000 U

Spending variance

$$\$178,500 - \$8,000 = \$110,000 + \$0.50X$$
$$\$0.50X = \$178,500 - \$8,000 - \$110,000$$
$$\$0.50X = \$60,500$$
$$X = 121,000 \text{ hours}$$

In this equation the spending variance is *subtracted* from the actual costs incurred because this variance is *unfavorable*.

2. A diagram is helpful in solving this problem. Let Y = Budgeted hours allowed for actual output achieved:

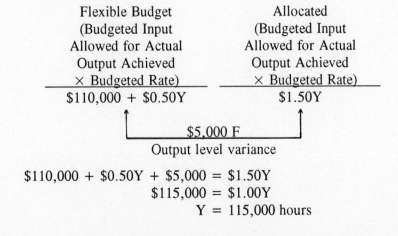

Flexible Budget (Budgeted Input Allowed for Actual Output Achieved × Budgeted Rate)	Allocated (Budgeted Input Allowed for Actual Output Achieved × Budgeted Rate)
$110,000 + $0.50Y	$1.50Y

$5,000 F

Output level variance

$$\$110,000 + \$0.50Y + \$5,000 = \$1.50Y$$
$$\$115,000 = \$1.00Y$$
$$Y = 115,000 \text{ hours}$$

In this equation the output level variance is *added* to the flexible-budget amount because this variance is *favorable*.

VII. Collier Corporation

1. $180,000 ÷ 4,000 = $45 per unit; (4,000 − 600) × $45 = $153,000
2. $16,000 U + $10,000 F = $6,000 U
3. $205,000 − $153,000 − $6,000 − $41,000 = $5,000
4. 600 × $45 = $27,000
5. ($180,000 + $6,000) ÷ 4,000 = $46.50 per unit;
   $205,000 − [(4,000 − 600) × $46.50] − $40,000 = $205,000 − $158,100 − $41,000 = $5,900
6. 600 × $46.50 = $27,900
7. $5,000 per (3) above. When standards are currently attainable, some accountants advocate that the variances should be immediately written off to cost of goods sold.
8. $27,900 per (6) above. When variances are prorated on the basis of the related standard costs in the accounts, the account balances after proration will be identical to those computed under actual costing.

CHAPTER 9

INCOME EFFECTS OF ALTERNATIVE INVENTORY-COSTING METHODS

MAIN FOCUS AND OBJECTIVES

This chapter examines and compares the effects of cost accounting system choices on the measurement of inventories and operating income. The chapter is divided into two major parts: (1) variable costing and absorption costing and (2) role of various denominator level concepts in absorption costing. We concentrate on how different system choices affect balance sheet and income statement numbers. These choices, however, have implications for many management decisions — including product mix, pricing, and making or buying components — as well as evaluation of managers' performance. Your overall objective for this chapter is to be able to make informed decisions on these system choices. Eight learning objectives are stated in the textbook (p. 308).

Give special attention to:

- the basic distinction between variable costing and absorption costing
- how the income statement format differs under variable costing and absorption costing
- why operating income can differ under variable costing and absorption costing
- the four alternative denominator-level concepts: theoretical capacity, practical capacity, normal utilization, and master-budget utilization

REVIEW OF KEY TERMS AND CONCEPTS

Part One: Variable Costing and Absorption Costing

A. One method of costing inventories of *manufacturing* companies is called variable costing.
1. Under **variable costing** all direct manufacturing costs and variable manufacturing overhead costs are included as inventoriable costs; *fixed* manufacturing overhead costs are *excluded* from inventoriable costs and treated as period costs.
   a. Inventoriable costs are initially recorded as an asset.
   b. When sales occur, inventoriable costs are expensed as cost of goods sold.
2. Variable costing is sometimes called *direct costing*, but the latter term is *not* descriptive.
   a. Variable costing does not include all direct costs as inventoriable costs (only direct *manufacturing* costs are included).
   b. Variable costing includes some indirect costs as inventoriable costs (variable manufacturing overhead costs are included).

3. Variable-costing income statements are presented in the contribution-margin format to highlight the distinction between variable costs and fixed costs.
   a. Exhibit 9-1 (Panel A) is an illustration.
   b. Note that in this type of income statement both variable manufacturing overhead and variable nonmanufacturing overhead are deducted from sales to arrive at contribution margin.
4. An output-level variance does not arise under variable costing because fixed manufacturing overhead is treated as a period cost.
5. Variable costing is used for *internal reporting only*; it is not acceptable for either income tax purposes or external financial reporting under generally accepted accounting principles.
   a. Therefore, variable costing must pass the *cost-benefit test*.
   b. As shown in the Surreys box (p. 318), 30% to 50% of companies around the world use variable costing.
6. Variable costing can be used with either actual costing, normal costing, budgeted costing, or standard costing. Exhibit 9-2 provides a helpful summary.
7. An extreme form of variable costing is called "*super-variable costing*" under which *only direct materials* are treated as inventoriable costs.

B. Another method of costing inventories of *manufacturing* companies is called absorption costing.
   1. Under **absorption costing** all direct manufacturing costs and all manufacturing overhead costs (that is, all manufacturing costs) are included as inventoriable costs; nonmanufacturing costs are treated as period costs.

Question: **Are different total amounts of fixed manufacturing overhead eventually written off in the income statement under variable costing and absorption costing?**
Answer: **No. The difference is in the *timing* of the writeoffs, which tends to be faster under variable costing.**

---

   2. The absorption-costing income statement is presented in the gross-margin format, as shown in Exhibit 9-1 (Panel B).
   3. An output level variance arises under absorption costing because fixed manufacturing overhead is treated as a period cost.

$$\text{Output level variance} = \left(\begin{array}{c} \text{Denominator} \\ \text{level in} \\ \text{output units} \end{array} - \begin{array}{c} \text{Actual} \\ \text{output units} \\ \text{achieved} \end{array} \right) \times \begin{array}{c} \text{Budgeted fixed} \\ \text{overhead rate} \\ \text{per output unit} \end{array}$$

   4. Absorption costing can be used with either actual costing, normal costing, budgeted costing, or standard costing. Exhibit 9-2 provides a helpful summary.
   5. Absorption costing is a generally accepted accounting principle.
   6. An extreme form of absorption costing, which is *not* a generally accepted accounting principle, is called "*super-absorption costing*" under which costs of *all* business functions in the value chain are treated as inventoriable costs.

> **Never overlook the heart of the matter. The difference between variable costing and absorption costing centers on how to account for fixed manufacturing overhead. If the level of finished goods inventory changes during the period, operating income will differ between these two costing methods.**

C. As Exhibit 9-1 shows, variable costing and absorption costing differ on how costs are classified in the income statement.
1. Variable costing classifies costs by cost behavior patterns thereby highlighting *contribution margin*.
2. Absorption costing classifies costs by business function (such as manufacturing and marketing), thereby highlighting *gross margin*.

> *Question*: **In Exhibit 9-1 (Panel B), why is there no output level variance?**
> *Answer*: **Because actual output units produced and the denominator level in output units are the same, 1,100,000 units.**

3. The basic differences between variable costing and absorption costing are illustrated by *Practice Test Question III (items 1-4)*.

D. Key Exhibit 9-3 shows comparative income statements, *with* an output level variance under absorption costing.

> **Carefully study Exhibit 9-3.**

1. A major point to understand is *why operating income for a given accounting period often differs between variable costing and absorption costing*.
   a. Example: In Exhibit 9-3, the operating income amounts are:

Method	January 19_4	February 19_4
Variable costing	$ 800	$21,800
Absorption costing	4,000	20,200

   b. Such differences can be explained by a *general case formula*:

$$\left(\begin{array}{c} \text{Absorption} \\ \text{costing} \\ \text{operating} \\ \text{income} \end{array} - \begin{array}{c} \text{Variable} \\ \text{costing} \\ \text{operating} \\ \text{income} \end{array}\right) = \left(\begin{array}{c} \text{Fixed manufacturing} \\ \text{OH in ending} \\ \text{FG inventory} \end{array} - \begin{array}{c} \text{Fixed manufacturing} \\ \text{OH in beginning} \\ \text{FG inventory} \end{array}\right)$$

$$\text{January 19\_4: } \$4,000 - \$800 = (200 \times \$16) - (0 \times \$16)$$
$$\$3,200 = \$3,200$$
$$\text{February 19\_4: } \$20,200 - \$21,800 = (100 \times \$16) - (200 \times \$16)$$
$$-\$1,600 = -\$1,600$$

c. The following *special case formula* can be used if three assumptions hold: (i) all manufacturing variances are written off as period costs, (ii) no change occurs in work in process inventory, and (iii) no change occurs in the budgeted manufacturing overhead rate between periods:

$$\begin{pmatrix} \text{Absorption} \\ \text{costing} \\ \text{operating} \\ \text{income} \end{pmatrix} - \begin{pmatrix} \text{Variable} \\ \text{costing} \\ \text{operating} \\ \text{income} \end{pmatrix} = \begin{pmatrix} \text{Units} \\ \text{produced} \\ \text{minus} \\ \text{units sold} \end{pmatrix} \times \begin{pmatrix} \text{Budgeted fixed} \\ \text{manufacturing} \\ \text{overhead rate} \end{pmatrix}$$

January 19_4: $4,000 - $800 = (600 - 400) \times 16
$3,200 = $3,200$
February 19_4: $20,200 - $21,800 = (650 - 750) \times 16
$-$1,600 = -$1,600$

d. As indicated by this example (the special case), absorption costing operating income *exceeds* variable costing operating income when inventory in units *increases* during the period. The reverse occurs when inventory decreases.

2. Another major point to understand is *how operating income is affected by changes in units sold and units produced.*

   a. Variable costing operating income increases (decreases) when units sold increase (decrease), given a constant unit contribution margin and constant fixed costs.

   $$\begin{array}{c} \textbf{Change in variable costing} \\ \textbf{operating income} \end{array} = \begin{array}{c} \textbf{Unit contribution} \\ \textbf{margin} \end{array} \times \begin{array}{c} \textbf{Change in} \\ \textbf{units sold} \end{array}$$

   $$\$21,800 - \$800 = (\$99 - \$39) \times (750 - 400)$$
   $$\$21,000 = \$60 \times 350$$
   $$\$21,000 = \$21,000$$

   b. Variable costing operating income would be unaffected by changes in *units produced*.

   c. Absorption costing operating income increases (decreases) when *units sold or units produced* increase (decrease) and the other unit level is held constant; of course, operating income increases (decreases) when both units sold and units produced increase (decrease).

   d. Exhibit 9-4 illustrates the effect of increasing production on absorption costing operating income.

3. **Breakeven point under variable costing** is computed as explained in Chapter 3:

   $$\text{Breakeven point in units} = \frac{\text{Total fixed costs}}{\text{Unit contribution margin}}$$

   a. There is *only one* level of units sold that is the breakeven point; the level of units produced is *not* used in the computation.

   b. Therefore, variable costing dovetails with CVP analysis discussed in Chapter 3.

4. **Breakeven point under absorption costing** is computed in a more complicated way:

$$\text{Breakeven sales in units} = \frac{\text{Total fixed costs} + \left[\text{Fixed manufacturing overhead rate}\left(\text{Breakeven sales in units} - \text{Units produced}\right)\right]}{\text{Unit contribution margin}}$$

a. In the textbook example (p. 321), a combination 291 units sold, 650 units produced, and an 800-unit denominator level results in an operating income of zero.

b. There are many, many combinations of units sold, units produced, and denominator levels that would result in an absorption costing operating income of zero (or some other specified amount). To illustrate, suppose the textbook example were changed in one respect: production is 500 units instead of 650 units. Then, breakeven sales (denoted by N) would be 346 units:

$$N = \frac{\$23,200 + \$16(N - 500)}{\$60}$$

$\$60N = \$23,200 + \$16N - \$8,000$

$\$44N = \$15,200$

$N = 346$ units (rounded)

> **Exhibit 9-5 provides a helpful comparison of income effects of variable costing and absorption costing.**

5. Variable costing is used by managers because the distinction between variable costs and fixed costs is essential for many decisions.

6. When absorption costing is used in performance evaluation, managers can increase operating income in the short run *solely* by increasing units produced (sometimes called "producing for inventory").

a. Such action would be manipulative by managers and undesirable for the company if the expected level of customer demand does not justify the increased production.

b. Some other production decisions would conflict with long-run company interests. See the three examples in the textbook (p. 322).

7. Two recent proposals for revising how the performance of managers is evaluated:

a. Reduce the types of costs that are inventoried, such as under "super-variable costing" where all costs except direct materials are treated as period costs.

b. Emphasize nonfinancial performance measures, such as attaining but not exceeding target inventory levels, meeting promised customer delivery dates, and abiding by plant maintenance schedules.

8. *See Practice Test Question III (items 5 and 6) and Problem IV.*

Part Two: Role of Various Denominator-Level Concepts in Absorption Costing

E. Alternative denominator-level concepts affect fixed manufacturing overhead rates and operating income under absorption costing.

1. Under absorption costing:

$$\text{Budgeted fixed manufacturing overhead rate} = \frac{\text{Budgeted fixed manufacturing overhead}}{\text{Denominator level}}$$

2. *Denominator level*: the preselected level of the cost allocation base used to set a budgeted fixed manufacturing overhead rate for allocating fixed manufacturing overhead costs to a product.

3. *Four alternative denominator-level concepts* that can be used to unitize fixed manufacturing overhead:

   a. **Theoretical capacity** (also called maximum capacity): the level of production output at maximum efficiency for 100% of the time.

   b. **Practical capacity**: the theoretical-capacity level reduced for unavoidable operating interruptions such as scheduled maintenance and shutdowns for holidays.

   c. **Normal utilization**: the level of capacity utilization that satisfies average customer demand over a period (say, two to three years) that includes seasonal, cyclical, and trend factors.

   d. **Master-budget utilization** (also called static-budget utilization): the anticipated level of capacity utilization for the coming budget period.

   e. Note that (a) and (b) are based on what a plant can *supply*, while (c) and (d) are based on *customer demand*. In many cases, demand is well below potential supply.

Question: **Which of the four denominator-level concepts would result in the lowest operating income?**

Answer: **Theoretical capacity (the highest denominator level) because the smallest portion of fixed overhead would be held back in inventory as a result of the budgeted fixed overhead rate being the lowest.**

See the comparative income statements in Exhibit 9-6.

---

4. A major reason for choosing master-budget utilization over normal utilization is the difficulty of forecasting normal utilization in many industries that have long-run cyclical patterns (for example, steel).

5. If theoretical capacity is used, the output level variance always would be unfavorable.

6. If practical capacity is used, the output level variance almost always would be unfavorable.

7. If normal utilization is used, unfavorable output level variances occurring in below-average production years would tend to be offset by favorable ones in above-average production years.

8. Using master-budget utilization as the denominator level (along with full proration of variances) is required for income tax reporting in the U.S.

a. U.S. companies are *not* required to use the same denominator-level concept for management purposes and for income tax purposes.

b. Nevertheless, recordkeeping costs and the desire for simplicity often lead companies to use master-budget utilization for internal reporting purposes.

9. *See Practice Test Question III (items 7 and 8) and Problem V.*

PRACTICE TEST QUESTIONS AND PROBLEMS

I. Complete each of the following statements.

Part One

1. Under _____ all direct manufacturing costs and variable manufacturing overhead costs are included as _____ _____ costs; fixed manufacturing overhead costs are treated as _____ costs.

2. For income statement purposes under variable costing, costs are divided into what two main groups? _____ and _____

3. An extreme form of variable costing is called "super-variable costing" under which only _____ are treated as inventoriable costs.

4. Which costs are inventoriable costs under absorption costing that are period costs under variable costing? _____ _____

5. For income statement purposes under absorption costing, costs are divided into what two main groups? _____ and _____

6. To compute the change in variable costing operating income, the change in units sold should be multiplied by _____ _____.

7. Absorption costing operating income decreases when either units sold or _____ decrease, or when they both decrease.

Part Two

8. The preselected level of the cost allocation base used to set a budgeted fixed manufacturing overhead rate is called the _____ _____.

9. The level of capacity utilization that satisfies average customer demand over a period (say, two to three years) that includes seasonal, cyclical, and trend factors is called _____ _____.

10. If practical capacity is used as the denominator level, the _____ _____ almost always would be unfavorable.

11. Using_____ as the denominator level (along with full proration of variances) is required for income tax reporting in the U.S.

II. Indicate whether each of the following statements is true or false by putting T or F in the space provided.

Part One

___ 1. Variable costing is sometimes called direct costing, but the latter term is not descriptive.

___ 2. In the variable costing income statement, all nonmanufacturing costs are deducted from contribution margin.

___ 3. An output level variance does not arise under variable costing.

___ 4. The cost-benefit test should be applied to variable costing.

___ 5. Variable costing can be used with standard costing but not with normal costing.

___ 6. Variable costing operating income would be unaffected by changes in units produced.

___ 7. Different total amounts of fixed manufacturing overhead are eventually charged as period costs under variable costing and absorption costing.

___ 8. Gross margin minus variable and fixed period costs equals operating income.

___ 9. Under "super-absorption costing" costs of all business functions in the value chain are treated as variable costs.

___ 10. Assume that a single-product company's selling price per unit is held constant and its fixed and variable costs follow their cost behavior patterns. If the company uses absorption costing, its operating income could not decrease if more units are sold.

___ 11. Suppose Enstrom Company uses absorption costing and determines that 10,000 units must be sold to break even in a particular month. If 10,500 units were actually sold in that month, Enstrom's operating income could be zero.

___ 12. Managers cannot manipulate absorption costing operating income in the short run solely by producing more units.

Part Two

___ 13. Choosing a denominator-level concept is only applicable to absorption costing.

___ 14. Using practical capacity rather than master-budget utilization would result in higher operating income.

___ 15. If normal utilization were used to compute the budgeted fixed manufacturing overhead rate, inventory unit costs would tend to fluctuate because of year-to-year differences in utilization of capacity.

III. Select the best answer for each of the following multiple-choice questions and put the identifying letter in the space provided.

Part One

___ 1. Vintage Co. made 4,000 units of a product during its first year of operations and sold 3,000 units for $600,000. There was no ending work in process. Total costs were $600,000: $250,000 for direct materials and direct manufacturing labor, $200,000 for manufacturing overhead (50% fixed), and $150,000 for marketing and administrative costs (100% variable). The cost of the 1,000 units of finished goods ending inventory under variable costing is:
   a. $112,500.
   b. $125,000.
   c. $87,500.
   d. none of the above.

___ 2. See item 1. The cost of the ending inventory under absorption costing is:

a. $112,500.
b. $150,000.
c. $25,000.
d. none of the above.

___ 3. See item 1. The contribution margin is:
   a. $337,500.
   b. $187,500.
   c. $100,000.
   d. none of the above.

___ 4. See item 1. The gross margin is:
   a. $100,000.
   b. $150,000.
   c. $262,500.
   d. none of the above.

___ 5. (CPA adapted) Indiana Corporation began its operations on January 1, 19_3, and produces a single product that sells for $9.00 per unit. One hundred thousand units were produced and 90,000 units were sold in 19_3. There was no work in process inventory at December 31, 19_3. Manufacturing, marketing, and administrative costs for 19_3 were as follows:

	Total Fixed Costs	Variable Costs Per unit
Direct materials		$1.75
Direct manufacturing labor		1.25
Manufacturing overhead	$100,000	.50
Marketing and administrative	70,000	.60

The cost driver for manufacturing costs is units produced, and the cost driver for marketing and administrative costs is units sold. What would be Indiana's operating income for 19_3 using variable costing?
   a. $181,000
   b. $271,000
   c. $281,000
   d. $371,000

___ 6. (CPA adapted) Operating income using variable costing as compared to absorption costing would be higher:
   a. when the amount of fixed manufacturing overhead in beginning inventory is greater than the amount in ending inventory.

b. when the amount of fixed manufacturing overhead in beginning inventory equals the amount in ending inventory.

c. when the amount of fixed manufacturing overhead in beginning inventory is less than the amount in ending inventory.

d. under no circumstances.

Part Two

___ 7. (CPA) The budgeted variable manufacturing overhead rate under the denominator-level concepts of normal utilization, practical capacity, and master-budget utilization would be:

a. the same except for normal utilization.

b. the same except for practical capacity.

c. the same except for master-budget utilization.

d. the same for all three denominator-level concepts.

___ 8. (CPA adapted) Dean Company is preparing a flexible budget for the coming year and the following practical capacity estimates for department M are available:

	At practical capacity
Direct manufacturing labor-hours (DMLH)	60,000
Variable manufacturing overhead	$150,000
Fixed manufacturing overhead	$240,000

Assume Department M's normal utilization, which is 80% of practical capacity, is used as the denominator level. What would be the total overhead rate, based on DMLH, in a flexible budget at normal utilization?

a. $6.00
b. $6.50
c. $7.50
d. $8.13

Part One

IV. (CMA adapted) Denham Company began operations on January 3, 19_3. Standard costs were established soon thereafter. The budgeted fixed manufacturing overhead rate was based on a denominator level of 160,000 units. However, Denham produced only 140,000 units of output and sold 100,000 units at a selling price of $180 per unit during 19_3. Variable costs totaled $7,000,000, of which 60% were manufacturing and 40% were marketing and administrative. Fixed costs totaled $11,200,000, of which 50% were manufacturing and 50% were marketing and administrative. Denham had no materials or work in process inventories at December 31, 19_3. Actual input prices per unit of output and actual input quantities per unit of output were equal to standard amounts.

1. Compute:
   a. Cost of finished goods inventory at December 31, 19_3 under variable costing.
   b. Cost of finished goods inventory at December 31, 19_3 under absorption costing.
   c. Operating income for 19_3 under variable costing.
   d. Output level variance for 19_3 under absorption costing.
   e. Operating income for 19_3 under absorption costing.
   f. The explanation by formula for the difference between operating income for 19_3 under variable costing and absorption costing, answers (c) and (e) above.
   g. Breakeven point sales in units for 19_3 under variable costing (show a proof of your answer).
   h. Breakeven point sales in units for 19_3 under absorption costing (show a proof of your answer).

2. Suppose in the coming year (19_4) sales volume increases 1,000 units and production volume increases 1,000 units. Assume that selling price per unit, variable costs per unit, total fixed costs, and denominator level remain the same. Without preparing an income statement, compute:

a. The effect of these changes on operating income from 19_3 to 19_4 under variable costing.
b. The effect of these changes on operating income from 19_3 to 19_4 under absorption costing.

Check figures: (1a) $1,200,000 (1b) $2,600,000 (1c) $1,000,000 (1d) $700,000 U (1e) $2,400,000 (1g) 91,804 units (1h) 72,414 units (2a) $122,000 increase (2b) $157,000 increase

---

Part Two

V. Bouchard Company furnished the following data.

Fixed manufacturing overhead for the year:

Budgeted	$720,000
Actual	$740,000
Practical capacity per year	20,000 machine-hours
Normal utilization per year	16,000 machine-hours
Master-budget utilization for the year	12,000 machine-hours
Budgeted input allowed for actual output achieved	13,000 machine-hours

1. Using master-budget utilization, compute:
   a. Budgeted fixed overhead rate
   b. Fixed overhead allocated
   c. Underallocated or overallocated fixed overhead
   d. Output level variance
2. Compute the output level variance:
   a. Under normal utilization
   b. Under practical capacity
3. Does master-budget utilization or normal utilization result in inventory cost that is more representative of the typical relationship between total fixed overhead and units produced beyond one year? Explain.

Check figures: (1a) $60 per machine-hour (1b) $780,000 (1c) $40,000 overallocated (1d) $60,000 F (2a) $135,000 U (2b) $252,000 U

CHAPTER 9 SOLUTIONS TO PRACTICE TEST

I. 1 variable costing, inventoriable, period; 2 variable costs, fixed costs; 3 direct materials; 4 fixed manufacturing overhead costs; 5 manufacturing costs, nonmanufacturing costs; 6 unit contribution margin; 7 units produced; 8 denominator level; 9 normal utilization denominator level; 10 output level variance; 11 master-budget utilization.

II.

1	T	5	F	9	T	13	T
2	F	6	T	10	F	14	F
3	T	7	F	11	T	15	F
4	T	8	T	12	F		

Explanations:

1 Direct costing is not a descriptive term for variable costing because (i) variable costing does not include all direct costs as inventoriable costs (only direct *manufacturing* costs are included) and (ii) variable costing includes some indirect costs as inventoriable costs (variable manufacturing overhead costs are included). (T)

2 All variable manufacturing and nonmanufacturing costs are deducted from sales to arrive at contribution margin, and all fixed manufacturing and nonmanufacturing costs are deducted from contribution margin to arrive at operating income. (F)

3 An output level variance does not arise under variable costing because fixed manufacturing overhead is treated as a period cost. (T)

4 Variable costing is not acceptable for income tax purposes or external financial reporting under generally accepted accounting principles. Variable costing is used for internal reporting only, so it should be subjected to the cost-benefit test. (T)

5 Variable costing (and also absorption costing) can be used with either actual costing, normal costing, budgeted costing, or standard costing. Exhibit 9-2 provides a helpful summary. (F)

6 Variable costing operating income is driven solely by units sold, given a constant unit contribution margin and constant fixed costs. (T)

7 The same total amount of fixed manufacturing overhead is eventually charged as period costs under variable costing and absorption costing. But there is a difference in the *timing* of these charges, which tends to be faster under variable costing. (F)

8 Fixed and variable *inventoriable costs* that relate to goods sold are written off in the current period. Sales minus these costs equals gross margin. Then all variable and fixed *period costs* are deducted from gross margin to arrive at operating income. (T)

9 The statement is true, but be aware that "super-absorption costing" is an extreme form of costing, which is *not* a generally accepted accounting principle. (T)

10 Under absorption costing, operating income is driven by both units sold *and* units produced. If the increase in operating income from a higher number of units sold was more than offset by the decrease in operating income from producing fewer units, the net effect would be a decrease in operating income. (F)

11 Three variables affect the calculation of breakeven point under absorption costing: units sold, units produced, and the denominator level. There are many, many combinations of these three variables that would result in an absorption costing operating income of zero. (T)

12 Managers can manipulate absorption costing operating income in the short run solely by producing more units because units produced is one of the drivers of absorption costing operating income. Producing more units would be manipulative by managers and undesirable for the company if the expected level of customer demand does not justify the increased production. (F)

13 A denominator-level concept is not chosen under variable costing because all fixed manufacturing overhead is written off as a period cost. (T)

14 Using practical capacity as the denominator level would give rise to lower operating income because a smaller portion of fixed manufacturing overhead is held back in inventory as a result of the budgeted fixed overhead rate being lower. (F)

15 The budgeted fixed manufacturing overhead rate is equal to budgeted fixed manufacturing overhead divided by the denominator level. Given that the denominator level is normal utilization, year-to-year differences in utilization of capacity would not affect the budgeted manufacturing overhead rate and, therefore, would not affect inventory unit costs. (F)

III.

1 c	4 c	7 d
2 a	5 b	8 c
3 b	6 a	

Explanations:

1 Total variable manufacturing costs = $250,000 + $200,000(.50) = $350,000, which is $87.50 per unit ($350,000 ÷ 4,000)
   Cost of ending finished goods inventory = (4,000 − 3,000) × $87.50 = $87,500 (c)

2 Total manufacturing costs per unit = ($250,000 + $200,000) ÷ 4,000 = $112.50
   Cost of ending finished goods inventory = (4,000 − 3,000) × $112.50 = $112,500 (a)

3 Variable cost of goods sold = $350,000 − $87,500 = $262,500

Contribution margin = $600,000 − ($262,500 + $150,000) = $187,500 (b)

Note that ending finished goods inventory of $87,500 is deducted in these computations because it is carried forward as an asset to the next accounting period.

4 Cost of goods sold = 3,000 × $112.50 = $337,500

Gross margin = $600,000 − $337,500 = $262,500 (c)

5 $9.00 − ($1.75 + $1.25 + $0.50 + $0.60) = $9.00 − $4.10 = $4.90; (90,000 × $4.90) − ($100,000 + $70,000) = $441,000 − $170,000 = $271,000 (b)

6 See the general case formula in section D(1b) of the chapter outline. (a)

7 The budgeted *variable* manufacturing overhead rate is unaffected by the choice of denominator-level concept. The budgeted *fixed* manufacturing overhead rate is affected by the choice. (d)

8 The budgeted variable overhead rate is the same within the relevant range.

$$\text{Budgeted variable overhead rate} = \frac{\$150,000}{60,000 \text{ DMLH}} = \$2.50 \text{ per DMLH}$$

$$\text{Budgeted variable overhead rate} = \frac{(.80)\$150,000}{(.80)60,000 \text{ DMLH}} = \frac{\$120,000}{48,000 \text{ DMLH}} = \$2.50 \text{ per DMLH}$$

$$\text{Budgeted fixed overhead rate} = \frac{\$240,000}{(.80)60,000 \text{ DMLH}} = \frac{\$240,000}{48,000 \text{ DMLH}} = \$5.00 \text{ per DMLH}$$

The budgeted total overhead rate = $2.50 + $5.00 = $7.50 per DMLH (c)

IV. Denham Company

1. (a) $7,000,000 × .60 = $4,200,000; $4,200,000 ÷ 140,000 = $30; (140,000 − 100,000) × $30 = $1,200,000

   (b) $11,200,000 × .50 = $5,600,000; $5,600,000 ÷ 160,000 = $35; (140,000 − 100,000) × ($30 + $35) = 40,000 × $65 = $2,600,000

   (c) $7,000,000 × .40 = $2,800,000; $2,800,000 ÷ 100,000 = $28;

Sales, 100,000 × $180	$18,000,000
Variable costs, 100,000 × ($30 + $28)	5,800,000
Contribution margin	12,200,000
Fixed costs	11,200,000
Operating income	$ 1,000,000

   (d) Budgeted fixed overhead = $11,200,000 × .50 = $5,600,000

   Budgeted fixed overhead rate = $5,600,000 ÷ 160,000 = $35 per unit

   Output level variance = (160,000 − 140,000) × $35 = $700,000 unfavorable

   (e)

Sales, 100,000 × $180		$18,000,000
Cost of goods sold		
At standard, 100,000 × ($30 + $35)	$6,500,000	
Add unfavorable output level variance	700,000	7,200,000
Gross margin		10,800,000
Marketing and administrative costs		
Variable, $7,000,000 × .40	2,800,000	
Fixed, $11,200,000 × .50	5,600,000	8,400,000
Operating income		$ 2,400,000

(f) $2,400,000 - $1,000,000 = (140,000 - 100,000) \times $35

$1,400,000 = $1,400,000

(g) Variable manufacturing costs per unit = ($7,000,000 \times .60) \div 140,000 = $30

Variable marketing and administrative costs per unit = ($7,000,000 \times .40) \div 100,000 = $28

Breakeven point sales in units = $11,200,000 \div [$180 - ($30 + $28)] = $11,200,000 \div $122 = 91,803.3 units rounded to 91,804 units

Proof:

Sales, 91,803.3 × $180	$16,524,594
Variable costs, 91,803.3 × ($30 + $28)	5,324,591
Contribution margin	11,200,003
Fixed costs	11,200,000
Operating income (not zero due to rounding error)	$ 3

(h) Budgeted fixed overhead rate = ($11,200,000 \times .50) \div 160,000 = $35 per unit

Using the formula in section D(4) of the chapter outline and letting X = Breakeven point sales in units:

$$X = \frac{\$11,200,000 + \$35(X - 140,000)}{\$180 - (\$30 + \$28)}$$

$$X = \frac{\$11,200,000 + \$35X - \$4,900,000}{\$122}$$

$$\$122X = \$6,300,000 + \$35X$$
$$\$87X = \$6,300,000$$
$$X = 72,413.8 \text{ units, rounded to } 72,414 \text{ units}$$

Proof:

Sales, 72,413.8 × $180		$13,034,484
Cost of goods sold		
At standard, 72,413.8 × ($30 + $35)	$4,706,897	
Add unfavorable output level variance, (160,000 − 140,000) × $35	700,000	5,406,897
Gross margin		7,627,587
Marketing and administrative costs		
Variable, 72,413.8 × $28	2,027,586	
Fixed, $11,200,000 × .50	5,600,000	7,627,586
Operating income (not zero due to rounding error)		$ 1

2. (a) Operating income under variable costing is driven by units sold alone (changes in units produced have no effect):

Effect on operating income under variable costing = 1,000 × [$180 − ($30 + $28)] = $122,000 increase

(b) Operating income under absorption costing is driven by both units sold and units produced:

Effect on operating income under variable costing = 1,000 × [$180 − ($30 + $28)] + 1,000($35) = $157,000 increase

V. Bouchard Company

1. (a) $\$720,000 \div 12,000 = \$60$ per machine-hour
   (b) $13,000 \times \$60 = \$780,000$
   (c) $\$740,000 - \$780,000 = \$40,000$ overallocated
   (d) $\$720,000 - (13,000 \times \$60) = \$720,000 - \$780,000 = \$60,000$ F

2. (a) and (b)

	Normal Utilization	Practical Capacity
Budgeted fixed overhead rate		
$\$720,000 \div 16,000; \$720,000 \div 20,000$	$\$45$	$\$36$
Fixed overhead allocated		
$13,000 \times \$45; 13,000 \times \$36$	$\$585,000$	$\$468,000$
Output level variance		
$(\$720,000 - \$585,000); (\$720,000 - \$468,000)$	$\$135,000$ U	$\$252,000$ U

3. Inventory cost is more representative of the typical relationship between total fixed overhead and average units produced over the next several years when normal utilization is used. Master-budget utilization relates to the current year only.

CHAPTER 10

DETERMINING
HOW COSTS BEHAVE

MAIN FOCUS AND OBJECTIVES

Knowing how costs behave and distinguishing fixed costs from variable costs are often keys to making good management decisions. This chapter examines cost estimation, which is the attempt to measure past cost relationships. Your overall objective for the chapter is to gain insight about estimating cost behavior patterns (cost functions). Nine learning objectives are stated in the textbook (p. 340). Give special attention to:

- the four approaches to cost estimation
- the six steps in estimating a cost function on the basis of quantitative analysis
- how regression analysis can be used to estimate cost functions
- the four criteria for choosing among cost functions
- the hierarchy of costs and cost drivers

Most cost functions are assumed to have a single cost driver and to be linear. The chapter Appendix explains multiple regression (using an example with two cost drivers) and provides additional details on regression analysis. A nonlinear cost function discussed in the chapter is the learning curve.

REVIEW OF KEY TERMS AND CONCEPTS

A. Knowledge of how costs behave helps managers make more accurate predictions of costs for decision making.
   1. **Cost estimation** is the attempt to measure *past* cost relationships.
   2. Managers use cost estimation to help make more accurate *cost predictions* (forecasts) of *future* costs.
   3. Cost estimation underlies many of the topics in the textbook, including CVP analysis, flexible budgets, and pricing.
   4. **Cost functions** are used to make cost predictions.
   5. Cost functions frequently are based on two simplifying assumptions:
      a. *Assumption 1*: Variations in a *single* cost driver explain variations in total costs.
      b. *Assumption 2*: A *linear* (straight-line) function adequately approximates cost behavior within the relevant range of the cost driver.
   6. Key terms in these assumptions:
      a. **Cost driver**: any factor that affects costs (that is, a change in the cost driver will cause a change in the total costs of a related cost object).

b. **Relevant range**: the range of the cost driver in which a specific relationship between total costs and the driver is valid.
7. Whether the single cost driver and linearity assumptions are acceptable for the purpose at hand depends on the cost of more sophisticated analysis versus the likelihood of improved decisions from more accurate cost estimates.
   a. Nonlinear cost functions are covered in section F of this chapter outline.
   b. Multiple regression using two cost drivers is discussed in the chapter Appendix.
8. Linear equation to estimate a cost function with one cost driver:

$$c = g + wD$$

   a. **c** is any *estimated amount of cost* (as distinguished from *actual cost amounts*).
   b. **D** is any *actual* amount of the cost driver within the relevant range.
   c. **g** is the **constant** or *vertical-axis intercept*.
   d. **w** is the **slope coefficient**, the amount of change in total costs (*c*) for each unit change in the cost driver (*D*).
   e. Note that, because the zero level of the cost driver (shutdown) is rarely within the relevant range, *the constant is usually not the fixed costs.*

> **Three types of linear cost functions are variable costs, fixed costs, and mixed costs. Graphs of these cost functions are in Exhibit 10-1.**

9. *Mixed costs (also called semivariable costs)* have both fixed and variable elements. Example: renting a photocopy machine for $50 per month plus $0.02 per copy made.
10. *The most important issue in estimating a cost function is to determine whether a cause-and-effect relationship exists between the cost driver and the costs.*
11. Whether a cost is fixed or variable depends on the cost object, the time span, and the relevant range.

B. Four approaches to cost estimation can be used individually or in combination.
   1. *Industrial-engineering method* (also called the work measurement method): analyzes the relationship between inputs and outputs in physical terms.
      a. This method is mostly used for direct cost categories such as materials and labor.
      b. The analysis is very time-consuming.
   2. *Conference method*: develops cost estimates on the basis of opinions gathered from various departments of an organization.
      a. The accuracy of the resulting cost estimates depends on the care and detail used by the people involved.
      b. This method is not time-consuming.
   3. *Account analysis method*: classifies cost accounts in the ledger as variable, fixed, or mixed with respect to the cost driver on the basis of qualitative (as distinguished from quantitative) analysis by managers.
      a. This method is widely used in practice and is often adequate for simple cost structures such as the one in Exhibit 10-2.
      b. Supplementing this method with the conference method improves its credibility.

4. *Quantitative analysis of cost relationships*: uses historical data to estimate cost functions. These data may be time-series data or cross-sectional data.
   a. Time-series data pertain to the same entity (company, activity area, and so on) over a sequence of past time periods.
   b. Cross-sectional data pertain to different entities for the same time period.
5. The first three methods require less historical data than do most quantitative analyses of cost relationships.

C. In estimating a cost function on the basis of quantitative analysis, six steps are used.

Step 1: **Choose the dependent variable (the particular cost to be predicted).**
Step 2: **Identify the cost driver(s).**
Step 3: **Collect data on the dependent variable and on the cost driver(s).**
Step 4: **Plot the data.**
Step 5: **Estimate the cost function.**
Step 6: **Evaluate the estimated cost function.**

---

1. These steps are used in the chapter example as follows:
   Step 1: The dependent variable is indirect manufacturing labor costs.
   Step 2: The cost driver is machine-hours.
   Step 3: The data are presented in Exhibit 10-3.
   Step 4: The data are plotted in Exhibit 10-4.
   Step 5: The estimated cost function is:

High-Low Method	*Regression Analysis Method*
$c = \$23.68 + \$14.92D$	$c = \$300.98 + \$10.31D$ (graphed in Exhibit 10-6)

Step 6: Evaluating the estimated cost function is covered in section D of this chapter outline.
2. Notes on using the six steps:
   a. The concept of *homogeneous cost pools* — where all costs in a cost pool have the same or a similar cause-and-effect relationship with the cost driver — should be used for determining how many indirect cost pools to form (steps 1 and 2).
   b. The general relationship between the dependent variable and the independent variable (such as a cost driver) is called *correlation*. In a homogeneous cost pool, there is high correlation between the indirect costs and the cost driver.
   c. Data collection (step 3) is usually the most difficult step.
   d. *Seven frequently encountered data problems*, ranging from missing or unreliable observations to distortions resulting from inflation, are discussed in the textbook (pp. 354-55).

e. Plotting the data (step 4):
   (1) Highlights extreme observations, which may be due to recording errors or unusual events such as a labor strike, that should be checked.
   (2) Provides insight about the relevant range and about whether the cost relationship is linear within that range.
f. The estimated cost function (step 5) can be used to make cost predictions. For example, suppose 80 machine-hours are budgeted for the coming week. Using the regression equation, budgeted indirect manufacturing labor costs would be:

$$c = \$300.98 + \$10.31(80) = \$1,125.78$$

   g. *See Practice Test Problem III (item 6).*
3. The **high-low method** is a very simplified way of estimating cost functions.
   a. This method simply calculates the formula for a straight line on the basis of two data points.
   b. See the textbook illustration (p. 349).
   c. Exhibit 10-5 illustrates the danger of mechanically picking the highest and lowest observations of the cost driver.
   d. *See Practice Test Question III (items 2-4) and Problem IV.*
4. **Regression analysis** is a statistical model that measures the average amount of change in the dependent variable that is associated with a unit change in one or more independent variables.
   a. *Simple regression analysis* uses only one independent variable.
   b. *Multiple regression analysis* uses more than one independent variable.
5. Regression uses all available data to estimate the cost function, thereby providing much more useful cost estimates than the high-low method.
6. Intelligent application of regression analysis requires knowledge of both operations and cost accounting.
7. The constant in the regression equation, $300.98, is *not* an estimate of fixed costs; instead, the constant is a component of the equation that gives the best linear approximation of how indirect manufacturing labor costs behave within the relevant range.

> **Exhibit 10-7 presents a convenient format for summarizing the regression results. The chapter Appendix elaborates on the statistics presented in this exhibit.**

D. Managers and accountants are often faced with choosing which particular regression cost function is the most appropriate.
   1. This situation arises because computer software programs make it quick and inexpensive to develop numerous simple and multiple regressions.
   2. Four criteria are relevant for choosing among cost functions:
      a. Economic plausibility
      b. Goodness of fit
      c. Significance of independent variable(s)
      d. Specification analysis of estimation assumptions

3. **Economic plausibility**: the relationship between the costs and the independent variable should make economic sense and be intuitive to both the operating manager and the accountant.
4. **Goodness of fit**: the closer the predicted amounts of c are to the actual cost amounts, the better the goodness of fit.
   a. A formal measure of goodness of fit is the *coefficient of determination* (r^2): measures the percentage of variation in the dependent variable (costs), explained by the independent variable.
   b. If the predicted costs exactly equal the actual costs, $r^2 = 1$.
   c. $r^2 \geq 0.30$ passes the goodness-of-fit test.
   d. Do not overemphasize the goodness-of-fit criterion; *all four criteria* need to be considered.

> **A high r^2 between two variables *does not prove* that a cause-and-effect relationship exists. Instead it indicates that those variables move together.**

5. *See Practice Test Problem V.*
6. **Significance of independent variable(s)**: that is, do changes in the independent variable(s) affect total costs?
   a. The key statistic is the t-value of the slope coefficient(s).
   b. If the t-value is less than 2.00, the independent variable is not a cost driver.
7. **Specification analysis of estimation assumptions**: refers to testing four assumptions underlying regression analysis.
   a. The assumptions are (i) linearity within the relevant range, (ii) constant variance of residuals, (iii) independence of residuals, and (iv) normality of residuals.
   b. A **residual** (residual term) is the difference between the predicted cost amount and the actual cost amount.
   c. If the regression model satisfies the four assumptions, confidence can be placed in the estimated cost function without using more complex statistical procedures.
8. Goodness of fit, significance of independent variable(s), and specification analysis of estimation assumptions are covered in more detail in the chapter Appendix.

> **Note that not all independent variables in regression analysis are cost drivers. To be a cost driver, an independent variable must satisfy the four criteria for choosing among cost functions.**

E. Managers are recognizing that the hierarchy of costs and cost drivers is a useful way to understand cost behavior and estimate cost functions.

> **Four hierarchical levels of costs:**
> - **Output unit-level costs**
> - **Batch-level costs**
> - **Product-sustaining costs**
> - **Facility-sustaining costs**

1. **Output unit-level costs**: the resources are used up on activities performed each time a unit of product or service is produced or sold. Examples are direct materials costs and (over the long run) machine maintenance costs.
2. **Batch-level costs**: the resources are used up on activities that are related to a batch of products or services. Examples are setup costs and purchase-order costs.
3. **Product (service)-sustaining costs**: the resources are used up on activities undertaken to support specific products (services). Examples are design costs and product-specific advertising costs.
4. **Facility-sustaining costs**: the resources are used up on activities that cannot be traced to specific services but support the organization as a whole. Examples are general administration costs and corporate-image advertising costs.

> **A major reason why low-volume products are often undercosted is that the batch-level and product-sustaining costs of those products should be allocated to the relatively few units of low-volume products, rather than allocated as output unit-level costs to all products.**

F. In practice, cost functions are not always linear.
   1. *Nonlinear cost function*: a single constant and a single slope coefficient do not adequately describe the behavior of costs for all changes in the level of the cost driver.
      a. Exhibit 10-8 shows how direct materials costs increase at a decreasing rate as a result of quantity discounts.
      b. Exhibit 10-9 illustrates a *step-variable cost function*. Example: clerical labor services cannot be obtained in as small fractional units as needed for use.
      c. Exhibit 10-10 shows a *step-fixed cost function*. Example: supervision costs remain constant over a wide range of the cost driver, but additional supervisors would be needed if a second shift is added.
      d. Learning curves for labor and labor-related costs are another nonlinear cost function. For example, see the graphs in Exhibit 10-11.
   2. **Learning curve**: a function that shows how labor-hours per unit decrease as units of output increase.
      a. This curve can be expressed as cumulative average-time per unit of output (left graph in Exhibit 10-11).
      b. This curve can be expressed as cumulative total time at various levels of output (right graph in Exhibit 10-11).
      c. Learning is more likely to occur with new products, new workers, and in labor intensive production situations.
   3. A broader application of the learning curve is called the *experience curve*: a function that shows how full product costs (all value chain costs expressed on a per unit basis) decline as units of output increase.
   4. Two models incorporate learning into the estimation of cost functions:
      a. The **cumulative average-time learning model** where cumulative average-time per unit declines by a constant percentage each time the cumulative quantity of units produced is doubled. Computations appear in Exhibits 10-12 and 10-15.

b. The **incremental unit-time learning model** where incremental unit time (the time needed to produce the last unit) declines by a constant percentage each time the cumulative quantity of units produced is doubled. Computations appear in Exhibit 10-14.

> *Question*: **Which learning-curve model is preferable?**
> *Answer*: **The one that more accurately approximates the behavior of labor-hours usage as output increases. The choice can only be made on a case-by-case basis.**

5. Important applications of the learning curve include setting standards for new production work, developing pricing strategy, and bidding for defense contracts.
6. *See Practice Test Question III (items 7 and 8) and Problem VI.*

G. (**Appendix**) When choosing among cost functions, it is important to know how the regression equation is derived and to understand several commonly used statistics.
   1. Regression analysis estimates the regression line that minimizes the sum of the squared deviations (distances) of each data point from the line.
   2. This calculation requires the use of two normal equations explained in the textbook (p. 365).
   3. The resulting regression equation is: $c = \$300.98 + \$10.31D$.
   4. To understand *goodness of fit* in regression analysis, it is helpful to express r^2 in a verbal formula:

   $$r^2 = 1 - \frac{\text{Unexplained variation}}{\text{Total variation}} = \frac{\text{Explained variation}}{\text{Total variation}}$$

   5. In evaluating *significance of the independent variable(s)*, a key statistic is the standard error of the estimated coefficient.
      a. This statistic indicates how much the estimated value of the slope coefficient, w, is likely to be affected by random factors.
      b. This statistic divided into w equals the t-value of the slope coefficient. Using the regression results in Exhibit 10-7:

      $$t\text{-value} = 10.31 \div 3.12 = 3.30$$

      c. If the t-value is *less than 2.00*, the independent variable is *not* a cost driver.
   6. *Specification analysis* tests four assumptions of regression analysis.
      a. *Assumption 1*: Linearity within the relevant range can be checked by studying the data on a scatter diagram. (A scatter diagram can be prepared only in the case of simple regression.)
      b. *Assumption 2*: Constant variance of residuals can be checked by studying the data on a scatter diagram.
      c. *Assumption 3*: Independence of residuals can be checked by studying a plot of the residuals.
         (1) When there is a systematic pattern in the *sequence* of residuals (such as in Panel B of Exhibit 10-18), this problem is called *serial correlation* or *autocorrelation*.

(2) Serial correlation is measured by the *Durbin-Watson statistic*. For samples of 10 to 20 observations, this statistic falling in the 1.30 to 2.70 range suggests that the residuals are independent.

d. *Assumption 4*: Normality of residuals can be checked by studying the frequency distribution of a plot of the residuals.

Assumption	Holds	Does Not Hold
Linearity within the relevant range	Exhibit 10-6	– –
Constant variance of residuals	Exhibit 10-17 (A)	Exhibit 10-17 (B)
Independence of residuals	Exhibit 10-18 (A)	Exhibit 10-18 (B)
Normality of residuals	– –	– –

7. It is often necessary to use an "imperfect" cost function because any particular cost function will not perfectly meet all the criteria for choosing among cost functions.

Question: **Which independent variable, machine-hours or direct manufacturing labor-hours, would be the better cost driver for a regression model used to predict indirect manufacturing labor costs?**
Answer: **Apply the four criteria for choosing among cost functions in each case and make a selection accordingly.**
See the Elegant Rugs example in the textbook (beginning p. 369):
- **Machine-hours is the independent variable in Exhibits 10–6 and 10–7.**
- **Direct manufacturing labor-hours is the independent variable in Exhibits 10–20 and 10–21.**
- **A comprehensive comparison of these variables is in key Exhibit 10–22. The regression model using machine-hours is preferable in this case.**
- ***See Practice Test Problem VII.***

---

8. The results of a **multiple regression** analysis with two independent variables— machine-hours and production batches—are presented in Exhibit 10-23.
   a. Note that this example is like the hierarchy of costs and cost drivers in the chapter: machine-hours is an output-unit-level cost driver and production batches is a batch-level cost driver.
   b. The regression equation is:

   $c = \$95.13 + \$4.99 \text{(machine–hours)} + \$47.38 \text{(production batches)}$

   c. As explained in the textbook, this model satisfies the four criteria among cost functions.
   d. A major concern that arises with multiple regression is multicollinearity.
      (1) *Multicollinearity* exists when two or more independent variables are highly correlated with each other.
      (2) Multicollinearity is at an unacceptable level when the coefficient of correlation (r) between any pair of independent variables exceeds 0.70.

PRACTICE TEST QUESTIONS AND PROBLEMS

I. Complete each of the following statements.

1. The attempt to measure past cost relationships is called _____.

2. Cost functions are used to make _____.

3. It is often assumed that a cost function is _____ within the relevant range of a _____ cost driver.

4. In the equation, $c = g + wD$, what do each of the symbols stand for?

_____

_____

_____

_____

5. The most important issue in estimating a cost function is to determine whether a _____ _____ exists between the cost driver and the costs.

6. Name the four approaches (methods) to cost estimation that can be used individually or in combination: _____

_____

_____

_____

7. The linear cost function that explains the cost of renting an automobile when the two pertinent factors are the specified rental period and miles driven is called a _____ _____.

8. A statistical method that measures the average amount of change in the dependent variable that is associated with a unit change in one or more independent variables is called _____ _____.

9. Name the four criteria that are relevant for choosing among cost functions:

_____

_____

_____

_____

10. Name the four hierarchical levels of cost:

_____

_____

11. (Appendix) Name the four assumptions of regression analysis tested under specification analysis: _____

_____

_____

12. (Appendix) When a systematic pattern exists in the sequence of residuals such that knowledge of the residual in period t conveys information about the residuals in $t + 1$, $t + 2$, and so on, this problem is called ____

_____.

II. Indicate whether each of the following statements is true or false by putting T or F in the space provided.

____ 1. The forecasting of future costs is called cost estimation.

____ 2. In the equation $c = g + wD$, the constant g is usually not the fixed costs.

____ 3. The account analysis method relies primarily on quantitative analysis.

____ 4. In cost estimation, the observed amounts of the cost driver should be plotted so that the dependent variable can be chosen.

____ 5. The most difficult step in estimating a cost function on the basis of quantitative analysis of cost relationships usually is data collection.

____ 6. When the high-low method is used, the constant in the cost function equation is always computed after the computation of the slope coefficient.

____ 7. The closer the predicted amounts of c in a cost function are to the actual cost amounts, the better the economic plausibility.

____ 8. A critical step in using simple regression is plotting the scatter diagram.

____ 9. A formal measure of goodness of fit is the coefficient of determination.

____ 10. Regression analysis is used in cost accounting to determine if cause-and-effect relationships exist between cost drivers and costs.

____ 11. Not all independent variables in regression analysis are cost drivers.

____ 12. Batch-level costs are the resources used up on activities performed each time a unit of product or service is produced or sold.

13. A major reason why low-volume products are often undercosted is that the batch-level and product-sustaining costs of those products are allocated as if they were output unit-level costs of all products.

14. The main purpose of the learning curve is to assist managers in developing techniques for increasing the speed and efficiency of production.

15. A broader application of the learning curve is called the experience curve.

16. (Appendix) The standard error of the estimated coefficient is a key statistic used to measure goodness of fit in regression analysis.

17. (Appendix) In simple regression, a scatter diagram can be used to check for constant variance of residuals.

18. (Appendix) A multiple regression model uses only one dependent variable.

19. (Appendix) Multicollinearity is measured by the Durbin-Watson statistic.

III. Select the best answer for each of the following multiple-choice questions and put the identifying letter in the space provided.

1. The main purpose for estimating cost functions is to:
   a. prove the validity of management decisions.
   b. improve the accuracy of cost predictions.
   c. correct errors in recording costs.
   d. develop precise mathematical equations.

2. (CPA) Jackson, Inc., is preparing a flexible budget for the coming year and requires the cost of steam used in its plant to be broken down into the fixed and variable elements. The following data on the cost of steam used and direct manufacturing labor-hours (DMLH) worked are available for the last six months of the current year:

Month	Cost of Steam	DMLH
July	$ 15,850	3,000
August	13,400	2,050
September	16,370	2,900
October	19,800	3,650
November	17,600	2,670
December	18,500	2,650
Total	$101,520	16,920

Assuming that Jackson uses the high-low method, the estimated variable cost of steam per DMLH would be:
   a. $4.00.
   b. $5.42.
   c. $5.82.
   d. $6.00.

3. See item 2. Assuming that Jackson uses the high-low method, the estimated amount of the constant is:
   a. $6,400.
   b. $0.
   c. $5,200.
   d. none of the above.

4. Under the high-low method, suppose the highest and lowest observations of the cost do not correspond with the same time period as the highest and lowest observations of the cost driver. Then the analyst should use the highest and lowest observations of:
   a. the cost.
   b. the cost driver.
   c. the constant.
   d. the slope coefficient.

5. In a step-cost function, as the steps become narrower, the cost behavior would approach the pattern of a:
   a. fixed cost.
   b. variable cost.
   c. mixed cost.
   d. semivariable cost.

6. (CPA) Adams Corporation has developed the following flexible budget formula for annual indirect manufacturing labor cost:

$$\text{Total cost} = \$4,800 + \$0.50(\text{Machine-hours})$$

Operating budgets for the current month are based on 20,000 hours of planned machine time. Indirect manufacturing labor cost included in the monthly budget would be:

a. $14,800.
b. $10,000.
c. $14,400.
d. $10,400.

____ 7. (CMA) Ace Manufacturing Corporation has found that the production of a certain product is subject to an 80% learning curve. The product is produced in lots of 100 units and 8 labor-hours are required for the first lot. Assuming Ace uses the cumulative average-time learning model, the total time required to produce 400 units would be:

a. 32 hours.
b. 20.48 hours.
c. 25.6 hours.
d. 19.52 hours.
e. none of the above.

____ 8. See item 7. Assuming Ace uses the cumulative average-time learning model, the incremental time required to produce the second lot of 100 units would be:

a. .0640 hours per unit.
b. 12.80 hours.
c. .0480 hours per unit.
d. none of the above.

____ 9. (Appendix) Serial correlation is measured by:

a. the standard error of the estimated coefficient.
b. the standard error of the residuals.
c. the t-value of the slope coefficient.
d. the Durbin-Watson statistic.

IV. Given the following data for a certain manufacturing overhead item of Rutledge Company:

	May	June
Direct manufacturing labor-hours (DMLH)	40,000	50,000
Total cost	$10,500	$13,000

Use the high-low method to compute:
1. The slope coefficient
2. The constant
3. Predicted cost when 42,000 DMLH are used

Check figures: (1) $0.25 (2) $500
(3) $11,000

V. Kenton Corporation predicts its monthly energy costs by using simple regression analysis. The cost driver is degree-days, defined as the absolute difference between 65 degrees and the average daily temperature. The regression results are as follows:

Constant	$2,000
Slope coefficient	$3
Standard error of the estimated coefficient	$1
Coefficient of determination	.73
Durbin-Watson statistic	1.82

1. Specify the regression equation.
2. What is the amount of increase in predicted energy costs from using one additional degree-day?
3. Compute the predicted energy costs when 320 degree-days are used in a particular month.
4. Would the constant in the regression equation be an acceptable estimate of the fixed cost of energy? Explain.
5. Comment on goodness of fit.
6. (Appendix) Compute the t-value of the estimated coefficient.
7. (Appendix) Comment on the significance of the independent variable.
8. (Appendix) Comment on the independence of residuals, assuming that 18 monthly observations were used in the regression model.

Check figures: (3) $2,960 (6) 3.00

VI. Addison Construction Company has begun paving roads for the Illinois highway system. Each paving project is similar. Recently, the company completed its first paving project in 20,000 hours. Direct labor is paid $20 per hour. The company needs to predict its direct labor costs for purposes of making a competitive bid on a group of three additional paving projects. Addison's experience indicates that a 90% learning curve is appropriate for these projects.

Using the cumulative average-time learning model:
1. Compute the predicted direct labor costs for the contract of three additional paving projects.
2. Disregard the 90% learning curve in the problem. Suppose 36,448 direct labor-hours were needed for these three paving projects. Compute the learning curve percentage.

Using the incremental unit-time learning model:
3. Compute the predicted direct labor costs for the contract of three additional paving projects, assuming a 90% learning curve.

Check figures: (1) $896,000 (2) 84%
  (3) $1,022,480

VII. Steve Kovzan was given the task of developing a cost function for predicting indirect manufacturing costs (manufacturing overhead) for the Kansas City personal computer plant of Electronic Horizons. The plant is highly automated. The following information has been collected:

Month	Indirect Manufacturing Costs	Machine-Hours	Direct Manufacturing Labor-Hours (DMLH)
January	$2,530	2,730	324
February	1,900	1,810	210
March	4,710	3,403	347
April	1,270	2,200	331
May	4,380	3,411	272
June	4,020	2,586	202
July	3,730	3,364	342
August	3,070	2,411	247
September	4,980	3,964	347
October	3,310	2,897	328
November	1,270	2,207	293
December	3,510	2,864	307

He estimates two cost functions using regression analysis:

Regression Model A: Indirect manufacturing costs = f(Machine-hours)

Variable	Coefficient	Standard Error	t-Value
Constant	−1,707.70	912.94	−1.87
Independent variable:			
Machine-hours	1.75	0.32	5.47

$r^2 = 0.75$; Standard error of residuals = 657.44; Durbin-Watson statistic = 2.59

Regression Model B: Indirect manufacturing costs = f(Direct manufacturing labor-hours)

Variable	Coefficient	Standard Error	t-Value
Constant	1,914.10	2,264.60	0.85
Independent variable:			
DMLH	4.43	7.55	0.59

$r^2 = 0.03$; Standard error of residuals = 1,300.77; Durbin-Watson statistic = 2.45

Which cost function should Kovzan use for predicting indirect manufacturing costs? Present your answer in the format of Exhibit 10-22.

Check figure: None

CHAPTER 10 SOLUTIONS TO PRACTICE TEST

I. 1 cost estimation; 2 cost predictions; 3 linear, single; 4 c is any estimated value of cost, g is the constant, w is the slope coefficient, D is any actual value of the cost driver within the relevant range; 5 cause-and-effect relationship; 6 industrial-engineering method, conference method, account analysis method, quantitative analysis of cost relationships; 7 mixed cost (semivariable cost); 8 regression analysis; 9 economic plausibility, goodness of fit, significance of independent variable(s), specification analysis of estimation assumptions; 10 output unit-level costs, batch-level costs, product-sustaining costs, facility-sustaining costs; 11 linearity within the relevant range, constant variance of residuals, independence of residuals, normality of residuals; 12 serial correlation (autocorrelation).

II.

1 F	6 T	11 T	16 F
2 T	7 F	12 F	17 T
3 F	8 T	13 T	18 T
4 F	9 T	14 F	19 F
5 T	10 F	15 T	

Explanations:

1 The forecasting of future costs is cost prediction. Cost estimation is the attempt to measure past cost relationships. (F)

2 The zero level of the cost driver (shutdown) is rarely within the relevant range, so the constant g is seldom the fixed costs. The constant is a component of the regression equation that gives the best linear approximation of how costs behave within the relevant range. (T)

3 The account analysis method classifies cost accounts in the ledger as variable, fixed, or mixed with respect to the cost driver on the basis of *qualitative* (as distinguished from *quantitative*) analysis by managers. (F)

4 In estimating a cost function on the basis of quantitative analysis, the first step is to choose the dependent variable (the particular cost to be predicted). The second step is to identify the cost driver(s). (F)

5 Seven frequently encountered data problems, ranging from missing or unreliable observations to distortions resulting from inflation, are discussed in the textbook (pp. 354-55). (T)

6 Under the high-low method, the first step is to compute the slope coefficient. In the second step, the slope coefficient is used to compute the constant in the equation of the cost function. (T)

7 The statement refers to goodness of fit, not economic plausibility. Economic plausibility means that the relationship between the costs and the independent variable should make economic sense and be intuitive to both the operating manager and the accountant. (F)

8 Plotting the data (i) highlights extreme observations, which may be due to recording errors or unusual events such as a labor strike, and (ii) provides insight about the relevant range and about whether the cost relationship is linear within that range. (T)

9 The coefficient of determination (r^2) needs to be at least 0.30 to pass the goodness-of-fit test. (T)

10 A high r^2 between two variables *does not prove* that a cause-and-effect relationship exists. Instead it indicates that those variables move together. Cause-and-effect relationships exist where the economic plausibility criterion is satisfied. (F)

11 To be a cost driver, an independent variable must satisfy the four criteria for choosing among cost functions: (i) economic plausibility, (ii) goodness of fit, (iii) significance of independent variable(s), and (iv) specification analysis of estimation assumptions. (T)

12 The definition in the statement refers to output unit-level costs. Batch-level costs are the resources used up on activities that are related to a batch of products or services. Examples are setup costs and purchase-order costs. (F)

13 Batch-level and product-sustaining costs of low-volume products should be allocated to the relatively few units of low-volume products, rather than allocated as output unit-level costs to all products. (T)

14 The learning curve is a function that shows how labor-hours per unit decline as units of output increase. The learning curve assists managers in setting standards and developing pricing strategy. (F)

15 The experience curve is a function that shows how full product costs (all value-chain costs expressed on a per unit basis) decline as units of output increase. (T)

16 The standard error of the estimated coefficient is a key statistic used to measure significance of the independent variable(s). This statistic divided into the slope coefficient equals the *t*-value of the coefficient. If the *t*-value is less than 2.00, the independent variable is not a cost driver. (F)

17 This use of the scatter diagram is illustrated in Exhibit 10-17. The scatter diagram also can be used to check for linearity within the relevant range. (T)

18 Multiple regression uses two or more independent variables but only one dependent variable. (T)

19 Multicollinearity exists when two or more independent variables are highly correlated with each other. Multicollinearity is at an unacceptable level when the coefficient of correlation (r) between any pair of independent variables exceeds 0.70. Serial correlation is measured by the Durbin-Watson statistic. (F)

III.

1 b	4 b	7 b
2 a	5 b	8 c
3 c	6 d	9 d

Explanations:

1 Cost estimation is the attempt to measure past cost relationships. Managers use cost estimation to help make more accurate cost predictions (forecasts) of future costs. (b)

2 The highest and lowest observations of DMLH are 3,650 and 2,050 respectively: ($19,800 − $13,400) ÷ (3,650 − 2,050) = $6,400 ÷ 1,600 = $4 per hour. (a)

3 $19,800 − 3,650($4) = $5,200, or $13,400 − 2,050($4) = $5,200 (c)

4 Because causality runs *from* the cost driver *to* the dependent variable in a cost function, choosing the highest and lowest observations of the cost driver is appropriate. (b)

5 The steps in a step-variable cost function are narrower than those in a step-fixed cost function (Exhibit 10-9 versus Exhibit 10-10). As the steps in a step-variable cost function become narrower, the cost behavior would approach the pattern of a variable cost. (b)

6 The key point in the question is that the equation is for a *year*, while the budget is for a *month*: $4,800 ÷ 12 = $400; $400 + 20,000($0.50) = $10,400 (d)

7

Cumulative Number of Units	Cumulative Average Hours Per Unit	Cumulative Total Hours
100	8 ÷ 100 = .0800	100 × .0800 = 8.00
200	.0800 × 80% = .0640	200 × .0640 = 12.80
400	.0640 × 80% = .0512	400 × .0512 = 20.48 (b)

8 Using amounts from the computations in the preceding answer, 12.80 − 8.00 = 4.80 hours; 4.80 ÷ the second lot of 100 units = .0480 hours per unit. (c)

9 Serial correlation is measured by the Durbin-Watson statistic. For samples of 10 to 20 observations, this statistic falling in the 1.30 to 2.70 range suggests that the residuals are independent. (d)

IV. Rutledge Company

1. ($13,000 − $10,500) ÷ (50,000 − 40,000) = $2,500 ÷ 10,000 = $0.25 per DMLH
2. $13,000 − 50,000($0.25) = $500, or $10,500 − 40,000($0.25) = $500
3. $c = $500 + 42,000($0.25) = $11,000

V. Kenton Corporation

1. $c = \$2,000 + \$3D$
2. $\$3$
3. $c = \$2,000 + \$3(320) = \$2,000 + \$960 = \$2,960$
4. No, unless the zero volume level of the cost driver is within the relevant range (which rarely is the case). Otherwise the constant is a component of the equation that provides the best available linear approximation of how the dependent variable behaves within the relevant range.
5. This regression meets the goodness of fit criterion because the r^2 of 0.73 satisfies the requirement of $r^2 \geq 0.30$.
6. $\$3 \div \$1 = 3.00$
7. The coefficient of the independent variable is significantly different than zero because the t-value is greater than 2.00, as computed in part 6.
8. The residuals are independent (that is, serial correlation is not a problem) because the Durbin-Watson statistic falls in the acceptable range of 1.30 to 2.70 for sample sizes between 10 and 20 observations.

VI. Addison Construction Company

1.

Cumulative Number of Projects	Cumulative Average Hours Per Project	Cumulative Total Hours
1	20,000	20,000
2	18,000 (20,000 × .90)	36,000
4	16,200 (18,000 × .90)	64,800

Predicted direct labor costs for the contract of three additional projects = $(64,800 - 20,000) \times \$20 = \$896,000$

2. Total hours to complete the first four projects = $36,448 + 20,000 = 56,448$; cumulative average hours per project = $56,448 \div 4 = 14,112$; Let X = Learning curve percentage

$14,112 = 20,000(X)(X)$; $X^2 = 14,112 \div 20,000$; $X^2 = .7056$; $X = .84$, or 84%

3.

Cumulative Number of Projects	Individual Project Hours for Xth Project	Cumulative Total Hours
1	20,000	20,000
2	18,000(20,000 × .90)	38,000
3	16,924*	54,924
4	16,200(18,000 × .90)	71,124

*This amount was computed by using logarithms (see bottom of Exhibit 10-14).

Predicted direct labor costs for the contract of three additional projects = $(71,124 - 20,000) \times \$20 = \$1,022,480$

VII. Electronic Horizons

Plots of the scatter diagram for each regression model are as follows:

Electronic Horizons - Regression Model A

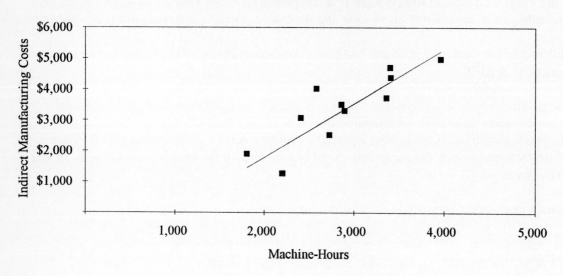

Electronic Horizons - Regression Model B

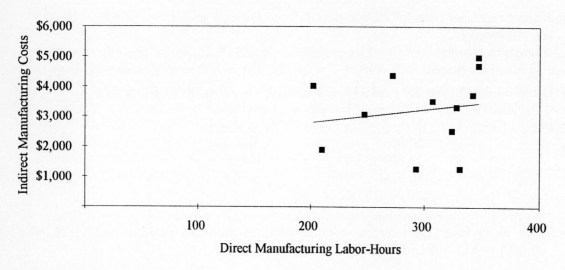

A comparison of the cost functions is on the next page.

A comparison of the cost functions is as follows:

Criterion	Regression Model A (Machine-hours)	Regression Model B (Direct manufacturing labor-hours)
1. Economic plausibility	Positive relationship between indirect manufacturing costs and machine-hours is economically plausible in a highly automated plant.	Positive relationship between indirect manufacturing costs and DMLH is economically plausible, but less so than machine-hours on a month-by-month basis.
2. Goodness of fit	$r^2 = 0.75$ Excellent goodness of fit.	$r^2 = 0.03$ Very poor goodness of fit.
3. Significance of independent variables	t-value for machine-hours of 5.47 is significant.	t-value for DMLH of 0.59 is not significant.
4. Specification analysis		
• Linearity within the relevant range	Appears reasonable from a plot of the data.	Appears questionable from a plot of the data.
• Constant variance of residuals	Appears reasonable, but inferences drawn from only 12 observations are not reliable.	Appears questionable, but inferences drawn from only 12 observations are not reliable.
• Independence of residuals	Durbin-Watson statistic = 2.59, thus the assumption of independence is not rejected.	Durbin-Watson statistic = 2.45, thus the assumption of independence is not rejected.
• Normality of residuals	Database is too small to make reliable inferences.	Database is too small to make reliable inferences.

Conclusion: The cost function using machine-hours as the cost driver is preferred. Note that a cost analyst often must make a choice among "imperfect" cost functions. That is, the data of any particular cost function will not perfectly meet one or more of the assumptions underlying regression analysis. In the comparison above, imperfection is present in both regression models for normality of residuals and in Model B for constant variance of residuals.

CHAPTER 11

RELEVANCE, COSTS, AND THE DECISION PROCESS

MAIN FOCUS AND OBJECTIVES

Cost data play a very important role in most management decisions. Accountants can help managers make better decisions by clearly distinguishing relevant revenues and costs from irrelevant ones. The chapter focuses on several types of decisions:

- accept or reject a one-time-only special order
- choose the product mix ✓
- insource or outsource (make or buy) a product or service
- keep or drop a customer
- keep or replace equipment

Your overall objective for this chapter is to understand and be able to apply the concept of relevance: the expected future costs and revenues that differ between alternative courses of action. Nine learning objectives are stated in the textbook (p. 386).

Give special attention to:

- the role of accounting information in the decision process
- the concept of relevance
- the distinction between quantitative factors and qualitative factors in decision making
- why certain per-unit data can mislead decision makers
- the concept of opportunity cost
- how managers' behavior is affected when conflicts arise between decision models and performance-evaluation models

To highlight and simplify various points throughout the chapter, we assume the amounts of expected future costs and revenues will occur with certainty. Consideration of the time value of money and income taxes are deferred to Chapters 20 and 21. The chapter Appendix applies linear programming to product mix decisions where multiple constraints exist.

REVIEW OF KEY TERMS AND CONCEPTS

A. The basic ideas underlying this chapter are in the first two exhibits.
   1. Exhibit 11-1 outlines a *five-step sequence* that highlights **the role of accounting information in the decision process**.

a. In this illustration, the choice is between two courses of action to reduce manufacturing labor costs on an assembly line: "do not rearrange" or "rearrange."

b. Information must be obtained for such decisions (step 1).

c. A management decision, such as this example, involves predictions of future costs (step 2).

d. Some management decisions involve predictions of *both* costs and revenues (step 2).

e. However, **only expected future costs and revenues that differ** among alternative courses of action are **relevant** to the decision.

f. Historical data themselves are **irrelevant** to the decision because *nothing can be done to change the past*.

g. The role of historical data is to aid prediction (the left arrow between steps 1 and 2).

h. *Decision model* (step 3): a formal method, frequently involving quantitative analysis, for choosing among alternative courses of action.

i. Implementation (step 4) occurs when the manager carries out the decision made in step 3.

j. *Performance-evaluation model* (step 5) is covered later in this chapter.

k. *Feedback* (from step 5) can affect the other four steps of the process in subsequent decisions.

2. Exhibit 11-2 presents the quantitative data that are applicable to "do not rearrange" and "rearrange."

a. The "all data" section of this exhibit includes *both relevant and irrelevant items*.

b. The other section is limited to *relevant items only*.

c. The $70,000 difference in total costs between the alternatives under *both* presentations is an **incremental cost** (also called *differential cost* or *net relevant cost*.)

3. *Both* quantitative factors and qualitative factors can be important to management decisions.

a. **Quantitative factors**: outcomes that are measured in numerical (financial or nonfinancial) terms. Examples: $100 per unit, 5% rate of defects.

b. **Qualitative factors**: outcomes that cannot be measured in numerical terms. Example: the desire to maintain a good business relationship with a supplier.

c. Decision analysis generally emphasizes quantitative factors that can be expressed in financial terms.

d. One way to explicitly tradeoff quantitative and qualitative factors is to calculate the quantitative difference in financial terms between two courses of action, and ask if management is willing to pay that amount to select the less financially desirable alternative for qualitative reasons.

Be sure to gain a good understanding of Exhibits 11-1 and 11-2 before proceeding.

B. Idle production capacity often permits the acceptance of a **one-time-only special order** at a reduced price.
   1. The phrase "one-time-only special order" is used to highlight the point that special orders are assumed to be short-run business that do not affect regular business.
   2. Unit costs do not necessarily serve as the proper basis for evaluating a special order, as explained below.
   3. The comparative *contribution income statements* in Exhibit 11-4 (as distinguished from the *absorption-costing format* in Exhibit 11-3) serve as the proper basis for evaluating a special order.
   4. The important point is that, in quantitative terms, those decisions should depend on the revenues and costs expected to *differ* between alternatives.

> *Question*: **In a one-time-only special order decision, are variable costs always relevant?**
> *Answer*: **No. For example, the variable marketing costs are irrelevant in Exhibit 11-4.**

   5. Fixed costs can be relevant or irrelevant to a one-time-only special decision, depending on whether their amount in total changes.
   6. **Unit costs** can mislead decision makers. This error occurs under either of two conditions.
      a. When irrelevant costs are included in unit costs—therefore, it is desirable to include *relevant costs only*.
      b. When unitized fixed costs are interpreted *as if* they behave like variable costs per unit—therefore, it is desirable to compare *total costs* of alternative actions.
   7. *Out-of-pocket costs* (also called *outlay costs*) are current or near-future cash disbursements made to meet costs incurred because of a specific decision.
   8. Exhibit 11-5 presents several *different types of unit costs*, which are based on the data in Exhibit 11-4.
      a. *Business function cost*: the sum of all the costs (variable costs and fixed costs) in a particular business function such as manufacturing or marketing.
      b. **Full product costs**: the sum of all the costs of a product in the business functions of the value chain.
      c. A company cannot survive if products are consistently sold for less than their full product cost.
   9. *See Practice Test Question III (item 1) and Problem IV.*

C. When a multiple product plant is being operated at capacity, managers must often make decisions regarding which products to emphasize (**product mix decisions**).
   1. Those decisions frequently have a short-run focus.
   2. The proper criterion that maximizes operating income at capacity is to obtain the *highest contribution margin per unit of the resource that constrains or limits the production or sale of a given product.*

> **Be sure to distinguish between (i) contribution margin per unit of the constraining resource and (ii) contribution margin per unit of product. In the textbook example (p. 394), the respective contribution margins of snowmobile engines are (i) $100 per machine-hour and (ii) $200 per unit.**

3. Examples of constraining resources: machine-hours, skilled labor-hours, cubic feet of display space.
4. *See Practice Test Question III (item 3) and Problem V.*
5. The chapter Appendix discusses *linear programming*, an optimization technique that can be used to determine the most profitable product mix in the short-run when multiple constraints exist.

D. A decision that faces all organizations is whether to insource or outsource products or services.
   1. **Insourcing**: making products or providing services within the organization rather than buying the same products or services from an outside supplier.
   2. **Outsourcing**: buying products or services from an outside supplier rather than making the same products or providing the same services within the organization.
   3. Examples:
      a. A manufacturer decides whether to make subassemblies or buy them from an outside supplier (often called a "make or buy" decision).
      b. A law firm decides whether to prepare its own payroll or hire the services of a payroll firm.
   4. Make or buy decisions depend on *both* quantitative and qualitative factors.
   5. Qualitative factors often important in make or buy decisions include the quality of the item in question, dependability of suppliers, and the ability to control product design and process technology.
   6. The analysis of relevant costs should not necessarily be restricted to variable costs; fixed costs also should be included if they are expected to be *avoided* when buying the item in question.

> **See the example in Exhibit 11-6.**

   7. The analysis in Exhibit 11-6 suggests that unless qualitative factors are worth $10,000, El Cerrito should make the part instead of buying it from an outside supplier.
   8. More generally, the choice in this textbook example is not fundamentally whether to make or buy; it is *how best to use available facilities*, giving consideration to alternatives such as:
      a. Leaving facilities idle (as assumed in the textbook example).
      b. Buying the item in question and renting out unused facilities.
      c. Buying the item in question and using released facilities for other purposes.

9. The contribution income statement, which separates variable and fixed costs, can be a useful starting point only for *short-run* decisions. Why? *Because it emphasizes costs that are variable in the short run. In the long run, all costs are variable.*

10. For longer time horizons, activity-based costing can be helpful in decisions that are affected by multiple cost drivers.

11. *See Practice Test Question III (item 2).*

E. In many decision-making situations, managers are faced with too many alternatives to be analyzed thoroughly. The concept of opportunity cost arises when there are multiple uses for resources and some alternatives are excluded from explicit consideration.

1. **Opportunity cost**: the contribution to income that is forgone (rejected) by not using a limited resource in its best *alternative* use.

2. Exhibit 11-7 illustrates a make or buy decision under a total alternatives approach (Panel A) and an opportunity cost approach (Panel B).

3. Opportunity costs are derived from transactions that *do not* actually occur.

4. Therefore, opportunity costs (i) are not ordinarily entered in the historical accounting records and (ii) do not entail cash receipts or disbursements.

5. Another textbook example of opportunity cost deals with the total costs of purchasing and carrying inventory (p. 400).

6. *See Practice Test Question III (items 4-6).*

F. The concept of relevance also applies to decisions where multiple cost drivers have been identified, as in activity-based costing.

1. This section relaxes the assumption made so far in the chapter that all costs are either variable or fixed with respect to a single cost driver, units of output.

2. The Allied West textbook example (beginning p. 400) illustrates the hierarchy of costs, described in section E of Chapter 10's outline (p. 129), in the decision context of keep or drop a customer.

> *Question*: **Should Allied keep Wisk as a customer?**
> *Answer*:
> - **No, if we decide on the basis of the profitability analysis in Exhibit 11-8; Wisk shows a loss of $20,000.**
> - **Yes, if we decide on the basis of the relevant cost analysis in Exhibit 11-9; Wisk accounts for operating income of $18,000.**
> - **Keeping Wisk is the correct decision because relevant cost analysis should be used.**

3. Notes about this example:
   a. The opportunity cost of keeping Wisk is zero.
   b. The decision could change if there were opportunity cost (for example, if freed-up warehouse space could be rented out).
   c. Qualitative factors must be considered, such as the effect the decision might have on Allied's reputation for developing stable, long-run business relationships.

4. Relevant cost analysis also is applicable to the decision to keep or drop a product or product line; *see Practice Test Problem VI.*

G. The last type of decision illustrated in the chapter is to **keep or replace equipment**.

1. The *book value of old equipment (original cost minus accumulated depreciation), is irrelevant* to a replacement decision. Why? Because the book value will be expensed either (i) as "Loss on Disposal" if the equipment is replaced or (ii) as "Depreciation Expense" if the equipment is kept.

2. The book value of old equipment is a past (historical) cost, sometimes called a **sunk cost**.

3. Either of two quantitative approaches can be used in the decision to keep or replace equipment:
   a. Include both relevant and irrelevant items in the analysis, illustrated in Exhibit 11-10.
   b. Include only relevant items in the analysis, illustrated in Exhibit 11-11.

4. What drives a manager's behavior in the decision to keep or replace equipment?

   a. Since replacement usually entails a "Loss on Disposal" in the year of replacement, the manager would likely be reluctant to replace because of the effect on his or her perceived performance (say, measured by operating income) in that year.
   b. In other words, managers often focus on the measures used in the **performance-evaluation model** (step 5 in Exhibit 11-1) instead of the **decision model** (step 3 in Exhibit 11-1).
   c. If there is an inconsistency between these two models, the performance-evaluation model tends to have more influence on managers' behavior.

5. *See Practice Test Question III (item 7) and Problem VIII.*

H. (**Appendix**) *Linear programming (LP) is an optimization technique that can be used to determine the most profitable product mix in the short-run where multiple constraints exist.*

1. The basic idea of LP was introduced in the chapter (p. 394): manufacture the product that provides the *highest contribution margin per unit of the constraining resource* (machine-hours).

2. However, *in practice there is usually more than one constraint—often many—and it is those situations for which LP is applicable.*

3. LP models depend on relevant cost data as inputs.

4. Three steps are used to formulate and solve the LP problem in the textbook:
   Step 1: Determine the objective (maximize total contribution margin).
   Step 2: Determine the basic relationships (the four constraint inequalities are listed on p. 411).
   Step 3: Compute the optimal solution (illustrated by the trial-and-error and graphic approaches).

5. The relevant input data for the LP model are presented in Exhibit 11-13.

> **Be sure you understand how the data in Exhibit 11-13 were used to construct the graph in Exhibit 11-14.**

6. The *trial-and-error solution approach* utilizes the coordinates of the corners of the **area of feasible solutions** in Exhibit 11-14. The optimal solution is 75 snowmobile engines and 90 boat engines.

7. The *graphic solution approach* seeks the equal contribution margin line (see the dashed lines in Exhibit 11-14) that is the farthest from the origin without leaving the area of feasible solutions. The same optimal solution of 75 snowmobile engines and 90 boat engines is found.

8. Note that the trial-and-error and graphic solution approaches can only be used in situations where there are two products and a small number of constraints.
   a. These approaches help develop intuition for the computation of the optimal solution.
   b. Computer software packages are used to solve more complex LP problems.

9. *See Practice Test Question III (items 8-10) and Problem IX.*

PRACTICE TEST QUESTIONS AND PROBLEMS

I. Complete each of the following statements.

1. The five steps that highlight the role of accounting information in the decision process are:_____

_____

_____

_____

2. To be relevant to a particular decision, a cost must meet two criteria: _____

_____

_____

3. The difference in the total costs between two alternative courses of action is called a(an) _____ cost.

4. Current or near-future cash disbursements made to meet costs incurred because of a specific decision are called _____

_____.

5. _____ is buying products or services from outside vendors rather than making the same products or providing the same services within the organization.

6. The contribution to income that is forgone (rejected) by not using a limited resource in its best alternative use is called _____

_____.

7. Managers often focus on the measures used in the _____ model instead of the decision model.

8. (Appendix) _____ is an optimization technique that can be used to determine the most profitable product mix in the short-run where multiple constraints exist.

9. (Appendix) The _____ is an LP graphic solution that shows the boundaries of those combinations of the two products that satisfy all constraints.

II. Indicate whether each of the following statements is true or false by putting T or F in the space provided.

____ 1. In the decision process, the prediction-method step precedes the decision-model step.

____ 2. In general, all variable costs are relevant to decisions, but all fixed costs are irrelevant to decisions.

____ 3. Historical costs can aid predictions of future costs.

____ 4. A car rental company is comparing two kinds of cars to add to its fleet. A qualitative factor in this decision is miles per gallon of fuel consumption.

____ 5. A company's total unit costs (all variable costs per unit plus all fixed costs per unit) are usually an appropriate basis for evaluating the desirability of accepting a one-time-only special order when there is idle plant capacity.

____ 6. A one-time-only special order that could be met from idle capacity should never be accepted at a selling price below the total manufacturing costs per unit.

____ 7. The absorption-costing income statement is a useful type of report for deciding whether to accept or reject a one-time-only special order.

8. Opportunity costs do not entail cash receipts or disbursements.

___ 9. In a decision to keep or replace equipment, book value of the old equipment is irrelevant.

___ 10. In deciding whether to keep or replace equipment, the analysis can include only relevant items or both relevant and irrelevant items.

___ 11. If there is an inconsistency between the decision model and the performance-evaluation model in a decision to keep or replace some old equipment, the manager's choice will tend to be influenced more by the decision model.

___ 12. (Appendix) The LP model is applicable to situations where there are more than three constraints.

___ 13. (Appendix) An equal total contribution margin line on an LP graph has the same slope as the objective function.

III. Select the best answer for each of the following multiple-choice questions and put the identifying letter in the space provided.

___ 1. Stokes Company's unit costs of manufacturing 9,000 units of a product for regular sale are $20 per unit. If Stokes manufactures 1,000 additional units to fill a one-time-only special order, the total manufacturing costs per unit would be $19. What is the selling price per unit for the order that would exactly cover the additional costs?
   a. $20
   b. $15
   c. $10
   d. none of the above

___ 2. (CMA) Dixon Company manufactures Part 347 for use in one of its products. Normal annual production for Part 347 is 100,000 units. The costs per 100-unit lot of the part are as follows:

Direct materials	$260
Direct manufacturing labor	100
Manufacturing overhead	
Variable	120
Fixed	160
Total manufacturing costs per 100 units	$640

Cext Company has offered to sell Dixon all 100,000 units it will need during the coming year for $600 per 100 units. If Dixon accepts the offer from Cext, the facilities used to manufacture Part 347 could be used in the production of Part 483. This change would save Dixon $90,000 in relevant costs. In addition, a $100,000 cost item included in fixed overhead is specifically related to Part 347 and would be eliminated.

Should Dixon Company accept the offer from Cext Company?
   a. No, Dixon should continue to make Part 347 because a savings of $20,000 can be achieved.
   b. No, Dixon should continue to make Part 347 because a savings of $30,000 can be achieved.
   c. Yes, Dixon should buy Part 347 because a savings of $150,000 can be achieved.
   d. Yes, Dixon should buy Part 347 because a savings of $70,000 can be achieved.

___ 3. Kent Company has a limited number of machine-hours that it can use for manufacturing two products, A and B. Each product has a selling price of $80 per unit, but product A has a 40% contribution margin and product B has a 70% contribution margin. One unit of B takes twice as many machine-hours to make as a unit of A. Assume that either product can be sold in whatever quantity is produced. Which product or products should the limited number of machine-hours be used for?
   a. A
   b. B
   c. both A and B
   d. cannot be determined from the information given

___ 4. (CMA) The opportunity cost of making a component part in a plant with excess capacity for which there is no alternative use is:
   a. zero.
   b. the variable manufacturing costs of the component.

c. the total manufacturing costs of the component.

d. the fixed manufacturing costs of the component.

___ 5. (CPA) Light Company has 2,000 obsolete light fixtures that are carried in inventory at a manufacturing cost of $30,000. If the fixtures are reworked for $10,000, they could be sold for $18,000. Alternatively, the light fixtures could be sold for $3,000 to a jobber. Assuming the fixtures are reworked and sold, the opportunity cost would be:

a. $3,000.
b. $10,000.
c. $5,000.
d. $30,000.

___ 6. (CPA) The manufacturing capacity of Jordan Company's facilities is 30,000 units of a product per year. A summary of operating results for the year ended December 31, 19_4 is as follows:

Sales,

18,000 units × $100	$1,800,000
Variable costs	990,000
Contribution margin	810,000
Fixed costs	495,000
Operating income	$ 315,000

A foreign distributor has offered to buy 15,000 units at $90 per unit during 19_5. Assume that all of Jordan's costs would have the same behavior patterns in 19_5 as in 19_4. If Jordan accepted this offer and rejected some business from regular customers so as not to exceed capacity, what would be the total operating income for 19_5?

a. $855,000
b. $840,000
c. $705,000
d. $390,000

___ 7. (CPA) Maxwell Company has an opportunity to acquire a new machine to replace one of its present machines. The new machine would cost $90,000 and has a five-year useful life, with a zero terminal disposal price. Variable operating costs would be $100,000 per year. The present machine has a book value of $50,000 and a remaining life of five years. Its disposal price now is $5,000 but would be zero after five years. Variable operating costs would be $125,000 per year. Considering the five years in total, but ignoring the time value of money and income taxes, what would be the difference in operating income by acquiring the new machine as opposed to retaining the present one?

a. $10,000 decrease
b. $15,000 decrease
c. $35,000 increase
d. $40,000 increase

___ 8. (Appendix, CMA) Pleasant Valley Company makes two products, ceramic vases (V) and ceramic bowls (B). Each vase requires two pounds of direct materials and three hours of direct manufacturing labor. Each bowl requires two pounds of direct materials and one hour of direct manufacturing labor. During the next production week, there will be 100 pounds of direct materials and 60 hours of labor available to make vases and bowls. Each pound of direct materials costs $4 and each hour of direct manufacturing labor costs $10. All manufacturing overhead is fixed and is estimated to be $200 for this production process for a week. Pleasant Valley sells vases for $50 each and bowls for $35 each. The objective function for total contribution margin would be:

a. $50V + $35B.
b. $12V + $17B.
c. $38V + $18B.
d. $12V + $17B − $200.

___ 9. See item 8. One of the constraints would be:

a. 2V + 2B ≤ 60.
b. 2V + 2B ≤ $400.
c. 3V + B ≤ 60.
d. V + 3B ≤ 100.
e. $8V + $8B ≤ 600.

___ 10. (Appendix, CPA) Williamson Manufacturing intends to produce two products, X and Y. Product X requires six hours of time on Machine 1 and 12 hours of time on Machine 2. Product Y requires four hours of time on Machine 1 and no time on Machine 2. Both machines are available for 24 hours. Assuming that the objective function of the total contribution margin is $2X + $1Y, what is the optimal product mix?

   a. No units of Product X and 6 units of Product Y.

   b. 1 unit of Product X and 4 units of Product Y.

   c. 2 units of Product X and 3 units of Product Y.

   d. 4 units of Product X and no units of Product Y.

IV. Sedona Corporation has an annual plant capacity of 2,800 units of output. Its predicted operations for the year are as follows:

Sales, 2,000 units at $38 each	$76,000
Manufacturing costs:	
Variable	$25 per unit
Fixed	$18,000
Marketing and administrative costs:	
Variable (sales commissions)	$6 per unit
Fixed	$2,000

Assuming there would be no effect on regular sales at regular prices, should the company accept a one-time-only special order for 600 units at a selling price of $32 each, subject to half the usual sales commission rate per unit? Show supporting computations.

Check figure: Yes, $2,400 incremental operating income

V. Edgewood Corporation has 1,440 machine-hours of plant capacity available during a particular period for manufacturing two products with the following characteristics:

	T	L
Selling price per unit	$42	$75
Variable costs per unit	$20	$25
Units that can be manufactured in one machine-hour	8	3

Compute the number of available machine-hours that should be used to manufacture the product(s).

VI. (CPA) The officers of Bradshaw Company are reviewing the profitability of the company's four products and the potential of several proposals for varying the product mix. An income statement and other data follow:

	Total	Product W	Product X	Product Y	Product Z
Sales	$62,600	$10,000	$18,000	$12,600	$22,000
Cost of goods sold	44,274	4,750	7,056	13,968	18,500
Gross margin	18,326	5,250	10,944	(1,368)	3,500
Operating costs	12,012	1,990	2,976	2,826	4,220
Operating income	$ 6,314	$ 3,260	$ 7,968	$ (4,194)	$ (720)
Units sold		1,000	1,200	1,800	2,000
Selling price per unit		$ 10.00	$ 15.00	$ 7.00	$ 11.00
Variable cost of goods sold per unit		$ 2.50	$ 3.00	$ 6.50	$ 6.00
Variable operating costs per unit		$ 1.17	$ 1.25	$ 1.00	$ 1.20

Each of the following proposals is to be considered independently. Consider only the product changes stated in each proposal; the production and sales levels of the other products remain the same.

1. Compute the effect on operating income if Y is discontinued.
2. Compute the total effect on operating income if Y is discontinued and a resulting loss of customers causes a decrease of 200 units in the production and sales of X.
3. Assume the part of the plant in which W is manufactured can easily be adapted to the production of Z, but changes in quantities produced would necessitate changes in selling prices. Compute the total effect on operating income if production of W is reduced to 500 units (to be sold at $12 each) and production of Z is increased to 2,500 units (to be sold at $10.50 each).

Check figures: (1) $900 increase (2) $1,250 decrease (3) $1,515 decrease

VII. (CMA) Sunnybrook Farms is a local grocery store that is currently open Monday through Saturday. Sunnybrook is considering opening on Sundays. The annual incremental marketing and administrative costs of Sunday openings are estimated at $24,960. Sunnybrook Farms' gross margin on sales is 20%. Sunnybrook estimates that 60% of its Sunday sales volume would be made to the same customers on other days if its store were not open on Sundays.

Compute the one-day volume of Sunday sales that would be necessary for Sunnybrook Farms to attain the same weekly operating income as the current six-day week.

Check figure: $2,400

VIII. Grimes Company has a machine with a book value of $102,000, a present disposal price of $15,000, and an estimated remaining life of ten years. A new machine that is available at a cost of $193,000 has the same capacity, but it would reduce energy costs by $19,000 per year. The new machine has an estimated useful life of ten years. Both machines would have a zero disposal price at the end of their useful lives. Ignoring income taxes and the time value of money, which of the two alternatives should the company select: keep the old machine or replace it with the new machine? Show supporting computations.

Check figure: $12,000 advantage of replacing

IX. (Appendix) Riedel Perfume Company can produce two kinds of perfume, Explore and Encore. Riedel furnishes the following data:

Product	Daily Capacity in Product Units		Contribution Margin per Unit of Output
	Process R	Process T	
Explore (X)	200	400	$7.00
Encore (Y)	400	160	$8.00

Severe material shortages for Encore will limit its production to a maximum of 150 units per day. The daily capacities in total machine-hours are 200 for Process R and 400 for Process T.

Compute:
1. Machine-hours required per unit of product Y in Process R.
2. Machine-hours required per unit of product Y in Process T.

Formulate the LP model:
3. Objective function
4. Constraints

Check figures: (1) .5 (2) 2.5

CHAPTER 11 SOLUTIONS TO PRACTICE TEST

I. 1 information, prediction method, decision model, implementation, performance-evaluation model; 2 it must be an expected future cost, and it must differ between the alternative courses of action under consideration; 3 incremental (differential, net relevant); 4 out-of-pocket costs (outlay costs); 5 Outsourcing; 6 opportunity cost; 7 performance-evaluation; 8 Linear programming (LP); 9 area of feasible solutions.

II.

1 T	5 F	9 T	13 T
2 F	6 F	10 T	
3 T	7 F	11 F	
4 F	8 T	12 T	

Explanations:

1. In the decision process, the five-step sequence is information, prediction method, decision model, implementation, and performance-evaluation model. (T)

2. Only *expected future costs and revenues* that *differ* between the alternative courses of action under consideration are relevant to a decision. Variable costs can be relevant or irrelevant (see Exhibit 11-4). Fixed costs can be irrelevant (see Exhibit 11-4) or relevant (see Exhibit 11-6). (F)

3. Historical costs themselves are not relevant to decisions about the future, but they can aid predictions of future costs. (T)

4. Miles per gallon of fuel consumption is a quantitative factor in the decision. An example of a qualitative factor in the decision would be customer comfort. (F)

5. Two possible errors can occur in using unit costs in a special order decision: (1) irrelevant costs may be included in the unit costs and (2) unitized fixed costs may be interpreted *as if* they behave like variable costs per unit. (F)

6. In the Fancy Fabrics example in the textbook (p. 390), total manufacturing costs are $12 per unit. At a selling price of $11 per unit, accepting the one-time-only special order *adds* $17,500 of operating income per month. (F)

7. The contribution income statement (Exhibit 11-4) is a useful type of report for deciding whether to accept or reject a one-time-only special order. (F)

8. Opportunity costs are derived from transactions that *do not* actually occur. Therefore (i) they are not ordinarily entered in the historical accounting records and (ii) they do not entail cash receipts or disbursements. (T)

9. Book value of equipment is original cost minus accumulated depreciation. The book value of old equipment is a past cost and, hence, irrelevant to a replacement decision. (T)

10. The "relevant items only" approach is illustrated in Exhibit 11-11. The "both relevant and irrelevant items" approach is illustrated in Exhibit 11-10. The difference in operating income in favor of replacement is $120,000 in both analyses. (T)

11. Managers tend to favor the decision alternative that makes their performance look best. Therefore, they focus on the measures used in the performance-evaluation model rather than the decision model .(F)

12. The LP model is applicable to situations where there are any number of constraints. When there are only two products and the number of constraints is manageable, the optimal solution can be computed by trial and error or graphically. When the LP problem is more complex, computer software packages are used to compute the optimal solution. (T)

13. In the textbook example, the slope of the objective function is computed to be $-4/5$, which is the slope of the equal total contribution margin line in Exhibit 11-14. Assuming no change in the objective function, all equal total contribution margin lines would have the same slope. (T)

III.

1 c	4 a	7 d	10 c
2 d	5 a	8 b	
3 a	6 c	9 c	

Explanations:

1. Total manufacturing costs of
   10,000 units, $19 × 10,000 $190,000
   Deduct total manufacturing costs
   of 9,000 units, $20 × 9,000   <u>180,000</u>
   Incremental cost of 1,000 units   <u>$ 10,000</u>

   Incremental cost per unit = $10,000 ÷ 1,000 = $10. Therefore, a selling price of $10 per unit for the order would exactly cover the additional costs. (c)

2.
Relevant Costs	Make	Buy
Direct materials, $260 × 1,000 lots	$260,000	
Direct manufacturing labor,		
$100 × 1,000 lots	100,000	
Manufacturing overhead		
Variable, $120 × 1,000 lots	120,000	
Avoidable fixed costs	100,000	
Outside purchase of the part,		
$600 × 1,000 lots		$600,000
Savings related to manufacturing Part 483		(90,000)
Total relevant costs	<u>$580,000</u>	<u>$510,000</u>

   Difference in favor of buying Part 347 $70,000 (d)

3. Two units of A can be produced for each unit of B. A: $80 × 40% × 2 = $64. B: $80 × 70% = $56. Therefore, A would produce a larger contribution margin per machine-hour. (a) Note that the amounts of $64 and $56 should *not* be called contribution margin per machine-hour in this case because the number of hours required per unit is not given in the question. Nevertheless, it is correct to conclude that A would produce a larger contribution margin per machine-hour than B.

4. Opportunity cost is the contribution to income that is forgone (rejected) by not using a limited resource in its best *alternative* use. In this case, there is no alternative use for the excess production capacity; therefore, the opportunity cost is zero. (a)

5. The following analysis shows there is a $5,000 advantage of reworking the fixtures:

Relevant Items	Rework and Sell	Sell As Is
Revenue	$18,000	$3,000
Deduct costs	<u>10,000</u>	<u>-0-</u>
Operating income	<u>$ 8,000</u>	<u>$3,000</u>

   Difference in favor of reworking $5,000

   However, the *difference* in operating income between the alternatives is *not* the opportunity cost. Opportunity cost is the contribution to income that is forgone (rejected) by not using a limited resource in its best *alternative* use. If the fixtures (a resource) are reworked and sold, the opportunity cost would be the rejected alternative of selling them "as is" for $3,000. (a) Note that the original cost of the fixtures ($30,000) is a past (historical or sunk) cost and, hence, irrelevant to the decision.

6. Sales, (15,000 × $100) + (15,000 × $90) $2,850,000
   Variable costs, ($990,000 ÷ 18,000) × 30,000   <u>1,650,000</u>
   Contribution margin   1,200,000
   Fixed costs   <u>495,000</u>
   Operating income   <u>$ 705,000</u> (c)

Note that although opportunity cost is *not explicitly shown* in this income statement, it is present in this situation because the short-run capacity of 30,000 units is insufficient to accommodate the regular business of 18,000 units and the special order of 15,000 units (that is, 3,000 units of regular business must be forgone in order to accept the special order). Knowing that the variable costs per unit are $990,000 ÷ 18,000 = $55, opportunity cost can be *explicitly shown* in an incremental analysis as follows:

Increase in contribution margin from the special order itself, 15,000 × ($90 − $55)	$525,000
Deduct forgone contribution margin from the regular business, 3,000 × ($100 − $55)	135,000
Increase in operating income from accepting the special order	390,000
Add operating income before considering the special order	315,000
Operating income	$705,000 (c)

7

Relevant Items	Keep	Replace
Variable operating costs,		
$125,000 × 5; $100,000 × 5	$625,000	$500,000
Cost of new machine		90,000
Disposal price of present machine		(5,000)
Total relevant costs	$625,000	$585,000

Difference in favor of replacing $40,000 (d)

Note that book value of the present machine is not included in the analysis because, being a past (historical or sunk) cost, it is irrelevant to the decision.

8

	Vase	Bowl
Selling price	$50	$35
Variable costs per unit		
Direct materials,		
2 lbs. × $4; 2 lbs. × $4	8	8
Direct manufacturing labor,		
3 hrs. × $10; 1 hr. × $10	30	10
Total variable costs per unit	38	18
Contribution margin per unit	$12	$17 (b)

9 Constraint for direct materials: $2V + 2B \le 100$
Constraint for direct manufacturing labor: $3V + B \le 60$ (c)
10 Constraint for Machine 1: $6X + 4Y \le 24$
Constraint for Machine 2: $12X \le 24$

Solving these inequalities as simultaneous equations:
$12X = 24, X = 2$
$6(2) + 4Y = 24$
$4Y = 24 - 12$
$Y = 3$ (c)

IV. Sedona Corporation

Yes, accept this special order:

Incremental sales, 600 × $32		$19,200
Incremental costs		
(all variable in this case):		
Manufacturing, 600 × $25	$15,000	
Sales commission, 600 × $3	1,800	16,800
Incremental operating income		$ 2,400

V. Edgewood Corporation

	T	L
Selling price per unit	$ 42	$ 75
Variable costs per unit	20	25
Contribution margin per unit	22	50
Multiply by number of units that		
can be manufactured per hour	× 8	× 3
Contribution margin per hour of		
plant capacity	$176	$150

All 1,440 machine-hours should be used to manufacture product T, because T has the higher contribution margin per unit of the constraining resource (machine-hours).

VI. Bradshaw Company

1. Effect on operating income of discontinuing Y:

Loss of revenue, 1,800 units × $7	$(12,600)
Savings of variable costs,	
1,800 units × ($6.50 + $1.00)	13,500
Increase in operating income	$ 900

This analysis includes *relevant items only*. The same answer could also be obtained by including *both* relevant and irrelevant items, albeit more time-consuming. Under that presentation (not shown), the company's income statement without Y would show operating income of $7,214, which is $900 more than the present level of $6,314. Note that when the product mix changes, total fixed costs (which are the same with or without Y) would merely be allocated (reallocated) to the new mix of products W, X and Z.

2. Effect on operating income of changes in Y and X:

Increase from discontinuing Y (from part 1)	$ 900
Loss of part of X's contribution	
margin, 200 units × ($15.00 − $3.00 − $1.25)	(2,150)
Decrease in operating income	$(1,250)

3. Effect on operating income of changes in W and Z:

Loss of present contribution margin	
W: 1,000 units × ($10.00 − $2.50 − $1.17)	$(6,330)
Z : 2,000 units × ($11.00 − $6.00 − $1.20)	(7,600)
Addition of proposed contribution margin	
W: 500 units × ($12.00 − $2.50 − $1.17)	4,165
Z : 2,500 units × ($10.50 − $6.00 − $1.20)	8,250
Decrease in operating income	$(1,515)

VII. Sunnybrook Farms

Three steps are used to obtain the answer:
First, compute each Sunday's incremental marketing and administrative costs:
$24,960 ÷ 52 weeks = $480.
Second, compute each Sunday's *incremental* sales volume needed to cover each Sunday's incremental marketing and administrative costs:
$480 ÷ .20 = $2,400
Third, compute each Sunday's *total* sales volume needed to obtain the same weekly operating income as in the current six-day week:
$2,400 ÷ (1 − .60) = $6,000
Note that of this amount, $3,600 ($6,000 × .60) would otherwise occur during the six-day week, and the remainder of $2,400($6,000 − $3,600) would cover each Sunday's incremental marketing and administrative costs.

VIII. Grimes Company

Cash outflow to buy the new machine	$193,000
Deduct cash inflow from	
sale of the old machine	15,000
Net cash outflow to change machines	178,000
Net cash inflow from annual savings in	
energy costs, $19,000 × 10	190,000
Difference in favor of	
replacing old machine	$ 12,000

Note that the book value of the present machine is not included in the analysis because, being a past (historical or sunk) cost, it is irrelevant to the decision.

IX. Riedel Perfume Company

1. 200 machine-hours ÷ 400 units of Y = .5 machine-hours per unit of Y
2. 400 machine-hours ÷ 160 units of Y = 2.5 machine-hours per unit of Y
3. Total contribution margin = $7X + $8Y
4. Process R constraint: $X + .5Y \leq 200$, or $2X + Y \leq 400$
   Process T constraint: $X + 2.5Y \leq 400$, or $.4X + Y \leq 160$
   Material shortage constraint: $Y \leq 150$

PRICING DECISIONS, PRODUCT PROFITABILITY DECISIONS, AND COST MANAGEMENT

MAIN FOCUS AND OBJECTIVES

Pricing and product profitability decisions are among the most challenging decisions facing managers. This chapter explains the important role that cost data can play in making those decisions. The relevant-revenue and relevant-cost framework outlined in the preceding chapter is used here. Your overall objective for this chapter is to understand how the time horizon and the context affect the costs that are relevant for pricing and product profitability decisions. Nine learning objectives are stated in the textbook (p. 428).

Give special attention to:

- full product costs
- the distinction between a market-based approach and a cost-plus approach to long-run pricing decisions
- target cost and its relationship to value engineering
- the distinction between locked-in costs and cost incurrence
- product life-cycle costing and budgeting

Be aware that a good working knowledge of cost behavior patterns and cost drivers can lead to better pricing and product profitability decisions. Always keep in mind, however, that costs are only one of the major influences on these decisions; the other major influences are customers and competitors.

REVIEW OF KEY TERMS AND CONCEPTS

A. The three major influences on pricing decisions are customers, competitors, and costs ("*the three C's*").
   1. A price increase may cause **customers** to choose a competitor's product or a substitute product.
   2. The presence of both domestic and international **competitors** weighs on pricing decisions.
   3. Knowing how **costs** behave provides insight into the predicted operating income from various price/volume combinations of a particular product.
   4. The three C's framework is consistent with the basic economic concept that *supply and demand* determine prices.
      a. Competitors and costs affect supply.
      b. Customers determine demand.

5. The role of cost data depends on the type of competition in the marketplace.
   a. In *perfect competition*, the company is a price-taker without pricing discretion. Cost data are used to determine the most profitable products.
   b. In *imperfect competition*, the company has some pricing discretion because products are differentiated. Here costs help managers make pricing decisions.
6. Deciding which product costs in the value chain are relevant to a particular situation depends on whether the time horizon is short run (say, six months or less) or long run.
   a. For *long-run pricing decisions*, managers want to know *all* the costs of *all* the business functions that are assigned to products; those costs are called **full product costs**:
      (1) Upstream (pre-manufacturing) costs—R&D and design.
      (2) Manufacturing costs.
      (3) Downstream (post-manufacturing) costs—marketing, distribution, and customer service.
   b. For *short-run pricing decisions,* managers want to know a *subset* of full product costs.

B. A short-run pricing decision, a one-time-only special order, is illustrated in the textbook (p. 431) and related Exhibits 12-2 and 12-3.

> **Carefully study Exhibits 12-2 and 12-3 and then note the key points listed below.**

1. In Exhibit 12-2:
   a. Output is the 250,000-barrel special order.
   b. Relevant costs consist of variable manufacturing costs (output unit-level costs) and fixed materials procurement and process changeover costs (batch-level costs or setup costs).
   c. Relevant costs total $9,050,000, or $36.20 per barrel, which is the proper cost to use in preparing a bid on the special order.
2. In Exhibit 12-3:
   a. Output is 600,000 barrels, which includes the 250,000-barrel special order.
   b. The *absorption-costing income statement* (Panel A) shows total manufacturing costs of $48 per barrel, an inappropriate figure to use for the decision because it (i) includes some irrelevant costs and (ii) excludes some relevant costs.
   c. The *contribution-income statement* (Panel B) shows contribution margin of $41 per barrel, an inappropriate figure to use for the decision because it (i) includes some irrelevant costs and (ii) excludes some relevant costs.
3. Note that a one-time-only special order pricing decision, by definition, has *no* long-run implications.
4. *See Practice Test Question III (item 2) and Problems IV and V.*

C. A long-run time horizon is appropriate for many pricing decisions.
1. When market forces set prices, knowledge of long-run product costs helps guide decisions about entering or remaining in the market.

2. When managers have some control, long-run full product costs can act as a base for this price.
3. See the Astel Computer example in the textbook (p. 435).

> **When Astel produces 150,000 Provalue computers, the activity-based product costs are:**
> - **Total manufacturing costs of $102 million, or $680 per unit (Exhibit 12-4)**
> - **All value-chain costs of $135 million, or $900 per unit (Exhibit 12-5)**

D. A market-based approach is often useful in long-run pricing decisions.
   1. **Market-based pricing** has a customer-driven external focus.
   2. The decision to enter or remain in a particular market often depends on the product's target price and target cost.
   3. *Target price*: the estimated price that potential customers are willing to pay for a product (or service).
   4. The target price leads to a target cost.
   5. **Target cost**: the estimated long-run cost of a product (or service) that when sold enables the company to achieve the target profit margin.
      a. Target cost is often lower than the existing full product cost.
      b. To achieve target cost, many Japanese companies use kaizen, their word for a process of continuous improvement.

> **Target costing dovetails with the management theme that customer satisfaction is priority one. Companies focus on what products will sell (at what prices) and *then* design them accordingly.**

   6. Determining target price and target cost requires four steps:
      Step 1: Develop a product that satisfies the needs of potential customers.
      Step 2: Choose a target price on the basis of customers' perceived value for the product and the expected response of competitors.
      Step 3: Derive target cost: Target cost = Target price − Target profit margin
      Step 4: Perform value engineering to achieve target cost.
   7. **Value engineering**: a systematic evaluation of all business functions in the value chain to "cost down" products (that is, reducing full product costs and still satisfying customers).
      a. Value engineering can result in improvements in product design, changes in materials specifications, or modifications in process methods.
      b. Cross functional teams perform value engineering.
   8. Study the four steps for determining target price and target cost in the textbook example of Astel's Provalue computer (pp. 438-39).
   9. Successful value engineering requires distinguishing between cost incurrence and locked-in costs.

a. **Cost incurrence**: arises when resources are actually sacrificed (such as when direct materials are used in manufacturing).

b. **Locked-in costs** (also called *designed-in costs*): costs that have not yet been incurred but which will be incurred in the future based on decisions already made (such as when the design of a product is finalized).

c. Exhibit 12-6 shows the wide divergence between when costs are locked-in and when costs are incurred.

d. Value engineering attempts to control costs *before* they are locked-in, within the constraints of customer satisfaction.

> *Question*: **Why is it important to distinguish between when costs are locked-in and when costs are incurred?**
>
> *Answer*: **Because it is difficult to reduce costs that have already been locked-in. Locked-in costs are often a large proportion of full product costs.**

---

10. Five examples of how design decisions affect full product costs are given in the textbook (p. 439).

11. **Caution**: Costs are *not* locked-in before manufacturing occurs in many cases.

a. In process industries, such as chemicals, oil, steel, and paper, some costs are locked-in and incurred at about the same time.

b. The key to lowering costs in these process industries is through improved efficiency and productivity rather than through better design.

12. The textbook example continues by comparing Provalue II, a new product, with Provalue.

a. Exhibit 12-7 shows that Provalue II is expected to reduce manufacturing costs per unit to $540 from Provalue's $680.

b. Exhibit 12-8 shows Provalue II's full product costs to be $720 per unit, the amount exactly equal to target costs.

c. Note that, contrary to this example, target cost is usually *not* achieved in one iteration. Typically, many iterations are necessary.

E. A cost-plus (cost-based) approach is often helpful in long-run pricing decisions.

1. **Cost-plus pricing** has an internal focus and is especially useful for products without observable market prices, such as buildings and submarines.

2. Accurate product costs, which can be determined with activity-based costing, are critically important in cost-plus pricing.

3. The general formula for cost-plus pricing is to add markup to the cost base:

Cost base	$ X
Markup	Y
Prospective selling price	$X + Y

4. Many different cost bases can be used in this formula; one example is full product costs. Other cost bases appear in the textbook (p. 444).

5. Managers often prefer that the cost base includes both fixed costs and variable costs because this is a simple approach to full cost recovery, price stability, and price justification.
6. One approach to choosing the amount of markup is a target return on investment.
   a. *Target return on investment*: the target operating income that a company expects to earn on the capital invested in a particular business subunit.

$$\text{Target return on investment} = \frac{\text{Target operating income}}{\text{Invested capital}}$$

   b. See the textbook example (p. 443).
   c. In the example, do not confuse the target return on investment (18%) with the markup (12% of the cost base).
7. In practice, companies choose cost bases and markup percentages on the basis of their past experiences in pricing products.
8. Note that cost-plus pricing is prospective in nature; managers should always consider consumer reaction to alternative prices as well as prices of similar competing products.
9. *See Practice Test Question III (items 5 and 6) and Problems VI and VII.*

F. Many pricing decisions are driven by factors other than costs.

Two non-cost factors in pricing decisions are price discrimination and peak-load pricing.

---

1. *Price discrimination*: the practice of charging some customers a higher price than is charged to other customers.
   a. The seller varies the price among different market segments to take advantage of different sensitivities to price exhibited by the segments.
   b. Pricing in these cases is largely divorced from the cost of the product.
   c. See the textbook example of hardcover and softcover books (p. 446).
2. Managers often make pricing decisions after taking capacity constraints into consideration.
   a. *Peak-load pricing*: the practice of charging a higher price for the same product or service when demand approaches physical capacity limits.
   b. Peak-load pricing is used in major industries including telephone, electric utilities, airlines, and lodging.
   c. Peak-load pricing is a form of price discrimination.

G. **Life-cycle costing** tracks and accumulates all costs attributable to each product from its initial research and development to its final customer service and support.
   1. Life-cycle reporting does not have the usual *calendar-based life focus.* Instead if fits the pattern of *each product's life cycle,* which can span from five to ten years for automobiles.
   2. The terms "cradle to grave costing" and "womb to tomb costing" convey the idea of reporting *all* costs associated with the product.

3. Life-cycle costing is an especially important concept in today's manufacturing environment, with the increased magnitude of upstream and downstream costs.
4. Life-cycle costing can report *budgeted amounts* and *actual results*.
5. Life-cycle budgeted costs can provide useful information for pricing decisions.
6. A product life-cycle budget highlights the importance of life-cycle revenues being large enough to cover the life-cycle costs of all business functions in the value chain rather than a subset of those functions.
7. Life-cycle budgeting is most helpful in cases where a product's revenues and the related costs occur in different reporting periods and are not well-matched by financial accounting procedures.
   a. For financial accounting purposes, R&D, marketing, distribution, and customer service costs are expenses in the period incurred, which is often *not* the period when the related revenue is earned.
   b. Some industries likely to benefit from life-cycle budgeting are computer software, publishing, and motion pictures.

> **See the computer software example in the textbook (p. 448) and related Exhibit 12-10. Note that:**
> - **both pre-manufacturing and post-manufacturing costs are a high proportion of total costs**
> - **the example does not consider the time value of money, a topic covered in Chapters 20 and 21**

8. Life-cycle costs further reinforce the importance of locked-in costs, target cost, and value engineering in pricing and cost management.
9. The earlier in a product's life-cycle that costs are locked-in (that is, before there is much information on the probability of the product being successful), the riskier the product is in terms of profitability.
10. Life-cycle reporting must be subjected to the *cost-benefit test*. It offers important benefits:
    a. The full set of costs (and revenues) associated with each product becomes visible. Typically in calendar-based reporting, manufacturing costs are more visible than those of other business functions in the value chain.
    b. Differences among products in the percentage of total costs incurred at early stages in the life-cycle are highlighted.
    c. Interrelationships across business-function cost categories are highlighted.
11. A different notion of life-cycle costs, *customer life-cycle costs*, focuses on the total costs to a customer of acquiring and using a product or service until it is no longer used.
12. *See Practice Test Problem VIII.*

H. Another factor sometimes affecting pricing decisions is the laws in the United States that prohibit predatory pricing, dumping, and collusive pricing.
   1. A company engages in *predatory pricing* when it deliberately sets low prices (below short-run marginal costs or average variable costs) to lessen or eliminate competition.

2. The car rental case discussed in the textbook (p. 451) shows that the courts are willing to use variable cost information in ruling on predatory pricing.
3. In conforming with the legal requirements, it is prudent for companies to have a system that incorporates the following procedures:
   a. Collect data so that variable costs can be compiled relatively easily.
   b. Review all proposed prices below variable costs, with a presumption of claims of predatory intent.
   c. Keep detailed records of all value-chain costs.
4. *Dumping* occurs when a foreign company sells a product in the U.S. at a price below the market value in the country of its creation, whereby this action materially injures or threatens to materially injure an industry in the U.S.
5. *Collusive pricing* occurs when companies in an industry conspire in their pricing and output decisions to achieve a price above the competitive price.

PRACTICE TEST QUESTIONS AND PROBLEMS

I. Complete each of the following statements.

1. The three major influences on pricing decisions are _____ _____.

2. When all the value chain costs are assigned to a product, the resulting unit cost is called _____.

3. _____ is the estimated long-run cost of a product (or service) that when sold enables the company to achieve the target profit margin.

4. A systematic evaluation of all aspects of the value chain to "cost down" products is called _____.

5. Costs are _____ at the time resources are actually sacrificed, but costs are _____ _____ at the point in the value chain that determines subsequent cost incurrence.

6. _____ pricing has an internal focus and is especially useful for products without observable market prices.

7. The practice of charging some customers a higher price than is charged to other customers is called _____.

8. _____ tracks and accumulates all costs attributable to each product from its initial research and development to its final customer service and support.

9. A company engages in _____ _____ when it deliberately sets low prices for the purpose of lessening or eliminating competition.

II. Indicate whether each of the following statements is true or false by putting T or F in the space provided.

___ 1. Cost behavior studies play an important role in pricing decisions.

___ 2. Relevant costs are expected future costs that will differ among alternative courses of action.

___ 3. Process changeover costs for a one-time-only special order are an example of output unit-level costs.

___ 4. Contribution margin per unit is an appropriate figure to use for decisions on one-time-only special orders.

___ 5. The decision to enter or remain in a particular market often depends on the product's target price and target cost.

___ 6. Value engineering can result in improvements in product design, changes in materials specifications, or modifications in process methods.

___ 7. Value engineering is usually constrained by locked-in costs.

___ 8. It is important for managers to distinguish between when costs are locked-in and when costs are incurred.

___ 9. In some cases, costs are not locked-in before manufacturing occurs.

___ 10. Managers often prefer that both fixed costs and variable costs be included in the cost base for cost-plus pricing decisions.

11. The target rate of return on investment for a product is a synonym for the product's markup as a percentage of cost.

___ 12. When the seller practices price discrimination, pricing is closely linked to the cost of the product.

___ 13. Under life-cycle costing, manufacturing costs are more visible than the costs of other business functions.

___ 14. Life-cycle budgeting is most helpful in cases where a product's revenues and the related costs occur in different reporting periods and are not well-matched by financial accounting procedures.

___ 15. Setting prices above average variable costs is regarded as pricing that is non-predatory.

___ 16. Collusive pricing occurs when a foreign company sells a product in the U.S. at a price below the market value in the country of its creation, whereby this action materially injures or threatens to materially injure an industry in the U.S.

III. Select the best answer for each of the following multiple-choice questions and put the identifying letter in the space provided.

___ 1. In reference to the basic economic concept of supply and demand, supply is affected by:
   a. customers, competitors, and costs.
   b. customers and competitors.
   c. customers and costs.
   d. competitors and costs.

___ 2. (CPA) Relay Corporation manufactures batons. Relay can manufacture 300,000 batons a year at variable costs of $750,000 and fixed costs of $450,000. Fixed costs will remain the same between 200,000 and 300,000 batons. Based on Relay's predictions, 240,000 batons will be sold at the regular price of $5.00 each. In addition, a one-time-only special order was received for 60,000 batons to be sold at a 40% discount off the regular price. By what amount would operating income be increased or decreased as a result of accepting the special order?
   a. $30,000 increase
   b. $60,000 decrease
   c. $36,000 increase
   d. $180,000 increase

___ 3. A manufacturing company assigns R&D, design, marketing, distribution, and customer service costs to products for:
   a. internal reporting purposes and external reporting purposes.
   b. internal reporting purposes but not external reporting purposes.
   c. external reporting purposes but not internal reporting purposes.
   d. neither internal reporting purposes nor external reporting purposes.

___ 4. Cost-plus pricing:
   a. has a customer-driven external focus and is especially useful for a toy manufacturer.
   b. has a customer-driven external focus and is especially useful for a maker of spacecraft equipment.
   c. has an internal focus and is especially useful for a maker of spacecraft equipment.
   d. has an internal focus and is especially useful for a toy manufacturer.

___ 5. (CPA) Purvis Company manufactures a product that has a variable cost of $50 per unit. Fixed costs total $1,000,000 and are allocated on the basis of the number of units produced. Selling price is computed by adding a 10% markup to full product costs. How much should the selling price be per unit for 100,000 units?
   a. $55
   b. $60
   c. $61
   d. $66

___ 6. (CPA) Diva Co. wants to establish a selling price that will yield a gross margin of 40% on sales of a product whose cost is $12.00 per unit. The selling price should be:
   a. $16.80.
   b. $19.20.
   c. $20.00.
   d. $30.00.

7. Peak-load pricing is:
   a. an illegal form of price discrimination.
   b. a legal form of price discrimination.
   c. illegal but is not a form of price discrimination.
   d. legal but is not a form of price discrimination.

IV. Solve Practice Test Problem IV in Chapter 11 (p. 152), which could have been placed here.

Check figure: Yes, $2,400 incremental operating income

V. (CMA adapted) E. Berg & Sons build custom-made pleasure boats that range in price from $30,000 to $250,000. For the past 30 years, Ed Berg, Sr., has determined the selling price of each boat by predicting the costs of materials, labor, an allocated portion of total overhead (which includes marketing and administrative costs), and adding a 20% markup to the total of those costs. For example, a recent price quotation was determined as follows:

Direct materials	$ 10,000
Direct manufacturing labor	16,000
Total overhead	4,000
Total predicted costs	30,000
20% markup	6,000
Selling price	$36,000

The total overhead figure was determined by budgeting total overhead costs for the year and allocating them at 25% of direct manufacturing labor.

If a customer rejected the price and business was slack, Ed Berg, Sr., would often be willing to reduce his markup to as little as 5% of total predicted costs. The average markup for the year is expected to be 15%.

Ed Berg, Jr., has just completed a course on pricing in which contribution margin was emphasized. He feels this approach would be helpful in determining the selling prices of their boats.

Total overhead for the year has been budgeted at $600,000 of which $360,000 is fixed and the remainder varies in direct proportion to direct manufacturing labor.

1. Assume the customer in the example rejected the $36,000 quotation and also rejected a $31,500 quotation (5% markup) during a slack period. The customer countered with a $30,000 offer. What is the minimum selling price Ed Berg, Jr., could quote without decreasing or increasing operating income?
2. What is the main disadvantage of emphasizing contribution margin in pricing decisions?

Check figure: (1) $27,600

VI. Silverthorne, Inc. needs to make a pricing decision on a new product. The company uses cost-plus pricing based on the target return on investment. The following information is available for the product:

Invested capital	$25 million
Target return on investment	20%
Full product costs (per unit) at the output level of 125,000 units	$200
Full product costs (per unit) at the output level of 80,000 units	$250

1. Compute the prospective selling price assuming the predicted output level is 125,000 units.
2. Compute markup as a percentage of full product costs assuming the predicted output level is 80,000 units.

Check figures: (1) $240 (2) 25%

VII. (CMA) Hall Company specializes in packaging bulk drugs in standard dosages for local hospitals. The company has been in business for nine years and has been profitable since its second year of operation. Don Greenway, Director of Cost Accounting, installed a standard cost system after joining the company three years ago.

Wyant Memorial Hospital has asked Hall to bid on the packaging of one million doses of medication at full cost plus a return on full cost of no more than 9% after income taxes. Wyant defines cost as including all variable costs of performing the service, a reasonable amount of fixed overhead, and reasonable administrative costs. The hospital will supply all packaging materials and ingredients. Wyant has indicated that any bid over $0.015 per dose will be rejected.

Greenway accumulated the following information prior to the preparation of the bid:

Direct manufacturing	
labor costs	$4.00/DMLH
Variable overhead costs	$3.00/DMLH
Fixed overhead costs	$5.00/DMLH
Administrative costs	$1,000 for the order
Production rate	1,000 doses/DMLH

Hall Company is subject to an income tax rate of 40%.

1. Compute the minimum price per dose Hall could bid for the Wyant job that would not change Hall's net income.
2. Compute the bid price per dose using the full cost criterion and the maximum allowable return specified by Wyant.

3. Without prejudice to your answer to part 2, assume that the price per dose that Hall computed using the cost-plus criterion specified by Wyant is greater than the maximum bid of $0.015 per dose allowed by Wyant. Discuss the factors that Hall should consider before deciding whether or not to submit a bid at the maximum price of $0.015 per dose that Wyant allows.
4. Discuss the factors that Wyant should have considered before deciding whether or not to employ cost-plus pricing.

Check figures: (1) $0.008 (2) $0.01495

VIII. Appletree, Inc., is analyzing the profitability and pricing policies for two of its accounting software packages. Summary data on the packages over their two-year product life cycle are as follows:

Package	Selling Price	Sales in Units
Quick Tax	$250	Year 1, 4,000
		Year 2, 16,000
Fast Audit	$200	Year 1, 10,000
		Year 2, 6,000

The life-cycle revenue and cost information is as follows (in thousands):

	Quick Tax		Fast Audit	
	Year 1	Year 2	Year 1	Year 2
Revenues	$1,000	$4,000	$2,000	$1,200
Costs:				
R&D	1,400	0	480	0
Product design	370	30	160	32
Manufacturing	150	450	286	130
Marketing	280	720	480	416
Distribution	30	120	120	72
Customer service	100	650	440	776

Appletree is particularly concerned with increases in R&D and product design costs for many of its software packages in recent years. Consequently, major efforts have been made to reduce these costs on the Fast Audit package.

1. Prepare a product life-cycle income statement for each software package.
2. Compare the two packages in terms of their profitability and cost structure. State your conclusions.

Check figure: (1) Operating income of Quick Tax $700,000

CHAPTER 12 SOLUTIONS TO PRACTICE TEST

I. 1 customers, competitors, costs; 2 full product cost; 3 target cost; 4 value engineering; 5 incurred, locked-in (designed-in); 6 Cost-plus; 7 price discrimination; 8 Life-cycle costing; 9 predatory pricing.

II.

1	T	5	T	9	T	13	F
2	T	6	T	10	T	14	T
3	F	7	F	11	F	15	T
4	F	8	T	12	F	16	F

Explanations:

1 Predictions of operating income from various price/volume combinations of a particular product are often based on knowledge of variable cost and fixed cost patterns. (T)

2 In a pricing decision, variable costs are not always relevant and fixed costs are not always irrelevant. In the one-time-only special order example in the textbook (p. 431), the variable marketing and distribution costs are irrelevant and the fixed costs of materials procurement and process changeover are relevant. (T)

3 Process changeover costs are setup costs and, therefore, are batch-level costs. Variable manufacturing costs are an example of output unit-level costs. (F)

4 As Exhibit 12-3 (Panel B) illustrates, contribution margin per unit can be an inappropriate figure to use for a one-time-only special order decision because it can (i) include some irrelevant costs and (ii) exclude some relevant costs. (F)

5 Target price is the estimated price that potential customers are willing to pay for a product (or service). The target price leads to a target cost. Target cost is the estimated long-run cost of a product (or service) that when sold enables the company to achieve the target profit margin. (T)

6 The results described in the statement can occur because value engineering systematically evaluates all business functions in the value chain to "cost down" products. Cross functional teams perform value engineering. (T)

7 Value engineering attempts to control costs *before* they are locked-in (designed-in), within the constraints of customer satisfaction. (F)

8 This distinction is important because it is difficult to reduce costs that have already been locked-in. Locked-in costs are often a large proportion of full product costs. (T)

9 In process industries, such as chemicals, oil, steel, and paper, costs are locked-in and incurred at about the same time. (T)

10 Including both fixed costs and variable costs in the cost base for cost-plus pricing decisions is a simple approach to full cost recovery, price stability, and price justification. (T)

11 These terms are not synonyms. In the textbook example (pp. 443-44), target return on investment is 18% while markup is 12% of the cost base. (F)

12 Price discrimination is the practice of charging some customers a higher price than is charged to other customers. The seller is simply taking advantage of the different sensitivities to price exhibited by the different market segments. Pricing in these cases is largely divorced from the cost of the product. (F)

13 One of the significant benefits offered by life-cycle reporting is that the full set of costs (and revenues) associated with each product becomes visible. Typically in *calendar-based reporting*, manufacturing costs are more visible that those of other business functions. Life-cycle costing is especially important in today's manufacturing environment, which has an increased magnitude of upstream and downstream costs. (F)

14 For financial accounting purposes, R&D, marketing, distribution, and customer service costs are expensed in the period incurred, which is often *not* the period when the related revenue is earned. (T)

15 A company engages in predatory pricing when it deliberately sets prices below short-run marginal costs or average variable costs to lessen or eliminate competition. (T)

16 The statement refers to dumping instead of collusive pricing. Collusive pricing occurs when companies in an industry conspire in their pricing and output decisions to achieve a price above the competitive price. (F)

III.

1 d	4 c	7 b
2 a	5 d	
3 b	6 c	

Explanations:

1 In terms of the forces of supply and demand, competitors and costs affect supply and customers determine demand. (d)

2 For the special order:

Selling price, $5.00(1 − .40)	$3.00 per baton
Incremental costs, $750,000 ÷ 300,000	2.50 per baton
Increase in operating income	$0.50 per baton × 60,000 = $30,000 (a)

Note that if the special order is accepted, *total* operating income would be:

Sales, (240,000 × $5) + (60,000 × $3)	$1,380,000
Variable costs, 300,000 × $2.50	750,000
Contribution margin	630,000
Fixed costs	450,000
Operating income	$ 180,000

3 As in the chapter example of Astel Computer, the upstream and downstream costs (that is, all value chain costs except manufacturing costs) are assigned to products only for internal reporting purposes. Those costs are expensed as period costs for external reporting purposes. (b)

4 Cost-plus pricing has an internal focus and is especially useful for products without observable market prices. Examples of such products are spacecraft equipment, buildings, and submarines. (c)

5 $50 + ($1,000,000 ÷ 100,000) = $50 + $10 = $60;
$60 + $60(.10) = $60 + $6 = $66 (d)

6 Let X = Selling price

$$X - \$12.00 = .40X$$
$$.60X = \$12.00$$
$$X = \$12.00 \div .60 = \$20.00 \text{ (c)}$$

Proof: $20.00 − $12.00 = $8.00, which equals 40% of $20.00

7 Peak-load pricing is the practice of charging a higher price for the same product or service when demand approaches physical capacity limits. Peak-load pricing is a legal form of price discrimination used in major industries including telephone, electric utilities, airlines, and lodging. (b)

IV. Sedona Corporation

See the solution to Practice Test Problem IV in Chapter 11 (p. 157).

V. E. Berg & Sons

1. Two steps are used to obtain the price that would have no effect on operating income. First, compute the budgeted variable overhead rate (denoted by X):

$$X = \frac{\text{Budgeted variable overhead costs}}{\text{Budgeted direct manufacturing labor costs}}$$

$$X = \frac{\$600,000 - \$360,000}{\$600,000 \div .25} = \frac{\$240,000}{\$2,400,000} = 10\%$$

Second, compute the variable cost of producing and selling the boat:

Direct materials	$10,000
Direct manufacturing labor	16,000
Variable overhead	
($16,000 × 10%)	1,600
Total	$27,600

2. Focusing exclusively on contribution margin in pricing decisions fails to explicitly recognize the fixed costs. Although fixed costs can be irrelevant in the short run, they must be recovered in the long run in order for the company to stay in business.

VI. Silverthorne, Inc.

1. Total target return on investment = $25,000,000 × .20 = $5,000,000
   Target return on investment per unit = $5,000,000 ÷ 125,000 = $40
   Prospective selling price = $200 + $40 = $240
2. Total target return on investment = $25,000,000 × .20 = $5,000,000
   Target return on investment per unit = $5,000,000 ÷ 80,000 = $62.50
   Markup as a percentage of full product costs = $62.50 ÷ $250 = 25%

VII. Hall Company

1. $$\text{DMLH required for job} = \frac{1{,}000{,}000 \text{ doses to be packaged}}{1{,}000 \text{ doses/DMLH}} = 1{,}000 \text{ DMLH}$$

Traceable out-of-pocket costs:

Direct manufacturing labor costs, $4.00 × 1,000	$4,000
Variable overhead costs, $3.00 × 1,000	3,000
Administrative costs	1,000
Total	$8,000

$$\text{Minimum price per dose} = \frac{\text{Total traceable out-of-pocket costs}}{1{,}000{,}000 \text{ doses}} = \frac{\$8{,}000}{1{,}000{,}000} = \$0.008$$

2. As in part 1, 1,000 DMLH are required for the job.

Direct manufacturing labor costs, $4.00 × 1,000	$ 4,000
Variable overhead costs, $3.00 × 1,000	3,000
Fixed overhead costs, $5.00 × 1,000	5,000
Administrative costs	1,000
Total (full) costs	13,000
Maximum allowable return before taxes (15%*)	1,950
Total bid price	$14,950

$$\text{Bid price per dose} = \frac{\text{Total bid price}}{1{,}000{,}000 \text{ doses}} = \frac{\$14{,}950}{1{,}000{,}000} = \$0.01495$$

$$*\begin{array}{c}\text{Maximum allowable} \\ \text{return before taxes}\end{array} = \frac{\text{Maximum allowable return after taxes}}{1 - \text{Tax rate}} = \frac{.09}{1 - .40} = \frac{.09}{.60} = .15$$

3. The factors that Hall should consider before deciding whether or not to submit a bid at the maximum allowable price include (i) whether Hall has excess capacity, (ii) whether there are available jobs for which profitability might be greater, and (iii) whether the maximum bid of $0.015 contributes toward recovering fixed costs.

4. The competitive environment of the industry should have been considered by Wyant to determine whether or not a lower price could be obtained through competitive bidding. The hospital should also have considered that cost-plus pricing is difficult to compute for products produced in "mass" quantity and is better suited for products that are unique and high priced.

VIII. Appletree, Inc.

1. and 2.	Quick Tax		Fast Audit	
Revenues (two-year totals)	$5,000		$3,200	
Costs (two-year totals):		%		%
R&D	1,400	32.5	480	14.1
Product design	400	9.3	192	5.7
Manufacturing	600	14.0	416	12.3
Marketing	1,000	23.3	896	26.4
Distribution	150	3.5	192	5.7
Customer service	750	17.4	1,216	35.8
Total costs	4,300	100.0	3,392	100.0
Operating income	$ 700		$ (192)	

Quick Tax is profitable, while Fast Audit is unprofitable. The relatively much lower upstream costs on Fast Audit might be the reason for this outcome. Quick Tax has 41.8% of its costs in R&D and product design compared to 19.8% for Fast Audit. Also, customer service costs are relatively much higher for Fast Audit (35.8% versus 17.4%), which suggests that problems should have been corrected prior to manufacturing. Product life-cycle reports highlight possible causal relationships among costs classified by business function.

CHAPTER 13

MANAGEMENT CONTROL SYSTEMS: CHOICE AND APPLICATION

MAIN FOCUS AND OBJECTIVES

Management control systems exist primarily to aid and coordinate the process of making planning and control decisions throughout organizations. This chapter presents an overview of management control systems, and emphasizes the behavior of the people who use those systems. Your overall objective for this chapter is to understand how motivation, goal congruence, and effort are related to the design, operation, and evaluation of management control systems. Eight learning objectives are stated in the textbook (p. 466).

Give special attention to:

- the discussion of value-added/nonvalue-added cost analysis
- how discretionary costs differ from engineered costs and infrastructure costs
- the control of discretionary costs by different types of negotiated static budgets
- how the engineered-cost approach can be used for some discretionary costs
- the use of financial and nonfinancial measures to promote and monitor effectiveness and efficiency in discretionary-cost centers (a portion of this material is discussed in the brief chapter Appendix)

This chapter provides guidance for identifying central issues when choosing management control systems and for weighing the costs and benefits of alternative systems. Keep in mind, however, that this subject matter is "softer" (there is less number crunching) than in most other chapters. Often there is no pat answer as to which management control system should be chosen; nonetheless, knowing how to identify the central issues is a skill in itself.

REVIEW OF KEY TERMS AND CONCEPTS

A. A **management control system** is a means of gathering information to aid and coordinate the process of making planning and control decisions throughout the organization.
   1. A management control system should include four types of information:
      a. Financial/internal
      b. Financial/external
      c. Nonfinancial/internal
      d. Nonfinancial/external
   2. Exhibit 13-1 gives specific examples of each of these types of information for Home Depot, Inc.

3. Financial/internal information has long been thought of as pivotal to an effective management control system; however, increased recognition is now being given to the importance of the other three types of information.
4. Because of the increased diversity of management responsibility, a well-functioning management control system is more important today than ever before.
5. The primary criterion for evaluating a management control system is whether it promotes the attainment of top management's goals in a cost-effective manner.
6. The system with the largest excess of benefits over costs should be chosen; however, determining the benefits and costs of individual systems can be an imposing task.
7. Two secondary criteria, goal congruence and effort, help make the cost-benefit test more specific.
   a. **Goal congruence** occurs when individuals and groups, working in their own perceived best interests, make decisions that further the overall goals of top management.
   b. **Effort** is physical and mental exertion toward a goal.
   c. Considered together, goal congruence and effort are elements of **motivation**: the desire to attain a selected goal (the goal-congruence aspect) combined with the resulting drive or pursuit toward that goal (the effort aspect).
   d. Although goal congruence and effort are often reinforcing aspects of motivation, be aware that each of these aspects can exist without the other.

B. Management control systems are varying combinations of formal and informal systems.
   1. *Formal control system*: the explicit rules, procedures, performance-evaluation measures, and incentive plans of an organization that guide the behavior of its managers and employees. Example: budgets.
   2. *Informal control system*: the shared values, loyalties, and mutual commitments among members of an organization and the unwritten norms about acceptable behavior for promotion.
   3. Different *risk-sharing arrangements* can change behavior; see the textbook example involving a subsidy given to an accounting firm that is bidding on a bank audit (p. 469).
   4. Rather than finding fault with a control system ("system bashing"), the focus should be on how the existing system (with all of its imperfections) can be improved.

> **A compensation plan for sales personnel illustrates the importance of motivation, goal congruence, and effort: see the helpful textbook example (p. 470) and related Exhibit 13-2.**

C. Value-added/nonvalue-added cost analysis is a key part of cost management.
   1. **Value-added activities**: those activities that customers perceive as increasing the utility (usefulness) of the products or services they purchase.
   2. **Nonvalue-added activities**: those activities that could be eliminated without the customer perceiving a deterioration in the performance, function, or other quality aspects of products or services.
   3. Some companies are using this classification to help identify which activities to keep and which to eliminate, thereby reducing costs.

4. General Electric's successful application of this cost management technique is described in the textbook (p. 473) and related Exhibit 13-3.
5. Exhibit 13-4 illustrates a reporting format for value-added/nonvalue-added costs.
6. *See Practice Test Problem IV.*

D. Differences among three types of costs—engineered, discretionary, and infrastructure—point to the need for different means of promoting effectiveness and efficiency.

Type of Cost	*Time Between Acquisition and Use of a Resource*	*Major Accounting Control Tool(s)*
Engineered	Short	Flexible budgets and standards
Discretionary	Short to longer	Negotiated static budgets
Infrastructure	Longest	Capital-expenditure budgets

1. **Engineered costs**: costs that result from a clear cause-and-effect relationship between inputs and outputs.
   a. Example: three pounds of direct materials are required to produce one finished unit.
   b. Engineered costs are most frequently found in the production function and, to a lesser extent, the distribution function in the value chain.
   c. In addition to flexible budgets and standards, nonfinancial measures are often helpful to control engineered costs (for example, monitoring direct materials waste).
2. **Discretionary costs**: costs that (i) arise from periodic (usually yearly) decisions regarding the maximum amount to be incurred and (ii) are not tied to a clear cause-and-effect relationship between inputs and outputs.
   a. Examples: advertising, public relations, executive training, health care.
   b. Discretionary costs are typically found in the R&D, design, marketing, and customer-service functions in the value chain.
   c. *The most noteworthy aspect of discretionary costs is that managers are seldom confident that the "correct" amounts are being spent.*
3. **Infrastructure costs**: costs that arise from having property, plant, equipment, and a functioning organization.
   a. Examples: depreciation, long-term lease rental.
   b. Infrastructure costs occur throughout the value chain.
   c. Since little can be done in the short run to change infrastructure costs, the key for managers is careful long-range planning.
   d. From a control standpoint, the objective is usually to increase current utilization of facilities. Why? Because this result will ordinarily increase operating income.

> **Exhibit 13-5 provides a detailed comparison of engineered costs and discretionary costs.**

E. Budgets are an important part of management control systems.
   1. Budgets help promote effectiveness and efficiency in discretionary-cost centers.
      a. *Effectiveness*: the degree to which a predetermined objective or target is met.
      b. *Efficiency*: the relative amount of inputs used to achieve a given level of output. (The fewer the inputs used to obtain a given output, the greater the efficiency.)
   2. The most common accounting technique for controlling discretionary costs is a negotiated static budget.
      a. **Negotiated static budget**: a fixed amount of costs is established through negotiations before the budget period begins.
      b. As defined in Chapter 7, a static budget is not adjusted after it is finalized, regardless of changes in output or input prices, quantities, or costs.
   3. Three types of negotiated static budgets:
      a. *Ordinary incremental budget* is essentially the previous period's budget adjusted for changes in the coming period.
      b. *Priority incremental budget* is essentially the previous period's budget adjusted for specific activities that might be added (dropped) if the current period's budget were increased (decreased) by a given percentage or amount. (Think of this type of budget as a simple and economical compromise between ordinary incremental budgeting and zero-based budgeting.)
      c. **Zero-base budgeting (ZBB)** is budgeting from the ground up, as though the budget were being prepared for the first time.
         (1) Managers must justify *every* proposed expenditure in *each* period's budget, so ZBB requires much more extensive work than other forms of budgeting.
         (2) ZBB forces managers to regularly and systematically explore alternative means of conducting each activity.
         (3) Very few companies adopt ZBB, but it could be used on a less regular basis and for only a subset of responsibility centers at any one time.

F. Alternative approaches are available to control some discretionary costs.
   1. The **engineered-cost approach** is work-measurement based and regards discretionary costs *as if* they were variable costs.
      a. *Work measurement*: the careful analysis of a task, its size, the methods used to perform it, and the efficiency with which it is performed.
      b. Work measurement seeks to determine the workload of an operation and the number of workers needed to perform the work efficiently.
      c. Two work measurement techniques are micromotion study and work sampling.
      d. *Control-factor unit*: the measure of workload used in work measurement (several examples are in the textbook, p. 479).
   2. The **discretionary-cost approach** regards discretionary costs as step-variable function costs.
      a. The primary means of control under this approach is the manager's personal observation; on the basis of experience, he or she decides what size of work force is needed.
      b. Peak workloads are often met by hiring temporary workers or by having regular employees work overtime.
      c. More reliance is placed on hiring capable people and less emphasis is given to monitoring their everyday performance.

> **The engineered-cost approach and the discretionary-cost approach are compared in Exhibit 13-6.**

3. Note that managers may regard some discretionary costs as discretionary for *cash-planning purposes* in the master budget but may use the engineered-cost approach for *control purposes* in preparing flexible budgets for performance evaluation.

4. *Question*: Is the engineered-cost approach better than the discretionary-cost approach?

   Answer: Which approach is better must be decided on a case-by-case basis, using the cost-benefit approach that focuses on how collective operating decisions will be improved.

5. *See Practice Test Problem V.*

6. Some organizations use benchmarking in their discretionary-cost centers.

   a. *Benchmarking*: the continuous process of measuring products, services, or activities against the best levels of performance that can be found inside or outside the organization.

   b. The illustration in the textbook (p. 482) and related Exhibit 13-7 describe benchmarking for hospital cost management.

   c. Benchmark reports are an attention-directing mechanism, but managers using these reports must be cautious. Why? Because the reliability of the cost data can be highly variable.

7. **(Appendix)** Exhibit 13-8 summarizes nine approaches used in various combinations to promote the effectiveness and efficiency of cost management in discretionary-cost centers.

   a. Approaches (1) and (2) are discussed in this chapter.

   b. Approaches (4), (5), and (6) are discussed in Chapters 25 and 26.

PRACTICE TEST QUESTIONS AND PROBLEMS

I. Complete each of the following statements.

1. What four types of information should be included in a management control system?

   _____

   _____

   _____

2. _____ occurs when individuals and groups, working in their own perceived best interests, make decisions that further the overall goals of top management.

3. The desire to attain a selected goal combined with the resulting drive or pursuit toward that goal is called _____.

4. Those activities that could be eliminated without the customer perceiving a deterioration in the performance, function, or other quality aspects of products or services are called _____ activities.

5. _____ are costs that (i) arise from periodic (usually yearly) decisions regarding the maximum amount to be incurred and (ii) are not tied to a clear cause-and-effect relationship between inputs and outputs.

6. The most common technique for controlling discretionary costs is a _____ _____.

7. Three types of negotiated static budgets are:

   _____

   _____

   _____ _____ .

8. The _____ approach is work-measurement based and regards discretionary costs as if they were variable costs, and the _____ approach regards discretionary costs as step-variable function costs.

9. The careful analysis of a task, its size, the methods used to perform it, and the efficiency with which it is performed is called ____

_____.

II. Indicate whether each of the following statements is true or false by putting T or F in the space provided.

___ 1. The cost-benefit test should be used when choosing among management control systems.

___ 2. Goal congruence and effort are often reinforcing aspects of motivation.

___ 3. An informal control system is likely to include a budget.

___ 4. Nonvalue-added costs are the costs of activities that could be eliminated without the customer perceiving a deterioration in the performance, function, or other quality aspects of products or services.

___ 5. The value-added/nonvalue-added cost classification appears to be desirable from a theoretical standpoint, but it has not been used successfully in practice at the time this edition of the textbook was written.

___ 6. Examples of engineered costs are fuel for an airline and handlebars for a bicycle manufacturer.

___ 7. The major accounting control tool for engineered costs is a negotiated static budget.

___ 8. Examples of discretionary costs are health care and property taxes.

___ 9. In contrast to infrastructure costs, discretionary costs are more easily influenced by management over shorter periods.

___ 10. The key to controlling infrastructure costs is careful planning by means of capital expenditure budgets.

___ 11. Effectiveness is the relative amount of inputs used to achieve a given level of output.

___ 12. When a negotiated static budget is, in essence, the previous period's budget adjusted for changes in the coming period, this type of budget is called a priority incremental budget.

___ 13. Work measurement is a fundamental aspect of the discretionary-cost approach.

___ 14. Managers may regard some discretionary costs as discretionary costs for cash-planning purposes but may use the engineered-cost approach for control purposes.

III. Select the best answer for each of the following multiple-choice questions and put the identifying letter in the space provided.

___ 1. Top management of a public accounting firm awarded its San Antonio branch office a subsidy equal to the difference between full billing rates and actual rates for two new clients, whose actual rates would probably be less than full rates because of intense competition. This procedure is aimed most specifically at achieving:
  a. goal congruence.
  b. maximum effort.
  c. risk sharing.
  d. lower infrastructure costs.

___ 2. A clear cause-and-effect relationship exists between inputs used and outputs achieved for:
  a. value-added costs.
  b. engineered costs.
  c. discretionary costs.
  d. infrastructure costs.

___ 3. (CMA) J. J. Motors Inc. employs 45 sales personnel to market their line of luxury automobiles. The average car sells for $23,000, and a 6% commission is paid to the salesperson. J. J. Motors is considering a change in the commission arrangement whereby the company would pay each salesperson a salary of $2,000 per month plus a commission of 2% of the sales made by that salesperson. The amount of total monthly car sales at which J. J. Motors would be indifferent as to which plan to select is:
  a. $2,250,000.
  b. $3,000,000.
  c. $1,500,000.
  d. $1,250,000.
  e. $4,500,000.

_____ 4. (CMA) Costs that arise from periodic budgeting decisions that have no strong input/output relationship are commonly called:
   a. infrastructure costs.
   b. discretionary costs.
   c. opportunity costs.
   d. engineered costs.
   e. differential costs.

_____ 5. (CMA adapted) A systematic approach known as zero-base budgeting (ZBB):
   a. presents the plan for only one level of activity and does not adjust to changes in the level of activity.
   b. presents a statement of expectations for a period of time but does not present a firm commitment.
   c. explores alternative means of conducting the activities under each manager's jurisdiction and ranks the importance of the activities.
   d. classifies budget requests by activity and estimates the benefits arising from each activity.
   e. commences with the present level of spending.

_____ 6. The objective of work measurement is to determine:
   a. the cost of doing the work with the available workers.
   b. which workers are most efficient at completing their tasks.
   c. the workload in an operation and the number of workers needed to perform the tasks efficiently.
   d. whether the work can be justified on a cost-benefit basis.

IV. For each of the following labor cost items in a manufacturing company, indicate the classification:
   V: value-added cost
   N: nonvalue-added cost

_____ 1. Reworking defective products
_____ 2. Assembling products
_____ 3. Moving component parts from the warehouse to the assembly line
_____ 4. Inserting an owner's manual in each product package

V. The Good Hands Insurance Company processes thousands of casualty claims from policyholders each month. Thirty claims adjusters work a five-day week at a salary of $600 per week. Travel costs are reimbursed at $20 per working day per adjuster. An average of four claims per day has been set as an appropriate work quota. Last week, 580 claims were processed by the adjusters.

1. Analyze last week's results using the discretionary-cost approach. How much is the flexible-budget variance and is it favorable or unfavorable?
2. Analyze last week's results using the engineered-cost approach. How much is the flexible-budget variance and is it favorable or unfavorable?
3. Should one adjuster be laid off? Explain.

Check figures: (1) $0 (2) $700 unfavorable

CHAPTER 13 SOLUTIONS TO PRACTICE TEST

I. 1 financial/internal, financial/external, nonfinancial/internal, nonfinancial/external; 2 Goal congruence; 3 motivation; 4 nonvalue-added; 5 Discretionary costs; 6 negotiated static budget; 7 ordinary incremental budgets, priority incremental budgets, zero-base budgets; 8 engineered-cost, discretionary-cost; 9 work measurement.

II.

1 T	5 F	9 T	13 F
2 T	6 T	10 T	14 T
3 F	7 F	11 F	
4 T	8 F	12 F	

Explanations:

1 The primary criterion for evaluating a management control system is how it promotes the attainment of top management's goals in a cost-effective manner. The system with the largest excess of benefits over costs should be chosen; however, determining the benefits and costs of individual systems can be an imposing task. (T)

2 Although this statement is true, be aware that goal congruence or effort can exist without the other. (T)

3 An informal control system is the shared values, loyalties, and mutual commitments among members of an organization and unwritten norms about acceptable behavior for promotion. Budgets are part of a formal control system. (F)

4 Some companies are using the value-added/nonvalue-added cost classification as a cost management tool to help identify which activities to keep and which to eliminate. (T)

5 As the textbook example explains (p. 473), General Electric has been successful in implementing the value-added/nonvalue-added approach to classify costs. (F)

6 Engineered costs are costs that result from a clear cause-and-effect relationship between inputs (such as fuel or handlebars) and outputs (such as miles traveled or bicycles produced). (T)

7 The major accounting control tools for engineered costs are flexible budgets and standards. Negotiated static budgets are the major control tool for discretionary costs. (F)

8 Discretionary costs are costs that (i) arise from periodic (usually yearly) decisions regarding the maximum amount to be incurred and (ii) are not tied to a clear cause-and-effect relationship between inputs and outputs. Health care costs satisfy this definition but property taxes do not. Property taxes are an infrastructure cost. (F)

9 See the table in section D of the chapter outline. (T)

10 Little can be done in the short run to change infrastructure costs that have been committed. As a result, it is usually desirable to increase current utilization of facilities in order to increase operating income. (T)

11 Effectiveness is the degree to which a predetermined objective or target is met. The definition in the statement is for efficiency. (F)

12 The statement describes an ordinary incremental budget. A priority incremental budget is essentially the previous period's budget adjusted for specific activities that might be added (dropped) if the current period's budget were increased (decreased) by a given percentage or amount. (F)

13 Work measurement seeks to determine the workload of an operation and the number of workers needed to perform the work efficiently. The engineered-cost approach is work-measurement based and regards discretionary costs *as if* they were variable costs. (F)

14 See the textbook example of personnel costs to process customer orders (pp. 480-81). (T)

III.
1	c	4	b
2	b	5	c
3	a	6	c

Explanations:

1 See the textbook example (p. 469). (c)

2 An example of an engineered cost is the use of two direct manufacturing labor-hours to produce one finished unit. (b)

3 Let S = Total amount of monthly car sales to be indifferent between the compensation plans

$$.06S = (\$2,000 \times 45) + .02S$$
$$.04S = \$90,000$$
$$S = \$2,250,000 \text{ (a)}$$

4 Examples of discretionary costs are advertising, public relations, executive training, and health care. The most noteworthy aspect of discretionary costs is that managers are seldom confident that the "correct" amounts are being spent. (b)

5 ZBB is budgeting from the ground up, as though the budget were being prepared for the first time. Managers must justify every proposed expenditure in each period's budget. (c)

6 Work measurement is the careful analysis of a task, its size, the methods used to perform it, and the efficiency with which it is performed. Work measurement is an integral part of the engineered-cost approach. (c)

IV. 1 N   3 N
      2 V   4 V

V. Good Hands Insurance Company

1. Actual results = $30 \times [\$600 + (5 \times \$20)] = 30 \times \$700 = \$21,000$; Flexible-budget amount = $21,000 (same computation as for actual results); Flexible-budget variance = $21,000 - $21,000 = $0

2. Budgeted costs per claim = $700 ÷ (4 × 5) = $700 ÷ 20 = $35; Flexible-budget amount = 580 × $35 = $20,300; Actual results = $21,000 (computed above); Flexible-budget variance = $21,000 - $20,300 = $700 unfavorable

3. One claim adjuster's quota would be 4 × 5 = 20 claims per week at $35 per claim. This weekly amount would be $35 × 20 = $700, which is equal to the unfavorable flexible-budget variance for last week. However, a claim adjuster should not necessarily be laid off, because that particular week may have been below-average in terms of claims processed. Moreover, individual claims may vary considerably in their size and complexity.

CHAPTER 14

COST ALLOCATION: I

MAIN FOCUS AND OBJECTIVES

This chapter and the next explain how costs are allocated to a variety of cost objects, including products, services, departments, divisions, contracts, and customers. Answers to cost allocation questions are debatable and seldom clearly right or clearly wrong. Your overall objective for this chapter is to obtain insight into cost allocation and to understand the dimensions of the questions, even if the answers are elusive. Eight learning objectives are stated in the textbook (p. 498).

The cornerstone of this topic is the four purposes of cost allocation:

- to provide information for economic decisions
- to motivate managers and employees
- to justify costs or compute reimbursement
- to measure income and assets for reporting to external parties

The key is to determine which purpose of cost allocation is dominant in a given situation.

Give special attention to:

- the concept of a homogeneous cost pool
- the single-rate and dual-rate methods of allocating costs from one department to another
- the direct, step-down, and reciprocal methods of allocating support department costs to operating departments

Keep in mind that cost allocation is a pervasive and inescapable problem – one that you undoubtedly will face many times in your career.

REVIEW OF KEY TERMS AND CONCEPTS

A. Nine key terms discussed in previous chapters are fundamental to the study of cost allocation: cost object, direct costs, indirect costs, cost tracing, cost allocation, cost assignment, cost pool, cost allocation base, and cost driver.

> **Review sections A and B(2) of Chapter 2's outline in the *Student Guide* (pp. 9-10) and section A(2) of Chapter 4's outline (pp. 37-38).**

B. Indirect costs are often a sizable percentage of the costs assigned to cost objects.
 1. Costing systems have multiple cost objects, which means that many individual costs are allocated and reallocated several times before becoming an indirect cost of a specific cost object.
 2. As a company produces a wider variety of products, more costs will be indirect costs of products.
  a. However, companies differ in how they classify costs.
  b. For example, energy cost is an indirect cost of products in some manufacturing plants and a direct cost of products, via metering, in other plants.
  c. Advances in information technology, such as metering and bar coding, have made it cost-effective to trace more costs directly to products.
 3. Different cost allocations may be appropriate depending on the specific purpose involved.

> **Key Exhibit 14-1 outlines and illustrates the four purposes of cost allocation.**

 4. Costs from different business functions of the value chain can be allocated for different purposes; examples are given in the textbook (p. 500).
 5. Managers must first choose the *primary purpose* that a particular cost allocation is to fulfill and then select the *appropriate criterion* for implementing the allocation.

> **Exhibit 14-2 explains four criteria used to guide decisions related to cost allocations.**

 6. The cause-and-effect and the benefits-received criteria guide most decisions related to cost allocations.
  a. The cause-and-effect criterion is superior when the purpose of cost allocation is economic decisions or motivation.
  b. *When the cause-and-effect criterion is not operational, the benefits-received criterion is often used.* For example, the fixed cost of rent typically is allocated to departments on the basis of square feet occupied.
 7. The *cost-benefit test* should be used when designing cost allocation systems.
  a. The costs, which include gathering data and educating managers about the chosen system, tend to be highly visible.
  b. The benefits, making a better collective set of operating decisions, are difficult to measure and usually are less visible than the costs.
  c. Cost allocation systems are becoming *more detailed*, primarily because of rapid reductions in the costs of collecting and processing information.

C. An individual cost item can be simultaneously a direct cost of one cost object and an indirect cost of another cost object.
 1. For example, consider the Microcomputer Manufacturing Division (MMD) of Computer Horizons in Exhibit 14-4.
  a. MMD's building costs are a direct cost of this division.

b. The building costs are an indirect cost of MMD's products.

c. Corporate headquarters costs are indirect costs of the MMD and indirect costs of MMD's products.

2. Three decisions are required when accumulating and subsequently allocating the indirect costs of MMD.

a. Which cost items from corporate headquarters and other divisions should be included in the indirect costs of MMD?

b. How many cost pools should be used when allocating corporate costs to MMD? The concept of homogeneity is important in making this decision.

c. Which cost allocation base should be used for each of the corporate cost pools when allocating these costs to MMD? Examples of cost pools and possible allocation bases are provided in the textbook (p. 505).

> *Question*: **When is a cost pool homogeneous?**
> *Answer*: **When all of the individual activities whose costs are included in the pool have the same or a similar cause-and-effect relationship or benefits-received relationship between the cost driver and the costs of the activity.**

3. *Example of homogeneity*: If the number of employees in a division is the cause for incurring both corporate payroll costs and corporate personnel costs, these cost pools can be aggregated before computing the combined payroll and personnel cost rate per employee.

4. The greater the degree of homogeneity, the fewer the number of cost pools required to accurately show differences in how products use resources of a company.

D. Costs are often allocated from one department to another. In so doing, managers must decide on three issues.

1. Should a single-rate method or dual-rate method be used?

a. **Single-rate method**: all costs are grouped in one cost pool and then allocated to cost objects using the same rate per unit of the single allocation base (no distinction is made between variable costs and fixed costs).

b. **Dual-rate method**: costs are grouped in two separate cost pools, each of which has a different allocation rate and may have a different allocation base (typically, the two cost pools are variable costs and fixed costs).

c. An obvious benefit of using a single-rate method is the low cost and simplicity of implementation; however, the textbook example (p. 507) explains that incorrect sourcing decisions may result.

d. *Use a dual rate when a single rate does not adequately describe the cost behavior pattern of the cost pool.*

2. Should the cost pool(s) be budgeted costs or actual costs?

a. *As a general rule, use budgeted costs.* Why? Two reasons:

(1) Because user departments know the cost rate(s) in advance, which helps in deciding how much service to request and (if the option exists) whether to source internally or externally.

        (2)   Because managers of support departments are motivated to improve efficiency (that is, cost variances are not allocated to user departments).

    b. As an alternative, the support and user departments may agree to share (through an explicit formula) the risk of variances from budgeted amounts.

3. Should the allocation base(s) be budgeted usage or actual usage?

    a. *Use budgeted usage for allocating fixed costs; use actual usage in the current period for allocating variable costs.*

    b. This choice for fixed costs prevents fluctuations of usage in one department from affecting the fixed costs allocated to other departments. (The other choice, using actual usage for allocating fixed costs, is illustrated in Exhibit 14-5.)

    c. Some managers will be tempted to underestimate their departments' long-run budgeted usage, so they would bear a smaller proportion of the total costs being allocated.

        (1)   Top management can counter this temptation by systematically comparing actual usage with budgeted usage.

        (2)   Subordinate managers can be rewarded for making accurate long-run forecasts or penalized for underestimating budgeted usage.

See the textbook example (pp. 507-08). Note that:
- **Both a single rate and dual rates are computed for illustrative purposes, using the italicized guidelines in 2a and 3a of the outline above.**
- **In particular, the cost allocations using dual rates are a means of getting subordinate managers to behave as top management desires.**

See Practice Test Problem IV.

E. Costs are accumulated in departments for planning and control purposes; then costs of support departments are allocated to operating departments to satisfy one or more of the four purposes of cost allocation in Exhibit 14-1.

1. Distinguish between operating departments and support departments.

    a. **Operating departments** (also called *production departments* in manufacturing companies): add value to products or services sold to customers.

    b. **Support departments** (also called *service departments*): provide services that maintain operating departments and other support departments in the organization.

2. Support department costs can be allocated to operating departments by the direct method, the step-down method, or the reciprocal method.

Note that the textbook example of Castleford Engineering illustrates these methods using a *single rate* for the allocations. The Problem for Self-Study (p. 517) illustrates these methods using *dual rates* for the allocations.

---

3. The **direct allocation method** (also called the **direct method**) is the most widely used method for allocating support department costs.
   a. This method allocates each support department's total costs directly to operating departments.
   b. Exhibit 14-7 illustrates the direct method using the data in Exhibit 14-6.
   c. Note that the method *ignores* any services rendered by one support department to another.
   d. The benefit of this method is its simplicity.
4. The **step-down allocation method** (also called the *step method* or *sequential method*) is more complex than the direct method because a sequence of allocations must be chosen.
   a. This method allocates costs of support departments to both operating and support departments, and thereby gives *partial recognition* of services rendered by support departments to other support departments.
   b. A popular step-down sequence begins with the support department that renders the highest percentage of its total services to other support departments.
   c. The allocation sequence continues in descending order, ending with the department rendering the lowest percentage of its total services to the other support departments.
   d. Exhibit 14-8 illustrates the step-down method.
   e. *Note that once a support department's costs have been allocated, no subsequent support department costs are allocated back to it.*
5. The **reciprocal allocation method** (also called the **reciprocal method**) *fully incorporates* the interdepartmental relationships among support departments.
   a. Three steps are used in the textbook example (pp. 513-14) to implement the reciprocal method.
   b. Note in step 1 that Plant Maintenance's total cost equals its own cost plus *its percentage use of Information Systems' services (not IS's percentage use of PM's services)*: Therefore, $PM = \$600,000 + .10IS$.
   c. Also note that *complete reciprocated cost* (for example, $624,082 for *PM* in step 2) is an *artificial cost* in the sense that it is always larger than the *actual cost* ($600,000) finally allocated.
   d. Exhibit 14-9 shows summary data pertaining to the reciprocal method.
   e. Because interdepartmental relationships are fully incorporated, the reciprocal method is the most defensible way of allocating support department costs to operating departments.
6. The costs allocated to each operating department constitute a cost pool that is then divided by an appropriate allocation base to compute the budgeted overhead rate.
   a. In the case of a *manufacturing company*, budgeted production department overhead rates are used *for inventory costing*.
   b. The budgeted overhead rates for the two production departments of Castleford Engineering under the direct, step-down, and reciprocal allocation methods are compared and discussed in the textbook (p. 515).

Be sure you can apply the direct, step-down, and reciprocal methods.
See Practice Test Question III (items 4-10) and Problem V.

F. **Common costs** are costs of operating a facility or other cost object shared by two or more users.
   1. For example, see the illustration of the FASB-GASB mailroom facility in the textbook (p. 515).
   2. There are several methods for allocating common costs to individual users:
      a. **Incremental method**: the incremental user (GASB) is charged with the *additional* ongoing costs arising from its participation with the primary user (FASB).
      b. **Stand-alone method**: each user is charged based on its proportion of the total costs that would be incurred if each were the sole user of the facility or a similar facility.
      c. Other allocation bases have been used for allocating common costs, such as revenues and estimates of long-run service requirements.
   3. *See Practice Test Problem VI.*

PRACTICE TEST QUESTIONS AND PROBLEMS

I. Complete each of the following statements.

1. Name the four purposes of cost allocation:

   _____

   _____

   _____

   _____

2. A cost pool is homogeneous when all of the costs included in the pool have the same or a similar_____relation-ship or _____ relationship between the cost driver and the costs of the activity.

3. Under the _____ method, costs typically are grouped in a variable cost pool and a fixed cost pool.

4. In allocating costs from one department to another, it is desirable to use _____ usage for allocating fixed costs and _____ usage in the current period for allocating variable costs.

5. _____ departments (also called production departments in manufacturing companies) add value to products or services sold to customers.

6. The_____method fully incorporates the interdepartmental relationships among support departments.

7. The_____method allocates costs of support departments to both operating and support departments, and thereby gives partial recognition of services rendered by support departments to other support departments.

8. _____ are costs of operating a facility or other cost object shared by two or more users.

II. Indicate whether each of the following statements is true or false by putting T or F in the space provided.

___ 1. The starting point in cost allocations is to choose the cost allocation base.

___ 2. The benefits-received criterion is superior to the other criteria used to guide cost allocation decisions when the purpose of the allocation is economic decisions or motivation.

___ 3. The cost-benefit test should be applied to cost allocation systems.

___ 4. The salary of a plant manager could be both a direct cost and an indirect cost.

___ 5. When the degree of homogeneity is greater, more cost pools are required to accurately show differences in how products use resources of a company.

___ 6. A good rule of thumb is to use the single-rate method unless the single rate does not adequately describe the cost behavior pattern of the cost pool.

___ 7. If the total of a support department's actual costs were allocated to user departments, the charges could be affected by factors beyond the control of the user-department managers.

___ 8. To allocate the fixed costs of a support department so that fluctuations of usage in one department do not affect charges to other departments, the allocation should be based on actual usage.

___ 9. Some managers will be tempted to underestimate their departments' long-run budgeted usage, so they would bear a smaller proportion of the total costs being allocated.

___ 10. Under the step-down method, once a support department's costs have been allocated, subsequent support department costs should never be allocated back to it.

___ 11. For a given support department serving other support departments, the complete reciprocated cost is always larger than the actual cost.

___ 12. A major reason for allocating support department costs to production departments in a manufacturing plant is to be able to compute budgeted department overhead rates.

___ 13. In general, when two users share a facility such as a mailroom, the primary user would prefer that the common costs be allocated under the incremental method.

III. Select the best answer for each of the following multiple-choice questions and put the identifying letter in the space provided.

___ 1. (CMA) Allocation of support department costs to production departments is necessary to:
   a. control costs.
   b. coordinate production activity.
   c. determine overhead rates.
   d. maximize efficiency.
   e. measure utilization of plant capacity.

___ 2. The most accurate and most widely used method for allocating support department costs is:
   a. the direct method.
   b. the step-down method.
   c. the reciprocal method.
   d. none of the above.

___ 3. The method that gives partial recognition of services rendered by support departments to other support departments is:

   a. the direct method.
   b. the step-down method.
   c. the reciprocal method.
   d. the dual-rate method.

___ 4. (CPA adapted) Boa Corp. allocates support department overhead costs to production departments X and Y by means of the reciprocal allocation method. Information for the month of June 19_5 is as follows:

| | Support Departments | |
	A	B
Overhead costs	$20,000	$10,000
Services provided to departments:		
A	–	10%
B	20%	–
X	40%	30%
Y	40%	60%
	100%	100%

The simultaneous equation to be used in the allocation of A's costs is:
   a. A = $20,000 + .20B.
   b. A = $10,000 + .10B.
   c. A = $10,000 + .20B.
   d. A = $20,000 + .10B.

___ 5. Bixler Manufacturing Company uses the step-down method to allocate its support department costs to production departments. The overhead costs of support Department A are to be allocated first, followed by the costs of B, and then those of C. The distribution of services is as follows:

Service Supplied By	Support Depts.			Production Depts.	
	A	B	C	X	Y
A	–	10%	50%	20%	20%
B	40%	–	15%	30%	15%
C	25%	25%	–	20%	30%

The percentage of B's costs that should be allocated to Y is:
   a. 15%.
   b. 33⅓%.
   c. 25%.
   d. none of the above.

___ 6. See item 5. The percentage of C's costs that should be allocated to B is:
   a. 0%.
   b. 20%.
   c. 33⅓%.
   d. none of the above.

___ 7. (CMA) The managers of Rochester Manufacturing are discussing ways to allocate the cost of support departments such as Quality Control and Maintenance to the Machining and Assembly production departments. To aid them in this discussion, the controller has provided the following information:

	Quality Control	Maintenance	Machining	Assembly	Total
Budgeted overhead costs before allocation	$350,000	$200,000	$400,000	$300,000	$1,250,000
Budgeted machine-hours	–	–	50,000	–	50,000
Budgeted direct manufacturing labor-hours	–	–	–	25,000	25,000
Budgeted units of service:					
Quality Control	–	7,000	21,000	7,000	35,000
Maintenance	10,000	–	18,000	12,000	40,000

If Rochester Manufacturing uses the direct method of allocating support department costs, the total support costs allocated to the Assembly Department would be:
a. $80,000.
b. $87,500.
c. $120,000.
d. $167,500.
e. $467,500.

___ 8. See item 7. Using the direct method, the budgeted total overhead rate per machine-hour at Rochester Manufacturing would be:
   a. $2.40.
   b. $5.25.
   c. $8.00.
   d. $9.35.
   e. $15.65.

___ 9. See item 7. If Rochester Manufacturing uses the step-down method of allocating service costs beginning with Quality Control, the Maintenance costs allocated to the Assembly Department would be:
   a. $70,000.
   b. $108,000.
   c. $162,000.
   d. $200,000.
   e. $210,000.

___ 10. See item 7. If Rochester Manufacturing uses the reciprocal method of allocating service costs, the complete reciprocated cost of Quality Control (rounded to the

nearest dollar) would be:
a. $284,211.
b. $336,842.
c. $350,000.
d. $421,053.
e. $469,473.

IV. Hanover Company's power plant provides electricity for its two operating departments, A and B. The 19_6 budget for the power plant shows:

Budgeted fixed costs	$80,000
Budgeted variable costs per kilowatt hour (KWH)	0.20

Additional data for 19_6:

	Budget (KWH)	Actual (KWH)
Department A	240,000	215,000
Department B	160,000	195,000

Actual power-plant costs: fixed $92,000, variable $88,000.

1. Compute the power-plant costs allocated to A and B using the single-rate method with budgeted usage as the allocation base.
2. Compute the power-plant costs allocated to A and B using the dual-rate method. Follow the approach that is helpful for economic decisions and motivation.
3. What is the main advantage of a single rate for allocating costs?
4. When should a dual rate be used?

Check figures: (1) $86,000 to A, $78,000 to B (2) $91,000 to A, $71,000 to B

V. Given for Zooker Manufacturing Company:

	Support Departments		Production Departments	
	T	V	1	2
Budgeted manufacturing overhead before allocation	$60,000	$80,000	$30,000	$25,000
Proportions of service provided by T	–	30%	50%	20%
Proportions of service provided by V	10%	–	60%	30%

Use the reciprocal method to compute the allocation of support department costs to Departments 1 and 2.

Check figures: Total overhead costs: Dept. 1 $125,670, Dept. 2 $69,330

VI. Adams Company and Baker Company are in non-competing lines of business and use a common database for marketing purposes. The variable costs of accessing the database are readily identifiable and kept in separate cost pools charged to each user. The fixed costs of maintaining the database, however, cannot be identified with each user on the basis of a cause-and-effect relationship. The fixed costs of maintaining the database for next year are budgeted at $55,000. If Baker did not use the database, the fixed costs to Adams would be $48,000. An outside vendor offers to provide Adams access to a comparable database for a fixed fee of $60,000 per year plus variable costs. The same vendor offers to provide Baker access to that database for a fixed fee of $20,000 per year plus variable costs.

1. Use the incremental common cost allocation method to compute how much of the $55,000 fixed costs of maintaining the database would be borne by each user, assuming Adams is regarded as the primary user.
2. Use the stand-alone common cost allocation method to compute how much of the $55,000 fixed costs of maintaining the database would be borne by each user.

Check figures: (1) Adams $48,000, Baker $7,000 (2) Adams $41,250, Baker $13,750

CHAPTER 14 SOLUTIONS TO PRACTICE TEST

I. 1 to provide information for economic decisions, to motivate managers and employees, to justify costs or compute reimbursement, to measure income and assets for reporting to external parties; 2 cause-and-effect, benefits-received; 3 dual-rate; 4 budgeted, actual; 5 Operating; 6 reciprocal (reciprocal allocation); 7 step-down (step-down allocation, sequential); 8 Common costs.

II.

1 F	5 F	9 T	13 F
2 F	6 T	10 T
3 T	7 T	11 T
4 T	8 F	12 T

Explanations:

1 The starting point in cost allocations is to choose the cost object. (F)

2 The cause-and-effect criterion is superior to the other criteria used to guide cost allocation decisions when the purpose of the allocation is economic decisions or motivation. When the cause-and-effect criterion is not operational, the benefits-received criterion is often used. (F)

3 The costs of a cost allocation system include gathering data and educating managers about the system. The benefits are making a better collective set of operating decisions. The costs of a cost allocation system are more visible and easier to measure than the benefits. (T)

4 Whether a particular cost is direct or indirect depends on the cost object chosen. The plant manager's salary would be a direct cost of the plant itself and would be an indirect cost of the products manufactured at the plant. (T)

5 When the degree of homogeneity is greater, *more* cost items will have the same or similar cause-and-effect relationships with the allocation bases. Therefore, *fewer* cost pools are required to accurately show differences in how products use resources of a company. (F)

6 This rule of thumb stems from the low cost and simplicity of implementing the single-rate method. (T)

7 The two main factors beyond the control of the user-department managers are the efficiency of the support departments and the usage by other departments. By using budgeted cost rates to allocate variable costs and budgeted usage to allocate fixed costs, the managers of support departments are motivated to improve efficiency, and the managers of user departments are motivated to use services wisely. (T)

8 Exhibit 14-5 shows that using actual usage does affect the allocation of fixed costs to departments when fluctuations in usage occur. The allocation would not be affected by fluctuations in usage if the allocation base is budgeted usage. (F)

9 Top management can counteract this temptation by systematically comparing actual usage with budgeted usage. Subordinate managers can be rewarded for making accurate long-run forecasts or penalized for underestimating budgeted usage. (T)

10 See Exhibit 14-8. (T)

11 See Exhibit 14-9. For the Information Systems Department, the complete reciprocated cost is $124,816 and the actual cost is $116,000. (T)

12 These budgeted department overhead rates are used for inventory costing purposes. (T)

13 For example, in the textbook illustration, the FASB (the primary user) was allocated $480,000 under the incremental method versus $375,000 under the stand-alone method. (F)

III.

1 c	4 d	7 d	10 d
2 d	5 c	8 e	
3 b	6 a	9 b	

Explanations:

1 Total budgeted overhead costs of each operating department (after allocation of all support department costs) are the numerator in the computation of the budgeted overhead rate. Examples of the denominator are machine-hours or labor-hours. See the table in the textbook (p. 515). (c)

2 The reciprocal method is the most accurate method for allocating support department costs because it fully incorporates the interdepartmental relationships among support departments. The direct method is the most widely used because of its simplicity. (d)

3 The direct method ignores services rendered by support departments to other support departments. (b)

4 The equation must include A's own costs plus its percentage use of B's services, 10%. (d)

5 $.15 \div (.15 + .30 + .15) = .15 \div .60 = .25$. (c)

6 Once a support department's costs have been allocated under the step-down method, no subsequent support department costs are allocated back to it. (a)

7 From Quality Control:

$$\frac{7,000}{21,000 + 7,000} \times \$350,000 = \qquad \$\ 87,500$$

From Maintenance

$$\frac{12,000}{18,000 + 12,000} \times \$200,000 = \qquad \underline{80,000}$$

Total support costs allocated to Assembly $\underline{\$167,500}$ (d)

8 From Quality Control:

$$\frac{21,000}{21,000 + 7,000} \times \$350,000 = \qquad \$262,500$$

From Maintenance:

$$\frac{18,000}{18,000 + 12,000} \times \$200,000 = \qquad \underline{120,000}$$

Total support costs allocated to Assembly $\underline{\$382,500}$

$$\text{Budgeted total overhead rate} = \frac{\$382,500 + \$400,000}{50,000} = \$15.65 \text{ per machine-hour (e)}$$

9

	Quality Control	Maintenance	Machining	Assembly	Total
Budgeted OH costs before allocation	$350,000	$200,000	$400,000	$300,000	$1,250,000
Allocation of QC (7/35, 21/35, 7/35)	(350,000)	70,000	210,000	70,000	
	$ 0	270,000			
Allocation of Maintenance (18/30, 12/30)		(270,000)	162,000	108,000 (b)	
		$ 0			
Total support costs allocated to production departments			$772,000	$478,000	$1,250,000

10   QC = $350,000 + .25M
      M = $200,000 + .20QC

     QC = $350,000 + .25($200,000 + .20QC)
     QC = $350,000 + $50,000 + .05QC
 .95QC = $400,000
     QC = $421,053 (d)

IV. Hanover Company

  1. Total cost pool (budgeted) = $80,000 + (240,000 + 160,000)$0.20 = $80,000 + $8...
       = $160,000;
     Cost per KWH for both A and B = $160,000 ÷ (240,000 + 160,000) = $0.4...
     Total costs allocated to A = 215,000 × $0.40 = $86,000
     Total costs allocated to B = 195,000 × $0.40 = $78,000

2. Fixed cost allocation:

   To A = [240,000 ÷ (240,000 + 160,000)] × \$80,000 = .60 × \$80,000 = \$48,000
   To B = [160,000 ÷ (240,000 + 160,000)] × \$80,000 = .40 × \$80,000 = \$32,000

   Total cost allocation:

   To A = \$48,000 + (215,000 × \$0.20) = \$48,000 + \$43,000 = \$91,000
   To B = \$32,000 + (195,000 × \$0.20) = \$32,000 + \$39,000 = \$71,000

3. The single-rate method has a low cost of implementation. It avoids the often expensive analysis necessary to classify individual cost items of a department into variable and fixed categories.

4. Use a dual rate when a single rate does not adequately describe the cost behavior pattern of the cost pool.

V. Zooker Manufacturing Company

	T	V	1	2	Total
Budgeted manufacturing overhead before allocation	\$60,000	\$ 80,000	\$ 30,000	\$25,000	\$195,000
Allocation of T: (see below)	(70,103)	21,031	35,051[a]	14,021[b]	
Allocation of V: (see below)	10,103	(101,031)	60,619[c]	30,309[d]	
	\$ 0	\$ 0			
Total budgeted manufacturing overhead of production departments			\$125,670	\$69,330	\$195,000

[a]50% × \$70,103 = \$35,051
[b]20% × \$70,103 = \$14,021
[c]60% × \$101,031 = \$60,619
[d]30% × \$101,031 = \$30,309

$T = \$60,000 + .10V$
$V = \$80,000 + .30T$

$T = \$60,000 + .10(\$80,000 + .30T)$
$T = \$60,000 + \$8,000 + .03T$
$.97T = \$68,000$
$T = \$70,103$

$V = \$80,000 + .30(\$70,103)$
$V = \$80,000 + \$21,031 = \$101,031$

VI. Adams Company and Baker Company

1. Adams, as the primary user, would bear \$48,000. Baker would bear \$55,000 − \$48,000 = \$7,000.

2. Total individual stand-alone costs = \$60,000 + \$20,000 = \$80,000
   Allocated to Adams = (\$60,000 ÷ \$80,000) × \$55,000 = \$41,250
   Allocated to Baker = (\$20,000 ÷ \$80,000) × \$55,000 = \$13,750

COST ALLOCATION: II

MAIN FOCUS AND OBJECTIVES

An important theme of the textbook, "different costs for different purposes," underlies this chapter. Several related questions are explored:

- How are value-chain costs assigned to products?
- Why might a company intentionally use cost allocation bases that are not cost drivers?
- What is the relationship between unused capacity costs and the downward demand spiral?
- What is the role of the Cost Accounting Standards Board?

Your overall objective for this chapter is to understand how decisions on cost allocation are guided by the cause-and-effect or benefits received criterion and the purpose for which cost information is desired. (The four purposes of cost allocation are presented in the preceding chapter's Exhibit 14-1.) Nine learning objectives are stated in the textbook (p. 536).

Give special attention to:

- the significance of deciding between a plantwide overhead rate and department overhead rates
- accounting for the costs of unused capacity
- cost allocations to determine contract reimbursements
- how cost allocation relates to the concept of cost hierarchies

REVIEW OF KEY TERMS AND CONCEPTS

A. *How are value-chain costs assigned to products?* Issues related to this challenging question are discussed by means of the textbook example, Consumer Appliances (beginning p. 536).
   1. A five-step general approach is used to assign costs to the deluxe refrigerator model.
      a. Three *direct costs* are *traced* to this product.
      b. Six *indirect costs* are *allocated* to this product.
   2. The allocation rate for each indirect cost pool is calculated as follows:

$$\text{Budgeted indirect cost rate} = \frac{\text{Budgeted total costs in indirect cost pool}}{\text{Budgeted total quantity of cost allocation base}}$$

3. Exhibit 15-1 provides an overview of Consumer Appliances' product-costing system.
4. The theme "different costs for different purposes" is reinforced in Exhibit 15-2.
    a. Full product costs (all value-chain costs) are used for long-run pricing and product emphasis decisions.
    b. Inventoriable costs (all manufacturing costs) and period costs (customer warranty, distribution, and marketing costs) are distinguished for financial reporting under generally accepted accounting principles.
5. Deciding what cost pools to form should be guided by *the concept of cost pool homogeneity*.
6. A cost pool is homogeneous when all of the individual activities whose costs are included in the pool have the same or a similar cause-and-effect relationship or benefits-received relationship between the cost driver and the costs of the activity.

Question: **Should a company producing many products allocate manufacturing overhead via a plantwide rate or department rates?**
Answer: **Department rates are preferable if (i) the plantwide overhead cost pool is *not* homogeneous and/or (ii) the individual products *differ significantly* in their usage of the resources of individual departments.**

---

7. Because the two conditions in the box are present in many companies, department rates are often used in manufacturing as well as other business functions in the value chain.
8. The Consumer Appliances example is continued (p. 539) to illustrate overhead allocation by a plantwide rate versus department rates. The results are much different.

Carefully study the textbook table (p. 540). Be aware why more accurate product costs are obtained under department rates:
- **Deluxe refrigerators are assigned more overhead because they make relatively high use of the machine-paced assembly and quality-testing departments (the plantwide rate would undercost this product).**
- **Clothes dryers are assigned less overhead because they make relatively low use of the machine-paced assembly and quality-testing departments (the plantwide rate would overcost this product).**

See Practice Test Problem IV.

B. Several trends are evolving in cost assignment practices that reflect developments in the business environment.
    1. Changes in a costing system should be considered when changes occur in information technology (such as metering and bar coding), in the underlying operations (such as increased automation), in the number of products manufactured, or in competition.

a. Companies are attempting to increase the percentage of total product costs that are classified as direct costs.

b. Companies are using a larger number of separate indirect cost pools and cost allocation bases (for example, a separate machining cost pool allocated on the basis of machine-hours).

2. The type of work environment often influences a company's choice of cost allocation bases.

a. *Labor-paced manufacturing environment*: worker dexterity and productivity determine the speed of production, and machines are tools that aid production workers.

b. Note that using direct manufacturing labor costs or hours as an allocation base may still capture cause-and-effect relationships in a labor-paced manufacturing environment, *even if operations are highly automated*.

c. *Machine-paced manufacturing environment*: machines conduct most or all phases of production, and workers may simultaneously operate more than one machine.

d. Machine-hours likely will better capture cause-and-effect relationships than direct manufacturing labor-hours in machine-paced manufacturing environments.

3. Some companies use nonfinancial variables as their cost allocation bases.

a. One example is *manufacturing lead time*: the amount of time from when an order is ready to start on the production line to when it is finished.

(1) The rationale for using this allocation base is that longer lead time frequently adds to a plant's indirect costs.

(2) Using this allocation base signals to operating personnel that reported product costs can be reduced by shortening manufacturing lead time.

b. Another example is cubic volume of product for allocating distribution and handling costs in retail companies.

4. If product costs result from allocation bases that do not capture cause-and-effect or benefits-received relationships, managers may make decisions that conflict with maximizing long-run company net income; four possible negative consequences of using direct labor costs as an allocation base in machine-paced manufacturing environments are described in the textbook example (p. 543).

> ***Question*: Why might a company intentionally use allocation bases that are not cost drivers (that is, do not meet the cause-and-effect criterion)?**
>
> ***Answer*: See the three reasons discussed in the textbook (p. 544).**

C. Accounting for the costs of unused capacity is an important topic because many organizations have excess capacity.

1. The costs of unused capacity are fixed costs of manufacturing plants, distribution networks, sales forces, and other resources.

2. Consider the following formula:

$$\text{Budgeted fixed cost rate} = \frac{\text{Budgeted fixed costs}}{\text{Budgeted quantity of cost allocation base}}$$

a. Managers are faced with several alternative choices for the denominator.

b. Two denominator alternatives (of the four discussed in section E(3) of Chapter 9's outline, p. 116):

    (1) *Practical capacity*: theoretical capacity reduced for unavoidable operating interruptions, such as scheduled maintenance time and shutdown for holidays.

    (2) *Master-budget utilization*: the anticipated level of capacity utilization for the coming budget period (often less than practical capacity).

3. In the textbook example of Rightway Foodmarkets (p. 545), fixed costs are $12,000,000, master-budget utilization is 5,000,000 ton miles, and practical capacity is 8,000,000 ton miles.

    a. Alternative fixed cost rates are: $12,000,000 ÷ 5,000,000 = $2.40 per ton mile, and $12,000,000 ÷ 8,000,000 = $1.50 per ton mile.

    b. The $2.40 rate based on the master-budget utilization level *excludes* the costs of unused capacity; therefore, fixed costs tend to be *fully allocated*.

    c. The $1.50 rate based on the practical capacity level *includes* the costs of unused capacity; therefore, fixed costs likely would be *underallocated*.

        (1) The costs of unused capacity can be reported as a line item in the income statement.

        (2) This approach highlights the costs of unused capacity, which are the responsibility of the manager authorized to determine capacity levels.

4. Related to the costs of unused capacity is the possibility of a downward demand spiral.

    a. **Downward demand spiral** (also called *black hole demand spiral*): the continuing reduction in demand that occurs when prices are raised and then raised again in an attempt to recover fixed costs from an ever-decreasing customer base.

    b. If Rightway Foodmarket uses the higher rate based on master-budget utilization and the option to outsource is available, managers may buy distribution services from an outside supplier.

    c. Outsourcing would cause a downward demand spiral — master-budget utilization for the next period decreases, rates increase, and more outsourcing occurs.

> **Another situation leading to the downward demand spiral is where a costing system overcosts high-volume products and undercosts low-volume products. Competitors may "cherry-pick" the high-volume products, leaving a company with the low-volume products. If the company spreads its costs over these products, the downward spiral will continue.**

D. Cost allocations are often used to determine reimbursement under contracts, both government contracts and contracts between companies.

1. The areas of dispute between the contract parties can be reduced by making the *"rules of the game"* as explicit as possible (and in writing) and well understood when the contract is signed.

2. Rules of the game include the definition of cost items allowed, the cost pools, and the permissible allocation bases.

a. **Allowable cost**: a cost that the parties to a contract agree to include in the costs to be reimbursed.

b. In U.S. government contracts, nonallowable costs include lobbying and alcoholic beverages.

3. The U.S. government reimburses most contractors in either of two ways:

a. Contractor is paid a preset price without analysis of actual contract cost data, such as in competitive bidding or established catalog prices.

b. Contractor is paid after analysis of actual contract cost data, such as a cost-plus contract or a fixed-price contract.

4. All contracts with any U.S. government agency must comply with cost accounting standards.

a. These standards are issued by the **Cost Accounting Standards Board (CASB)**.

b. The aim of the CASB is to achieve *uniformity* and *consistency* in cost accounting practices for contracts under its authority.

c. Exhibit 15-3 lists the titles of selected standards issued by the CASB that are incorporated into Federal Acquisition Regulations (FARs).

d. FARs are procurement regulations with which government contractors must comply.

e. The CASB prohibits *double counting*, which occurs when a cost item is included both as a direct cost of a contract and as part of an indirect cost pool allocated to this contract.

f. Exhibit 15-4 provides examples of the allocation bases used in Standard 403 for home office expenses.

E. There is growing interest in cost assignment related to several types of cost hierarchies.

1. **Cost hierarchies**: categorizations of costs into different cost pools on the basis of different classes of cost drivers or different degrees of difficulty in determining cause-and-effect relationships.

2. Four types of cost hierarchies are discussed in the textbook.

3. One type of cost hierarchy is where the cost object is a product.

a. The *four hierarchical levels of costs* in this case are output unit-level costs, batch-level costs, product-sustaining costs, and facility-sustaining costs.

b. This cost hierarchy is discussed in section E of Chapter 10's outline (pp. 129-30).

4. A second type of hierarchy is an *organization-structure cost hierarchy*.

a. In this case, costs are classified according to *organization subunits* or *segments* (for example, plants, divisions, corporate).

> **Exhibit 15-5 illustrates cost assignment under an organization-structure cost hierarchy.**

b. Note these important points about Exhibit 15-5:

(1) A contribution income statement is used.

(2) The four key line items are numbered.

(3) Line item (2) measures the *segment manager's performance*.

(4) Line item (3) measures the *performance of the segment as an economic investment*.

(5) $135,000 of fixed costs is *not* allocated to divisions; examples include corporate income taxes and interest on company debt.

    d. *See Practice Test Question III (items 4-6) and Problems V and VI.*

5. A third type of hierarchy is a *customer cost hierarchy*.
    a. Given that customer satisfaction is priority one in the modern management approach, companies desire to refine their customer costing systems.
    b. Customer costing systems are discussed in the textbook (pp. 118-24) and in section F of Chapter 4's outline (p. 42).
    c. Exhibit 15-6 illustrates a customer cost hierarchy that has three levels:
        (1) Customer-specific costs (includes both direct and indirect costs)
        (2) Customer-line costs (allocated to direct sale line and retail-outlet line)
        (3) Company costs (not allocated to customer lines or individual customers)
    d. The information in Exhibit 15-6 helps managers make decisions that affect different levels of operations, such as which customers to emphasize or downplay and how to allocate the marketing budget between the direct sale and retail-outlet lines.
    e. More information on customer-costing is in section F of Chapter 4's outline (p. 42).

6. A fourth type of hierarchy is a *brand cost hierarchy*.
    a. In this case, costs are classified into three categories:
        (1) Individual product-level costs
        (2) Related product-line costs
        (3) Brand-level costs
    b. See the textbook example that applies this hierarchy to Nestlé Company (p. 552).

PRACTICE TEST QUESTIONS AND PROBLEMS

I. Complete each of the following statements.

1. For assigning costs to products, a budgeted indirect cost pool is divided by a _____ _____ to calculate the _____.

2. In a _____, worker dexterity and productivity are tools that aid production workers.

3. The amount of time from when an order is ready to start on the production line to when it is finished is called _____ _____.

4. _____ is theoretical capacity reduced for unavoidable operating interruptions, such as scheduled maintenance time and shutdown for holidays.

5. The anticipated level of capacity utilization for the coming budget period is called ____ _____.

6. _____ is the continuing reduction in demand that occurs when prices are raised and then raised again in an attempt to recover fixed costs from an ever-decreasing customer base.

7. A cost that the parties to a contract agree to include in the costs to be reimbursed is called a(an) _____.

8. CASB stands for _____ _____.

9. _____ are categorizations of costs into different cost pools on the basis of different classes of cost drivers or different degrees of difficulty in determining cause-and-effect relationships.

II. Indicate whether each of the following statements is true or false by putting T or F in the space provided.

____ 1. Full product costs are used for the purpose of financial reporting under generally accepted accounting principles.

___ 2. In many cases homogeneity of cost pools likely would be increased by increasing the number of cost pools.

___ 3. Department overhead rates will provide more accurate product costs than a plantwide overhead rate if the individual products are the same or similar in their usage of the resources of individual departments.

___ 4. Changes in a costing system should be considered when changes occur in the number of products manufactured or in competition.

___ 5. Increased automation necessarily means that direct labor would be an inappropriate cost allocation base.

___ 6. If direct labor is used as a cost allocation base in a machine-paced manufacturing environment and the option to outsource is available, managers would tend to make excessive use of external vendors for parts with high direct labor content.

___ 7. Using manufacturing lead time as a cost allocation base can be an effective way to motivate managers to reduce product costs.

___ 8. A company may prefer to use direct manufacturing labor-hours as a base for product costing even if management knows that the cause-and-effect relationship is not good.

___ 9. The costs of unused capacity are fixed costs that relate exclusively to manufacturing plants.

___ 10. Budgeted fixed overhead rates based on the master-budget utilization level include the costs of unused capacity.

___ 11. To highlight the costs of unused capacity, these costs can be reported as a line item in the income statement.

___ 12. Budgeted fixed overhead rates based on the practical capacity level are more likely to lead to a downward demand spiral than those based on the master-budget utilization level.

___ 13. In U.S. government contracts, lobbying costs are a nonallowable cost.

___ 14. If a company is using an organization-structure cost hierarchy and a particular cost cannot be allocated to divisions in a meaningful way, the cost should be allocated to divisions on the basis of their respective revenues.

III. Select the best answer for each of the following multiple-choice questions and put the identifying letter in the space provided.

___ 1. (CPA) Of most relevance in deciding how indirect costs should be allocated to products is the degree of:
  a. avoidability.
  b. causality.
  c. controllability.
  d. linearity.

___ 2. (CMA) Because of changes that are occurring in the basic operations of many companies, all of the following represent trends in the way indirect costs are allocated *except*:
  a. treating direct manufacturing labor as an indirect cost in an automated plant.
  b. using manufacturing lead time as an allocation base to increase awareness of the costs associated with lengthened production time.
  c. preferring plantwide allocation rates that are based on machine-hours rather than more detailed allocations.
  d. using several machine cost pools to measure product costs on the basis of time in a machine center.
  e. using cost drivers as allocation bases to increase the accuracy of reported product costs.

___ 3. (CMA adapted) The Cost Accounting Standards Board's purpose is to:
  a. develop accounting principles and standard practices for industry.
  b. develop uniform cost accounting standards to be used in pricing, administration, and settlement of negotiated government contracts.
  c. work in conjunction with the Securities and Exchange Commission in examining registration forms and statements filed by corporations.
  d. aid the Financial Accounting Standards Board in establishing accounting standards.

4. (CPA) Gata Co. plans to discontinue a segment with a $48,000 contribution to overhead, and allocated overhead of $96,000, of which $42,000 cannot be eliminated. What would be the effect of this discontinuance on Gata's operating income?
   a. Increase of $6,000
   b. Decrease of $6,000
   c. Increase of $48,000
   d. Decrease of $48,000

5. (CMA) Generally, the appropriate basis on which to evaluate the performance of a division manager is the division's:
   a. contribution margin.
   b. revenue minus controllable division costs.
   c. gross margin.
   d. net income minus the division's fixed costs.
   e. revenue minus variable division costs.

6. The performance of a segment as an economic investment is best measured by:
   a. operating income.
   b. contribution margin.
   c. contribution margin minus fixed costs controllable by the segment manager.
   d. contribution controllable by the segment manager minus allocated fixed costs controllable by others.

IV. Harjo Company manufactures two products, T-68 and K-71. Manufacturing overhead is allocated to these products on the basis of direct manufacturing labor-hours (DMLH). The following information is available for 19_3:

Production Department	Budgeted Overhead	Budgeted DMLH
J	$360,000	10,000
P	150,000	15,000
	$510,000	25,000

	T-68	K-71
DMLH required:		
Department J	6	1
Department P	2	5
R&D and product design costs	$ 10	$ 12
Direct materials costs	140	200
Direct manufacturing labor costs	110	110
Marketing, distribution, and customer-service costs	70	78

At the end of 19_3, finished goods inventory was 150 units of T-68 and 500 units of K-71. There was no work in process. Harjo's selling prices are equal to full product costs plus a markup of 30% of full product costs.

1. Compute the cost of finished goods inventory of each product at the end of 19_3:
   a. Using a budgeted plantwide overhead rate.
   b. Using budgeted department overhead rates.
2. Compute the selling price of each product:
   a. Using a budgeted plantwide overhead rate.
   b. Using budgeted department overhead rates.
3. Should Harjo prefer a plantwide overhead rate or department overhead rates? Explain.

Check figures: (1) T-68 using plantwide rate, $61,980; K-71 using department rates, $198,000 (2) T-68 using department rates, $735.80; K-71 using plantwide rate, $679.12

V. From the following data (in thousands) for Hawthorne Company, use an organization-structure cost hierarchy to prepare a controllability-based contribution income statement by divisions.

	Company As a Whole	Alpha Division	Omega Division
Net revenues	$900	$500	$400
Fixed costs:			
Controllable by segment manager(s)	140	60	80
Controllable by others	70	30	40
Variable costs:			
Manufacturing cost of goods sold	450	300	150
Marketing and administrative costs	130	60	70
Unallocated costs	75	–	–

Check figure: Contribution by Alpha Division $50,000

VI. (CMA) Cosmo Inc.'s income statement by segments for November 19_4 is as follows:

	Total	Mall Store	Town Store
Sales	$200,000	$80,000	$120,000
Variable costs	116,000	32,000	84,000
Contribution margin	84,000	48,000	36,000
Direct fixed costs	60,000	20,000	40,000
Contribution by store	24,000	28,000	(4,000)
Indirect fixed costs	10,000	4,000	6,000
Operating income	$ 14,000	$24,000	$(10,000)

Additional information regarding Cosmo's operations is as follows:

- One-fourth of each store's direct fixed costs would continue through December 31, 19_5, if either store were closed.
- Cosmo allocates indirect fixed costs to each store on the basis of sales dollars. These costs are regarded as unavoidable.
- Management estimates that closing the Town Store would result in a 10% decrease in Mall Store sales, while closing the Mall Store would not affect Town Store sales.
- The operating results for November 19_4 are representative of all months.

1. Compute the increase (decrease) in Cosmo's monthly operating income during 19_5 if the Town Store is closed.
2. Suppose Cosmo is considering a promotion campaign at the Town Store that would not affect the Mall Store. Compute the increase (decrease) in Cosmo's monthly operating income during 19_5, assuming annual promotion costs at the Town Store are increased by $60,000 and its sales increase by 10%.
3. Suppose 50% of Town Store's sales are from items sold at variable cost in order to attract customers to the store. Cosmo is considering the deletion of these items, a move that would reduce the Town Store's direct fixed costs by 15% and result in the loss of 20% of its remaining sales. This change would not affect the Mall Store. Compute the increase (decrease) in Cosmo's monthly operating income during 19_5, assuming the items sold at variable cost are eliminated.

Check figures: (1) $10,800 decrease (2) $1,400 decrease (3) $1,200 decrease

CHAPTER 15 SOLUTIONS TO PRACTICE TEST

I. 1 budgeted cost allocation base, budgeted indirect cost rate; 2 labor-paced manufacturing environment; 3 manufacturing lead time; 4 Practical capacity; 5 master-budget utilization; 6 Downward demand spiral (Black hole demand spiral); 7 allowable cost; 8 Cost Accounting Standards Board; 9 cost hierarchies.

II.

1 F	5 F	9 F	13 T
2 T	6 T	10 F	14 F
3 F	7 T	11 T	
4 T	8 T	12 F	

Explanations:

1 Full product costs (all value-chain costs) are used for long-run pricing and product emphasis decisions. Inventoriable costs (all manufacturing costs) and period costs (all nonmanufacturing costs) are used for the purpose of financial reporting under generally accepted accounting principles. (F)

2 A cost pool is homogeneous when all of the individual activities whose costs are included in the cost pool have the same or a similar cause-and-effect relationship or benefits-received relationship between the cost driver and the costs of the activity. When a given cost pool is not homogeneous, more accurate product costs can be computed by separating this pool into two or more cost pools. This approach helps managers find better cause-and-effect or benefits-received relationships. (T)

3 Department overhead rates are preferable to a plantwide overhead rate if (i) the individual products *differ significantly* in their usage of the resources of individual departments and/or (ii) the plantwide overhead cost pool is *not* homogeneous. (F)

4 The statement is true. Changes in a costing system also should be considered when changes occur in information technology (such as metering or bar coding) or in the underlying operations (such as increased automation). (T)

5 The key to whether direct labor would be an appropriate cost allocation base is the type of manufacturing environment, not the extent of automation per se. In labor-paced manufacturing environments, worker dexterity and productivity determine the speed of production. In machine-paced manufacturing environments, machines conduct most or all phases of production. Direct labor may be an appropriate cost allocation base in labor-paced manufacturing even if operations are highly automated. (F)

6 If direct labor is used as a cost allocation base in a machine-paced manufacturing environment, a part with high direct labor content would be overcosted. Therefore, external vendors' selling prices for this part would be attractive to managers. (T)

7 The rationale for using this allocation base is that longer manufacturing lead time frequently adds to a plant's indirect costs. Using this allocation base signals to operating personnel that reported product costs can be reduced by shortening manufacturing lead time. (T)

8 Direct manufacturing labor-hours may be preferred in this situation because improving the accuracy of individual product costs is less important to the company than other goals. For example, management may view increased automation as a strategic necessity to remain competitive in the long run. Using direct manufacturing labor-hours as the allocation base motivates product designers to decrease the direct labor content of the products they design. (T)

9 The costs of unused capacity are fixed costs of manufacturing plants, distribution networks, sales forces, and other resources. (F)

10 Budgeted fixed overhead rates based on the master-budget utilization level *exclude* the costs of unused capacity. Budgeted fixed overhead rates based on the practical capacity level *include* the costs of unused capacity. See the textbook example of Rightway Foodmarkets (p. 545) for a numerical illustration. (F)

11 This approach dovetails with responsibility accounting. The costs of unused capacity are the responsibility of the manager authorized to determine capacity levels. (T)

12 Budgeted fixed overhead rates based on the master-budget utilization level are usually *higher* than those based on the practical capacity level. Because of this higher rate, managers may outsource rather than buy internally. If so, a downward demand spiral begins—master-budget utilization for the next period decreases, rates increase, and more outsourcing occurs. (F)

13 The statement is true. Another example of a nonallowable cost in U.S. government contracts is alcoholic beverages. (T)

14 This cost should not be allocated to divisions. An example is the $135,000 at the bottom of Exhibit 15-5. (F)

III.
1	b	4	a
2	c	5	b
3	b	6	d

Explanations:

1 Decisions on cost allocation are guided by the cause-and-effect criterion. That is, it is desirable that all individual activities whose costs are included in a cost pool have the same or a similar cause-and-effect relationship between the cost driver and the costs of the activity. (b)

2 In most cases, a plantwide overhead rate is *not* preferred over more detailed allocations such as department overhead rates. (c)

3 The purpose of the CASB is to promulgate cost accounting standards in order to achieve *uniformity* and *consistency* in the cost accounting principles followed by contractors under its authority. (b) Note that answer (a) is incorrect because only cost accounting standards (as distinguished from *financial* accounting standards) are promulgated by the CASB.

4

	Before Discontinuance	After Discontinuance
Contribution to overhead	$ 48,000	$ 0
Deduct allocated overhead	96,000	42,000
Operating income of segment	$(48,000)	$(42,000)
Difference in favor of discontinuing the segment	$6,000 (a)	

5 The performance of a division manager should be evaluated on the basis of the items he or she can control, namely revenues and controllable fixed costs. The corresponding figure for Division B in Exhibit 15-5 is $300,000. (b)

6 For an example of this performance measure, see Exhibit 15-5; the contribution of Division A is a negative $10,000. (d)

IV. Harjo Company

1. Plantwide rate = $510,000 ÷ 25,000 = $20.40 per DMLH
   Department rates:
   Department J = $360,000 ÷ 10,000 = $36 per DMLH
   Department P = $150,000 ÷ 15,000 = $10 per DMLH

	T-68		K-71	
	(a) Plantwide Rate	(b) Dept. Rates	(a) Plantwide Rate	(b) Dept. Rates
Direct materials costs	$140.00	$140.00	$ 200.00	$ 200.00
Direct manufacturing labor costs	110.00	110.00	110.00	110.00
Manufacturing overhead costs,				
$(6 + 2) \times \$20.40$; $(1 + 5) \times \$20.40$	163.20		122.40	
$(6 \times \$36) + (2 \times \$10)$; $(1 \times \$36) + (5 \times \$10)$		236.00		86.00
Inventoriable (total manufacturing) costs per unit	$413.20	$486.00	$ 432.40	$ 396.00
Multiply by units of ending finished goods	× 150	× 150	× 500	× 500
Ending finished goods inventory	$61,980	$72,900	$216,200	$198,000
Difference due to the way overhead is allocated	$10,920		$18,200	

2.

	$413.20	$486.00	$432.40	$396.00
Total manufacturing costs per unit (from part 1)	$413.20	$486.00	$432.40	$396.00
R&D and product design costs	10.00	10.00	12.00	12.00
Marketing, distribution and customer-service costs	70.00	70.00	78.00	78.00
Full product costs	493.20	566.00	522.40	486.00
Markup (at 30%)	147.96	169.80	156.72	145.80
Selling price	$641.16	$735.80	$679.12	$631.80
Difference due to the way overhead is allocated	$94.64		$47.32	

3. Department overhead rates should be preferred because (i) the production departments differ significantly in their cost structures in relation to DMLH, indicating that the plantwide overhead cost pool is not homogeneous and (ii) the two products differ significantly in their usage of the resources of the production departments.

V. Hawthorne Company (in thousands)

	Total	Alpha Division	Omega Division
Net revenues	$900	$500	$400
Variable manufacturing cost of goods sold	450	300	150
Manufacturing contribution margin	450	200	250
Variable marketing and administrative costs	130	60	70
Contribution margin	320	140	180
Fixed costs controllable by division manager(s)	140	60	80
Contribution controllable by division manager(s)	180	80	100
Fixed costs controllable by others	70	30	40
Contribution by division	110	$ 50	$ 60
Unallocated costs	75		
Operating income	$ 35		

VI. Cosmo Inc.

1. Compare the company's total operating income at present, $14,000, with the amount of operating income from the proposed situation of operating only the Mall Store:

		Proposed Situation
Contribution margin of Mall Store, $48,000 × 90%		$43,200
Deduct:		
Direct fixed costs of Mall Store	$20,000	
Unavoidable direct fixed costs of Town Store, $40,000 × 25%	10,000	
Indirect fixed costs of company as a whole	10,000	
Total fixed costs		40,000
Operating income of company as a whole		$ 3,200

Therefore, by closing the Town Store, operating income for the year would decrease by $14,000 − $3,200 = $10,800.

2. The two items affected in the proposed situation are the Town Store's contribution margin and its promotion costs. Monthly contribution margin would increase by $36,000 × 10% = $3,600. *Monthly* promotion costs would be $60,000 ÷ 12 = $5,000. Therefore, monthly operating income of the Town Store would decrease by $5,000 − $3,600 = $1,400.

3. Compare the Town Store's contribution at present, −$4,000, with the amount of its contribution with the proposed changes:

Town Store		Proposed Situation
Sales, .50 × $120,000 × (1 − .20)		$48,000
Deduct:		
Variable costs		
50% of original sales of $120,000 are variable costs and would be avoided; also there will be a 20% reduction in the *remainder* of the original variable costs, ($84,000 − $60,000) × (1 − .20)	$19,200	
Direct fixed costs, $40,000 × (1 − .15)	34,000	
Total costs		53,200
Contribution by store		$ (5,200)

Therefore, the proposed situation would result in the Town Store's contribution decreasing from −$4,000 to −$5,200. This $1,200 decrease is also the effect on the company's operating income because indirect fixed costs, regardless of how they are allocated between the two stores, would remain the same in total.

CHAPTER 16

COST ALLOCATION: JOINT PRODUCTS AND BYPRODUCTS

MAIN FOCUS AND OBJECTIVES

Many industries have processes that yield two or more products simultaneously. For example, in the lumber industry logs yield finished lumber of various grades, bark, wood chips, and sawdust. Such industries classify their products as joint or main products, byproducts, and scrap – with the distinction depending on the relative sales values. In this chapter, the focus is on allocating joint costs to individual products for the purpose of measuring income and assets for reporting to external parties.

Your overall objective for this chapter is to understand the methods for allocating joint costs to products and to be able to apply the concept of relevance (introduced in Chapter 11) to decisions of whether joint products and byproducts should be sold at the splitoff point or processed further. Seven learning objectives are stated in the textbook (p. 570).

Give special attention to four methods for allocating joint costs:

- sales value at splitoff
- physical measure
- estimated net realizable value (NRV)
- constant gross-margin percentage NRV

Also give special attention to:

- why joint costs, however allocated, are irrelevant in deciding whether to process an individual product beyond splitoff
- four methods of accounting for byproducts

REVIEW OF KEY TERMS AND CONCEPTS

A. Allocating joint costs to products can be thought of as a *special case* of cost allocation because the cause-and-effect criterion is not operational in this case.
   1. Seven key terms are applicable to this topic.
      a. **Joint costs**: the costs of a single process that yields multiple products simultaneously.
      b. **Splitoff point**: the juncture in the process where the products become separately identifiable.

> **Exhibit 16-1 provides examples of joint-cost situations in diverse industries.**

c. **Separable costs**: the costs incurred beyond the splitoff point that are assignable to individual products.

d. **Joint products** have relatively high sales value and are not separately identifiable as individual products until the splitoff point. The special case in a joint-products situation occurs when there is only one joint product, which is called a main product.

e. A **main product** arises when a single process yielding two or more products yields *only one* product with a relatively high sales value.

f. **Byproducts** have relatively low sales value compared with the sales value of the main or joint product(s).

g. **Scrap** has minimal (frequently zero) sales value.

h. Note that *"sales value"* is an integral part of the definitions of the last four terms—joint products, main product, byproducts, and scrap.

i. Also note that the classification of a given product on the basis of its sales value can change if its market price fluctuates widely over time.

> **Exhibit 16-2 gives an overview of the distinctions among joint and main product(s), byproducts, and scrap.**

2. In joint-cost situations, no individual product can be produced without the accompanying products appearing, although sometimes the proportions can be varied.

3. The two main purposes for allocating joint costs to individual products or services:

a. To measure income and assets for reporting to external parties, such as computing cost of goods sold and inventory costs under generally accepted accounting principles.

b. To justify costs or compute reimbursement, such as government contracts, settlement of insurance claims, or rate regulation of electric utilities.

4. Since no cause-and-effect relationship exists between individual products and joint costs, *managers should be reluctant to use joint-cost allocations for purposes of economic decisions or motivation.*

B. In joint-cost situations, there are three basic approaches to computing cost of goods sold and inventory costs.

> *Approach 1*: **Allocate costs using market selling-price data. Three common methods are used in applying this approach:**
> - **sales value at splitoff method**
> - **estimated net realizable value (NRV) method**
> - **constant gross-margin percentage NRV method**
>
> *Approach 2:* **Allocate costs using a physical measure.**
>
> *Approach 3:* **Do not allocate costs; use market selling-price data to guide inventory costing.**

1. The **sales value at splitoff method** allocates joint costs on the basis of each product's relative sales value at the splitoff point.

> **Exhibit 16-3's format for organizing the quantity, cost, and revenue data is helpful to visualize both the production process and the cost allocation process.** *Routinely sketch such diagrams in joint-cost situations.*

    a. See the textbook computations (p. 573) and the related product-line income statement (Exhibit 16-4).

    b. Note that this method uses the sales value of the *entire production of the period including the unsold portion*, not just the actual sales of the period.

    c. Advantages: the revenue-generating power of the products at splitoff is a simple and meaningful allocation base that does not presuppose any management decisions on further processing.

    d. Disadvantage: limited to situations where all products are salable at splitoff.

    e. *See Practice Test Question III (items 2 and 3).*

2. The **physical measure method** allocates joint costs on the basis of their relative proportions at splitoff, using a common weight or volume base such as pounds or gallons.

    a. See the textbook computations (p. 574) and the related product-line income statement (Exhibit 16-5).

    b. The major argument against this method is that it ignores the revenue-generating power of the individual products, which can result in showing unrealistically large gross margins on some products and consistent losses on others.

    c. However, the physical measure method is sometimes preferred to sales value methods in rate-regulation situations to set a fair selling price; the physical measure method avoids the circular reasoning of using selling prices to allocate joint costs that in turn serve as a basis for setting selling prices.

    d. *See Practice Test Question III (item 4).*

3. The **estimated net realizable value method** allocates joint costs on the basis of the relative estimated net realizable value (NRV).

$$\begin{array}{c} \text{NRV of a} \\ \text{product} \end{array} = \begin{array}{c} \textbf{Expected final sales value} \\ \textbf{in the ordinary course} \\ \textbf{of business} \end{array} - \begin{array}{c} \textbf{Expected separable} \\ \textbf{costs of production} \\ \textbf{and marketing} \end{array}$$

    a. See the textbook computations (p. 576) and the related product-line income statement (Exhibit 16-7).

    b. This method uses the NRV of the *entire production of the period*, not the NRV of actual final sales of the period.

    c. Advantage: can be used when one or more of the products is not salable at splitoff.

    d. Disadvantage: presupposes the exact number of further-processing steps to be undertaken, but managers may change these steps to exploit fluctuations in separable costs or selling prices.

    e. *See Practice Test Question III (items 5 and 6) and Problem IV (parts 1 and 2).*

4. The **constant gross-margin percentage NRV method** allocates joint costs in such a way that the overall gross-margin percentage is identical for all of the individual products.

a. This method entails a three-step procedure:

   Step 1: Compute the overall gross-margin percentage.

   Step 2: Use the overall gross-margin percentage and deduct the gross margin from the final sales values to obtain the total costs that each product should bear.

   Step 3: Deduct the expected separable costs from the total costs that each product should bear to obtain the joint-cost allocation.

   b. Exhibit 16-8 illustrates this three-step procedure; the related product-line income statement is in Exhibit 16-9.

   c. One rationale for this method is that, given the arbitrary nature of joint cost allocation, none of the products show a loss.

   d. The major argument against this method is that its underlying assumption is unrealistic; a uniform relationship between sales value and the costs of individual products is rare or virtually nonexistent for multiple-product situations not involving joint costs.

   e. *See Practice Test Problem IV (part 3).*

5. Many companies producing joint products **do not allocate the joint costs at all**.

   a. See the income statement in Exhibit 16-10.

   b. In these cases, inventories are carried at estimated net realizable value, thereby recognizing income when production is completed (*before* sales are made).

   c. Reducing estimated net realizable value by a normal profit margin avoids the usual accounting criticism of recognizing income before sales are made.

   d. Industries using variations of this practice include meat packing, canning, and mining.

   e. Some advocates of the no allocation approach believe that arbitrary allocations of joint costs could cause managers to make poor decisions.

C. The amount of joint costs incurred up to the splitoff point and how it is allocated are *both irrelevant* in deciding whether to process an individual product beyond splitoff.

   1. Why are the joint costs irrelevant? Because they are the same amount whether or not further processing is done.

   2. Therefore, the methods of joint-cost allocation (discussed in section B above) would mislead managers that rely on unit-cost data to guide their sell or process further decisions.

   3. *The only costs that are relevant to* **further processing decisions** *are the costs beyond the splitoff point.*

   4. It is profitable to process beyond splitoff if the *incremental revenue* is more than the *incremental costs* from such processing.

Example 3 in the textbook (p. 580) deals with the sell or process further decision. Carefully study this illustration.

---

5. Do not assume that separable costs are always incremental costs. Why? Because some separable costs may be allocated manufacturing costs that *do not differ* between the sell or process further alternatives.

6. *See Practice Test Question III (items 7 and 8) and Problem IV (parts 4 and 5).*

D. **Byproduct accounting** is an area where there is much inconsistency in practice and where the use of some methods is justified on the basis of expediency rather than theoretical soundness.
1. Byproducts have relatively low sales value compared with the sales value of the main or joint product(s).
2. Four methods can be used to account for byproducts.
   a. These methods are labeled A through D in the descriptive listing in the textbook (p. 583).
   b. Choosing one of these methods is not a particularly important decision because *the dollar amounts involved are, by definition, immaterial.*

> **Exhibit 16-13 illustrates methods A through D.**

3. Methods A and B recognize byproducts in the general ledger at the time they are *produced*.
   a. A small portion of the joint costs is allocated to the byproduct(s).
   b. The unsold quantity of byproduct(s) is inventoried at estimated net realizable value plus separable manufacturing costs incurred (if any).
4. Methods C and D recognize byproducts in the general ledger at the time they are *sold*.
   a. No joint costs are allocated to the byproduct(s).
   b. The unsold quantity of byproduct(s) is assigned zero cost for financial reporting to external parties.
5. *See Practice Test Question III (items 9 and 10) and Problem V.*

PRACTICE TEST QUESTIONS AND PROBLEMS

I. Complete each of the following statements.

1. The costs incurred beyond the _____ point that are assignable to individual products are called _____.
2. When two or more products of a single process have relatively high _____ and are not separately identifiable as individual products until the splitoff point, these products are called _____. When there is only one such product, it is called a _____.
3. _____ have relatively low sales value compared with the sales value of main or joint product(s).
4. The _____ method allocates joint costs on the basis of their relative proportions at splitoff using a common weight or volume.
5. _____ of a product is equal to expected final sales value in the

ordinary course of business minus expected separable costs of production and marketing.
6. The _____ _____ method allocates joint costs in such a way that the overall _____ _____ percentage is identical for all of the individual products.
7. Of the methods for allocating joint costs to products, name the three that use market selling price data: _____ _____ _____ _____.

II. Indicate whether each of the following statements is true or false by putting T or F in the space provided.

___ 1. Joint products have relatively high sales value and must be salable at the splitoff point.

___ 2. Because no cause-and-effect relationship exists between individual products and joint costs, managers should be reluctant to use joint-cost allocations for purposes of economic decisions or motivation.

___ 3. The size of the joint costs to be allocated should have an influence on choosing the allocation method.

___ 4. The joint-cost allocation method that recognizes the revenue-generating power of the individual products and presupposes management decisions on further processing is the sales value at splitoff method.

___ 5. The method of allocating joint costs that is sometimes preferred to set a fair selling price in rate-regulation situations, because it avoids the circular reasoning of other methods, is constant gross-margin percentage NRV.

___ 6. The constant gross-margin percentage NRV method of allocating joint costs is generally used when each of the joint products has the same gross-margin percentage.

___ 7. The estimated net realizable value method of allocating joint costs uses in its computations the entire production of the period as distinguished from the actual sales of the period.

___ 8. The allocation of joint costs assists managers in deciding whether joint or main product(s) should be sold at splitoff or processed further.

___ 9. Expediency is a major factor influencing the selection of a byproduct accounting method.

___ 10. Under some byproduct accounting methods, no joint costs are allocated to the byproduct(s).

III. Select the best answer for each of the following multiple-choice questions and put the identifying letter in the space provided.

___ 1. Joint costs ordinarily are:
  a. direct materials costs.
  b. prime costs.
  c. manufacturing costs.
  d. costs throughout the value chain.

___ 2. (CPA) O'Connor Company manufactures Product J and Product K from a joint process. For Product J, 4,000 units were produced having a sales value at splitoff of $15,000. If Product J were processed further, the separable costs would be $3,000 and the final sales value would be $20,000. For Product K, 2,000 units were produced having a sales value at splitoff of $10,000. If Product K were processed further, the separable costs would be $1,000 and the final sales value would be $12,000. Using the sales value at splitoff method, the portion of the total joint costs allocated to Product J was $9,000. What were the total joint costs?
  a. $14,400
  b. $15,000
  c. $18,400
  d. $19,000

___ 3. (CPA adapted) Ohio Corporation manufactures liquid chemicals A and B from a joint process. Joint costs are allocated on the basis of sales value at splitoff. It costs $13,680 to process 500 gallons of A and 1,000 gallons of B up to the splitoff point. The sales value at splitoff is $10 per gallon for A and $14 per gallon for B. B requires additional processing beyond splitoff at separable costs of $1 per gallon before it can be sold. Assuming that the 1,000 gallons of B were processed further and sold for $18 per gallon, what is Ohio's gross margin on this sale?
  a. $7,920
  b. $7,420
  c. $7,880
  d. $6,920

___ 4. (CMA) Sonimad Sawmill manufactures two lumber products from a joint milling process. The two products are mine support braces (MSB) and unseasoned commercial building lumber (CBL). A production run results in 60,000 units of MSB and 90,000 units of CBL at the splitoff point. The joint costs are $300,000. MSB and CBL can be sold at splitoff for $2 per unit and $4 per unit, respectively. If the physical measure method is used, the total joint costs allocated to CBL would be:

a. $75,000.
b. $180,000.
c. $225,000.
d. $120,000.
e. none of the above.

___ 5. See item 4. Assume CBL is not salable at the splitoff point but must be further planed and sized at separable costs of $200,000. During this process, 10,000 units are unavoidably lost; these units of scrap have zero sales value. The good units of CBL can be sold at $10 per unit. The MSB is coated with a tar-like preservative at separable costs of $100,000. MSB then can be sold for $5 per unit. Using the estimated net realizable value method, the inventoriable costs of each unit of CBL would be:
a. $2.92.
b. $5.625.
c. $2.50.
d. $5.3125.
e. none of the above.

___ 6. (CPA) Actual sales values at the splitoff point for joint Products Y and Z are not known. However, for purposes of allocating joint costs to Products Y and Z, the estimated net realizable value method is used. Suppose an increase in the separable costs beyond splitoff for Product Z occurs, while those of Product Y remain constant. If the selling prices of finished Products Y and Z remain constant, the percentage of the total joint costs allocated to Product Y and Product Z would:
a. decrease for both products.
b. increase for Y and decrease for Z.
c. decrease for Y and increase for Z.
d. increase for both products.

___ 7. (CPA) From a particular joint process, Watkins Company produces three products, X, Y, and Z. Each product may be sold at splitoff or processed further. Additional processing requires no special facilities, and separable costs of further processing are entirely variable and traceable to the products involved. In 19_3, all three products were processed beyond splitoff. Joint production costs for the year were $60,000. Sales values and costs for 19_3 are as follows:

	Product		
	X	Y	Z
Units produced	6,000	4,000	2,000
Sales value at splitoff	$25,000	$41,000	$24,000
Sales value and costs if processed further			
Final sales value	$42,000	$45,000	$32,000
Separable costs	$9,000	$7,000	$8,000

Joint costs are allocated to the products in proportion to the relative physical volume of output. The relevant cost per unit for a decision to sell Product Z or process it further is:
a. $4.
b. $5.
c. $9.
d. $12.

___ 8. See item 7. To maximize operating income, Watkins should subject the following products to additional processing:
a. X only.
b. X, Y, and Z.
c. Y and Z only.
d. Z only.

___ 9. (CPA) Crowley Company produces joint Products A and B from a process that also yields a byproduct, Y. The byproduct requires additional processing before it can be sold. The cost assigned to the byproduct is its market value minus additional costs incurred after splitoff. Information concerning a batch produced in January 19_3 at joint costs of $40,000 is as follows:

Product	Units Produced	Market Value	Costs After Splitoff
A	800	$44,000	$4,500
B	700	32,000	3,500
Y	500	4,000	1,000

How much of the joint costs should be allocated to the joint products?
a. $35,000
b. $36,000
c. $37,000
d. $39,000

____ 10. (CPA) Abel Corp. manufactures a product that yields the byproduct Yum. The only costs associated with Yum are selling costs of $0.10 for each unit sold. Abel accounts for sales of Yum by deducting Yum's selling costs from Yum's sales, and then deducting this net amount from the main product's cost of goods sold. Yum's sales were 100,000 units at $1 each. If Abel changes its method of accounting for Yum's sales by showing the net amount realized as additional sales revenue, then Abel's gross margin would:

a. increase by $90,000.
b. increase by $100,000.
c. increase by $110,000.
d. be unaffected.

IV. The Tri-Ken Corporation produced the following products in a single process at joint costs of $3,000.

	Product T	Product K
Quantity produced and processed beyond splitoff point	150 units	400 units
Separable costs	$1,000	$1,500
Selling price of a fully processed unit	$40	$10

1. Compute the amount of joint costs allocated to each product using the estimated net realizable value method.
2. Based on your allocation of joint costs in part 1, compute the gross margin of Product T, Product K, and both products together, assuming all units are sold.
3. Compute the amount of joint costs allocated to each product using the constant gross-margin percentage NRV method.
4. If the selling prices at splitoff were $4 per unit for Product K and $34 per unit for Product T, would it be profitable to further process either or both products? Assume separable costs are incremental costs. Show supporting computations.
5. Based on your further processing decisions in part 4, compute the total gross margin that would be realized from the sales of all units of both products.

Check figures: (1) $2,000 to T (2) $3,000 for T (3) $2,300 to T (4) $100 loss for T (5) $4,600

V. The Cambridge Chemical Company presents the following data:

Total manufacturing costs of main product and byproduct	$ 75,000
Total sales of main product	100,000
Estimated net realizable value of byproduct (including ending inventory of byproduct)	2,000
Beginning inventories	none

Ending inventory of the main product is 10% of the quantity produced. Ending inventory of the byproduct is 30% of the quantity produced.

Compute the gross margin of the main product, assuming the byproduct is recognized in the general ledger when produced and its net revenue is treated as a reduction of manufacturing costs (Method A in the textbook).

Check figure: $34,360

CHAPTER 16 SOLUTIONS TO PRACTICE TEST

I. 1 splitoff, separable costs; 2 sales value, joint products, main product; 3 Byproducts; 4 physical measure; 5 Net realizable value (NRV); 6 constant gross-margin percentage NRV, gross margin; 7 sales value at splitoff method, estimated NRV method, constant gross-margin percentage NRV method.

II.

1 F	4 F	7 T	10 T
2 T	5 F	8 F	
3 F	6 F	9 T	

Explanations:
1 Joint products have relatively high sales value and are not separately identifiable as individual products until the splitoff point. Joint products may be, but need not be, salable at the splitoff point. (F)
2 The two main purposes for allocating joint costs to individual products or services are (i) to measure income and assets for reporting to external parties and (ii) to justify costs or compute reimbursement. Therefore, managers should be reluctant to use joint-cost allocations for purposes of economic decisions or motivation. (T)
3 The size of the joint costs to be allocated has no bearing on the choice of allocation method. The method chosen depends on factors such as the revenue-generating power of the products and whether all products are salable at splitoff. (F)
4 The statement applies to the estimated net realizable value method. The sales value at splitoff method recognizes the revenue-generating power of individual products at the splitoff point and, consequently, does *not* presuppose management decisions on further processing. (F)
5 The sales value methods—sales value at splitoff, estimated net realizable value, and constant gross-margin percentage NRV—involve circular reasoning for setting prices: the use of selling prices to allocate joint costs that, in turn, serve as a basis for setting selling prices. The only method that avoids this circular reasoning is the physical measure method, because no selling price data are used. (F)
6 The allocation of joint costs must be made *before* the gross-margin percentages of the products can be computed, not vice versa. The *effect* of using the constant gross-margin percentage NRV method is that the overall gross-margin percentage is identical for all of the individual products. (F)
7 See the textbook example (p. 576): the joint-cost allocation is based on production of 20 gallons of butter cream and 50 gallons of condensed milk; actual sales of 12 gallons and 45 gallons, respectively, are used in the income statement in Exhibit 16-7. (T)
8 The allocation of joint costs is irrelevant in deciding whether joint or main product(s) should be sold at splitoff or processed further, because the *total* amount of the joint costs remains the same under both alternatives. Only revenues and costs that are *incremental beyond splitoff* are relevant to the decision. (F)
9 Byproduct accounting methods are almost always chosen on the basis of expediency rather than theoretical soundness. The decision is not particularly important because the dollar amounts involved are, by definition, immaterial. (T)
10 Methods C and D in the textbook use the approach described in the statement. Under these methods, the unsold quantity of byproduct(s) is assigned zero cost for financial reporting to external parties; for example, see the bottom line of Exhibit 16-13. (T)

III.

1 c	4 b	7 a	10 d
2 b	5 d	8 a	
3 d	6 b	9 c	

Explanations:
1 Joint costs are the costs of a single process that yields multiple products simultaneously. These costs ordinarily consist of direct materials, direct manufacturing labor, and manufacturing overhead incurred up to the splitoff point. (c)
2 Total sales value at splitoff of the two products together = $15,000 + $10,000 = $25,000; portion of joint costs allocated to Product J = $15,000 ÷ $25,000 = 60%; total joint costs = $9,000 ÷ .60 = $15,000. (b) Of course, it is a coincidence that the sales value at splitoff of Product J happens to be the same amount as total joint costs, $15,000. Note that when the sales value at splitoff method is used, the information regarding further processing of the products is ignored in the computations.

3 Sales value at splitoff:

A, 500 × $10	$ 5,000
B, 1,000 × $14	14,000
Total	$19,000

Cost of Product B (fully processed):

Allocation of joint costs,	
($14,000 ÷ $19,000) × $13,680	$10,080
Separable costs, 1,000 × $1	1,000
Total	$11,080
Sales, 1,000 × $18	$18,000
Cost of goods sold	11,080
Gross margin	$ 6,920 (d)

4 [90,000 ÷ (60,000 + 90,000)] × $300,000 = (90,000 ÷ 150,000) × $300,000 = .60 × $300,000 = $180,000 (b)

5 Estimated net realizable value:

MSB, (60,000 × $5) − $100,000	$200,000
CBL, [(90,000 − 10,000) × $10] − $200,000	600,000
Total	$800,000

Joint costs allocated to CBL = ($600,000 ÷ $800,000) × $300,000 = .75 × $300,000 = $225,000

Inventoriable costs per unit of CBL = ($225,000 + $200,000) ÷ 80,000 = $425,000 ÷ 80,000 = $5.3125 (d)

6 An effective way to answer this question is to use any set of "before change" figures you desire and then incorporate an increase in the separable costs of Product Z. Select any reasonable amount for the increase ($2,000 is used in the following example). Then calculate "after change" figures:

	Before Change	
	Y	Z
Final sales value	$9,000	$6,000
Deduct separable costs	3,000	2,000
Estimated net realizable value	$6,000	$4,000
Joint cost allocation		
percentage:		
$6,000 ÷ ($6,000 + $4,000)	60%	
$4,000 ÷ ($6,000 + $4,000)		40%

	After Change	
	Y	Z
Final sales value	$9,000	$6,000
Deduct separable costs	3,000	4,000
Estimated net realizable value	$6,000	$2,000
Joint cost allocation		
percentage:		
$6,000 ÷ ($6,000 + $2,000)	75%	
$2,000 ÷ ($6,000 + $2,000)		25%

The percentage of total joint costs allocated to Product Y increases (to 75% from 60%) and decreases for Product Z (to 25% from 40%). (b)

7 The relevant unit cost for the decision is the incremental cost: $8,000 ÷ 2,000 = $4. (a) Note that if the incremental revenue related to further processing of Z exceeds $4 per unit, further processing would be profitable.

8

Relevant Items	X	Y	Z
Incremental revenue,			
$42,000 − $25,000	$17,000		
$45,000 − $41,000		$ 4,000	
$32,000 − $24,000			$8,000
Incremental costs	9,000	7,000	8,000
Effect on operating income of further processing	$ 8,000	$(3,000)	$ -0-

Since Z has a zero effect on operating income, the company would be indifferent with regard to further processing of this product. (a)

9 This question illustrates using the estimated net realizable value to cost byproduct inventory (Methods A and B in Exhibit 16-13). The joint cost allocated to the joint products = $40,000 − ($4,000 − $1,000) = $37,000. (c) Note that the cost of byproduct inventory = ($3,000 + $1,000) ÷ 500 units = $8 per unit.

10 The net amount in question = 100,000 × ($1.00 − $0.10) = $90,000. Regardless of whether the $90,000 is treated as additional sales revenue or a reduction in cost of goods sold, gross margin would be the same. (d)

IV. Tri-Ken Corporation

1.

	T	K	Total
Final sales value,			
150 × $40; 400 × $10	$6,000	$4,000	$10,000
Deduct separable costs	1,000	1,500	2,500
Estimated net realizable value	$5,000	$2,500	$ 7,500
Allocation of $3,000 joint costs:			
To T: (5,000 ÷ 7,500) × $3,000	$2,000		
To K: (2,500 ÷ 7,500) × $3,000		$1,000	

2.

	T	K	Total
Final sales value	$6,000	$4,000	$10,000
Deduct cost of goods sold:			
Joint costs (computed above)	2,000	1,000	3,000
Separable costs	1,000	1,500	2,500
Total	3,000	2,500	5,500
Gross margin	$3,000	$1,500	$ 4,500

3.

		Total
Final sales value		$10,000
Deduct:		
Total joint costs	$3,000	
Total separable costs	2,500	5,500
Overall gross margin		$ 4,500
Overall gross margin %,		
$4,500 ÷ $10,000		45%

	T	K	Total
Final sales value	$6,000	$4,000	$10,000
Deduct gross margin at 45%	2,700	1,800	4,500
Total manufacturing costs	3,300	2,200	5,500
Deduct separable costs	1,000	1,500	2,500
Joint costs allocated	$2,300	$ 700	$ 3,000

4.

	T	K
Incremental revenue beyond splitoff, ($40 − $34) × 150; ($10 − $4) × 400	$ 900	$2,400
Incremental costs beyond splitoff	1,000	1,500
Operating income (loss) from further processing	$ (100)	$ 900

5.

		Total
Sales, ($34 × 150) + ($10 × 400)		$9,100
Deduct total manufacturing costs:		
Joint costs	$3,000	
Separable costs of further processing K	1,500	4,500
Gross margin		$4,600

Note that this gross margin is $100 greater than the $4,500 gross margin based on the further processing of both products as computed in part 2 above.

V. Cambridge Chemical Company

Sales		$100,000
Cost of goods sold:		
Total manufacturing costs	$75,000	
Deduct net revenue of byproduct sold, 70% × $2,000	1,400	
Net manufacturing costs	73,600	
Deduct:		
Main product inventory, 10% × $73,600	$7,360	
Byproduct inventory, 30% × $2,000	600	7,960	65,640
Gross margin		$ 34,360

CHAPTER 17

PROCESS-COSTING SYSTEMS

MAIN FOCUS AND OBJECTIVES

Process-costing systems are used for costing like or similar units of products that are often mass produced. Process costing was introduced in Part Two of Chapter 5. The introduction assumed no beginning inventory. Here that assumption is relaxed. We focus on two alternative process-costing methods:

- the weighted-average method
- the first-in, first-out (FIFO) method

A third method of process costing – using standard costs – is also discussed. Your overall objective for this chapter is to understand how to use the five-step approach in process-costing systems. Eight learning objectives are stated in the textbook (p. 598).

The key concept in process costing is averaging costs over like or similar units. This average is often computed by using equivalent units. The quantity of equivalent units is affected by the presence of beginning and ending work in process inventories and by the process-costing method chosen.

This chapter has 20(!) exhibits, far more than almost any other chapter in the textbook. This presentation signals that process costing is highly procedural. Take time to carefully study the exhibits. It is also helpful to categorize process-costing problems as dealing with either a first process or a subsequent process. The latter situation is more difficult because of transferred-in costs and the related units.

REVIEW OF KEY TERMS AND CONCEPTS

A. Process-costing computations are much more complex when beginning work in process inventory is present in a process or department.
   1. With or without this beginning inventory, a five-step approach is used to effectively solve process-costing problems.

> *Step 1:* **Summarize the flow of physical units of a product (output) in a process.**
> *Step 2:* **Compute output in terms of equivalent units.**
> *Step 3:* **Summarize the total costs to account for, which are all the costs debited to the Work in Process account.**
> *Step 4:* **Compute equivalent unit costs.**
> *Step 5:* **Assign total costs to units completed and to units in ending work in process.**

a. The first two steps measure what is occurring in a process in terms of *units*.

b. The last three steps measure what is occurring in terms of *costs*.

c. The overall objective of the five-step approach is to compute how much of the total costs in a process are assigned to (i) *units completed* and (ii) *ending work in process inventory*.

2. The components of physical units (step 1) can be expressed as an equation:

Where did the units come from? = Where did the units go?

$$\begin{array}{c} \text{Beginning} \\ \text{inventory} \end{array} + \begin{array}{c} \text{Units} \\ \text{started} \end{array} = \begin{array}{c} \text{Units} \\ \text{completed} \end{array} + \begin{array}{c} \text{Ending} \\ \text{inventory} \end{array}$$

3. **Equivalent units** (step 2): the measure of output in terms of the quantities used of each of the factors of production.

a. Equivalent units are usually computed *separately* for (i) *transferred-in costs*, (ii) *direct materials*, and (iii) *conversion costs*. Why? Because these three cost components are often added at *different* stages of production.

b. Equivalent unit costs (step 4) are computed by dividing equivalent unit totals (step 2) into the appropriate cost totals (step 3).

> *Question:* When is the extra accuracy of equivalent unit computations most likely to result in dollar differences that are material in amount?
>
> *Answer:* When work in process inventory is large in dollar amount and fluctuates widely over time.

4. The total costs of units completed and transferred out of a process (step 5) are used in a journal entry to credit the Work in Process account.

a. The debit is to the subsequent process or to Finished Goods.

b. The total costs assigned to units completed and transferred out and to ending inventory (step 5) *must equal* the total debits in the Work in Process account (step 3).

5. *See Practice Test Question III (item 1).*

B. Two alternative methods for computing unit costs are weighted average and first in, first out (FIFO).

1. **Weighted-average process-costing method**: focuses on the total costs and total equivalent units completed *to date*; no distinction is made between work done during the preceding period on the beginning inventory and work done during the current period.

> In this definition, the effect of the phrase "to date" is that the stage of completion of beginning work in process is *not* used in computing equivalent units.

a. Steps 1 and 2 under this method are illustrated as follows:
   (1) Exhibit 17-3 covers the Assembly Department, *a first process*.
   (2) Exhibit 17-14 covers the Testing Department, *a subsequent process*.

> **The computations for a subsequent process are always more complicated because of transferred-in costs (also called previous-department costs) and the related units. Transferred-in costs are like direct materials costs that are added at the beginning of a process.**

b. Steps 3, 4, and 5, which collectively are called a *production-cost worksheet*, are illustrated as follows:
   (1) Exhibit 17-7 covers the Assembly Department.
   (2) Exhibit 17-15 covers the Testing Department.
   (3) In these exhibits, note in step 4 that *the costs incurred to date (step 3) are matched to the equivalent units to date* (step 2).
   (4) Also note that in the Testing Department direct materials ($13,200,000) are added at the *end* of the process.
c. The flow of costs through the general ledger accounts is shown in Exhibit 17-8.
d. **Carefully study the specified exhibits**.
e. *See Practice Test Question III (items 5 and 7) and Problem IV (part 1).*

2. **First-in, first-out (FIFO) process-costing method**: computes unit costs by confining equivalent units to work done *during the current period only*; costs of the current period are separately identified so that the unit costs are related only to the current period's work.

> **In this definition, the effect of the phrase "during the current period only" is that the stage of completion of beginning work in process *is* used in computing equivalent units. Therefore, it is necessary to distinguish between completed units that are (i) from beginning inventory and (ii) started and completed during the current period.**

a. Step 1 is the same under weighted average and FIFO, but all other steps are affected by the choice of method.
b. Steps 1 and 2 under FIFO are illustrated as follows:
   (1) Exhibit 17-9 covers the Assembly Department.
   (2) Exhibit 17-18 covers the Testing Department.
c. Steps 3, 4, and 5, collectively called a production-cost worksheet, are illustrated as follows:
   (1) Exhibit 17-10 covers the Assembly Department.
   (2) Exhibit 17-19 covers the Testing Department.
   (3) Note in step 4 that *the costs incurred during the current period only (step 3) are matched to the current period's equivalent units* (step 2).
   (4) Also note that the costs of beginning inventory are *not* used in computing equivalent unit costs.

d. The flow of costs through the general ledger accounts would be like that shown for the weighted-average method in Exhibit 17-8, except the *transferred-out costs* would be $43,610,000 instead of $43,680,000, and ending inventory would be $1,500,000 instead of $1,430,000.

e. **Carefully study the specified exhibits**.

f. *See Practice Test Question III (items 2, 4, and 6) and Problem IV (part 2).*

3. A straightforward way to compare equivalent unit computations is: FIFO equivalent units (work done during the current period only) equal weighted-average equivalent units (total work done to date) minus work done during the preceding period on the current period's beginning inventory. *See Practice Test Question III (item 3).*

Question: **Under what conditions will the results materially differ between the FIFO and weighted-average methods?**

Answer: **When (1) direct materials or conversion costs per unit vary greatly from period to period and (2) work in process inventory is large in relation to the total number of units transferred out or this inventory changes greatly from period to period.**

C. **Standard costing** (first discussed in Chapter 7) is especially useful in process-costing situations where there are numerous combinations of materials, operations, and product sizes. Examples: steel, textiles, paints, and packaged foods.

1. *Standard costs in process costing are the costs per equivalent unit.*

2. Therefore, the computations under standard costing are relatively much simpler than those under weighted average or FIFO.

a. The standard cost of units completed and transferred out is the actual quantity completed multiplied by the standard cost per unit.

b. The standard cost of ending inventory is computed by multiplying the equivalent units for each cost element by the respective standard cost per equivalent unit.

3. Standard costing uses "work done during the current period only" (*the same measure used under FIFO*) as a basis for comparing actual costs of the current period with standard costs of the current period.

a. The differences between actual costs and standard costs are variances.

b. Standard costing serves two purposes: product costing and management control.

Exhibits 17-11 and 17-13 respectively illustrate a production-cost worksheet under standard costing and the flow of costs through the general ledger accounts. Carefully study these exhibits. *See Practice Test Question III (item 8).*

PRACTICE TEST QUESTIONS AND PROBLEMS

I. Complete each of the following statements.

1. The key concept in process costing is _____ _____ costs over like or similar units.

2. The overall objective of the five-step approach in process costing is to compute how much of the total costs in a process are assigned to _____ and to _____.

3. The measure of output in terms of the quantities used of each of the factors of production is called _____.

4. The weighted-average process-costing method focuses on the total costs and total equivalent units completed _____, whereas the FIFO process-costing method computes unit costs by confining equivalent units to work done _____.

5. Conversion costs are defined as _____ _____.

6. The computations for a subsequent processing department are always more complicated than those for a first processing department because of _____ _____.

7. The journal entry to transfer completed goods out of Painting, the final processing department, would be:
Debit: _____
Credit: _____

8. Using standard costs in process costing serves what two purposes? _____ _____.

II. Indicate whether each of the following statements is true or false by putting T or F in the space provided.

____ 1. In terms of the five-step approach used in process-costing systems, it is necessary to compute output in terms of equivalent units before costs are allocated to units completed and to units in ending work in process inventory.

____ 2. In a particular process, physical units will always be equal to or greater than equivalent units.

____ 3. In terms of physical units in a processing department, work completed and transferred out minus beginning inventory is equal to work started and completed during the current period, assuming work completed and transferred out is greater than beginning inventory.

____ 4. When the weighted-average process-costing method is used, the divisor for computing equivalent unit costs for a period should exclude the equivalent units of work done during the preceding period on the current period's beginning inventory.

____ 5. When the FIFO process-costing method is used, the costs of beginning inventory are not used in computing equivalent unit costs for the current period.

____ 6. For a processing department, total costs to account for should be equal to the sum of total costs of units started in production plus costs assigned to ending work in process inventory.

____ 7. Transferred-in costs for Process Two in the current period cannot include conversion costs that were incurred by Process One in the current period.

____ 8. When standard costs are used in process costing, "work done during the current period only" is the basis for comparing actual costs to standard costs for control purposes.

____ 9. Standard costing has limited usefulness in process-costing situations where there are numerous combinations of materials, operations, and product sizes.

III. Select the best answer for each of the following multiple-choice questions and put the identifying letter in the space provided.

____ 1. (CPA) Kew Co. had 3,000 units in work in process at April 1, 19_4, which were 60% complete as to conversion costs. During April, 10,000 units were completed. At April 30, 4,000 units remained in work in process and were 40% complete as to conversion costs. Direct materials are added at the beginning of the process. Assuming Kew uses the weighted-average method, how many units were started during April?

a. 9,000
b. 9,800
c. 10,000
d. 11,000

2. (CPA) Under which of the following conditions will the first-in, first-out method of process costing produce the same equivalent unit costs as the weighted-average method?
   a. When units produced are homogeneous in nature.
   b. When there is no beginning inventory.
   c. When there is no ending inventory.
   d. When beginning and ending inventories are each 50% complete.

3. (CPA) Walton, Incorporated, had 8,000 units of work in process in Department A on October 1, 19_4. These units were 60% complete as to conversion costs, which are added evenly throughout the process. Direct materials are added at the beginning of the process. During the month of October, 34,000 units were started and 36,000 units completed. Walton had 6,000 units of work in process on October 31, 19_4. These units were 80% complete as to conversion costs. By how much did the equivalent units for the month of October using the weighted-average method exceed the equivalent units for the month of October using the first-in, first-out method?

	Direct Materials	Conversion Costs
a.	0	3,200
b.	0	4,800
c.	8,000	3,200
d.	8,000	4,800

4. (CPA) The Cutting Department is the first stage of Mark Company's production cycle. Conversion costs for this department, which are added evenly throughout the process, were 80% complete for the beginning work in process and 50% complete for the ending work in process. Information as to conversion costs in the Cutting Department for January 19_4 is as follows:

	Units	Conversion Costs
Work in process at January 1, 19_4	25,000	$ 22,100
Units started and costs incurred during January	135,000	$143,000
Units completed and transferred to next department during January	100,000	

Using the FIFO method, how much is the conversion costs component of the work in process inventory in the Cutting Department at January 31, 19_4?
   a. $33,000
   b. $38,100
   c. $39,000
   d. $45,000

5. (CPA) The Wiring Department is the second stage of Flem Company's production cycle. On May 1, 19_4, the beginning work in process inventory consisted of 25,000 units that were 60% complete as to conversion costs. During May, 100,000 units were transferred in from the first stage of Flem's production cycle. On May 31, 19_4, the ending work in process inventory consisted of 20,000 units that were 80% complete as to conversion costs. Direct materials costs were added at the end of the process, and conversion costs were added evenly throughout the process. Using the weighted-average method, the equivalent units were:

	Transferred-in Costs	Direct Materials	Conversion Costs
a.	100,000	125,000	100,000
b.	125,000	105,000	105,000
c.	125,000	105,000	121,000
d.	125,000	125,000	121,000

6. (CPA) An error was made in the computation of the percentage of completion of the current year's ending work in process inventory. The error resulted in assigning a lower percentage of completion to each component of the inventory than actually was the case. What is the resulting effect of this error on:

1. the computation of equivalent units in total?
2. the computation of costs per equivalent unit?
3. costs assigned to work completed during the period?

	1	2	3
a.	Understate	Overstate	Overstate
b.	Understate	Understate	Overstate
c.	Overstate	Understate	Understate
d.	Overstate	Overstate	Understate

____ 7. Additions are always made at the beginning of any process subsequent to the first process:
   a. for any direct materials costs and for transferred-in costs.
   b. for any direct materials costs but not for transferred-in costs.
   c. for neither any direct materials costs nor for transferred-in costs.
   d. for transferred-in costs but not for any direct materials costs.

____ 8. (CPA) When standard costs are used in a process-costing system, how, if at all, are equivalent units used in the production-cost worksheet?
   a. equivalent units are not used.
   b. actual equivalent units are multiplied by the standard cost per unit.
   c. standard equivalent units are multiplied by the standard cost per unit.
   d. standard equivalent units are multiplied by the actual cost per unit.

IV. Given for Ozark Company's Cooking Process for January 19_4:

	Units
Inventory in process, January 1, 40% complete	300
Transferred in during January	600
Completed and transferred out during January	700
Inventory in process, January 31, 50% complete	200

January 1 inventory costs:	
Transferred-in costs	$28,200
Conversion costs	5,560
Current costs in January:	
Transferred-in costs	51,000
Conversion costs	36,040

No direct materials are added in this process.

1. Using the weighted-average method, compute:
   a. Physical units to account for
   b. Equivalent units of transferred-in costs and conversion costs
   c. Cost per equivalent unit of transferred-in costs and conversion costs
   d. Cost of units completed and transferred out
   e. Cost of work in process inventory, January 31
2. Repeat part 1 using the first-in, first-out method.

   Check figures: (1a) 900 (1b) 900, 800 (1c) $88, $52 (1d) $98,000 (1e) $22,800 (2a) 900 (2b) 600, 680 (2c) $85, $53 (2d) $98,500 (2e) $22,300

CHAPTER 17 SOLUTIONS TO PRACTICE TEST

I. 1 averaging; 2 units completed, ending work in process inventory; 3 equivalent units; 4 to date, during the current period only; 5 all manufacturing costs other than direct materials costs; 6 transferred-in costs and the related units; 7 Finished Goods, Work in Process – Painting; 8 product costing, management control.

II.

1 T	4 F	7 F
2 T	5 T	8 T
3 T	6 F	9 F

Explanations:
1 Equivalent units are computed in step 2 of the five-step approach. Costs are assigned to units completed and to ending work in process inventory in step 5. (T)

2 Physical units measure output by ignoring the percentage of completion, while equivalent units incorporate the percentage of completion by measuring output in terms of the quantities used of each of the factors of production. In the extreme case, then, equivalent units would be equal to physical units. Otherwise, equivalent units would be less than physical units. (T)

3 For example in Exhibit 17-2, $(100 + 380) - 100 = 380$. (T)

4 Under the weighted-average process-costing method, the divisor for computing equivalent unit costs should *include* the equivalent units of work done on the beginning inventory during the preceding period. For example, in Exhibit 17-3 the 100 physical units of beginning inventory are included as 100 equivalent units in the computations. (F)

5 For example, look at the $5,110,000 beginning inventory figure in Exhibit 17-10. It is not used in computing the equivalent unit costs. (T)

6 Total costs to account for (step 3) are equal to the sum of beginning inventory costs plus costs added during the current period. An example is the $45,110,000 shown for step 3 in Exhibit 17-7. (F)

7 Transferred-in costs always include conversion costs incurred in the preceding process. Those conversion costs would have been incurred in either the preceding period or the current period. (F)

8 For example, consider direct materials in Exhibit 17-11. Current output at standard costs assigned of $21,200,000 is equal to equivalent units of work done in the current period only multiplied by standard cost per equivalent unit: $400 \times \$53,000 = \$21,200,000$. The difference between actual costs incurred and this amount is the total variance: $\$22,000,000 - \$21,200,000 = \$800,000$ unfavorable. (T)

9 Standard costing is especially useful in the process-costing situations described in the question. Examples of these situations are steel, textiles, paints, and packaged foods. (F)

III.
1 d	4 c	7 d
2 b	5 c	8 b
3 d	6 a	

Explanations:

1 Physical units to account for $= 10,000 + 4,000 = 14,000$; Units started $= 14,000 - 3,000 = 11,000$. This answer is *not* affected by the process-costing method used. (d)

2 Either of two conditions must be met for the two methods to produce the same equivalent unit costs: (i) no beginning inventory or (ii) no period-to-period changes in the costs of direct materials and conversion costs. Condition (i) was assumed in the introduction to process costing in Part Two of Chapter 5. Condition (ii) rarely exists. (b)

3 The differences in equivalent units are attributable to work done in the *preceding* period. Therefore, the differences can be computed directly by multiplying physical units in October 1 inventory by the percentage of work done in September.

　　Direct materials: $8,000 \times 100\% = 8,000$
　　Conversion costs: $8,000 \times 60\% = 4,800$ (d)

Alternatively, the answer can also be obtained by comparing equivalent units computed under each method. These comparisons are as follows (detailed computations not shown):

	Direct Materials	Conversion Costs
Equivalent units under weighted average	42,000	40,800
Equivalent units under FIFO	34,000	36,000
Difference in equivalent units	8,000	4,800 (d)

4 Equivalent units of conversion costs = 25,000(20%) + (100,000 − 25,000)(100%) + (25,000 + 135,000 − 100,000)(50%) = 5,000 + 75,000 + 30,000 = 110,000

Conversion costs per equivalent unit = $143,000 ÷ 110,000 = $1.30

Conversion costs component of ending inventory = (25,000 + 135,000 − 100,000)(50%) × $1.30 = 30,000 × $1.30 = $39,000 (c)

Note that the conversion costs completed and transferred out during January are:

Work in process:

Balance on January 1	$ 22,000
Completed during January, 5,000 × $1.30	6,500
Started and completed units, 75,000 × $1.30	97,500
Total	$126,000

Alternatively, this amount can be computed by subtracting the cost of ending inventory from the total costs to account for: $22,000 + $143,000 − $39,000 = $126,000.

5

	(Step 1)	(Step 2) Equivalent Units		
	Physical	Trans.-in	Direct	Conversion
Flow of Production	Units	Costs	Materials	Costs
Work in process, May 1	25,000			
Transferred in during May	100,000			
To account for	125,000			
Completed and transferred out during May, 125,000 − 20,000	105,000	105,000	105,000	105,000
Work in process, May 31, 20,000 × 100%; 0%; 80%	20,000	20,000	-0-	16,000
Accounted for	125,000			
Work done to date		125,000	105,000	121,000

The equivalent units of direct materials for the May 31 inventory is zero because materials are added at the *end* of the process. (c)

6 Regardless of whether the FIFO or weighted-average method is used, the effects of this error will be the same because *both methods treat ending inventory exactly alike*. To illustrate the effects of this error, use assumed figures to satisfy the situation described. Suppose ending inventory is computed to be 50% complete as to conversion costs instead of the correct figure of 70%. *Using assumed figures*, the effect of this error on each of the three items specified in the question is as follows:

(1) Equivalent units would be understated:

		Equivalent Units	
	Physical	Before	After
	Units	Correction	Correction
Work in process, beginning	-0-		
Started during current period	1,100		
To account for	1,100		
Completed and transferred out during current period	900	900	900
Work in process, ending, 200 × 50%; 200 × 70%	200	100	140
Accounted for	1,100	1,000	1,040

(2) Costs per equivalent unit would be overstated:

Before correction: $2,080 ÷ 1,000 = $2.08 per unit

After correction: $2,080 ÷ 1,040 = $2.00 per unit

(3) Cost of work completed and transferred out would be overstated:

Before correction: 900 units × $2.08 = $1,872
After correction: 900 units × $2.00 = $1,800

If the illustration above were based on *direct materials* instead of *conversion costs*, the conclusions would be the same; however, an error in computing the percentage of completion of direct materials is much less likely to occur because direct materials are usually added at either the beginning or the end of a process. (a)

7 Transferred-in costs are *always added at the beginning of a subsequent process.* If direct materials are added in that process, this addition can occur at *whatever stage* is dictated by the nature of production. For example, packaging materials could be added at or near the *end* of a subsequent process, while a chemical ingredient could be added at or near the *beginning* of a subsequent process. (d)

8 Under standard costing, costs are computed by multiplying actual equivalent units of each cost component by the respective standard cost per unit. For example, see Exhibit 17-11. (b)

IV. Ozark Company

1. (a) $300 + 600 = 900$
   (b) Equivalent units:
   Transferred-in costs $= 700 + 200 = 900$
   Conversion costs $= 700 + 200(50\%) = 800$
   (c) Cost per equivalent unit:
   Transferred-in costs $= (\$28,200 + \$51,000) \div 900 = \$79,200 \div 900 = \$88$
   Conversion costs $= (\$5,560 + \$36,040) \div 800 = \$41,600 \div 800 = \$52$
   (d) $700(\$88 + \$52) = \$98,000$
   (e) $200(\$88) + 200(50\%)(\$52) = \$17,600 + \$5,200 = \$22,800$

2. (a) Same as 1(a) above, 900
   (b) Equivalent units:
   Transferred-in costs $= (700 - 300) + 200 = 600$
   Conversion costs $= 300(60\%) + (700 - 300)(100\%) + 200(50\%) =$
   $180 + 400 + 100 = 680$
   (c) Cost per equivalent unit:
   Transferred-in costs $= \$51,000 \div 600 = \$85$
   Conversion costs $= \$36,040 \div 680 = \$53$
   (d) $(\$28,200 + \$5,560) + 300(60\%)(\$53) + (700 - 300)(\$85 + \$53) =$
   $\$33,760 + \$9,540 + \$55,200 = \$98,500$
   (e) $200(\$85) + 200(50\%)(\$53) = \$17,000 + \$5,300 = \$22,300$

CHAPTER 18

SPOILAGE, REWORKED UNITS, AND SCRAP

MAIN FOCUS AND OBJECTIVES

In almost all manufacturing operations, some outputs either do not meet established production standards or otherwise emerge in an undesirable form. Such outputs are called spoilage, reworked units, and scrap. All of these outputs have received increasing management attention in recent years as companies worldwide focus on improving product quality. Managers have learned that a rate of defects regarded as normal in the past is no longer tolerable. Accounting systems that record the costs of spoilage, rework, and scrap in a timely and detailed way help managers make more informed decisions. Your overall objective for this chapter is to understand how spoilage, rework, and scrap are recorded in accounting systems. Seven learning objectives are stated in the textbook (p. 632).

Give special attention to:

- the distinction between normal spoilage and abnormal spoilage
- accounting for spoilage in process-costing systems under the weighted-average and first-in, first-out (FIFO) methods
- accounting for spoilage, rework, and scrap in job costing systems

The brief chapter Appendix explores how the timing of inspection affects the amount of normal and abnormal spoilage.

REVIEW OF KEY TERMS AND CONCEPTS

A. Definitions of spoilage, reworked units, and scrap vary considerably in practice. This chapter uses the following definitions:
   1. **Spoilage**: unacceptable units of production that are discarded or sold for net disposal proceeds.
      a. Partially completed or fully completed units may be spoiled.
      b. Net spoilage costs are the total of the costs assigned to the product up to the point of rejection (plus disposal costs or minus net disposal proceeds).
   2. **Reworked units**: unacceptable units of production that are subsequently reworked and sold as acceptable finished goods (through either regular distribution channels or alternative channels).
   3. **Scrap**: a product that has minimal (frequently zero) sales value.
      a. Scrap may be either sold, otherwise disposed of, or reused.
      b. Examples: wood shavings, metal filings.

B. The most economical production method or process usually includes an allowance for spoilage.
   1. In recent years, many companies have decreased their spoilage allowances, and thereby achieved lower overall costs and higher sales.
   2. **Normal spoilage** arises under *efficient* operating conditions (that is, normal spoilage is inherent in the chosen production process).
      a. Therefore, normal spoilage is planned spoilage and is *uncontrollable* in the short run.
      b. The net cost of normal spoilage typically is included as a necessary part of the cost of good (unspoiled) production (that is, it is an *inventoriable cost*).
      c. However, some companies adhere to a perfection standard of zero defects; none of their spoilage is regarded as normal—all of it is abnormal.
   3. **Abnormal spoilage** is not expected to arise under efficient operating conditions.
      a. Therefore, abnormal spoilage is *controllable*.
      b. Generally, the net cost of abnormal spoilage should be excluded from the cost of good production and should be debited to the Loss from Abnormal Spoilage account. Why? Because it is a *period cost*, not an inventoriable cost.
   4. Spoilage typically is assumed to occur at the stage of completion *where inspection takes place* because spoilage is not detected until that point.

> *Question*: **In computing normal spoilage rates, what base should be used?**
>
> *Answer*: **Total *good* units of output because total *actual* units of input can include both normal and abnormal spoilage.**

C. In process-costing systems, the computation of equivalent units either includes spoilage (the accurate approach) or ignores spoilage (the inaccurate approach).
   1. Exhibit 18-1 illustrates both of these approaches.
   2. *Two keys to computing equivalent units and allocating spoilage costs:*
      a. The product-costing method used—weighted average or first-in, first out (FIFO).
      b. The stage of completion for conversion costs where inspection occurs—*spoilage is not detected until inspection takes place.*

> **Exhibits 18-3 and 18-4 illustrate the weighted-average and FIFO methods of process costing, respectively. Carefully study these exhibits. Note that:**
> - **The five-step approach from the preceding chapter is used with slight modification to incorporate spoilage.**
> - **Both normal spoilage and abnormal spoilage are included in the computation of equivalent units.**
> - **Inspection occurs in this example at the *end* of the process.**
> - **To simplify FIFO computations, spoiled units are accounted for *as if* they were started during the current period.**

   3. After the computation of equivalent unit costs, costs applicable to spoiled units may then be determined and accounted for.

a. The cost of abnormal spoilage is debited to Loss from Abnormal Spoilage and credited to Work in Process.

b. No normal spoilage costs of the process would be allocated to the ending work in process inventory, if (as in Exhibits 18-3 and 18-4) those units have not yet reached the inspection point.

4. *See Practice Test Question III (item 1) and Problem IV.*

5. Inspection may or may not occur at the *end* of the production process.

a. Managers should have inspection take place as early in the production process as is technically feasible, and thereby preventing further work from being done on spoiled units.

b. *Normal spoilage cost is allocated to units of ending work in process inventory only if those units have been inspected.*

c. (**Appendix**) The effects of inspection occurring at three stages of completion for conversion costs are illustrated in the textbook (p. 646) and related Exhibit 18-6.

D. Accounting for spoilage, rework, and scrap in *job costing systems* involves more detailed classifications (due to identifiable jobs) than are required in process-costing systems.

Classification of Spoilage, Rework, and Scrap	*Spoilage Costs*	*Rework Costs*	*Scrap Value Recovered*
Normal: common to all jobs	1	4	7
Normal: attributable to specific jobs	2	5	8
Abnormal	3	6	9

1. Journal entries are required for each of the nine numbered cells in the table.

2. **Entries for spoilage**, keyed to cells 1; 2, and 3 (using the textbook figures, p. 641), are as follows:

Entry 1: Normal Spoilage Common to All Jobs

Materials Control (disposal value)	$150	
Manufacturing Dept. Overhead Control (net cost)	350	
Work in Process Control (gross cost)		$500

Note that the net cost of this spoilage has been allocated to production via a budgeted manufacturing overhead rate, which includes a provision for normal spoilage.

Entry 2: Normal Spoilage Attributable to Specific Jobs

Materials Control (disposal value)	$150	
Work in Process Control (disposal value)		$150

Entry 3: Abnormal Spoilage

Materials Control (disposal value)	$150	
Loss from Abnormal Spoilage (net cost)	350	
Work in Process Control (gross cost)		$500

3. **Entries for rework**, keyed to cells 4, 5, and 6 (using the textbook figures, p. 641), are as follows:

Entry 4: Normal Rework Common to All Jobs

Manufacturing Dept. Overhead Control (rework cost)	$190	
Materials Control		$ 40
Wages Payable Control		100
Manufacturing Overhead Allocated		50

Entry 5: Normal Rework Attributable to Specific Jobs

Work in Process Control (rework cost)	$190	
Materials Control		$ 40
Wages Payable Control		100
Manufacturing Overhead Allocated		50

Entry 6: Abnormal Rework

Loss from Abnormal Spoilage (rework cost)	$190	
Materials Control		$ 40
Wages Payable Control		100
Manufacturing Overhead Allocated		50

4. **Entries for scrap**, keyed to cells 7, 8, and 9 (using the textbook figures, p. 643), are as follows:

Entry 7a: Normal Scrap Common to All Jobs: Scrap Sold

Cash or Accounts Receivable (net proceeds)	$45	
Sales of Scrap		$45

Alternatively, many companies credit Manufacturing Dept. Overhead Control.

Entry 7b: Normal Scrap Common to All Jobs: Scrap Returned to Storeroom and Reused

Materials Control (net realizable value)	$45	
Manufacturing Dept. Overhead Control		$45
Work in Process Control	$45	
Materials Control		$45

Entry 8a: Normal Scrap Attributable to Specific Jobs: Scrap Sold

Cash or Accounts Receivable (net proceeds)	$45	
Work in Process Control		$45

Entry 8b: Normal Scrap Attributable to Specific Jobs: Scrap Returned to Storeroom and Reused

Materials Control (net realizable value)	$45	
Work in Process Control		$45
Work in Process Control	$45	
Materials Control		$45

Entry 9: Abnormal Scrap

Loss from Abnormal Scrap (net cost)	$45	
Work in Process Control		$45

> These journal entries are for a job costing system. Similar entries can be made in a process-costing system. Of course, cells 2, 5, and 8 relate to *specific jobs* and are not applicable to process costing.

5. *See Practice Test Question III (items 2-5) and Problem V.*
6. Notes on accounting for scrap:
   a. There are two main purposes of accounting for scrap:
      (1) Management control, including physical tracking.
      (2) Inventory costing, including when and how to affect operating income.
   b. Detailed records of physical quantities of scrap are often kept at different stages of the production process.
   c. Scrap reports not only help measure efficiency but also spotlight what may be a tempting source of theft.

PRACTICE TEST QUESTIONS AND PROBLEMS

I. Complete each of the following statements.

1. Unacceptable units of production that are discarded or sold for net disposal proceeds are called _____.
2. _____ is a product that has minimal (frequently zero) sales value.
3. _____ spoilage arises under efficient operating conditions, is _____ in the short run, and is a(an) _____ _____ cost.
4. _____ spoilage is not expected to arise under efficient operating conditions, is debited to the _____ account, and is a(an) _____ cost.
5. Managers should have _____ take place as early in the production process as is technically feasible, and thereby preventing further work from being done on spoiled units.
6. Accounting for spoilage, rework, and scrap involves what three necessary classifications in job costing systems? _____ _____ _____
7. The net cost of normal spoilage common to all jobs is allocated to production via a(an) _____, which includes a provision for normal spoilage.
8. When normal scrap common to all jobs is sold, the account credited can be either _____ or _____ _____.

II. Indicate whether each of the following statements is true or false by putting T or F in the space provided.

___ 1. The most economical production method or process usually includes no allowance for normal spoilage.

___ 2. It is more accurate in computing equivalent units to include both normal and abnormal spoilage.

___ 3. The appropriate base to use in computing normal spoilage is actual units of input.

___ 4. If a company adheres to a goal of zero defects, all of its spoilage is regarded as abnormal.

___ 5. Normal spoilage cost never should be allocated to units in ending work in process inventory.

___ 6. Accounting for spoilage, rework, and scrap involves more detailed classifications in job costing systems than in process-costing systems.

___ 7. Detailed records of physical quantities of scrap are often kept at different stages of the production process.

III. Select the best answer for each of the following multiple-choice questions and put the identifying letter in the space provided.

___ 1. (CMA) During March 19_4, Mercer Company completed 50,000 units costing $600,000, exclusive of spoilage allocation. Of these completed units,

25,000 were sold during the month. An additional 10,000 units, costing $80,000, were 50% complete at March 31. All units are inspected between the completion of manufacturing and transfer to finished goods inventory. For the month, normal spoilage was $20,000 and abnormal spoilage was $50,000. The portion of total spoilage costs that should be charged against revenue in March is:

- a. $50,000.
- b. $20,000.
- c. $70,000.
- d. $60,000.
- e. $30,000.

___ 2. When spoilage is incurred that is normal and common to all jobs, Work in Process Control should be credited with:
- a. nothing.
- b. the disposal value of the spoiled goods.
- c. the net spoilage cost.
- d. the gross spoilage cost.

___ 3. In a job costing system, Work in Process Control would ordinarily be debited with the cost of reworked units that are:
- a. abnormal.
- b. normal and common to all jobs.
- c. normal and attributable to specific jobs.
- d. discarded.

___ 4. (CPA) Simpson Company manufactures electric drills to the exacting specifications of various customers. During April 19_3, Job 403 for the production of 1,100 drills was completed at the following costs per unit:

Direct materials	$10
Direct manufacturing labor	8
Manufacturing overhead allocated	12
Total manufacturing costs	$30

Final inspection of Job 403 disclosed 50 defective units and 100 units of normal spoilage. The defective drills were reworked at a total cost of $500 and the spoiled drills were sold to a jobber for $1,500. What would be the unit cost of the good units produced on Job 403?

- a. $33
- b. $32
- c. $30
- d. $29

___ 5. (CPA) The sale of scrap from a manufacturing process usually would be recorded as a(an):
- a. decrease in Manufacturing Department Overhead Control.
- b. increase in Manufacturing Department Overhead Control.
- c. decrease in Finished Goods.
- d. decrease in Work in Process.

IV. (CMA) JC Company employs a process-costing system. A unit of product passes through three departments—Molding, Assembly, and Finishing—before it is completed. The following activity took place in the Finishing Department during May:

	Units
Work in process, May 1	1,400
Transferred in from the Assembly Department	14,000
Spoilage	700
Completed and transferred out to finished goods inventory	11,200

Direct materials are added at the beginning of the processing in the Finishing Department without changing the number of units being processed. Conversion costs are added evenly throughout the process. The work in process inventory was 70% complete as to conversion costs on May 1 and 40% complete as to conversion costs on May 31. All spoilage is detected at final inspection, which occurs immediately after the units are completed; 560 of the units spoiled were within the allowance considered normal.

JC Company employs the weighted-average costing method. The equivalent units and the costs per equivalent unit of production for each cost factor in May are as follows:

	Equivalent Units	Cost per Equivalent Unit
Transferred-in costs	15,400	$5.00
Direct materials	15,400	1.00
Conversion costs	13,300	3.00
		$9.00

Compute:

1. Equivalent units of transferred-in costs, direct materials, and conversion costs.
2. Costs of units completed and transferred from the Finishing Department to finished goods inventory during May.
3. Cost assigned to the Finishing Department's work in process inventory on May 31.
4. Cost of abnormal spoilage.
5. Total transferred-in costs from the Assembly Department to the Finishing Department during May, assuming the transferred-in costs component of the work in process inventory of the Finishing Department on May 1 amounted to $6,300.

Check figures: (1) Conversion costs 13,300 (2) $105,840 (3) $25,200 (4) $1,260 (5) $70,700

V. Given for Chesser & Delton, Inc., which uses a job costing system:

Spoiled work:

Gross cost incurred	$900
Disposal value	200
Cost incurred to rework units	600
Scrap value recovered	150

Enter the appropriate dollar amounts in the following table to indicate the journal entries for each of the six situations.

Situation	Entry	Materials Control	Work in Process Control	Manufacturing Department Overhead Control	Loss from Abnormal Spoilage
1. Abnormal spoilage	Debit				
	Credit				
2. Normal scrap attributable to specific jobs (scrap returned to storeroom)	Debit				
	Credit				
3. Normal rework common to all jobs	Debit				
	Credit	$600*			
4. Normal spoilage attributable to specific jobs	Debit				
	Credit				
5. Normal spoilage common to all jobs	Debit				
	Credit				
6. Normal rework attributable to specific jobs	Debit				
	Credit	$600*			

*Credit Materials Control, Wages Payable Control, and Manufacturing Overhead Allocated for a total of $600.

Check figures: None

SPOILAGE, REWORKED UNITS, AND SCRAP 237

CHAPTER 18 SOLUTIONS TO PRACTICE TEST

I. 1 spoilage; 2 Scrap; 3 Normal, uncontrollable, inventoriable; 4 Abnormal, Loss from Abnormal Spoilage, period; 5 inspection; 6 normal and common to all jobs, normal and attributable to specific jobs, abnormal; 7 budgeted manufacturing overhead rate; 8 Sale of Scrap, Manufacturing Department Overhead Control.

II. 1 F   4 T   7 T
         2 T   5 F
         3 F   6 T

Explanations:

1 Normal spoilage is inherent in the chosen production process. Therefore, companies usually include an allowance for normal spoilage in their budgets. In recent years, however, many companies have decreased their spoilage allowances, and thereby achieved lower overall costs and higher sales. (F)

2 See Exhibit 18-1. (T)

3 The appropriate base to use in computing normal spoilage is total units of *good* output. Actual units of input is an inappropriate base because it can include both normal and abnormal spoilage. (F)

4 Under a zero-defects philosophy, normal spoilage does not exist; therefore, any spoilage occurring would be regarded as abnormal. (T)

5 Normal spoilage cost should be allocated to units in ending work in process inventory only if those units have been inspected. For example, if inspection occurs at the 50% stage of completion and ending work in process inventory is 70% completed, normal spoilage cost should be allocated to it. The chapter Appendix illustrates the effects of inspection occurring at three stages of completion for conversion costs. (F)

6 Job costing systems require the added detail because each job is identifiable. Therefore, it is necessary to distinguish between spoilage, rework, and scrap that is (i) normal and common to all jobs, (ii) normal and attributable to specific jobs, or (iii) abnormal. In process-costing systems, it is only necessary to distinguish between spoilage, rework, and scrap that is (i) normal or (ii) abnormal. (T)

7 Such records aid management control. Scrap reports not only help measure efficiency but also spotlight what may be a tempting source of theft. (T)

III. 1 d   4 b
          2 d   5 a
          3 c

Explanations:

1 Normal spoilage included in cost of goods sold,
   ($20,000 ÷ 50,000) × 25,000 $10,000
   Abnormal spoilage   50,000
   Total spoilage costs charged against revenue $60,000 (d)

2 See Entry 1 in section D of the chapter outline. (d)

3 See Entry 5 in section D of the chapter outline. (c)

4 Since the electric drills were manufactured to the exacting specifications of various customers, the rework and normal spoilage are *attributable specifically to Job 403*. Rework costs would increase the cost of good units produced, and the disposal value of spoilage would decrease the cost of good units produced. Therefore, the per unit cost of good units produced is [(1,100 × $30) + $500 − $1,500] ÷ (1,100 − 100) = $32,000 ÷ 1,000 = $32. (b) Note that if the rework and normal spoilage were *common to all jobs*, an allowance for these costs would be

included in the budgeted manufacturing overhead rate. In that case, the per unit cost of good units produced would be $[(1,100 \times \$30) - (100 \times \$30)] \div (1,100 - 100) = \$30,000 \div 1,000 = \$30$.

5 The sale of scrap can be credited to either Manufacturing Department Overhead Control or Sale of Scrap (Entry 7a in section D of the chapter outline). (a)

IV. JC Company

1.

| | (Step 1) | (Step 2) Equivalent Units | | |
Flow of Production	Physical Units	Trans.-in Costs	Direct Materials	Conversion Costs
Work in process, May 1	1,400			
Transferred in during May	14,000			
To account for	15,400			
Good units completed and transferred out	11,200	11,200	11,200	11,200
Normal spoilage	560	560	560	560
Abnormal spoilage, 700 − 560	140	140	140	140
Work in process, May 1, 15,400 − 140 − 560 − 11,200	3,500			
3,500 × 100%; 100%; 40%		3,500	3,500	1,400
Accounted for	15,400			
Work done to date		15,400	15,400	13,300

2. Since spoilage is detected at the completion of work in the Finishing Department, the cost of all normal spoilage should be allocated to the good units completed and transferred out of the Finishing Department: $(11,200 \times \$9.00) + (560 \times \$9.00) = \$105,840$. This amount would be debited to Finished Goods and credited to Work in Process − Finishing Department.

3. Using the equivalent unit amounts for the May 31 inventory from part 1 above, the costs of that inventory are: $(3,500 \times \$5) + (3,500 \times \$1) + (1,400 \times \$3) = \$17,500 + \$3,500 + \$4,200 = \$25,200$.

4. $140 \times \$9.00 = \$1,260$. This amount would be debited to Loss from Abnormal Spoilage and credited to Work in Process − Finishing Department.

5. Under the weighted-average method, equivalent unit costs are computed by dividing costs incurred to date by work done to date.

Let X = Transferred-in costs of the Finishing Department during May (that is, costs transferred out of the Assembly Department)

$$(X + \$6,300) \div 15,400 = \$5.00$$
$$X + \$6,300 = 15,400(\$5.00)$$
$$X = \$77,000 - \$6,300$$
$$X = \$70,700$$

V. Chesser & Delton, Inc.

Situation	Entry	Materials Control	Work in Process Control	Manufacturing Department Overhead Control	Loss from Abnormal Spoilage
1. Abnormal spoilage	Debit	$200			$700
	Credit		$900		
2. Normal scrap attributable to specific jobs (scrap returned to storeroom)	Debit	$150			
	Credit		$150		
3. Normal rework common to all jobs	Debit			$600	
	Credit	$600*			
4. Normal spoilage attributable to specific jobs	Debit	$200			
	Credit		$200		
5. Normal spoilage common to all jobs	Debit	$200		$700	
	Credit		$900		
6. Normal rework attributable to specific jobs	Debit		$600		
	Credit	$600*			

*Credit Materials Control, Wages Payable Control, and Manufacturing Overhead Allocated for a total of $600.

CHAPTER 19

OPERATION COSTING, BACKFLUSH COSTING, AND PROJECT CONTROL

MAIN FOCUS AND OBJECTIVES

This chapter builds on the discussion of product-costing systems in several previous chapters. The chapter is divided into two independent parts: (1) operation costing and backflush costing systems, and (2) control of projects. Your overall objective for this chapter is to understand how the underlying production systems affect the design of product-costing systems. Seven learning objectives are stated in the textbook (p. 656).

Give special attention to:

- the procedures used in operation costing systems
- how just-in-time production systems differ from traditional systems
- the procedures used in different versions of backflush costing systems
- computing and interpreting project performance cost variances and project schedule cost variances

REVIEW OF KEY TERMS AND CONCEPTS

Part One: Operation Costing and Backflush Costing Systems

A. Product-costing systems should be tailored to the underlying production systems.
1. Job costing systems and process-costing systems are best visualized as ends of a continuum.
    a. Job costing systems accompany custom-made manufacturing of relatively heterogeneous (different) products.
    b. Process-costing systems accompany mass production and continuous-flow manufacturing of homogeneous (uniform) products.
2. *Hybrid costing systems* are blends of characteristics from both job costing systems and process-costing systems.
    a. Hybrid costing systems develop because there are hybrid production systems.
    b. Example: cars may be manufactured in a continuous flow, but each car may be customized with a particular combination of motor, transmission, radio, and so on.

> **Exhibit 19-1 shows the variety of costing system choices available to management. The choice of a costing system depends on the underlying production system and managers' desires regarding cost management and accuracy in product costing.**

241

B. **Operation costing** is a hybrid costing system for batches (production runs) of similar products.

1. Each batch is often a variation of a basic product design and requires a particular sequence of standard operations. *All batches do not pass through each operation.*
   a. Product examples: clothing, shoes.
   b. **Operation**: a standardized method or technique that is performed routinely regardless of the distinguishing features of the finished good.
   c. Examples of operations in suit making: cutting, stitching, finishing.
   d. The term "operation" is often loosely used; it may be a synonym for a department or process.

2. Operation costing blends features of job costing and process costing.
   a. *The job costing feature*: direct materials are traced to specific batches.
   b. *The process-costing feature*: within each operation, identical amounts of conversion costs are allocated to each product unit.
   c. A single average conversion cost per unit is used in each operation.

3. Journal entries in an operation costing system focus on a Work in Process account for a batch of similar products.

> **Carefully study the textbook example of accounting for the production of wool and polyester blazers (p. 658). It is helpful to work through the related journal entries. Normal costing is used in the example.**

4. *See Practice Test Problem IV.*

C. **Just-in-time (JIT) production** is a system in which each component on a production line is produced immediately as needed by the next step in the production line.

1. JIT production lines operate on a *demand-pull basis*: manufacturing activity at any particular workstation is prompted by the use of that station's output at downstream stations.

2. Ideally, the sale of a unit of finished goods triggers the completion of a unit in final assembly, and so forth, backward in the sequence of manufacturing steps all the way to the delivery of materials (that is, *ideally JIT production systems operate with zero inventories*).

> **Key features of JIT production systems:**
> - **Inventory is regarded as evil because of its nonvalue-added nature.**
> - **Production activities are simplified. Nonvalue-added activities are spotlighted and then reduced or eliminated.**
> - **Emphasis is placed on reducing the manufacturing lead time, resulting in faster response to changes in customer demand and lower work in process inventory.**
> - **Production stops if component parts are absent or defects are discovered.**

3. *Nonvalue-added activities*: those activities that could be eliminated without the customer perceiving a deterioration in the utility (usefulness) of products.
4. *Manufacturing lead time*: the time from when a product is ready to start on the production line to when it becomes a finished good.
5. JIT has many potential financial benefits including lower investment in inventories, less risk of obsolete inventories, less plant space used for inventories, and less paperwork.

D. Backflush costing is a simplified and streamlined budgeted or standard costing system that began to receive attention in the 1980's.
  1. Traditional budgeted or standard costing systems often use an expensive form of recordkeeping called sequential tracking.
  2. **Sequential tracking**: the timing of accounting entries is synchronized with the movement of production from materials, through work in process, to finished goods.
  3. **Backflush costing** (also called *delayed costing, endpoint costing,* or *post-deduct costing*) delays recording changes in the movement of production until good finished units are produced or sold (that is, sequential tracking is *not* used); it then uses budgeted or standard costs to work backward to assign manufacturing costs to these units.
     a. Under backflush costing, typically no record of work in process inventory appears in the accounting system.
     b. *The trigger points for inventory costing journal entries are delayed until the completion of production or sale*, and then costs are "flushed back" through the accounting system.
     c. Backflush costing accompanies JIT production systems, although backflush costing can be coupled with any production system.
  4. Three conditions often met by companies adopting backflush costing:
     a. Management wants a simple accounting system.
     b. Each product has a budgeted or standard cost.
     c. Backflush costing yields approximately the same financial results as sequential tracking (which would occur if inventories are *low or constant*).
  5. The textbook illustrates backflush costing with three examples that differ in terms of the number and placement of **journal entry trigger points**.

Example 1 has two trigger points: (i) purchase of raw (direct) materials and (ii) completion of good finished units of product.
Example 2 has two trigger points: (i) purchase of raw (direct) materials and (ii) sale of good finished units of product.
Example 3 has one trigger point: (i) completion of good finished units of product.

---

  6. **Example 1** (p. 663) illustrates how backflush costing can eliminate the need for a separate Work in Process account.
     a. Six steps result in journal entries labeled (a) through (d) to assign costs to units sold and to inventories.

b. Note the new account, *Inventory: Raw and In-Process*, which is the combination of materials and work in process inventories.

c. In particular, see the discussion of *entry (c)*, which appears in steps 3, 4, and 5.

d. Exhibit 19-2 shows the entries posted to the T-accounts in this version of backflush costing.

7. Accounting for variances in backflush costing systems is similar to the discussion in Chapters 7 and 8.

a. Three variances highlighted are materials price variance, materials efficiency variance, and total overhead variance.

b. These variances are often immediately written off to Cost of Goods Sold rather than prorated. Why? Because companies that use backflush costing typically have low inventories and proration would not yield materially different results.

8. **Example 2** (p. 665) illustrates a backflush costing system that is a more dramatic departure from a sequential tracking system than Example 1.

a. In this case, the second trigger point is the *sale*, not the *production*, of finished units.

b. Managers have no incentive to produce for inventory, as under the sequential tracking approach of absorption costing; they can focus on a plantwide goal of selling units.

c. Note that a single inventory account, called *Inventory*, is used; it is restricted solely to raw (direct) materials, whether they are in storerooms, in process, or in finished goods.

d. This version of backflush costing is called "super-variable costing" because only materials costs are inventoried; conversion costs are treated as period costs.

e. Journal entries (a) through (d) are posted to T-accounts in Exhibit 19-3.

9. **Example 3** (p. 666) illustrates the most extreme and simplest version of backflush costing.

a. There is only one trigger point for recording inventory: completion of finished goods.

b. This version of backflush costing *does not* inventory direct materials and *does not* record accounts payable for direct materials until the related products are completely through the manufacturing process!

10. The accounting procedures illustrated in Examples 2 and 3 do not strictly adhere to generally accepted accounting principles of external reporting and do not provide sufficient information for audit trails.

a. However, the accounting principle of *materiality* works in favor of these more extreme versions of backflush costing if inventories are low.

b. Also, an adjustment can be recorded to make the backflush numbers satisfy external reporting requirements, if necessary.

11. *See Practice Test Problem V.*

Part Two: Control of Projects

E. The planning and control of jobs and projects have common characteristics, but projects are larger and more challenging than jobs.

1. In general, a **project** is a complex job that often takes months or years to complete and requires the work of many different departments, divisions, or subcontractors.

2. Examples of projects: building bridges, developing and introducing new product models such as automobiles, conducting complex lawsuits.
3. Compared to jobs, projects have more uncertainties, involve more skills and specialties, and require more coordination over a longer time period.
4. Managers control projects by focusing on four critical success factors: scope (the technical description of the final product), quality, time schedule, and costs.
5. The U.S. Department of Defense, which spends huge amounts of money on projects, requires those expenditures to be monitored by cost (and schedule) performance reporting (CPR).

Exhibit 19-4 presents a cost and schedule performance report. Note the new terms:
- **BCWS: budgeted costs of work scheduled to date**
- **BCWP: budgeted costs of work performed to date**
- **ACWP: actual costs of work performed to date**

---

6. In Exhibit 19-4, the "time now" label helps managers see what has been accomplished and what remains to be done.
7. Two variances of specific interest in project costing:
   a. **Project performance cost variance**: the difference between ACWP and BCWP (an unfavorable variance is called a cost overrun).
   b. **Project schedule cost variance**: the difference between BCWP and BCWS.
8. *See Practice Test Question III (items 4 and 5) and Problem VI.*

PRACTICE TEST QUESTIONS AND PROBLEMS

I. Complete each of the following statements.

Part One

1. Hybrid costing systems are blends of characteristics from both _____ and _____.
2. A hybrid costing system for batches of similar products is called a(an) _____ _____ system.
3. _____ is a system of production in which each component on a production line is produced immediately as needed by the next step in the production line.
4. When the timing of accounting entries is synchronized with the movement of production from materials, through work in process, to finished goods, this set of procedures is called _____.

5. _____ delays recording changes in the movement of production until good finished units are produced or sold; it then uses budgeted or standard costs to work backward to assign manufacturing costs to units produced or sold.

Part Two

6. In general, a _____ is a complex job that often takes months or years to complete and requires the work of many different departments, divisions, or subcontractors.
7. Under cost performance reporting, what does each of these sets of initials stand for?

   BCWS _____
   _____

   BCWP _____
   _____

   ACWP _____
   _____

8. The difference between BCWP and BCWS is a _____ variance; the difference between ACWP and BCWP is a _____ variance.

II. Indicate whether each of the following statements is true or false by putting T or F in the space provided.

Part One

___ 1. Production systems should be tailored to the product-costing system in use.

___ 2. Hybrid costing systems blend characteristics from both job costing systems and process-costing systems.

___ 3. In operation costing systems, all batches of production pass through each operation.

___ 4. Under an operation costing system, identical amounts of conversion costs are allocated to each product unit within each operation used.

___ 5. JIT production lines operate on a demand-pull basis.

___ 6. Ideally, JIT production systems operate with low inventories.

___ 7. A key feature of backflush costing is that it avoids sequential tracking of costs.

___ 8. Under backflush costing, each product has a budgeted or standard cost.

___ 9. Under a backflush costing system when a single inventory account is used, this account is restricted solely to raw (direct) materials, whether they are in storerooms, in process, or in finished goods.

___ 10. The backflush costing system that is the most extreme departure from sequential tracking of costs has a trigger point when raw (direct) materials are purchased and another trigger point when finished goods are sold.

___ 11. If a backflush costing system does not strictly adhere to generally accepted accounting principles, the accounting principle of materiality may work in favor of backflush costing.

Part Two

___ 12. In general, a project is a complex job that often takes months or years to complete.

___ 13. As used in cost and schedule performance reporting, BCWS stands for budgeted cost of work slippage to date.

___ 14. An unfavorable project schedule cost variance is called a cost overrun.

III. Select the best answer for each of the following multiple-choice questions and put the identifying letter in the space provided.

Part One

___ 1. JIT production systems usually entail:
   a. lower inventory levels and more paperwork.
   b. lower inventory levels and longer manufacturing lead time.
   c. simplified production activities and less paperwork.
   d. shorter manufacturing lead time and more paperwork.

___ 2. Which of the following actions is least likely to be a trigger point in backflush costing systems?
   a. Purchase of raw (direct) materials.
   b. Issuance of raw (direct) materials to production.
   c. Completion of good finished units of product.
   d. Sale of good finished units of product.

___ 3. Backflush costing systems can differ in terms of:
   a. the number of trigger points but not in the placement of trigger points.
   b. neither the number of trigger points nor the placement of trigger points.
   c. the placement of trigger points but not the number of trigger points.
   d. both the number of trigger points and the placement of trigger points.

Part Two

___ 4. Shamrock Engineering has a major project underway. The project was started four months ago and is scheduled for completion ten months from now.

The following information is available for the project:

Budgeted costs of work scheduled to date	$836,000
Budgeted costs of work performed to date	804,000
Actual costs of work performed to date	915,000

The project performance cost variance is:

a. $32,000 unfavorable.
b. $79,000 unfavorable.
c. $111,000 unfavorable.
d. none of the above.

___ 5. See item 4. The project schedule cost variance is:

a. $32,000 unfavorable.
b. $79,000 unfavorable.
c. $111,000 unfavorable.
d. none of the above.

Part One

IV. Metaxes Company manufactures two models of aircraft subassemblies, X and Y. Given the following data:

	Production Orders	
	2,000 Units of Model X	1,000 Units of Model Y
Direct materials	$48,000	$64,000
Conversion costs (allocated on the basis of machine-hours used)		
Operation 1	20,000	10,000
Operation 2	?	?
Operation 3	–	5,000
Total manufacturing costs	$?	$?

Operation 2 is highly automated. Manufacturing costs include a budgeted allocation rate for conversion costs based on machine-hours. The budgeted costs for 19_4 were $200,000 for direct manufacturing labor and $880,000 for manufacturing overhead. Budgeted machine-hours were 36,000. Each product unit required 10 minutes of machine time in Operation 2.

1. Compute the total costs of processing each model in Operation 2.
2. Compute the total manufacturing costs and the unit costs of each model in finished form.

3. Suppose at the end of the year that 100 Model X units were in process through Operation 1 only and 200 Model Y units were in process through Operation 2 only. Assume that no direct materials are added in Operation 2 and that $8,000 (of the $64,000) direct materials are to be added to the 1,000 units processed in Operation 3. Compute the cost of ending work in process inventory.
4. Prepare journal entries that track the costs of all 1,000 Model Y units through each operation to Finished Goods.

Check figures: (1) X $10,000 (2) X $39 per unit (3) $17,600 (4) debit Finished Goods $84,000

V. Cumberland Inc. produces video cameras. For November, there were no beginning inventories of raw (direct) materials and no beginning and ending work in process. Cumberland uses a JIT production system and backflush costing. The November standard costs per unit are: direct materials $52, conversion costs $30. The following data are for November manufacturing:

Raw materials and components purchased	$21,200,000
Conversion costs incurred	$12,320,000
Number of finished units manufactured	400,000
Number of finished units sold	384,000

Assume there are no raw materials variances.

1. Prepare summary journal entries for November (without disposing of underallocated or overallocated conversion costs), assuming there are two trigger points: (i) purchase of raw materials and components and (ii) completion of finished goods. The inventory accounts used are Inventory: Raw and In-Process and Finished Goods.
2. Prepare summary journal entries for November, assuming there are two trigger points: (i) purchase of raw materials and components and (ii) sale of finished goods. The only inventory account, called Inventory, is restricted solely to raw materials and components (whether they are in storerooms, in process, or in finished goods). Underallocated or overallocated conversion costs are written off at the end of each month.

3. Refer to part 2. Suppose that conversion costs are regarded as being material in amount. Show how your journal entries in part 2 would be changed.
4. Repeat part 1 with one change. There is only one trigger point, the completion of finished units. This change means that there is only one inventory account, Finished Goods.

Check figures: (1) credit Finished Goods $31,488,000 (2) debit Cost of Goods Sold $31,488,000, $800,000 (3) debit Inventory $480,000 (4) debit Finished Goods $32,800,000

Part Two

VI. Given at August 31 for the Sigma Project, which had an original budget of 20,000 hours at $100 per hour:

Budgeted hours of work scheduled to date	12,000 hours
Budgeted hours of work performed to date	10,000 hours
Actual hours of work performed to date	11,000 hours

No price variance has occurred to date, but an unfavorable price variance of $18,000 is expected during the remainder of the project.

1. Compute the project performance cost variance and the project schedule cost variance.
2. Prepare a revised budget that is designed to predict actual final costs of the project. Assume that the project performance cost variance will continue to be unfavorable at the same rate as shown to date.

Check figures: (1) $100,000 U, $200,000 U (2) $2,218,000

CHAPTER 19 SOLUTIONS TO PRACTICE TEST

I. 1 job costing systems, process-costing systems; 2 operation costing; 3 Just-in-time (JIT) production; 4 sequential tracking; 5 Backflush costing; 6 project; 7 budgeted costs of work scheduled to date, budgeted costs of work performed to date, actual costs of work performed to date; 8 project schedule cost, project performance cost.

II.

1 F	5 T	9 T	13 F
2 T	6 F	10 F	14 F
3 F	7 T	11 T	
4 T	8 T	12 T	

Explanations:
1 The statement is reversed. Product-costing systems should be tailored to the underlying production systems. (F)
2 Hybrid costing systems develop because there are hybrid production systems. For example, cars may be manufactured in a continuous flow, but each car may be customized with a particular combination of motor, transmission, radio, and so on. (T)
3 All batches of production do not pass through each operation. In the textbook illustration, for example, work order 423 (for wool blazers) did not use operation 5, sewing collars and lapels by machine. (F)
4 This statement describes the process-costing feature of operating costing. (T)
5 In JIT production systems, manufacturing activity at any particular workstation is prompted or "pulled" by the use of that station's output at downstream stations. (T)
6 Ideally, JIT production systems operate with *zero* inventories. That is, ideally the sale of a unit of finished goods triggers the completion of a unit in final assembly, and so forth, backward in the sequence of manufacturing steps all the way to the delivery of materials. (F)
7 Backflush costing avoids sequential tracking by first focusing on output and then working backward to assign manufacturing costs to units sold and to inventories. (T)

8   This statement names one of the three conditions often met by companies adopting backflush costing. The other two conditions are (i) management wants a simple accounting system and (ii) inventories are low or constant. (T)

9   See textbook Example 2. (T)

10 This statement describes textbook Example 2. A more extreme departure from sequential tracking of costs is Example 3, where the only trigger point is completion of finished goods. (F)

11 The difference in results between backflush costing and sequential tracking of costs would tend to be immaterial in amount if materials and work in process inventories are *low* or *constant*. (T)

12 A project often requires the work of many different departments, divisions, and subcontractors. Compared to jobs, projects have more uncertainties, involve more skills and specialties, and require more coordination over a longer time period. (T)

13 BCWS stands for budgeted costs of work *scheduled* to date. (F)

14 An unfavorable project performance cost variance is called a cost overrun. The project performance cost variance is the difference between actual cost of work performed to date (ACWP) and budgeted cost of work performed to date (BCWP). (F)

III. 1 c   4 c
          2 b   5 a
          3 d

Explanations:

1   Key features of JIT production systems are listed in the box in section C of the chapter outline. JIT has many potential financial benefits including lower investment in inventories, less risk of obsolete inventories, less plant space used for inventories, and less paperwork. (c)

2   In the textbook illustration, Example 1 has trigger points (a) and (c); Example 2 has trigger points (a) and (d); Example 3 has trigger point (c). (b)

3   See the preceding explanation. (d)

4   Project performance cost variance = ACWP − BCWP = $915,000 − $804,000 = $111,000 U (c)

5   Project schedule cost variance = BCWS − BCWP = $836,000 − $804,000 = $32,000 U (a)

IV. Metaxes Company

1. $\text{Budgeted allocation rate for conversion costs} = \dfrac{\$200,000 + \$880,000}{36,000} = \$30 \text{ per machine-hour}$

    Production per hour = 60 minutes ÷ 10 minutes per unit = 6 units
    Cost per unit = $30 ÷ 6 = $5
    Cost of 2,000 units of Model X = 2,000 × $5 = $10,000
    Cost of 1,000 units of Model Y = 1,000 × $5 = $5,000

2.

	Model X	Model Y
Direct materials	$48,000	$64,000
Conversion costs:		
Operation 1	20,000	10,000
Operation 2	10,000	5,000
Operation 3	–	5,000
Total manufacturing costs	$78,000	$84,000
Divide by number of units	÷2,000	÷1,000
Cost per unit	$ 39	$ 84

3.

	Model X	Model Y
Direct materials:		
$48,000 \times (100 \div 2,000)$	$2,400	
$($64,000 - $8,000) \times (200 \div 1,000)$		$11,200
Conversion costs:		
Operation 1:		
$20,000 \times (100 \div 2,000)$	1,000	
$10,000 \times (200 \div 1,000)$		2,000
Operation 2:		
$5,000 \times (200 \div 1,000)$		1,000
Ending work in process ($17,600)	$3,400	$14,200

4.

Work in Process, Operation 1	$56,000	
Materials Inventory Control		$56,000
Work in Process, Operation 1	$10,000	
Conversion Costs Allocated		$10,000
Work in Process, Operation 2	$66,000	
Work in Process, Operation 1		
($64,000 - $8,000 + $10,000)		$66,000
Work in Process, Operation 2	$5,000	
Conversion Costs Allocated		$5,000
Work in Process, Operation 3	$71,000	
Work in Process, Operation 2		
($66,000 + $5,000)		$71,000
Work in Process, Operation 3	$8,000	
Materials Inventory Control		$8,000
Work in Process, Operation 3	$5,000	
Conversion Costs Allocated		$5,000
Finished Goods	$84,000	
Work in Process, Operation 3		
($71,000 + $8,000 + $5,000)		$84,000

V. Cumberland, Inc.

1.

Inventory: Raw and In-Process	$21,200,000	
Accounts Payable Control		$21,200,000
Conversion Costs Control	$12,320,000	
Various Accounts		$12,320,000
Finished Goods		
$(400,000 \times $52) + (400,000 \times $30)$	$32,800,000	
Inventory: Raw and In-Process		
($400,000 \times 52)		$20,800,000
Conversion Costs Allocated		
($400,000 \times 30)		12,000,000
Cost of Goods Sold	$31,488,000	
Finished Goods		
$384,000 ($52 + $30)$		$31,488,000

2. | | | |
    |---|---|---|
    | Inventory | $21,200,000 | |
    | Accounts Payable Control | | $21,200,000 |
    | Conversion Costs Control | $12,320,000 | |
    | Various Accounts | | $12,320,000 |
    | Cost of Goods Sold | | |
    | (384,000 × $52) + (384,000 × $30) | $31,488,000 | |
    | Inventory (384,000 × $52) | | $19,968,000 |
    | Conversion Costs Allocated | | |
    | (384,000 × $30) | | 11,520,000 |
    | Conversion Costs Allocated | $11,520,000 | |
    | Cost of Goods Sold | 800,000 | |
    | Conversion Costs Control | | $12,320,000 |

3. All journal entries in part 2 would be the same except the last one. It should now include some conversion costs in Inventory, 16,000 units × $30 = $480,000:

Conversion Costs Allocated	$11,520,000	
Inventory	480,000	
Cost of Goods Sold	320,000	
Conversion Costs Control		$12,320,000

4. | | | |
    |---|---|---|
    | Finished Goods | | |
    | (400,000 × $52) + (400,000 × $30) | $32,800,000 | |
    | Accounts Payable Control | | |
    | (for materials: 400,000 × $52) | | $20,800,000 |
    | Conversion Costs Allocated | | |
    | (400,000 × $30) | | 12,000,000 |

VI. Sigma Project

1. Project performance cost variance = ACWP − BCWP = $100(11,000 − 10,000) = $100,000 U
    Project schedule cost variance = BCWS − BCWP = $100(12,000 − 10,000) = $200,000 U

2. | | |
    |---|---|
    | Original budgeted costs, 20,000 hours × $100 | $2,000,000 |
    | Add unfavorable project performance | |
    | cost variance to date | 100,000 |
    | Subtotal | 2,100,000 |
    | Add: | |
    | Additional unfavorable project performance | |
    | cost variance expected | 100,000* |
    | Unfavorable price variance expected | 18,000 |
    | Revised budget, final costs | $2,218,000 |

*11,000 − 10,000 = 1,000 hours, which is 10% of 10,000;
10% × 20,000 × $100 = $200,000; $200,000 − $100,000 = $100,000

CHAPTER 20

CAPITAL BUDGETING AND COST ANALYSIS

MAIN FOCUS AND OBJECTIVES

This chapter and the next explain the role of accounting data in decision models for capital budgeting. Capital budgeting involves making investment decisions on projects that usually span several years or more. Capital-budgeting decisions frequently deal with large dollar amounts and have uncertain outcomes. Your overall objective for this chapter is to be able to apply the concept of relevant costs and revenues (introduced in Chapter 11) to the decision models for capital budgeting. Ten learning objectives are stated in the textbook (p. 684).

Give special attention to:

- the distinction between two discounted cash-flow methods: net present value and internal rate of return
- the four main categories of cash flows for the discounted cash-flow methods
- the payback method
- the accrual accounting rate-of-return method

Keep in mind two points as you study this chapter. First, income determination and the planning and control of operations primarily focus on the current accounting period, while capital budgeting focuses on projects that typically cover a much longer time span. This contrast can lead to conflicts between decision making and performance evaluation. Second, income taxes are either ignored in or do not apply to the examples in this chapter. Income taxes are included in the next chapter.

REVIEW OF KEY TERMS AND CONCEPTS

A. The revenues and costs specifically associated with a capital-budgeting project should be measured over its life and compared with the required investment.
   1. A project's life tends to be much longer than the one-year accounting period, as shown in Exhibit 20-1.
   2. Therefore, the planning and control tools used for year-to-year operating decisions are not well suited for capital-budgeting decisions.
   3. Capital budgeting has six stages: (i) identification, (ii) search, (iii) information acquisition, (iv) selection, (v) financing, and (vi) implementation and control.
   4. The textbook focuses on the *information-acquisition stage* and emphasizes the role of quantitative factors that can be expressed in financial terms.
   5. *The analysis should include only relevant items: future cash flows that differ between the "invest" and "do not invest" alternatives.*

6. In the selection stage, conclusions reached on the basis of quantitative analysis are then re-evaluated, taking into account *qualitative factors* such as employee morale.
7. Keep in mind that acceptance or rejection of specific capital-budgeting projects often depends on how persuasive individual managers are in "selling" their own projects to the decision makers.
8. Several of the capital-budgeting methods weigh the time value of money.
   a. The *time value of money* takes into account that, because interest can be earned on investments, a dollar received today is worth more than a dollar received at any time in the future.
   b. Note that the time value of money is usually ignored in short-run decisions, such as most of the material in Chapter 11, because the interest involved is unlikely to be material in amount over short time periods.
   c. Various aspects of the time value of money are explained in Appendix C at the back of the textbook.

> **Be sure you have a good working knowledge of the compound interest and present value tables in Appendix C.** *See Practice Test Questions II (item 2) and III (item 1).*

B. **Discounted cash-flow (DCF) methods** measure the *expected cash inflows and outflows* of a project as if they occurred at a single point in time.
   1. Since DCF methods weigh the time value of money, they are usually considered to be better (more comprehensive) than other capital-budgeting methods.
   2. Two main DCF methods: net present value and internal rate of return.
   3. **Net present value (NPV)** is the expected net gain or loss from a project after discounting all expected future cash inflows and outflows to the present point in time (referred to as *year 0*), using the required rate of return.
      a. The *required rate of return* (also called the *discount rate, hurdle rate,* or *cost of capital*) is the minimum acceptable rate of return on an investment.
      b. The NPV method is illustrated in Exhibit 20-2. Note two key points:
         (1) The *"sketch of relevant cash flows"* in this and other exhibits is a very helpful step in the analysis. For simplicity, all of the cash flows are assumed to occur either at the beginning or at the end of each period.
         (2) The $20,200 positive NPV indicates that the manager would likely buy the machine *unless* there were adverse qualitative factors that outweigh this net gain.
      c. *Decision rule*: a project is acceptable in financial terms if its NPV is positive or zero.

> **Do not proceed until you thoroughly understand Exhibit 20-2.** *See Practice Test Question III (item 2) and Problem IV.*

   4. **Internal rate of return (IRR)** is the discount rate at which the present value of expected cash inflows of a project equals the present value of expected cash outflows of the project.

a. IRR is the discount rate that makes *NPV = $0*.
b. IRR can be determined by using a calculator, a computer, or the two-step trial-and-error approach explained in the textbook (p. 690).
c. The IRR method is illustrated in Exhibit 20-3.
d. *Decision rule*: a project is acceptable in financial terms if its IRR exceeds or equals the required rate of return.
e. *See Practice Test Question III (item 3) and Problem V.*

5. The textbook emphasizes NPV; three advantages are discussed (p. 692).
6. NPV and IRR focus exclusively on a project's *future incremental cash flows*, regardless of their sources or uses and regardless of how they are accounted for under accrual accounting.
7. A project's future incremental cash flows can be classified in four main categories.

Cash-Flow Category	*Relevant Cash Inflows (Outflows) Shown in Exhibit 20-5*
1. Initial investment	
a. Purchase of new fixed asset	$(372,890) at end of year 0
b. Working capital	$(10,000) at end of year 0
2. Current disposal price of old fixed asset	$3,790 at end of year 0
3. Recurring operating cash flows	$100,000 in years 1-5
4. Terminal disposal price	
a. Sale of new fixed asset	$0 at end of year 5
b. Working capital	$10,000 at end of year 5

8. *Special notes on the cash-flow categories*:
   a. Items 2, 3, and 4(a) can have income tax effects, which are discussed in Chapter 21.
   b. The book value of old equipment (original cost minus accumulated depreciation) is irrelevant to the replacement decision because it is a sunk cost.
   c. Working capital, items 1(b) and 4(b), is defined as current assets minus current liabilities (for example, a cash outflow to increase the investment in inventory).
      (1) Working capital is often required at the beginning of a project and is recovered at the end of the project, as illustrated in Exhibit 20-5.
      (2) Some projects *reduce* working capital, such as when factory automation decreases work in process inventory; in those cases, the timing of the cash outflows and inflows is reversed.
      (3) *See Practice Test Question III (item 4).*

C. Sensitivity analysis can help managers cope with the uncertainty in capital-budgeting decisions.
   1. *Sensitivity analysis* (introduced in Chapter 3) is a "what if" technique that examines how a result for a project would change if the original predicted data are not achieved or if an underlying assumption changes.

2. Two uses of sensitivity analysis:
   a. Compute the amount of change needed in annual cash operating savings to reach the point of indifference for a project (NPV = $0); see the textbook example (p. 693).
   b. Compute how NPV is affected by various "what if" scenarios, as shown in Exhibit 20-4.
3. By providing an immediate financial measure of the effects of uncertainty, sensitivity analysis can help managers focus on the more sensitive variables before decisions are made.
4. Errors in forecasting terminal disposal prices of new fixed assets are seldom critical because the present value of amounts to be received in the distant future is usually small.
5. Given the rapid pace of technological change, managers may find that estimating a project's useful life is one of the most challenging aspects of capital budgeting.

D. Another method for analyzing the financial aspects of projects is payback.
   1. **Payback** measures the time it will take to recoup, in the form of net cash inflows, the net amount invested in a project.
   2. When the annual cash inflows are uniform:

$$\text{Payback} = \frac{\text{Net initial investment}}{\text{Uniform increase in annual cash flow}}$$

   3. *See Practice Test Question III (item 5) and Problem VI (part 1).*
   4. When the annual cash inflows are *not uniform*, payback is reached when the cumulative total of those amounts equals the net initial investment.
   5. Projects with shorter paybacks are preferable, if all other things are equal.
   6. Strengths: highlights liquidity and is easily understood.
   7. Weaknesses: does not consider profitability and ignores the time value of money.
   8. **Bailout payback** measures the time it will take to recoup the net initial investment in a project by using the sum of (i) cumulative annual cash flow from operations, (ii) disposal price at the end of a particular year, and (iii) recovery of working capital at the end of that year.
      a. Bailout payback examines the downside protection if the project is disbanded.
      b. Projects with shorter bailout paybacks are preferable, if all other things are equal.
      c. See the textbook example (p. 700) and related Exhibit 20-6.
      d. *See Practice Test Problem VI (part 2).*

E. The last capital-budgeting method discussed is **accrual accounting rate of return (AARR)**.

$$\text{AARR} = \frac{\text{Increase in expected average annual operating income}}{\text{Net initial investment}}$$

   1. The numerator is equal to cash flow from operations minus depreciation.
   2. As an alternative to net initial investment, the denominator may be expressed as *average* increase in investment.
      a. Average increase in investment = (Net initial investment + Terminal disposal price of new fixed asset + Recovery of working capital at the end of the project's life) ÷ 2

b. When the average increase in investment is used, the net initial investment tends to be about cut in half, which about doubles AARR.
3. *See Practice Test Question III (items 6 and 7) and Problem VI (parts 3 and 4).*
4. Projects with higher AARR's are preferable, if all other things are equal.
5. Strengths: is easily understood and weighs profitability.
6. Weakness: ignores the time value of money.
7. *Note that there is an inconsistency between citing DCF methods as being best for capital-budgeting decisions and then evaluating subsequent performance on AARR.*
    a. For example, a manager might reject a project with a positive NPV because it lowers AARR in the *short run*.
    b. Several factors could cause such short-run decreases, including a loss from disposing of the old fixed asset at the start of a project, a higher net initial investment, and higher depreciation in the early years of a project.
    c. The short-run bias from using AARR to evaluate performance is heightened when income is important in managers' compensation plans.

F. The focus in this chapter is on the financial aspects of capital-budgeting projects.
1. Most textbook examples ignore the complexity in practice associated with *identifying the project* and *predicting its outcomes*.
2. Some of this complexity is illustrated in the interesting textbook example of computer-integrated manufacturing (CIM) technology (pp. 704-05) and related Exhibit 20-7.
3. In this example, two important factors are (i) recognizing the full set of benefits and costs and (ii) recognizing the full time horizon of the project.

PRACTICE TEST QUESTIONS AND PROBLEMS

I. Complete each of the following statements.

1. Capital-budgeting decisions frequently deal with large dollar amounts and have _____ _____ outcomes.
2. The textbook discussion focuses on the ____ _____ stage of capital budgeting and emphasizes the role of quantitative factors that can be expressed in _____ _____ terms.
3. The _____ takes into account that, because interest can be earned on investments, a dollar received today is worth more than a dollar received at any time in the future.
4. What do these initials stand for?

    DCF: _____

    NPV: _____

    IRR: _____

    AARR: _____

5. _____ is the discount rate that makes NPV equal to zero.
6. In a capital-budgeting project, the investment that might be required for accounts receivable and inventories is called _____ _____.
7. _____ is a technique that examines how a result for a project would change if the original predicted data are not achieved or if an underlying assumption changes.
8. The downside protection if a project is disbanded is examined by the _____ _____ method.

II. Indicate whether each of the following statements is true or false by putting T or F in the space provided.

____ 1. The planning and control tools used for year-to-year operating decisions are not well suited for capital-budgeting decisions.

2. The present value of $1 million to be received ten years from now would be lower if computed at a discount rate of 10% rather than 14%.

___ 3. The required rate of return is also called the discount rate.

___ 4. A project is acceptable if NPV is positive or zero.

___ 5. A required rate of return of 12% is used to compute the NPV of a project. If NPV is negative, IRR is greater than 12%.

___ 6. The NPV method is more appropriate than the IRR method for deciding whether a combination of mutually exclusive projects would be acceptable.

___ 7. Errors in forecasting terminal disposal prices of new fixed assets are often important in capital-budgeting decisions.

___ 8. Depreciation is not a cash flow.

___ 9. The payback method considers the profitability of capital-budgeting projects.

___ 10. The bailout payback time for a project is reached when the cumulative operating savings minus the sum of disposal price and recovery of working capital at the end of a particular year equals the net initial investment.

___ 11. The accrual accounting rate of return weighs a project's profitability.

___ 12. It is consistent to cite DCF methods as being best for capital-budgeting decisions and then to evaluate subsequent performance on the basis of accrual accounting rate of return.

___ 13. Computer-integrated manufacturing (CIM) technology is a case where there is considerable complexity involved in predicting the outcomes of capital-budgeting projects.

III. Select the best answer for each of the following multiple-choice questions and put the identifying letter in the space provided.

___ 1. (CPA adapted) John Kent wishes to find the present value of an annuity of $1 payable at the *beginning* of each period at 10% for eight periods. He has only one present value table, which shows the present value of an annuity of $1 payable at the *end* of each period. To compute the present value factor he

needs, Kent would use the present value factor in the 10% column for:
a. seven periods.
b. nine periods and subtract $1.
c. eight periods.
d. seven periods and add $1.

___ 2. (CMA) Making the common assumption in capital-budgeting analysis that cash inflows occur in lump sums at the end of individual years during the life of an investment project when in fact they flow more or less continuously during those years:
a. results in increasingly overstated estimates of NPV as the life of the investment project increases.
b. is done because present value tables for continuous flows cannot be constructed.
c. results in a higher estimate for the IRR on the investment.
d. will result in inconsistent errors being made in estimating NPVs such that projects cannot be evaluated reliably.
e. results in understated estimates of NPV.

___ 3. (CPA adapted) Herman Hospital, a non-profit institution not subject to income taxes, is considering the purchase of new equipment at a cost of $46,600. The equipment has an estimated life of ten years. There is no terminal disposal price. Annual cash flow from operations is estimated to be $10,000 at the end of each year. The following amounts appear in the interest table for the present value of an annuity of $1 at year-end for ten years:

16%	4.83
18%	4.49
20%	4.19

What is the IRR of the project?
a. 16%
b. 17%
c. 18%
d. 19%

___ 4. (CMA) Fast Freight Inc. is planning to purchase equipment to make its operations more efficient. This equipment has an estimated life of six years. As part of this acquisition, a $75,000 investment in working capital is required. In a discounted cash flow analysis, this investment in working capital:

a. should be amortized over the useful life of the equipment.
b. can be disregarded because no cash is involved.
c. should be treated as a recurring annual cash outflow that is recovered at the end of six years.
d. should be treated as an immediate cash outflow.
e. should be treated as an immediate cash outflow that is recovered at the end of six years.

___ 5. (CPA adapted) Apex Corp. is considering the purchase of a machine costing $100,000. The machine's expected useful life is five years. The estimated annual cash flow from operations is: $60,000 in year 1, $30,000 in year 2, $20,000 in year 3, $20,000 in year 4, and $20,000 in year 5. Assuming the cash flows will be received evenly during each year, the payback is:

a. 2.50 years.
b. 3.00 years.
c. 3.33 years.
d. none of the above.

___ 6. (CPA adapted) The Gravina Company is planning to spend $6,000 for a machine that it will depreciate on a straight-line basis over a ten-year period with no terminal disposal price. The machine will generate cash flow from operations of $1,200 a year. Ignoring income taxes, what is the accrual accounting rate of return on the net initial investment?

a. 5%
b. 10%
c. 15%
d. 20%

___ 7. (CPA adapted) If income tax considerations are ignored, how is depreciation used in the following capital-budgeting techniques?

	IRR	AARR
a.	Excluded	Excluded
b.	Excluded	Included
c.	Included	Excluded
d.	Included	Included

IV. Given for Talihina Co.:

Net initial investment for a special-purpose machine	$152,000
Estimated useful life	12 years
Estimated terminal disposal price	$10,000
Estimated net annual cash operating savings	$30,000
Required rate of return	16%

Compute NPV of the machine, using the interest tables in Appendix C at the back of the textbook.

Check figure: $5,590

V. Given for a project under consideration by Fasken, Inc.:

Net initial investment	$180,000
Estimated useful life	15 years
Estimated terminal disposal price	none
Estimated cash flow from operations	$30,000

Compute IRR of the project to the nearest tenth of a percent, using the interest tables in Appendix C at the back of the textbook.

Check figure: 14.5%

VI. Given for Sisco Industries:

Net initial investment for materials-handling equipment	$125,000
Estimated useful life	8 years
Estimated disposal price at end of year 1	$84,000
Estimated decrease in disposal price each year for years 2 through 8	$12,000
Estimated terminal disposal price	$10,000
Estimated annual cash operating savings	$35,000
Required rate of return	10%
Depreciation method: straight-line	

Compute (using the interest tables in Appendix C at the back of the textbook as needed):
1. Payback
2. Bailout payback
3. Accrual accounting rate of return based on net initial investment
4. Accrual accounting rate of return based on average increase in investment

Check figures: (1) 3.57 years (2) 1.26 years (3) 16.5% (4) 30.56%

CHAPTER 20 SOLUTIONS TO PRACTICE TEST

I. 1 uncertain; 2 information-acquisition, financial; 3 time value of money; 4 discounted cash flow, net present value, internal rate of return, accrual accounting rate of return; 5 Internal rate of return (IRR); 6 working capital; 7 Sensitivity analysis; 8 bailout payback.

II.

1 T	5 F	9 F	13 T
2 F	6 T	10 F	
3 T	7 F	11 T	
4 T	8 T	12 F	

Explanations:

1 Operating decisions focus on a time period of one year or less, while capital-budgeting projects typically span a much longer time (see textbook Exhibit 20-1). Consequently, the time value of money is much more important in capital-budgeting decisions. (T)

2 Using Table 2 in Appendix C at the back of the textbook:
At 10%, $1,000,000 × 0.386 = $386,000
At 14%, $1,000,000 × 0.270 = $270,000 (F)

3 Other synonyms for the required rate of return are hurdle rate and cost of capital. (T)

4 A project is acceptable if its NPV is positive or zero. Whether a project is actually accepted depends on (i) knowledge of adverse qualitative factors that outweigh the NPV and (ii) availability of funding. (T)

5 In Exhibit 20-3, NPV = $0 when a 10% discount rate is used. That is, IRR is 10%. If a discount rate of 12% were used in Exhibit 20-3, the present value factors would be smaller and NPV would be negative. (F)

6 This statement refers to one of the three advantages of the NPV method discussed in the textbook (p. 692). (T)

7 Errors in forecasting terminal disposal prices are usually not critical because the combinations of relatively small disposal prices and long useful lives result in small present values of these expected cash inflows. (F)

8 Depreciation itself does not affect an organization's Cash account. However, when income taxes are considered (as in the next chapter), depreciation is included in the computation of cash flow from operations, net of income taxes, because depreciation reduces the payments for income taxes. (T)

9 The payback method does not consider profitability and ignores the time value of money. Nonetheless, the payback method is widely used (at a minimum as a screening device) because it highlights liquidity and is easily understood. (F)

10 To make the statement true, the word "minus" needs to be changed to "plus." For an illustration, see Exhibit 20-6. (F)

11 AARR also is easily understood. Its main disadvantage is that it ignores the time value of money. (T)

12 It is inconsistent to cite DCF methods as being best for capital-budgeting decisions and then to evaluate subsequent performance on the basis of AARR. For example, a manager might reject a project with a positive NPV because it lowers AARR in the short run. (F)

13 See the textbook discussion of the complexities regarding CIM (pp. 704-05). (T)

III.

1 d	4 e	7 b
2 e	5 a	
3 b	6 b	

Explanations:

1 The *beginning* of a given period is the same point in time as the *end* of the preceding period. Therefore, the present value factor would be $1 payable at the beginning of the first period plus the present value of the $1 annuity payable at the end of each of the seven periods. (d)

2 Although present value tables for continuous cash flows are available, they are seldom used. Present value tables for end-of-the-period cash flows are used for convenience. Since *some* cash flows occur only once *sometime during* a period, it is simply convenient to assume that *all* cash flows occur at the *end* of a period. Under this assumption, cash inflows that occur more or less continuously during a period are discounted at the end of a period. As a result, the true present value of those inflows will be *understated*, which in turn will understate NPV and IRR. Since the errors introduced by making the end-of-the-period assumption tend to be reasonably consistent, projects can be evaluated with a satisfactory degree of reliability. (e)

3   Let F = Present value factor for 10 years in Table 4 of Appendix C
$10,000F = $46,600
    F = 4.66, which lies between 4.83(16%) and 4.49(18%)

16%	4.83	4.83
IRR		4.66
16%	4.49	
Difference	0.34	0.17

IRR = 16% + (0.17 ÷ 0.34)2%
IRR = 16% + (.50)2% = 17% (b)

4 In Exhibit 20-5, the $10,000 cash outflow for working capital occurs in year 0 and is recovered in year 5. (e)

5 Cumulative cash flow from operations:

Year 1	$ 60,000
Year 2	30,000
Subtotal	90,000
Year 3	20,000
Total	$110,000

Payback = 2 + [($100,000 − $90,000) ÷ ($110,000 − $90,000)]
Payback = 2 + ($10,000 ÷ $20,000) = 2.50 years (a)

6 $\text{AARR} = \dfrac{[\$1,200 - (\$6,000 \div 10)]}{\$6,000} = \dfrac{\$600}{\$6,000} = 10\%$ (b)

7 If income tax considerations are ignored, depreciation is excluded under IRR (see Exhibit 20-3) and is included under AARR (see the calculations in item 6 above). (b)

IV.   Talihina Co.

Present value of net annual cash operating savings, $30,000 × 5.197	$155,910
Present value of terminal disposal price, $10,000 × 0.168	1,680
Total present value	157,590
Net initial investment	(152,000)
NPV	$ 5,590

V. Fasken, Inc.

Let F = Present value factor for 15 years in Table 4 of Appendix C
$30,000 F = $180,000
F = 6.000, which lies between 6.142 (14%) and 5.575 (16%)

14%	6.142	6.142
IRR		6.000
16%	5.575	
Difference	0.567	0.142

IRR = 14% + (0.142 ÷ 0.567)2%
IRR = 14% + (.25)2% = 14.5%

VI. Sisco Industries

1. $125,000 ÷ $35,000 = 3.57 years

2.

At End of	Cumulative Cash Operating Savings	Disposal Price	Cumulative Total Cash Inflows
Year 1	$35,000	$84,000	$119,000
Year 2	70,000	72,000	142,000

$$\text{Bailout payback} = 1 + \frac{(\$125,000 - \$119,000)}{(\$142,000 - \$119,000)} = 1 + \frac{\$6,000}{\$23,000} = 1.26 \text{ years}$$

3. Annual depreciation = ($125,000 − $10,000) ÷ 8 = $14,375;
   AARR = ($35,000 − $14,375) ÷ $125,000 = $20,625 ÷ $125,000 = 16.5%

4. Average increase in investment = ($125,000 + $10,000) ÷ 2 = $67,500;
   AARR = ($35,000 − $14,375) ÷ $67,500 = $20,625 ÷ $67,500 = 30.56%

CHAPTER 21

CAPITAL BUDGETING:
A CLOSER LOOK

MAIN FOCUS AND OBJECTIVES

The preceding chapter introduced basic aspects of capital budgeting. This chapter extends that coverage by explaining how managers analyze the effects of income taxes, inflation, and investment risk for projects under consideration. These economic realities, however, do not change the fundamental ideas underlying discounted cash-flow analysis. Your overall objective for this chapter is to understand how each of the additional topics affects capital budgeting. Nine learning objectives are stated in the textbook (p. 720).

Give special attention to:

- how income taxes affect both the amount and the timing of cash flows
- the three methods to compute cash flow from operations, net of income taxes, which are illustrated in key Exhibit 21-1
- why depreciation deductions for tax purposes increase cash flow from operations
- the total project approach and the incremental approach to capital-budgeting decisions
- the nominal approach to incorporating inflation in capital-budgeting analysis and its equivalence to the real approach

Keep in mind that this chapter focuses only on a general approach to incorporating income taxes in capital-budgeting analysis because tax laws are very detailed and frequently change. The chapter Appendix summarizes some key provisions of U.S. tax rules for depreciable assets.

REVIEW OF KEY TERMS AND CONCEPTS

A. Income taxes can sizably reduce the net cash inflows from individual projects and thereby change their relative desirability.
   1. Income tax is an expense that affects both the *amount* and *timing* of cash inflows and outflows.
   2. Three methods are used to compute **cash flow from operations, net of income taxes**. Using the data from Exhibit 21-1, the three methods produce identical results:
      a. *Receipts minus disbursements method*:
         $100,000 − $62,000 − $8,000 = $30,000
      b. *Income statement method* (net income plus depreciation):
         $12,000 + $18,000 = $30,000

c. *Item-by-item method*:

Cash items subject to tax $\times$ (1 − Tax rate) = \$38,000(1 − .40) = \$22,800
Noncash items subject to tax $\times$ Tax rate = \$18,000 $\times$ .40 = 7,200
Cash flow from operations, net of income taxes $\underline{\underline{\$30,000}}$

Carefully study key Exhibit 21-1. It shows how cash flow from operations, net of income taxes, of \$30,000 is computed under each of the three methods.

---

3. Depreciation itself has *no direct cash-flow effect* (as explained in the preceding chapter); however, because of its deductibility for tax purposes, depreciation *indirectly increases cash flow from operations* by decreasing the current cash outflow for income tax expense.

 a. Therefore, *the tax savings from depreciation is equivalent to a cash inflow.*

Question: How do we measure the cash inflow from depreciation?
Answer: Multiply the depreciation deduction by the tax rate, as in the bottom portion of Exhibit 21-1: \$18,000 $\times$ .40 = \$7,200.

---

 b. Income tax rules cover three factors that influence depreciation deductions:
  (1) The amount allowable for depreciation.
  (2) The time period over which the fixed asset is to be depreciated.
  (3) The pattern of allowable depreciation.

 c. The present value of the tax savings from depreciation is higher under accelerated depreciation than under straight-line depreciation. Why? Because the larger tax savings in the earlier years of a project's life are discounted over a shorter period of time than the smaller tax savings in the later years.

 d. *Note that using working capital for capital-budgeting projects (such as accounts receivable and inventories) involves cash flows that are not subject to income tax.*

4. *See Practice Test Questions II (item 3) and III (items 1 and 6).*

5. The detailed textbook example (p. 725) highlights the effect of the tax deductibility of depreciation on the net present value (NPV) of a project—whether to keep or replace an old machine.

 a. Exhibits 21-2 and 21-3 illustrate the *total project approach*, which includes *all* the cash inflows and outflows associated with the two alternatives.

 b. Exhibit 21-4 illustrates the *incremental approach*, which includes *only* those cash inflows and outflows that *differ* between the two alternatives.

 c. Both approaches result in the same NPV of \$100,324 in favor of replacing the old machine:
  (1) The total project approach is longer but clearer.
  (2) The incremental approach is more efficient if only two alternatives are compared; otherwise, it is cumbersome.

Carefully study the five numbered categories of after-tax cash flows in key Exhibits 21-2 through 21-4.

---

6. *Special notes on Exhibits 21-2 through 21-4*:
   a. Depreciation is based on the *straight-line method* for the old machine and the *double-declining balance method* for the new machine. The latter method is illustrated in the textbook (p. 728).
   b. Exhibit 21-3 shows the *advantage of accelerated depreciation*—the sooner the depreciation deduction, the higher the present value of the tax savings.
   c. Exhibit 21-3 shows after-tax cash flow from current disposal of the old machine of $33,200. *This figure includes the tax savings from the loss on disposal*: $24,000 × .30 = $7,200.
   d. Exhibit 21-3 shows after-tax cash flow from terminal disposal of the new machine of $14,000. This figure results from proceeds of $20,000, which is also the amount of taxable gain on disposal: $20,000 − ($20,000 × .30) = $14,000.
   e. Depreciation and book value of the old machine are *irrelevant* to the replacement decision.
7. *See Practice Test Question III (items 3-5) and Problems V and VI.*
8. The textbook emphasizes only a general approach to analyzing income tax effects in capital budgeting because tax rules are very detailed and frequently change.
   a. The tax rules governing depreciation in the U.S. (in effect at the time this edition was written) are called the Modified Accelerated Cost Recovery System (MACRS).
   b. Some key provisions of MACRS are summarized in the chapter Appendix; see section E of this outline.
9. The preceding chapter discussed payback, accrual accounting rate of return, and sensitivity analysis.
   a. In this chapter, the effect of income taxes is included in those computations.
   b. *See Practice Test Problems IV and VII.*

B. The cash flows used in the discounted cash-flow methods should be adjusted for the effects of inflation.
   1. **Inflation**: the decline in the general purchasing power of the monetary unit.
   2. When considering inflation, distinguish between two rates of return.
      a. **Real rate of return**: the rate of return demanded to cover investment risk disregarding inflation; this rate of return consists of a risk-free element and a business-risk element.
      b. **Nominal rate of return**: the rate of return demanded to cover both investment risk and inflation risk.
      c. The relationship between these rates of return:
         (1) *Nominal rate = (1 + Real rate)(1 + Inflation rate) − 1*
         (2) This formula is used in a textbook example (p. 732).
      d. *See Practice Test Question III (item 7).*
   3. Two internally consistent approaches for incorporating inflation under the DCF methods:
      a. *Nominal Approach*: Express all cash flows in *nominal dollars* and discount them at a *nominal rate*.
         (1) All dollar amounts must *first* be expressed in terms of future values, using the compounded inflation rate factor; *then* discount them back to present value, using the nominal discount rate.

(2) **Carefully study Exhibit 21-5—an illustration of the nominal approach**.

    b. *Real Approach*: Express all cash flows in *real dollars* and discount them at a *real rate*, as shown in Exhibit 21-6.

    c. The project in question has an NPV of $230,475 under both approaches.

    d. Note that the tax savings from depreciation is treated differently under the two approaches.

        (1) In Exhibit 21-5, *the tax savings is not adjusted for inflation* because the amount is expressed in nominal dollars.

        (2) In Exhibit 21-6, *the tax savings is adjusted to real dollars* to eliminate the effect of inflation.

Question: **What is the most common error when accounting for inflation in capital-budgeting analysis?**

Answer: **Keeping cash inflows and outflows in *real* terms and using a *nominal* discount rate, which is not an internally consistent approach.**

---

4. Many managers find the nominal approach easier to understand. Why? Because it uses the same type of financial numbers that will be recorded in the accounting system—dollars that include the impact of inflation.

5. *See Practice Test Problem VIII.*

C. The discount rate used in DCF analysis is the *required rate of return* (also called hurdle rate or cost of capital).

    1. The required rate of return varies with the *risk* of each project. For example, petroleum companies use higher required rates of return for exploration than for office equipment.

    2. Approaches to recognizing risk:

        a. Using a shorter required payback for riskier projects.

        b. Using a higher required rate of return for riskier projects.

        c. Reducing estimates of cash inflows for riskier projects (called the certainty equivalent approach).

        d. Using sensitivity analysis to identify and evaluate key assumptions for a project.

        e. Estimating the probability distribution of future cash inflows and outflows.

D. The NPV method is the best general guide for choosing among capital-budgeting projects.

    1. Theoretically, all projects with positive or zero NPV's should be accepted.

    2. In practice, however, there is often a restriction on the total funds available for capital-budgeting purposes.

    3. Exhibit 21-7 illustrates the selection of projects when the total funds available are limited.

    4. A tool for selecting projects is the *excess present value index* or *profitability index*.

        a. This index is equal to a project's total present value of future net cash inflows divided by the net initial investment.

b. Optimal decisions will not always result from using this index, as demonstrated by the textbook example (p. 739).
5. Exhibit 21-8 shows that NPV and IRR can result in *conflicting rankings* of mutually exclusive projects that have unequal lives or require different initial investments.
  a. *Question*: What causes these conflicting rankings?
     Answer: NPV and IRR make different implicit assumptions as to the rate of return on reinvestment of cash proceeds at the end of the shortest-lived project.
     (1) NPV assumes that the reinvestment rate is equal to the project's required rate of return.
     (2) IRR assumes that the reinvestment rate is equal to the indicated rate of return for the shortest-lived project.
  b. NPV and IRR can be reconciled in these cases either (i) by using a common terminal date for alternative projects or (ii) by making explicit assumptions as to reinvestment rates.

E. (**Appendix**) The income tax rules governing depreciation in the U.S. (in effect at the time this edition was written) are called the *Modified Accelerated Cost Recovery System (MACRS)*.
1. MACRS applies to assets acquired after 1986.
2. Changes in MACRS have occurred from time to time.
3. Some highlights of the current version of MACRS:
  a. The amount allowable for depreciation is the original cost of the asset; terminal disposal price does not affect the amount allowable for depreciation.

Note that under MACRS the term "cost recovery" is used to describe the amount allowable each year as a "depreciation" deduction.

---

  b. The time period over which the asset is to be depreciated is specified in a table of allowable lives (called *recovery periods*).
     (1) Recovery periods range from 3 to 31.5 years.
     (2) Recovery periods do not necessarily reflect the estimated useful lives of the assets.
  c. The depreciation method is a function of the recovery period (see textbook, p. 744).

PRACTICE TEST QUESTIONS AND PROBLEMS

I. Complete each of the following statements.

1. Income tax is an expense that affects both the _____ and the _____ of cash flows in capital-budgeting analysis.
2. When working capital does not change during the year, net income plus depreciation equals

_____
_____.

3. The decline in the general purchasing power of the monetary unit is called _____.
4. The rate of return that consists of a risk-free element and a business-risk element is called the _____.
5. The _____ rate of return is the rate of return that covers both investment risk and inflation risk.

6. For incorporating inflation in the NPV model, managers find the _____ approach easier to understand: express cash flows in _____ dollars and discount them at a(an) _____ rate.

7. The _____ is equal to a project's total present value of future net cash inflows divided by the net initial investment.

8. (Appendix) The income tax rules governing depreciation in the U.S. (in effect at the time this edition of the textbook was written) are called the _____

_____ .

II. Indicate whether each of the following statements is true or false by putting T or F in the space provided.

___ 1. Cash flow from operations, net of income taxes, may be computed by adding net income and the income tax savings from depreciation.

___ 2. Depreciation itself has no cash flow effect.

___ 3. If the income tax rate for a profitable company is 30%, depreciation of $10,000 results in a tax savings of $7,000.

___ 4. The cash flows regarding the use and recovery of working capital in capital budgeting are subject to income tax.

___ 5. If properly applied, the incremental approach and the total project approach will result in the same NPV of a project.

___ 6. Under conditions of inflation, the nominal rate of return would be higher than the real rate of return.

___ 7. If properly applied, the nominal approach and the real approach are internally consistent with regard to incorporating inflation under the NPV method.

___ 8. Higher risks of some capital-budgeting projects can be recognized by increasing the required rate of return or increasing the required payback.

___ 9. In the absence of a restriction on the total funds available for capital budgeting, all projects should be undertaken that have an excess present value index of 100% or more.

___ 10. When alternative projects have unequal lives, the NPV method assumes that the rate of return on the reinvestment of cash proceeds at the end of the shortest-lived project is the required rate of return.

___ 11. (Appendix) Under MACRS, the term "cost recovery" is used to describe the amount allowable each year as a "depreciation deduction."

III. Select the best answer for each of the following multiple-choice questions and put the identifying letter in the space provided.

___ 1. Suppose a profitable business pays $10,000 for advertising and has depreciation of $10,000. If the income tax rate is 40%, the after-tax effects on cash would be:
   a. a net inflow of $4,000 for advertising and a net inflow of $4,000 for depreciation.
   b. a net inflow of $6,000 for advertising and a net inflow of $6,000 for depreciation.
   c. a net outflow of $4,000 for advertising and a net inflow of $6,000 for depreciation.
   d. a net outflow of $6,000 for advertising and a net inflow of $4,000 for depreciation.

___ 2. In contrast to the use of the double-declining-balance depreciation method, the use of the straight-line depreciation method would result in a present value of tax savings that is:
   a. larger.
   b. smaller.
   c. the same.
   d. not determinable from the information given.

___ 3. Sunray Corporation sold an old piece of equipment for $44,000 cash. It was purchased eight years ago for $130,000 and was being depreciated on a straight-line basis over a useful life of 10 years, with a predicted terminal disposal price of $10,000. The after-tax cash flow from the sale of the old equipment, assuming a 40% income tax rate, would be:

a. $40,000.
b. $17,600.
c. $26,400.
d. none of the above.

4. See item 3. Suppose the old equipment were sold for $30,000 instead of $44,000. The after-tax cash flow from the sale of the old equipment, assuming a 40% income tax rate, would be:
   a. $30,000 gain.
   b. $28,400 loss.
   c. $26,000 gain.
   d. none of the above.

5. (CMA) Superstrut is considering replacing an old press that cost $80,000 six years ago with a new one that would cost $225,000. Shipping and installation would cost an additional $20,000. The old press has a book value of $15,000 and could be sold currently for $5,000. The increased production of the new press would increase inventories by $4,000, accounts receivable by $16,000, and accounts payable by $14,000. Superstrut's net initial investment for analyzing the acquisition of the new press, assuming a 40% income tax rate, would be:
   a. $256,000.
   b. $242,000.
   c. $250,000.
   d. $245,000.
   e. $236,000.

6. (CMA) Brownel Inc. currently has annual cash revenues of $240,000 and annual operating costs of $185,000 (all cash items except depreciation of $35,000). The company is considering the purchase of a new mixing machine costing $120,000 that would increase cash revenues to $290,000 per year and operating costs (including depreciation) to $205,000 per year. The new machine would increase depreciation to $50,000 per year. Using a 40% income tax rate, Brownel's annual incremental after-tax cash flow from the new mixing machine would be:

a. $33,000.
b. $24,000.
c. $30,000.
d. $18,000.
e. $68,000.

7. If the nominal rate of interest is 16% and the inflation rate is 5%, the real rate of interest (rounded to the nearest tenth of a percent) would be:
   a. 11.0%.
   b. 11.6%.
   c. 10.5%.
   d. none of the above.

IV. The Willet Company provides the following data:

Purchase price of special-purpose equipment	$100,000
Predicted useful life	10 years
Predicted annual savings in cash operating costs	$30,000
Predicted terminal disposal price	none
Depreciation method	straight-line
Required rate of return	10%
Income tax rate	30%

Compute the following items on an after-tax basis (use the interest tables in Appendix C at the back of the textbook as needed):

1. Payback
2. NPV
3. IRR (to the nearest tenth of a percent)
4. Accrual accounting rate of return on net initial investment (to the nearest tenth of a percent)

   Check figures: (1) 4.17 years (2) $47,480 (3) 20.2% (4) 14%

V. (CMA adapted) Ander Company can invest $49,800 in a piece of equipment with a three-year useful life. The predicted annual cash savings from operations, net of income taxes, is $25,000. The required rate of return is 10% and the present value of an annuity of $1.00 for three years is 2.49.

Compute the amount by which annual cash flow from operations, net of income taxes, could decrease before the company would be indifferent about acquiring the equipment.

   Check figure: $5,000

VI. Clayton Company acquired a machine for $72,000. It has a predicted useful life of eight years with zero terminal disposal price.

1. Compute the second year's depreciation, using the:
   a. Straight-line method
   b. Double-declining-balance method
2. Assuming a 40% income tax rate, compute the second year's tax savings from depreciation, using the:
   a. Straight-line method
   b. Double-declining-balance method

   Check figures: (1a) $9,000 (1b) $13,500 (2a) $3,600 (2b) $5,400

VII. (CPA) Dillon, Inc., purchased a new machine for $60,000 on January 1, 19_3. The machine is being depreciated on the straight-line basis over five years with zero terminal disposal price. The accrual accounting rate of return is expected to be 15% on the net initial investment.

Compute annual cash flow from operations, net of income taxes, assuming that operations are uniform each year of the new machine's useful life.

Check figure: $21,000

VIII. Massey Company's discount rate of 20% for capital budgeting includes a 10% inflation rate. The present value of $1 at 20% is .833. Assume a 40% income tax rate.

Compute the present value (expressed in nominal dollars) of:

1. Predicted cash operating savings before taxes of $100,000 (expressed in year 0 dollars) one year from now.
2. Depreciation of $70,000 one year from now.

Check figures: (1) $54,978 (2) $23,324

CHAPTER 21 SOLUTIONS TO PRACTICE TEST

I. 1 amount, timing; 2 cash flow from operations, net of income taxes; 3 inflation; 4 real rate of return; 5 nominal; 6 nominal, nominal, nominal; 7 excess present value index (profitability index); 8 Modified Accelerated Cost Recovery System (MACRS).

II.

1 F	4 F	7 T	10 T
2 T	5 T	8 F	11 T
3 F	6 T	9 T	

Explanations:

1 Assuming no change in working capital, one method to compute cash flow from operations, net of income taxes, is net income plus depreciation. Exhibit 21-1 illustrates the three methods to compute cash flow from operations, net of income taxes. (F)

2 To record depreciation, the journal entry increases depreciation expense and decreases net fixed assets, so there is *no direct cash-flow effect*. However, because of its deductibility for tax purposes, depreciation *indirectly increases cash flow from operations* by decreasing the current outflow for income tax expense. (T)

3 $10,000 × .30 = $3,000 (F)

4 Working capital for capital-budgeting projects (such as accounts receivable and inventories) involves cash flows that are not subject to income tax. (F)

5 Total project approach NPV

Exhibit 21-2 (keep old machine)	$(539,997)
Exhibit 21-3 (buy new machine)	(439,673)
Advantage in favor of replacement	$ 100,324

Exhibit 21-4 shows the same NPV advantage in favor of replacement under the incremental approach. (T)

6 The real rate of return expresses investment risk disregarding inflation. The nominal rate of return includes both the investment risk and the inflation risk, so it is higher than the real rate of return. (T)

7 Compare the NPV's in Exhibits 21-5 and 21-6. (T)

8 Higher risks on some projects can be recognized by increasing the required rate of return or decreasing the required payback. Other approaches to recognizing risk are listed in section C(2) of the chapter outline. (F)

9 When there is no restriction on the total funds available for capital budgeting (which is rarely the case), the excess present value index (also called the profitability index) is an appropriate guide for choosing among investments of different sizes. The index is equal to a project's total present value of future net cash inflows divided by the net initial investment. When the index is exactly 100%, NPV = $0. When the index is above 100%, NPV is positive. (T) Note that when there is a restriction on the total funds available, NPV is the better guide for choosing among investments of different sizes. See Exhibit 21-7.

10 This statement correctly describes the reinvestment assumption under NPV. In contrast, IRR assumes that the reinvestment rate is equal to the indicated rate of return for the shortest-lived project. (T)

11 Under MACRS, the amount allowable each year as a depreciation deduction is called cost recovery. The total cost recovery during the recovery period is the original cost of the asset. Terminal disposal price does not affect the amount of cost recovery. (T)

III. 1 d   4 d   7 c
      2 b   5 b
      3 a   6 a

Explanations:

1 Advertising: $-\$10,000 \times (1 - .40) = -\$6,000$
Depreciation: $\$10,000 \times .40 = \$4,000$ (d)

2 Compared to the double-declining-balance method, the straight-line method shows less depreciation in earlier years of a project's life and more in later years. The smaller tax savings in earlier years are discounted over a shorter period of time than the larger tax savings in later years; therefore, the present value of the tax savings is smaller. (b)

3 Four steps are used to obtain the answer. First, compute the annual depreciation: $(\$130,000 - \$10,000) \div 10 = \$12,000$. Second, compute the book value of the equipment: $\$130,000 - (\$12,000 \times 8) = \$130,000 - \$96,000 = \$34,000$. Third, compute the gain or loss on the sale of equipment before income taxes: $\$44,000 - \$34,000 = \$10,000$ gain. The fourth step is to compute the after-tax cash flow from the sale of the old equipment $= \$44,000 - \$10,000(.40) = \$40,000$ (a)

4 $\$30,000 - \$34,000$(book value) $= \$4,000$ loss; $\$30,000 + (\$4,000 \times .40) = \$30,000 + \$1,600 = \$31,600$ (d)

5
Cost of new press		$225,000
Shipping and installation		20,000
Working capital		
Increase in accounts receivable	$16,000	
Increase in inventories	4,000	
Increase in accounts payable	(14,000)	6,000
Subtotal		251,000
Deduct after-tax cash inflow		
from sale of old press,		
$5,000 + ($15,000 − $5,000)(.40)		9,000
Net initial investment of new press		$242,000 (b)

6

Annual Amounts	Present Situation	Proposed Situation	Cash-Flow Difference
Cash revenues	$240,000	$290,000	$50,000
Operating costs:			
Cash operating costs (does not include depreciation)			
$185,000 − $35,000	150,000		} (5,000)
$205,000 − $50,000		155,000	
Depreciation	35,000	50,000	
Total operating costs	185,000	205,000	
Operating income	55,000	85,000	
Income tax (40%)	22,000	34,000	(12,000)
Net income	$ 33,000	$ 51,000	
Cash-flow difference			$33,000 (a)

Alternatively, this answer can be obtained two other ways.
First,

Incremental net income, $51,000 − $33,000	$18,000
Incremental depreciation, $50,000 − $35,000	15,000
Incremental cash flow from operations, net of income taxes	$33,000 (a)

Second,

Incremental revenues × (1 − Tax rate), $50,000 × (1 − .40)	$30,000
Deduct incremental cash operating costs × (1 − Tax rate), ($155,000 − $150,000) × (1 − .40)	(3,000)
Add incremental depreciation × Tax rate, ($50,000 − $35,000) × .40	6,000
Incremental cash flow from operations, net of income taxes	$33,000 (a)

7   Nominal rate = (1 + Real rate)(1 + Inflation rate) − 1
$\qquad$ .16 = (1 + Real rate)(1 + .05) − 1
$\qquad$ .16 = (1 + Real rate)(1.05) − 1
$\qquad$ .16 = 1.05 + 1.05(Real rate) − 1
$\quad$ 1.05(Real rate) = 1 − 1.05 + .16
$\quad$ 1.05(Real rate) = .11
$\qquad$ Real rate = .11 ÷ 1.05 = .1048, or 10.5% (c)

IV. Willet Company

1. Annual cash flow from operations, net of income taxes = $30,000 × (1 − .30) + [($100,000 ÷ 10) × .30] = $21,000 + ($10,000 × .30) = $21,000 + $3,000 = $24,000; Payback = $100,000 ÷ $24,000 = 4.17 years
2. NPV = $24,000 (from part 1) × 6.145 − $100,000 = $147,480 − $100,000 = $47,480

3.   Let F = Present value factor for 10 years in Table 4 of Appendix C
$24,000F = $100,000
        F = 4.167, which lies between 4.192(20%) and 3.923(22%)

20%	4.192	4.192
IRR		4.167
22%	3.923	
Difference	0.269	0.025

IRR = 20% + (0.025 ÷ 0.269)2%
IRR = 20% + (.093)2% = 20.2%

4. Operating income = $30,000 − ($100,000 ÷ 10) = $30,000 − $10,000 = $20,000;
Net income = $20,000 − ($20,000 × .30) = $20,000 − $6,000 = $14,000;
Accrual accounting rate of return = $14,000 ÷ $100,000 = 14%

V. Ander Company

Let X = Annual cash flow from operations, net of income taxes, that would produce an NPV
        of $0
2.49X = $49,800
    X = $20,000

Therefore, the amount by which annual cash flow from operations, net of income taxes, could
decrease before the company would be indifferent about acquiring the equipment = $25,000 −
$20,000 = $5,000. Note that computing the point of indifference (i.e., NPV = $0) is an example
of using sensitivity analysis.

VI. Clayton Company

1. (a) $72,000 ÷ 8 = $9,000
   (b) 100% ÷ 8 = 12.5%; 12.5% × 2 = 25%;
       First year's depreciation = $72,000 × 25% = $18,000;
       Second year's depreciation = ($72,000 − $18,000) × 25% = $54,000 × 25% = $13,500
2. (a) $9,000 × .40 = $3,600
   (b) $13,500 × .40 = $5,400

VII. Dillon, Inc.

Two steps are used to obtain the answer. First, compute the increase in annual net income
expected from the new machine (denoted by X):

Accrual accounting rate of return = X ÷ Net initial investment
15% = X ÷ $60,000
X = $60,000(15%) = $9,000

The second step is to compute annual cash flow from operations, net of income taxes (denoted by
Y):

Y = Net income + Depreciation
Y = $9,000 + ($60,000 ÷ 5)
Y = $9,000 + $12,000 = $21,000

Recap: AARR = [$21,000 − ($60,000 ÷ 5)] ÷ $60,000 = $9,000 ÷ $60,000 = 15%

VIII. Massey Company

1. $100,000 × 1.10 = $110,000; $110,000 × (1 − .40) = $66,000;
    $66,000 × .833 = $54,978
2. $70,000 × .40 = $28,000; $28,000 × .833 = $23,324

CHAPTER 22

MEASURING MIX, YIELD, AND PRODUCTIVITY

MAIN FOCUS AND OBJECTIVES

This chapter extends the discussion of variance analysis introduced in Chapter 7 and explains how accounting information can be used to measure productivity. The chapter is divided into three independent parts: (1) sales variances, (2) input variances, and (3) productivity measurement. A useful columnar format is used in all three parts. Your overall objective for this chapter is to understand how multiple products or multiple materials and labor inputs make the analyses more complex. Nine learning objectives are stated in the textbook (p. 754).

Give special attention to computing and interpreting:

- sales-quantity and sales-mix variances
- market-size and market-share variances
- yield and mix variances for materials and labor inputs
- partial productivity and total factor productivity measures

To focus on basic concepts, the illustrations in this chapter are limited to two products or two inputs. When there are multiple products or inputs, computer software packages can greatly reduce the computational burden.

REVIEW OF KEY TERMS AND CONCEPTS

Part One: Sales Variances

A. When a company markets more than one product or service, the sales quantities, the sales mix, or both can differ from the budget.
   1. Terminology regarding sales variances is far from uniform, so be aware of the definitions used in a particular situation.
   2. **Sales-volume variance**: the difference between the flexible budget amount and the static budget amount; unit selling prices, unit variable costs, and fixed costs are held constant.
      a. This variance is measured in terms of contribution margin (that is, sales minus variable costs) because fixed costs are the same in the flexible budget and static budget.
         (1) The flexible budget is the budget for actual output achieved.
         (2) The static budget is the budget for expected output.
      b. The sales-volume variance assumes that units sold is the sole driver of budgeted contribution margin.

c. Most managers want detail on *individual* products, which is not available in Exhibit 22-1.

d. Such detail is shown in Exhibit 22-2. *Carefully study this key exhibit.*

e. The main point of Exhibit 22-2 is that, *despite actual total sales and budgeted total sales being equal at 1,600 units, each individual product has a sales-volume variance. Why? Because the original sales mix of the products changed.*

f. **Sales mix** is the relative combination of the quantities of products that constitute total sales.

g. For an individual product:

$$\begin{array}{c} \text{Sales-} \\ \text{volume} \\ \text{variance} \end{array} = \left(\begin{array}{c} \text{Actual} \\ \text{sales quantity} \\ \text{in units} \end{array} - \begin{array}{c} \text{Budgeted} \\ \text{sales quantity} \\ \text{in units} \end{array} \right) \times \begin{array}{c} \text{Budgeted individual} \\ \text{product contribution} \\ \text{margin per unit} \end{array}$$

3. To obtain more detail, the sales-volume variance can be divided into the sales-quantity variance and sales-mix variance.

a. For an individual product:

$$\begin{array}{c} \text{Sales-} \\ \text{quantity} \\ \text{variance} \end{array} = \left(\begin{array}{c} \text{Actual} \\ \text{units of all} \\ \text{products sold} \end{array} - \begin{array}{c} \text{Budgeted} \\ \text{units of all} \\ \text{products sold} \end{array} \right) \times \begin{array}{c} \text{Budgeted} \\ \text{sales mix} \\ \text{percentage} \end{array} \times \begin{array}{c} \text{Budgeted unit} \\ \text{contribution} \\ \text{margin} \end{array}$$

b. This variance arises because the total quantity of units actually sold differs from the static budget (sales mix is held constant).

c. For an individual product:

$$\begin{array}{c} \text{Sales-} \\ \text{mix} \\ \text{variance} \end{array} = \left(\begin{array}{c} \text{Actual} \\ \text{sales mix} \\ \text{percentage} \end{array} - \begin{array}{c} \text{Budgeted} \\ \text{sales mix} \\ \text{percentage} \end{array} \right) \times \begin{array}{c} \text{Actual units} \\ \text{of all} \\ \text{products sold} \end{array} \times \begin{array}{c} \text{Budgeted unit} \\ \text{contribution} \\ \text{margin} \end{array}$$

d. This variance arises because the mix of individual products actually sold differs from the budgeted mix (sales quantity is held constant).

e. In computing both the sales-quantity and sales-mix variances, budgeted selling prices and budgeted unit variable costs are held constant.

f. These variances are measured in terms of contribution margin because fixed costs are the same in the flexible budget and static budget.

4. *See Practice Question III (items 3 and 4) and Problem IV (parts 1-3).*
5. To obtain even more detail, the sales-quantity variance can be divided into the market-size variance and market-share variance.

   a. **Market-size variance** measures the effect of actual industry sales volume in units differing from budgeted industry sales volume in units.

$$\begin{array}{c} \text{Market-} \\ \text{size} \\ \text{variance} \end{array} = \left(\begin{array}{c} \text{Actual} \\ \text{market size} \\ \text{in units} \end{array} - \begin{array}{c} \text{Budgeted} \\ \text{market size} \\ \text{in units} \end{array}\right) \times \begin{array}{c} \text{Budgeted} \\ \text{market} \\ \text{share} \end{array} \times \begin{array}{c} \text{Budgeted average} \\ \text{contribution margin} \\ \text{per unit} \end{array}$$

   b. **Market-share variance** measures the effect of actual market share percentage differing from budgeted market share percentage.

$$\begin{array}{c} \text{Market-} \\ \text{share} \\ \text{variance} \end{array} = \begin{array}{c} \text{Actual} \\ \text{market size} \\ \text{in units} \end{array} \times \left(\begin{array}{c} \text{Actual} \\ \text{market} \\ \text{share} \end{array} - \begin{array}{c} \text{Budgeted} \\ \text{market} \\ \text{share} \end{array}\right) \times \begin{array}{c} \text{Budgeted average} \\ \text{contribution margin} \\ \text{per unit} \end{array}$$

   c. Note that *the market-size and market-share variances are computed for all products together* but not for each product individually.

   d. Exhibit 22-4 illustrates these variances in a columnar format.

   e. Note these important points about Exhibit 22-4:

     (1) A key figure, *budgeted (weighted) average contribution margin of $2.50 per unit*, is computed in one of the exhibit's footnotes.

     (2) The zero sales-quantity variance hides the fact that, although the overall wine market has grown, Party Wholesaler's share has declined.

     (3) The static budget (column 3) = 20,000 × 0.08 × $2.50 = $4,000. This same amount is computed in a different way in the static budget in Exhibit 22-3 (column 3) = (1,600 × 0.75 × $1) + (1,600 × 0.25 × $7) = $1,200 + $2,800 = $4,000.

   f. The industry statistics needed to compute market-size and market-share variances often are not easy to obtain, but they are readily available for some products including automobiles, television sets, and soft drinks.

> **Exhibit 22-5 shows the big picture of sales variances. Always consider possible interdependencies among these individual variances.**

---

6. *See Practice Test Question III (items 5 and 6) and Problem IV (parts 4-6).*
7. Marketing managers want to know why actual sales differ from budgeted sales.

   a. If the sales-quantity variance is primarily due to uncontrollable changes in market size, the company may need to expand, downsize, or shift to new product markets.

   b. In contrast, market share is more controllable. Why? Because pricing and promotion decisions are more likely to affect market share than total market size.

   c. The sales-mix variance indicates whether the mix is shifting toward high or low margin products.

> *Question:* Do accountants need to understand variance analysis, given that computers usually calculate the variances?
>
> *Answer:* Yes, because accountants' primary role is thinking. They must determine *what* the computer should calculate and *interpret* the resulting calculations.

Part Two: Input Variances

B. Manufacturing processes often entail the combination of different types of direct materials and different direct labor skills to make various products. Merchandising and service organizations often can combine different types of labor to supply their goods and services.

> Keep in mind that the interpretation of an input variance will depend on the source of the budgeted (or standard) figures(s) used in computing it. A list of sources is in the textbook (p. 764).

1. The least detailed analysis of inputs is to compute their price variances and efficiency variances.
   a. *Price variance for materials or labor:* the difference between actual price and budgeted price multiplied by the actual quantity of input in question.
   b. *Efficiency variance for materials or labor:* the difference between the actual quantity of input used and the budgeted quantity of input that should have been used, multiplied by the budgeted price.
   c. These variances are computed for multiple inputs of materials and labor in Exhibits 22-6 (a manufacturing company) and 22-8 (a service firm).
   d. Such information is useful to managers in situations where *no substitutions are permitted in the physical mix of inputs.*
2. Where managers have *discretion to make substitutions among types of materials or among types of labor*, more detail in the form of yield and mix variances can provide valuable insight.
   a. **Materials yield (labor yield) variance:** the difference between actual and budgeted total quantity of inputs for actual output achieved, multiplied by budgeted prices (budgeted mix is held constant).
   b. **Materials mix (labor mix) variance:** the difference between actual and budgeted mix for the total quantity of inputs used, multiplied by budgeted prices (total quantity of inputs used is held constant).
   c. *The yield and mix variances are the two parts of the efficiency variance.*
   d. The intuition for the yield and mix variances is analogous to the intuition for the sales-quantity and sales-mix variances discussed in Part One of this chapter.

> **Exhibits 22-7 and 22-9 show in a columnar format the computation of yield and mix variances for materials (in a manufacturing company) and labor (in a service firm), respectively. Carefully study these exhibits. To understand where the yield and mix variances fit in the big picture, see the diagram in the textbook (p. 769).**

    e. *Question*: What is the proper interpretation of the variances in Exhibit 22-7? *Answer*: There was a tradeoff among materials (California tomatoes and Florida tomatoes) that reduced the cost of the mix of tomatoes used ($3,250 F) but hurt yield ($8,250 U). The net effect is that the budgeted (weighted) average unit cost of all tomatoes is higher than expected (an efficiency variance of $5,000 U).

3. *See Practice Test Question III (items 7-9) and Problem V.*

Part Three: Productivity Measurement

C. Productivity improvement is consistently cited by chief operating officers as one of the most important issues requiring their attention.
1. **Productivity** measures the relationship between actual inputs used and actual outputs achieved; the lower the quantity of inputs used for a given set of output achieved or the higher the quantity of outputs achieved for a given set of inputs used, the higher the level of productivity.
2. Productivity measures evaluate two aspects of the relationship between inputs and outputs:
    a. Whether more inputs than necessary have been used to produce output.
    b. Whether the best mix of inputs has been used to produce output.
3. Although yield variances address 2(a) and mix variances address 2(b), those variances are only applicable when substitutions can be made *within a given factor of production*, such as substituting more experienced welders for less experienced welders.
4. Productivity embraces the broader idea of substitutions *between factors of production*, such as capital invested in automation to replace labor.
5. The discussion in this chapter focuses on how productivity can be used to describe the actual performance of an organization over time, which is a useful way to monitor efforts regarding continuous improvement.
6. One measure of productivity is called partial productivity.

$$\textbf{Partial productivity} = \frac{\textbf{Quantity of output produced}}{\textbf{Quantity of input used}}$$

    a. This measure of productivity is "partial" in the sense that it includes the output produced per unit of a *single factor of production*.
    b. Standing alone, a partial productivity measure has limited usefulness. However, it becomes meaningful when comparisons are made to examine productivity changes (i) over time, (ii) among different facilities, or (iii) relative to a benchmark.

c. Note that partial productivity is measured in terms of *physical inputs and outputs*; therefore, *fluctuations in input prices do not affect partial productivity measures*.

d. Exhibit 22-10 illustrates that partial productivity is not affected by changes in output levels under the condition of constant returns to scale.

> ***Question*: Can a company have an unfavorable efficiency variance in a reporting period when partial productivity improved?**
>
> ***Answer*: Yes, as shown in Exhibit 22-11. The reason for this difference lies in the benchmarks used for comparison—a budgeted or standard amount to measure the efficiency variance and last period's actual performance to measure the change in partial productivity.**

e. Two uses of partial productivity measures are described in the textbook (p. 777).

f. *Question*: What is the most serious deficiency of a partial productivity measure?
   Answer: It does not consider the productivity of all inputs simultaneously. That is, the effect of substitutions between factors of production is ignored.

g. *See Practice Problem VI (part 1).*

7. Another measure of productivity is called total factor productivity.

   a. **Total factor productivity**: the ratio of the quantity of output produced to the quantity of *all* inputs used, where the costs of inputs are computed on the basis of current period prices.

   b. By formula:

$$\textbf{Total factor productivity (TFP)} = \frac{\textbf{Quantity of output produced}}{\textbf{Costs of all inputs used}}$$

   c. This measure of productivity is "total" in the sense that it combines the productivity of the inputs used from *all factors of production* to produce output by taking into account the *relative prices of inputs*.

   d. TFP considers all inputs simultaneously and evaluates tradeoffs among inputs on the basis of input prices.

   e. The textbook example (p. 778) explains the computation of TFP.
      (1) In 19_5 TFP = 0.51 units of output per dollar of inputs.
      (2) In 19_4 TFP = 0.50 units of output per dollar of inputs.
      (3) Therefore, *in 19_5 TFP increased 2%* [(0.51 − 0.50) ÷ 0.50].

   f. TFP increases if (i) a company uses fewer physical quantities of all inputs in the second period to produce the same quantity of output that it produced in the first period or (ii) a company uses a less expensive mix of inputs to produce output in the second period than in the first period.

   g. A major advantage of TFP is that it explicitly evaluates substitution possibilities among inputs.

   h. Two disadvantages of TFP:
      (1) It measures the ratio of output to *all* inputs but operating personnel only have control over *some* inputs, such as their labor or the materials they add to the products. (As a result, workers' bonuses are often tied to partial productivity measures rather than TFP.)

(2) Comparisons across more than two periods are more difficult to make than with partial productivity measures.

> **Exhibit 22-12 is a helpful learning tool. The columnar format shows that the actual cost change for inputs between two periods is explained by three components—productivity change, input price change, and output adjustment. Each of these components is discussed in the textbook (p. 780).**

 i. Special notes about Exhibit 22-12:
   (1) The productivity change component compares the cost to produce output in 19_5 with what it would have cost to produce the same level of output in 19_4 at 19_5 input prices.
   (2) *TFP can be computed by using the two figures in Panel C that explain productivity change: $20,000 F ÷ $1,000,000 = +0.02, or an increase of 2%, which is the same result computed in section 7(e) of the outline above.*
 j. *See Practice Test Question III (items 10-12) and Problem VI (parts 2 and 3).*

PRACTICE TEST QUESTIONS AND PROBLEMS

I. Complete each of the following statements.

Part One

1. The sales-volume variance assumes that _____ is the sole driver of budgeted contribution margin.
2. In a multiple-product company, the sales-volume variance can be divided into what two variances? _____ _____. These variances are measured in terms of _____ _____ because fixed costs are the same in the flexible budget and static budget.
3. The sales-quantity variance can be divided into what two variances? _____ _____.

Part Two

4. The _____ is the difference between the actual quantity of input used and the budgeted quantity of input that should have been used, multiplied by the _____.
5. The direct labor efficiency variance can be divided into what two variances? _____ _____.
6. In computing the _____, the two items held constant are total quantity of materials used and budgeted prices.

Part Three

7. What are the two measures of productivity called? _____ _____

8. To compute partial productivity, the quantity of output produced is divided by the _____ _____.

9. _____ is the ratio of the quantity of output produced to the quantity of all inputs used, where the costs of inputs are computed on the basis of current period prices.

II. Indicate whether each of the following statements is true or false by putting T or F in the space provided.

Part One

____ 1. The sales-volume variance is the difference between the flexible budget amount and the static budget amount; unit selling prices, unit variable costs, and fixed costs are held constant.
____ 2. A sales-volume variance can arise if actual total sales in units is equal to budgeted total sales in units.

___ 3. The sales-volume variance plus the sales-mix variance is equal to the sales-quantity variance.

___ 4. Market-size and market-share variances can be computed for all products together as well as for each product individually.

___ 5. The sales-quantity variance can hide the fact that, although an overall product-line market has grown, the company's market share has declined.

___ 6. Marketing managers generally find that the market-size variance is more controllable than the market-share variance.

Part Two

___ 7. One possible source of the budgeted (or standard) figures used in the computation of input variances is internally generated actual costs of the most recent reporting period adjusted for expected improvement.

___ 8. It is always desirable to divide the efficiency variance into yield and mix variances.

___ 9. The analysis of input variances is applicable only to the manufacturing sector.

___ 10. In computing the yield variance, the difference between actual and budgeted quantities of inputs for actual output achieved is multiplied by budgeted prices.

Part Three

___ 11. The lower the quantity of inputs used for a given set of outputs, the higher the level of productivity.

___ 12. Productivity is only applicable when substitutions can be made within a given factor of production, such as substituting more nitrogen for less phosphorus in manufacturing fertilizer.

___ 13. Standing alone, a partial productivity measure has little usefulness.

___ 14. Fluctuations in input prices can affect partial productivity measures.

___ 15. A company can have an unfavorable materials efficiency variance in a reporting period when partial productivity of materials increases.

___ 16. Total factor productivity combines the productivity of the inputs used from all factors of production to produce output by taking into account the relative prices of inputs.

III. Select the best answer for each of the following multiple-choice questions and put the identifying letter in the space provided.

Part One

___ 1. The difference between the total amount of contribution margin in the flexible budget and that amount in the static budget is:
   a. the sales-volume variance.
   b. the sales-quantity variance.
   c. the sales-mix variance.
   d. the market-size variance.

___ 2. A sales-mix variance is attributable to the change in:
   a. quantity of units sold.
   b. prices of units sold.
   c. a combination of quantity and prices of units sold.
   d. none of the above.

___ 3. The following data are for Eucha Corp. for the first quarter of 19_4:

	Static Budget	Actual Results
Unit sales:		
Product X	40,000	15,000
Product Y	60,000	65,000
Total	100,000	80,000
Unit contribution margin:		
Product X	$5	$4
Product Y	$2	$3

The sales-quantity variance for Product Y would be:
   a. $40,000 favorable.
   b. $40,000 unfavorable.
   c. $24,000 unfavorable.
   d. none of the above.

___ 4. See item 3. The sales-mix variance for both products together would be:
   a. $51,000 unfavorable.
   b. $64,000 unfavorable.
   c. $115,000 unfavorable.
   d. none of the above.

___ 5. See item 3. The amount of the budgeted (weighted) average contribution margin per unit would be:
a. $3.50.
b. $3.20.
c. $2.5625.
d. none of the above.

___ 6. See item 3. If actual market size was
480,000 units and budgeted market size
was 500,000 units, the market-share
variance would be:
a. $12,800 unfavorable.
b. $8,534 unfavorable.
c. $51,200 unfavorable.
d. none of the above.

Part Two

___ 7. (CPA adapted) The excess cost of direct
labor resulting from the premium paid
for overtime will be disclosed in the:
a. direct labor yield variance.
b. direct labor mix variance.
c. direct labor price variance.
d. none of the above.

___ 8. The following data are for Kershaw
Company for April 19_4:

Budgeted labor mix at budgeted prices
for actual output achieved
3,825 skilled hours at $16 per hour
1,275 unskilled hours at $12 per hour
5,100 total hours

Actual results
4,000 skilled hours at $19 per hour
1,000 unskilled hours at $9 per hour
5,000 total hours

The yield variance for both types of
labor together would be:
a. $1,500 favorable.
b. $1,000 unfavorable.
c. $500 favorable.
d. none of the above.

___ 9. See item 8. The mix variance for
skilled labor would be:
a. $1,200 favorable.
b. $4,000 unfavorable.
c. $2,800 unfavorable.
d. none of the above.

Part Three

___ 10. Pandora, Inc. manufactures a mineral-
based product using direct materials and
direct manufacturing labor as substitutable inputs. The company reports the
following data for the last two years of
operations:

	19_4	19_5
Output in units	212,500	255,000
Direct manufacturing labor-hours (DMLH) used	17,000	18,700
Wage rate per DMLH	$12	$13
Direct materials used in pounds	85,000	109,750
Direct materials cost per pound	$3.10	$3.00

Using the format of Exhibit 22-12, the
change in productivity for direct manufacturing labor from 19_4 to 19_5 in
dollars would be:
a. $20,400 unfavorable.
b. $20,400 favorable.
c. $22,100 unfavorable.
d. none of the above.

___ 11. See item 10. Using the format of Exhibit 22-12, the change in productivity
for direct materials from 19_4 to 19_5
in dollars would be:
a. $24,025 unfavorable.
b. $23,250 unfavorable.
c. $23,250 favorable.
d. none of the above.

___ 12. See item 10. The change in total factor
productivity from 19_4 to 19_5 in percent would be (rounded to the nearest
tenth of a percent):
a. a decrease of 0.2%.
b. an increase of 0.2%.
c. a decrease of 2.0%.
d. none of the above.

Part One

IV. (CMA) Given the following information for Xerbert Company (in thousands):

	Static Budget for 19_3			Actual Results for 19_3		
	Xenox	Xeon	Total	Xenox	Xeon	Total
Units sold	150	100	250	130	130	260
Sales	$900	$1,000	$1,900	$ 780	$1,235	$2,015
Variable costs	450	750	1,200	390	975	1,365
Contribution margin	$450	$ 250	700	$ 390	$ 260	650
Fixed costs:						
Manufacturing			200			190
Marketing			153			140
Administration			95			90
Total fixed costs			448			420
Operating income			$ 252			$ 230

Using a columnar format:
1. Compute the individual product and the total sales-volume variances for 19_3.
2. Compute the individual product and the total sales-mix variances for 19_3.
3. Compute the individual product and the total sales-quantity variances for 19_3.
4. Suppose Xerbert's budgeted market share for 19_3 was 10% and actual industry volume was 2,580,000 units. Compute the market-size variance.
5. Compute the market-share variance.
6. Compute the percentage of the company's increased sales volume that is due to improved market share.

> Check figures: (1) Xenox $60,000 U (2) Xeon $65,000 F (3) Xenox $18,000 F (4) $22,400 F (5) $5,600 F (6) 20%

Part Two

V. (CMA adapted) LAR Chemical Co. manufactures a wide variety of chemical compounds and liquids for industrial uses. The budgeted mix of direct materials for producing a single batch of 500 gallons of a particular chemical compound is as follows:

Material Input	Quantity (in gallons)	Cost (per gallon)	Total Cost
Maxan	100	$2.00	$200
Salex	300	.75	225
	400		$425

There is a 15% budgeted loss in liquid volume during processing due to evaporation. The finished chemical compound is put into 8-gallon bottles for sale. Thus, the budgeted materials cost for an 8-gallon bottle is $425 \div [(400 \times .85) \div 8] = $425 \div 42.5 = 10.00.

The actual quantities of direct materials and the respective cost of the materials placed in production during November were as follows:

Material Input	Quantity (in gallons)	Total Cost
Maxan	8,480	$17,384
Salex	25,200	17,640
	33,680	$35,024

No inventories of direct materials are kept. Purchases are made as needed, so all price variances relate to materials placed in production.

A total of 4,250 bottles (34,000 gallons) was produced during November.

For each of the direct materials and then both together, use a columnar format to:
1. Compute the price variance for November.
2. Compute the efficiency variance for November.
3. Compute the yield variance for November.
4. Compute the mix variance for November.

Check figures: (1) Maxan $424 U (2) Salex $900 U (3) Maxan $840 U (4) Salex $45 F

Part Three

VI. Dapper Industries makes a chemical product using direct materials and direct manufacturing labor as substitutable inputs. The company reports the following data for the last two years of operations:

	19_4	19_5
Output in units	8,500	10,200
Direct manufacturing labor-hours (DMLH) used	700	800
Wage rate per DMLH	$14	$15
Direct materials used in kilograms	5,700	7,000
Direct materials cost per kilogram	$3.20	$3.00

1. Compute the partial productivity ratios for each input for each year.
2. Using your answers in part 1, can it be determined whether total factor productivity increased in 19_5 compared with 19_4? Explain.
3. Compute the change in total factor productivity from 19_4 to 19_5 (rounded to the nearest tenth of a percent).

Check figures: (1) Labor for 19_4 12.14, Materials for 19_5 1.46 (3) Increase of 0.4%

CHAPTER 22 SOLUTIONS TO PRACTICE TEST

I. 1 units sold; 2 sales-quantity variance, sales-mix variance, contribution margin; 3 market-size variance, market-share variance; 4 materials efficiency variance, budgeted price; 5 direct labor yield variance, direct labor mix variance; 6 materials mix variance; 7 partial productivity, total factor productivity; 8 quantity of input used; 9 Total factor productivity.

II.

1 T	5 T	9 F	13 T
2 T	6 F	10 T	14 F
3 F	7 T	11 T	15 T
4 F	8 F	12 F	16 T

Explanations:
1 The formula for the sales-volume variance of an individual product is given in section A(2g) of the chapter outline. (T)

2 For example, see Exhibit 22-2; actual total sales and budgeted total sales are both 1,600 units and the sales-volume variances are $100 U for regular wine, $700 F for premium wine, and $600 F for both products together. (T)

3 Sales-volume variance *minus* sales-mix variance is equal to sales-quantity variance. That is, sales-volume variance is equal to the sum of sales-mix variance and sales-quantity variance. (F)

4 Market-size and market-share variances can be computed for all products together but not for each product individually. This point is illustrated in Exhibit 22-4. (F)

5 This statement describes the situation in Exhibit 22-4; sales-volume variance is $0, market-size variance is $1,000 F, and market-share variance is $1,000 U. (T)

6 The market-share variance generally is more controllable than the market-size variance. Pricing and promotion decisions are more likely to affect market share than total market size. (F)

7 Several other sources of budgeted (or standard) figure(s) used in computing input variances are listed in the textbook (p. 764). (T)

8 No, the efficiency variance is an appropriate level of detail in situations where no substitutions are permitted in the physical mix of inputs. However, in cases where managers have discretion to make substitutions among types of materials or among types of labor, more detail in the form of yield and mix variances can provide valuable insight. (F)

9 In Exhibits 22-8 and 22-9, the analysis is for Lee and Associates, an architectural firm. (F)

10 The other key aspect of computing the yield variance is that budgeted mix of the inputs is held constant. (T)

11 Productivity measures the relationship between actual inputs used and actual outputs achieved. Productivity increases if fewer inputs are used for a given set of outputs achieved, or if more outputs are achieved for a given set of inputs used. (T)

12 The statement refers to yield and mix variances rather than productivity. Productivity embraces the broader idea of substitutions *between* factors of production, such as capital invested in automation to replace labor. (F)

13 A partial productivity measure only becomes meaningful when comparisons are made to examine productivity changes over time, among different facilities, or relative to a benchmark. (T)

14 Partial productivity is measured only in terms of physical inputs and outputs. (F)

15 The truth of this statement is illustrated in Exhibit 22-11. The reason for this difference lies in the benchmarks used for comparison – a budgeted or standard amount to measure the efficiency variance and last period's actual performance to measure partial productivity. (T)

16 See the example of computing TFP in the textbook (p. 778). (T)

III.
1	a	4	a	7	c	10	d
2	d	5	b	8	a	11	b
3	c	6	c	9	b	12	a

Explanations:

1 For example, see Exhibit 22-3: the difference between column 1 and column 3. (a)

2 The sales-mix variance arises because the mix of individual products actually sold differs from the budgeted mix. Items held constant in computing this variance are budgeted selling prices, budgeted unit variable costs, budgeted fixed costs, and actual units of all products sold. For example, see Exhibit 22-3: the difference between column 1 and column 3. (d)

3 For brevity and illustrative purposes, *formulas* are used to answer items 3-6. A *columnar format* is used to compute the variances in Practice Test Problem IV.

Let SQV-Y = Sales-quantity variance for Product Y

$$\text{SQV-Y} = (80,000 - 100,000) \times (60,000 \div 100,000) \times \$2$$
$$\text{SQV-Y} = -20,000 \times 0.60 \times \$2$$
$$\text{SQV-Y} = -\$24,000, \text{ or } \$24,000 \text{ U (c)}$$

4 Let SMV-X = Sales-mix variance for Product X
   Let SMV-Y = Sales-mix variance for Product Y
   Let SMV-T = Sales-mix variance for both products together

   SMV-X = (15,000 ÷ 80,000) − (40,000 ÷ 100,000) × 80,000 × \$5
   SMV-X = (0.1875 − 0.40) × \$400,000
   SMV-X = −0.2125 × \$400,000
   SMV-X = −\$85,000, or \$85,000 U

   SMV-Y = (65,000 ÷ 80,000) − (60,000 ÷ 100,000) × 80,000 × \$2
   SMV-Y = (0.8125 − 0.60) × \$160,000
   SMV-Y = 0.2125 × \$160,000
   SMV-Y = \$34,000, or \$34,000 F

   SMV-T = SMV-X + SMV-Y
   SMV-T = \$85,000 U + \$34,000 F = \$51,000 U (a)

5 [(40,000 × \$5) + (60,000 × \$2)] ÷ 100,000 = (\$200,000 + \$120,000) ÷ 100,000 = \$320,000 ÷ 100,000 = \$3.20 (b)

6 Actual market share = 80,000 ÷ 480,000 = 16.6667%
   Budgeted market share = 100,000 ÷ 500,000 = 20%
   Budgeted (weighted) average contribution margin per unit = \$3.20 (from item 5 above)
   Market-share variance = 480,000 × (0.166667 − 0.200000) × \$3.20
   Market-share variance = 480,000 × −0.033333 × \$3.20
   Market-share variance = −\$51,200 (rounded), or \$51,200 U (c)

7 Overtime premium increases the hourly wage rate and, hence, results in a direct labor price variance. (c)

8 A diagram is helpful in answering this question and the next:

	(Actual Quantities of All Inputs Used × Actual Input Mix) × Budgeted Prices	(Actual Quantities of All Inputs Used × Budgeted Input Mix) × Budgeted Prices	Flexible Budget (Budgeted Inputs Allowed for Actual Outputs Achieved × Budgeted Prices)
Skilled	5,000 × 0.80 × \$16 $64,000	5,000 × 0.75 × \$16 $60,000	5,100 × 0.75 × \$16 $61,200

↑   \$4,000 U   ↑   \$1,200 F
Mix Variance   Yield Variance
↑   \$2,800 U
Efficiency Variance

Unskilled	5,000 × 0.20 × \$12 $12,000	5,000 × 0.25 × \$12 $15,000	5,100 × 0.25 × \$12 $15,300

↑   \$3,000 F   ↑   \$300 F
Mix Variance   Yield Variance
↑   \$3,300 F
Efficiency Variance

All Labor	\$76,000	\$75,000	\$76,500

↑   \$1,000 U   ↑   \$1,500 F (a)
Mix Variance   Yield Variance
↑   \$500 F
Efficiency Variance

Actual labor mix:
  Skilled = 4,000 ÷ 5,000 = 80%
  Unskilled = 1,000 ÷ 5,000 = 20%

Budgeted labor mix:
  Skilled = 3,825 ÷ 5,100 = 75%
  Unskilled = 1,275 ÷ 5,100 = 25%

9 See the preceding answer. The mix variance for skilled labor is $4,000 U. (b)

10 A diagram is helpful in answering this question and the next:

	Actual Costs for 19_5 (Actual Units of Inputs Used to Produce 19_5 Output × 19_5 Prices)	(Actual Units of Inputs That Would Have Been Used in 19_4 to Produce 19_5 Output × 19_5 Prices)
Direct Manu-facturing Labor	18,700 × $13 $243,100	20,400[†] × $13 $265,200

$$\uparrow \quad \text{\underline{\$22,100 F (d)}} \quad \uparrow$$
Productivity change

Direct Materials	109,750 × $3.00 $329,250	102,000[‡] × $3.00 $306,000

$$\uparrow \quad \text{\underline{\$23,250 U}} \quad \uparrow$$
Productivity change

Both Inputs	$572,350	$571,200

$$\uparrow \quad \text{\underline{\$1,150 U}} \quad \uparrow$$
Productivity change

[†] 17,000 × (255,000 ÷ 212,500) = 17,000 × 1.20 = 20,400
[‡] 85,000 × (255,000 ÷ 212,500) = 85,000 × 1.20 = 102,000

11 See the preceding answer. The change in productivity for direct materials is $23,250 U. (b)

12 TFP for 19_5 = 255,000 ÷ [(18,700 × $13) + (109,750 × $3)] =
255,000 ÷ ($243,100 + $329,250) = 255,000 ÷ $572,350 = 0.4455 units of output per dollar of inputs

TFP for 19_4 = 212,500 ÷ [(17,000 × $13) + (85,000 × $3)] =
212,500 ÷ ($221,000 + $255,000) = 212,500 ÷ $476,000 = 0.4464 units of output per dollars of inputs

The change in TFP from 19_4 to 19_5 = (0.4455 − 0.4464) ÷ 0.4464 = −0.0020, or a decrease of 0.2%. (a)

Alternatively, the change in TFP can be computed by using the dollar amounts for "both inputs" in answer 10 above: $1,150 U ÷ $571,200 = −0.002, or a decrease of 0.2%. (a)

IV. Xerbert Company

1., 2., and 3.

	Flexible Budget: (Actual Units Sold of All Products Sold × Actual Sales Mix) × Budgeted Unit Contribution Margin	(Actual Units of All Products Sold × Budgeted Sales Mix) × Budgeted Unit Contribution Margin	Static Budget: (Budgeted Units of All Products Sold × Budgeted Sales Mix) × Budgeted Unit Contribution Margin
Xenox	(260,000 × 0.50) × \$3.00	(260,000 × 0.60) × \$3.00	(250,000 × 0.60) × \$3.00
	\$390,000	\$468,000	\$450,000

    ↑——— \$78,000 U ———↑——— \$18,000 F ———↑

       Sales-mix variance   Sales-quantity variance

    ↑——————— \$60,000 U ———————↑

          Sales-volume variance

Xeon	(260,000 × 0.50) × \$2.50	(260,000 × 0.40) × \$2.50	(250,000 × 0.40) × \$2.50
	\$325,000	\$260,000	\$250,000

    ↑——— \$65,000 F ———↑——— \$10,000 F ———↑

       Sales-mix variance   Sales-quantity variance

    ↑——————— \$75,000 F ———————↑

          Sales-volume variance

All Products	\$715,000	\$728,000	\$700,000

    ↑——— \$13,000 U ———↑——— \$28,000 F ———↑

       Sales-mix variance   Sales-quantity variance

    ↑——————— \$15,000 F ———————↑

          Sales-volume variance

Actual sales mix:
Xenox = 130,000 ÷ 260,000 = 50%
Xeon = 130,000 ÷ 260,000 = 50%

Budgeted sales mix:
Xenox = 150,000 ÷ 250,000 = 60%
Xeon = 100,000 ÷ 250,000 = 40%

Budgeted unit contribution margin:
Xenox = \$450,000 ÷ 150,000 = \$3.00
Xeon = \$250,000 ÷ 100,000 = \$2.50

4. and 5.

(Actual Market Size × Actual Market Share) × Budgeted Average Unit Contribution Margin	(Actual Market Size × Budgeted Market Share) × Budgeted Average Unit Contribution Margin	Static Budget: (Budgeted Market Size × Budgeted Market Share) × Budgeted Average Unit Contribution Margin
(2,580,000 × .1007752) × \$2.80	(2,580,000 × .10) × \$2.80	(2,500,000 × .10) × \$2.80
260,000 × \$2.80	258,000 × \$2.80	250,000 × \$2.80
\$728,000	\$722,400	\$700,000

    ↑——— \$5,600 F ———↑——— \$22,400 F ———↑

      Market-share variance   Market-size variance

    ↑——————— \$28,000 F ———————↑

         Sales-quantity variance

See the supporting computations at the top of the next page.

Actual market share: 260,000 ÷ 2,580,000 = 10.07752%
Budgeted market share: 10% (given)
Budgeted average unit contribution margin: $700,000 ÷ 250,000 = $2.80
Budgeted market size: 250,000 units ÷ .10 = 2,500,000

6 Total increase in the company's sales volume = 260,000 − 250,000 = 10,000 units; amount of total increase in the company's sales volume due to improved market share = 260,000 − (2,580,000 × .10) = 260,000 − 258,000 = 2,000 units; percentage of increase in the company's sales volume due to improved market share = 2,000 ÷ 10,000 = 20%

V. LAR Chemical Co.

1. and 2.

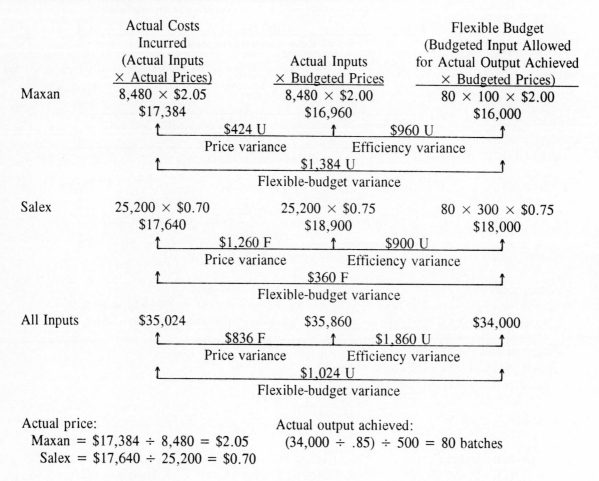

	Actual Costs Incurred (Actual Inputs × Actual Prices)	Actual Inputs × Budgeted Prices	Flexible Budget (Budgeted Input Allowed for Actual Output Achieved × Budgeted Prices)
Maxan	8,480 × $2.05 $17,384	8,480 × $2.00 $16,960	80 × 100 × $2.00 $16,000
	$424 U Price variance	$960 U Efficiency variance	
	$1,384 U Flexible-budget variance		
Salex	25,200 × $0.70 $17,640	25,200 × $0.75 $18,900	80 × 300 × $0.75 $18,000
	$1,260 F Price variance	$900 U Efficiency variance	
	$360 F Flexible-budget variance		
All Inputs	$35,024	$35,860	$34,000
	$836 F Price variance	$1,860 U Efficiency variance	
	$1,024 U Flexible-budget variance		

Actual price:
  Maxan = $17,384 ÷ 8,480 = $2.05
  Salex = $17,640 ÷ 25,200 = $0.70

Actual output achieved:
  (34,000 ÷ .85) ÷ 500 = 80 batches

3. and 4.

	(Actual Quantities of All Inputs Used × Actual Input Mix) × Budgeted Prices	(Actual Quantities of All Inputs Used × Budgeted Input Mix) × Budgeted Prices	Flexible Budget (Budgeted Inputs Allowed for Actual Output Achieved × Budgeted Prices)
Maxan	(33,680 × 0.25178) × $2.00	(33,680 × 0.25) × $2.00	80 × 100 × $2.00
	8,480 × $2.00	8,420 × $2.00	8,000 × $2.00
	$16,960	$16,840	$16,000

↑————— $120 U —————↑————— $840 U —————↑
Mix variance　　　　　　　Yield variance

↑———————————— $960 U ————————————↑
Efficiency variance

Salex	(33,680 × 0.74822) × $0.75	(33,680 × 0.75) × 0.75	80 × 300 × $0.75
	25,200 × $0.75	25,260 × $0.75	24,000 × $0.75
	$18,900	$18,945	$18,000

↑————— $45 F —————↑————— $945 U —————↑
Mix variance　　　　　　　Yield variance

↑———————————— $900 U ————————————↑
Efficiency variance

All Materials	$35,860	$35,785	$34,000

↑————— $75 U —————↑————— $1,785 U —————↑
Mix variance　　　　　　　Yield variance

↑———————————— $1,860 U ————————————↑
Efficiency variance

Actual materials mix:　　　　　　Budgeted materials mix:
　Maxon = $8,480 ÷ 33,680 = 25.178%　　Maxon = 100 ÷ 400 = 25%
　Salex = $25,200 ÷ 33,680 = 74.822%　　Salex = 300 ÷ 400 = 75%

Actual output achieved:
(34,000 ÷ .85) ÷ 500 = 80 batches

VI. Dapper Industries

1. Partial productivity of direct manufacturing labor:
    19_4 = 8,500 ÷ 700 = 12.14 units of output per DMLH
    19_5 = 10,200 ÷ 800 = 12.75 units of output per DMLH
   Partial productivity of direct materials:
    19_4 = 8,500 ÷ 5,700 = 1.49 units of output per kilogram of direct materials
    19_5 = 10,200 ÷ 7,000 = 1.46 units of output per kilogram of direct materials
2. Partial productivity of direct manufacturing labor increased 5.0% [(12.75 − 12.14) ÷ 12.14 = +0.050]. Partial productivity of direct materials decreased 2.0% [(1.46 − 1.49) ÷ 1.49 = −0.020]. Partial productivities, per se, do not reveal total factor productivity. The partial productivity of labor increased but the partial productivity of direct materials deceased.
3. TFP for 19_5 = 10,200 ÷ [(800 × $15) + (7,000 × $3)] = 10,200 ÷ ($12,000 + $21,000) = 10,200 ÷ $33,000 = 0.3091 units of output per dollar of inputs
   TFP for 19_4 = 8,500 ÷ [(700 × $15) + (5,700 × $3)] = 8,500 ÷ ($10,500 + $17,100) = 8,500 ÷ $27,600 = 0.3080
   The change in TFP from 19_4 to 19_5 = (0.3091 − 0.3080) ÷ 0.3080 = +0.04, or an increase of 0.4%.

CHAPTER 23

COST MANAGEMENT: QUALITY AND TIME

MAIN FOCUS AND OBJECTIVES

Quality and time are two key success factors that are part of the newly evolving management approach (see textbook Exhibit 1-2, p. 6). This chapter examines how management accounting can provide information to assist managers in taking initiatives in the areas of quality and time. Your overall objective for this chapter is to understand that quality and time issues relate directly to a company's ability to compete in the marketplace and involve interdependencies across the entire value chain. Nine learning objectives are stated in the textbook (p. 794).

Give special attention to:

- the distinction between quality of design and conformance quality
- the four categories of the costs of quality
- financial and nonfinancial measures of quality performance
- new product development time and breakeven time
- customer-response time and on-time performance
- the theory of constraints

The concept of relevant revenues and relevant costs (introduced in Chapter 11) is used in several of the chapter's illustrations.

REVIEW OF KEY TERMS AND CONCEPTS

A. Companies increasingly emphasize manufacturing or delivering high-quality products or services. Why? Because quality improvement programs can result in sizable cost savings and higher sales revenue.
1. **Quality**: the conformance of a product or service with a preannounced or pre-specified standard.
2. The costs of quality are significant, ranging from 15% to 20% of sales in many companies.
3. Two basic aspects of quality are quality of design and conformance quality.
   a. **Quality of design** measures how closely the characteristics of products (or services) match the needs and wants of customers.
   b. **Conformance quality** is making the product according to design, engineering, and manufacturing specifications.
4. **Costs of quality (COQ)** encompass costs incurred to prevent poor quality from occurring and costs incurred because poor quality has occurred. Four COQ classifications are often distinguished:

a. **Prevention costs**: costs incurred in preventing the production of products that do not conform to specifications.

b. **Appraisal costs**: costs incurred in detecting which of the individual units of product do not conform to specifications.

c. **Internal failure costs**: costs incurred when a nonconforming product is detected *before* being shipped to customers.

d. **External failure costs**: costs incurred when a nonconforming product is detected *after* being shipped to customers.

> **Exhibit 23-1 provides examples of individual cost items in each of the four COQ classifications. In addition, two overlay categories are specified:**
> - *Category A* **is cost items generally included in COQ reports.**
> - *Category B* **is cost items generally not included in COQ reports (mainly forgone contribution margin on lost sales resulting from poor quality).**

e. Category B costs are more difficult to measure, but they can be larger in amount than category A costs.

f. If all category B costs are not included in COQ reports, managers will likely underestimate failure costs, and thereby underinvest in the activities of prevention and appraisal.

5. The textbook example of Photon (beginning p. 796) uses a five-step activity-based approach to determine category A costs.

a. The results of this analysis are shown in Exhibit 23-2 (Panel A).

b. Exhibit 23-2 (Panel B) shows the category B external failure costs of $12 million arising from forgone contribution margin on lost sales.

c. Note that COQ are incurred across the entire value chain.

   (1) Most prevention costs are incurred in R&D and design.

   (2) Appraisal and internal failure costs are incurred in manufacturing.

   (3) External failure costs are incurred in marketing, distribution, and customer service.

6. *See Practice Test Question III (items 1 and 2) and Question IV.*

7. In a situation where competitors are improving quality, a company that does not invest in quality improvement will likely suffer a decline in sales.

8. Two trends occur in successful quality programs:

a. COQ as a percentage of sales decreases over time.

b. The sum of internal and external failure costs as a percentage of the total COQ decreases over time.

9. Three methods that organizations use to identify quality problems are control charts, Pareto diagrams, and cause-and-effect diagrams.

a. A *control chart*—a graph of a series of successive observations of a particular operation or production step taken at regular time intervals—is a key tool of statistical quality control.

(1) The purpose of control charts is to distinguish between random variation and other sources of variation in an operating process.

(2) Exhibit 23-3 presents control charts for the defect rates observed at Photon's three production lines.

b. A *Pareto diagram* indicates how frequently each type of failure (defect) occurs. Exhibit 23-4 is a Pareto diagram for the failures of Photon's photocopying machines.

c. A *cause-and-effect diagram* (also called a *fishbone diagram*) helps to identify potential causes of failure. Exhibit 23-5 is a cause-and-effect diagram for the quality problem of fuzzy and unclear copies.

Carefully study Exhibit 23-6. It shows Photon's analysis of the relevant revenues and relevant costs of quality improvement. The difference in favor of redesigning the machine's frame (versus inspecting the frame) is $972,000. Note that in this decision, qualitative factors (such as gaining expertise about a product or process) should also be considered.

---

10. Customer satisfaction is an important element in quality programs. Producing a defect-free, high-quality product is profitable only if it satisfies customers.

a. Motorola's program of total customer satisfaction is described in the textbook (p. 804).

b. Most organizations use both financial and nonfinancial measures of customer satisfaction.

(1) *Financial measures* include warranty repair costs and forgone contribution margin on lost sales.

(2) *Nonfinancial measures* include number of customer complaints and customer-response time.

11. Examples of nonfinancial measures of internal quality are defect rate, process yield, and manufacturing lead time.

12. *Half-life method*: the amount of time it takes for a defect rate to be reduced by 50%.

a. This method can be used to set targets for rates of quality improvement.

b. See the numerical example in the textbook (p. 805).

Exhibit 23-7 gives a summary of financial and nonfinancial measures of customer satisfaction and internal performance. Advantages of using these measures are listed in the textbook (p. 806).

---

13. Some organizations include both financial and nonfinancial measures of quality performance in a single report, often called a *balanced scoreboard*. This approach helps top management evaluate whether lower-level managers have improved one performance aspect (such as net income) at the expense of others (such as on-time delivery).

B. Companies increasingly view time as a key variable in competition. Several measures of time are used.
   1. **New product development time**: the amount of time from when the initial concept for a new product is approved by management to its market introduction.
      a. Shortened product life cycles make it necessary to introduce new products more quickly.
      b. To reduce new product development time, the business functions in the value chain must proceed simultaneously (and in a coordinated manner) rather than sequentially.
      c. Many companies have reported spectacular reductions in new product development time.
   2. Breakeven time measures how long it takes to recover the investment made in new product development (that is, how quickly new ideas are converted into profitable products).
      a. **Breakeven time (BET)**: the amount of time from when the initial concept for a new product is approved by management until the time when the cumulative present value of net cash inflows from the project equals the cumulative present value of net investment outflows.
      b. New product proposals with shorter BET's are preferred to those with longer BETs, if all other things are equal.
      c. BET is most important for companies that experience rapid technological change; they want to recoup their investments quickly, before the products become obsolete.

BET is computed in two alternative ways in the textbook example. Using the figures in Exhibit 23-8 (dollar amounts in millions):

- **Panel A: 3 years (through 19_7)** $+ \dfrac{\$10.524 - \$9.920}{\$5.920} = 3.10$ **years**

- **Panel B: 3 years (through 19_7)** $+ \dfrac{\$0.604}{\$5.920} = 3.10$ **years**

---

   d. Special notes:
      (1) In BET computations, *year 0 is when the initial concept for a new product receives management approval*. Under the payback period, year 0 is when the initial investment occurs.
      (2) Only relevant cash flows are used to compute BET.
      (3) The limitations of BET (see textbook p. 811) are the same as those of the payback method except that BET incorporates the time value of money.
   e. *See Practice Test Problem V.*
   3. Two operational measures of time—customer-response time and on-time performance—reveal respectively how quickly and how reliably an organization supplies its products or services to customers.

a. **Customer-response time**: the amount of time from when a customer places an order to when delivery occurs.

b. In many service and merchandising industries (such as banking, fast-food, and groceries), the critical component of customer-response time is how much time, on average, a customer spends in line waiting for a product or service.

c. *Time driver*: any factor that causes a change in the speed with which an activity is undertaken when the factor itself changes.

   (1) Two important time drivers are (i) uncertainty about when customers will order products or services and (ii) limited capacity and bottlenecks.

   (2) *Bottleneck*: an operation, such as a machine on a production line, where the work required to be performed approaches or exceeds the available capacity.

d. *See Practice Test Question III (items 3-5).*

e. In manufacturing industries, a key component of customer-response time is manufacturing lead time.

   (1) **Manufacturing lead time** (also called *manufacturing cycle time*): the amount of time from when an order is ready to start on the production line (ready to be set up) to when it is finished.

   (2) Manufacturing lead time for a production order = Waiting time (if any) + Manufacturing time (See the textbook diagram, p. 813.)

The textbook example of **Falcon Works (p. 812)** illustrates the computation of *average waiting time* when there is one product (A22) and then two products (A22 and C33). The introduction of product C33 would increase average waiting time by 117% [(325 − 150) ÷ 150].

---

   (3) Intuitively, when setup time is relatively small, average waiting time is less for processes that have many small jobs then for processes that have few large jobs.

   (4) *Average waiting time is inversely related to the amount of unused capacity*; that is, the more unused capacity, the greater the likelihood that an order will arrive when the process is not being used.

   (5) Think of unused capacity as a cushion for absorbing the shocks of variability and uncertainty in the arrival of customer orders.

f. **On-time performance** refers to situations in which the product or service is actually delivered to the customer on schedule.

Be aware that there is a tradeoff between customer-response time and on-time performance; on-time performance can be improved simply by promising longer customer-response times.

---

g. An interesting textbook example (pp. 812-13) considers whether product C33 should be introduced.

   (1) The relevant revenues and relevant costs for this decision are shown in Exhibit 23-9.

(2) Note that manufacturing lead times affect revenues (customers are willing to pay a small premium for faster delivery) and costs (more inventory needs to be carried).

(3) Introducing C33 is rejected even though this product has a positive contribution margin and machine capacity is available. Why? Because that contribution margin is more than offset by increased inventory carrying costs and lost contribution margin on product A22.

h. When demand uncertainty is high, some excess capacity of the bottleneck resource is desirable.

C. The **theory of constraints (TOC)** focuses on revenue and cost management when manufacturing involves multiple parts and multiple machines.

1. TOC defines three measures:
   a. *Throughput contribution*: sales dollars minus direct materials costs.
   b. *Investments (inventory)*: the sum of materials costs (in all inventories including materials inventory), R&D costs, and equipment/building costs.
   c. *Other operating costs*: all operating costs (except direct materials costs) incurred to earn throughput contribution.

2. The objective of TOC is to increase throughput contribution while decreasing investments and operating costs; the time horizon is short run and the other operating costs are considered to be fixed.

3. Key steps in managing the production bottlenecks are described in the textbook (p. 817). Note that:
   a. The bottleneck machine determines throughput contribution of the plant as a whole.
   b. Producing more nonbottleneck output creates more inventory but does not increase throughput contribution.
   c. The bottleneck machine should set the pace for the nonbottleneck machines.
   d. Actions should be taken to increase bottleneck efficiency and capacity.

4. *See Practice Test Problem VI.*

PRACTICE TEST QUESTIONS AND PROBLEMS

I. Complete each of the following statements.

1. _____ measures how closely the characteristics of products or services match the needs and wants of customers.

2. Costs of quality (COQ) are divided into what four categories? _____
   _____
   _____

3. A(An) _____, which is a graph of a series of successive observations of a particular operation or production step taken at regular time intervals, is a tool used to identify quality problems.

4. The measurement of both new product development time and breakeven time begins when the initial concept of a new product is _____
   _____.

5. The amount of time from when a customer places an order to when delivery occurs is called _____.

6. A(An) _____ is an operation, such as a machine on a production line, where the work required to be performed approaches or exceeds the available capacity.

7. The amount of time from when an order is ready to start on the production line (ready to set up) to when it is finished is called _____
   _____.

8. Situations in which the product or service is actually delivered to the customer on schedule is referred to as _____.

9. Under the theory of constraints, _____ _____ is equal to sales dollars minus direct materials costs.

II. Indicate whether each of the following statements is true or false by putting T or F in the space provided.

___ 1. Conformance quality measures how closely the characteristics of products or services match the needs and wants of customers.

___ 2. The costs of quality incurred in detecting which of the individual products do not conform to specifications are called internal failure costs.

___ 3. The four categories of costs of quality are interdependent.

___ 4. All of the costs of quality entail cash outlays (including the outlays for quality-related equipment).

___ 5. Costs of quality are incurred across the entire value chain.

___ 6. In successful quality programs, the costs of quality as a percentage of sales declines over time.

___ 7. A Pareto diagram helps to identify the potential causes of product failure.

___ 8. A financial measure of internal quality is called the half-life method.

___ 9. Customer-response time is an example of a nonfinancial measure of performance used in quality programs.

___ 10. New product development time can be reduced by proceeding with the business functions in the value chain simultaneously (and in a coordinated manner) rather than sequentially.

___ 11. BET is most important for companies that experience rapid technological change.

___ 12. For BET computations, year 0 is when the initial investment occurs.

___ 13. Average waiting time is inversely related to the amount of unused capacity.

___ 14. There is a tradeoff between customer-response time and on-time performance.

___ 15. Considering only quantitative factors, it may be desirable to not introduce a new product that has a positive contribution margin, even though machine capacity is available.

___ 16. It is undesirable to have excess capacity at the bottleneck resource in a manufacturing plant.

___ 17. The objective of the theory of constraints is to increase throughput contribution while decreasing investments and operating costs.

III. Select the best answer for each of the following multiple-choice questions and put the identifying letter in the space provided.

___ 1. (CMA adapted) The costs of rework in a quality costing system are categorized as:
a. external failure costs.
b. internal failure costs.
c. training costs.
d. prevention costs.
e. appraisal costs.

___ 2. (CMA) The costs of statistical quality control in a quality costing system are categorized as:
a. external failure costs.
b. internal failure costs.
c. training costs.
d. prevention costs.
e. appraisal costs.

___ 3. Merediths is a small grocery store with a single checkout lane. It takes an average of 5 minutes for the cashier to check out a customer at the store. The store is open 8 hours per day (480 minutes) and attracts an average of 56 customers per day. The cashier is paid $10 per hour. How long, on average, will a customer wait in line before being served?
a. 7.0 minutes
b. 3.5 minutes
c. 0.7 minutes
d. none of the above

___ 4. See item 3. Merediths is considering carrying a new product. This action is expected to increase the average number of customers to 66 per day. If the new product is introduced, how long, on average, will a customer wait in line before being served?

    a. 5.5 minutes
    b. 1.1 minutes
    c. 11.0 minutes
    d. none of the above

___ 5. See items 3 and 4. Suppose Merediths decides to carry the new product but has concern about excessive waiting time. If the store remains open one more hour per day, how long, on average, will a customer wait in line before being served?

    a. 0.79 minutes
    b. 4.51 minutes
    c. 7.86 minutes
    d. none of the above

IV. For each of the following items in Kronner Manufacturing Company's costs of quality program, indicate the proper classification.

    P: Prevention costs
    A: Appraisal costs
    I : Internal failure costs
    E: External failure costs

___ 1. Cost of product returned by customers
___ 2. Cost of reworking defective products detected at the company's plant
___ 3. Cost of conformance tests at the company's plant
___ 4. Cost of inspection tests at the company's assembly department
___ 5. Cost of "Vendor Day," a seminar to inform vendors of new quality requirements being used by the company

V. Advanced Medical Devices is considering the development of a new surgical instrument, SI-107. Management approval of this project is expected at the end of 19_3, but work on the project would not start until the end of 19_4. The following cash flows are projected (in thousands):

Year	Investment Cash Outflows	Product Cash Inflows
19_4	$1,000	
19_5		$500
19_6		800
19_7		300

Product cash inflows are the cash flow from operations. The company uses a 14% required rate of return for this type of project.

Compute the breakeven time for SI-107 using the interest tables in Appendix C at the back of the textbook.

Check figure: 2.91 years

VI. Huntington Industries makes VCRs in two departments—machining and assembly. The capacity per month is 30,000 units in the machining department and 20,000 units in the assembly department. The only variable costs of the product are direct materials costs of $100 per unit. All direct materials costs are incurred in the machining department. All other costs of operating the two departments are fixed costs. Huntington can sell as many VCRs as it produces at a selling price of $300 per unit.

Assuming any defective units produced in either department must be scrapped:

1. Compute the loss that occurs when a defective unit is produced in the machining department.
2. Compute the loss that occurs when a defective unit is produced in the assembly department.
3. Do your answers in parts 1 and 2 relate to the theory of constraints? Explain.

Check figures: (1) $100 (2) $300

CHAPTER 23 SOLUTIONS TO PRACTICE TEST

I. 1 Quality of design; 2 prevention costs, appraisal costs, internal failure costs, external failure costs; 3 control chart; 4 approved by management; 5 customer-response time; 6 bottleneck; 7 manufacturing lead time (manufacturing cycle time); 8 on-time performance; 9 throughput contribution.

II.

1 F	5 T	9 T	13 T	17 T
2 F	6 T	10 T	14 T	
3 T	7 F	11 T	15 T	
4 F	8 F	12 F	16 F	

Explanations:

1 The statement describes quality of design. Conformance quality is making the product according to design, engineering, and manufacturing specifications. (F)

2 The statement describes appraisal costs. Internal failure costs are incurred when a nonconforming product is detected *before* being shipped to customers. (F)

3 For example, incurring more prevention costs would likely reduce external failure costs. (T)

4 Category B items in Exhibit 23-1 do not entail cash outlays — forgone contribution margin on lost sales resulting from poor quality production, lower unit sales, and lower selling prices. (F)

5 Most prevention costs are incurred in R&D and design. Appraisal and internal failure costs are incurred in manufacturing. External failure costs are incurred in marketing, distribution, and customer service. (T)

6 Another trend in successful quality programs is that the sum of internal and external failure costs as a percentage of the total costs of quality decreases over time. (T)

7 The statement describes a cause-and-effect diagram (also called a fishbone diagram); see Exhibit 23-5. A Pareto diagram indicates how frequently each type of failure (defect) occurs; see Exhibit 23-4. (F)

8 The half-life method is a nonfinancial measure. It reveals how long is required for a defect rate to be reduced by 50%. (F)

9 Exhibit 23-7 gives a summary of financial and nonfinancial measures of customer satisfaction and internal performance. (T)

10 For example, design should begin *during* R&D instead of waiting until R&D is completed. (T)

11 These companies want to recoup their investment quickly, before the products become obsolete. (T)

12 For BET computations, year 0 is when the initial concept for a new product receives management approval. (F)

13 The more unused capacity, the greater the likelihood that an order will arrive when the process is not being used. Unused capacity can be thought of as a cushion for absorbing the shocks of variability and uncertainty in the arrival of customer orders. (T)

14 On-time performance can be improved simply by promising longer customer-response times. (T)

15 Yes, because the new product's contribution margin may be more than offset by increased inventory carrying costs and lost contribution margin on existing products. This point is illustrated in the textbook example of products C33 and A22 (pp. 812-13). (T)

16 When demand uncertainty is high, some excess capacity of the bottleneck resource is desirable. Increasing the capacity of the bottleneck resource can reduce average waiting time and inventories. (F)

17 The theory of constraints has a short-run time horizon. Other operating costs (all operating costs except direct materials costs) are considered to be fixed. (T)

III.

1 b	4 a		
2 e	5 d		
3 b			

Explanations:

1 The costs incurred when a nonconforming product (such as reworked units) is detected before being shipped to the customer are called internal failure costs. (b)

2 The costs incurred in detecting which of the individual units of product do not conform to specifications (such as the costs of control charts used in statistical quality control) are called appraisal costs. (e)

3 Let W = Average waiting time in minutes

$$X = \frac{\left(\begin{array}{c}\text{Average number}\\ \text{of customers}\end{array}\right) \times \left(\begin{array}{c}\text{Time to serve}\\ \text{each customer}\end{array}\right)^2}{2 \times \left[\begin{array}{c}\text{Available}\\ \text{capacity}\end{array} - \left(\begin{array}{c}\text{Average number}\\ \text{of customers}\end{array}\right) \times \left(\begin{array}{c}\text{Time to serve}\\ \text{each customer}\end{array}\right)\right]}$$

$$X = \frac{56 \times 5^2}{2 \times [480 - (56 \times 5)]} = \frac{56 \times 25}{2(480 - 280)} = \frac{1,400}{400} = 3.5 \text{ minutes (b)}$$

4 Using the formula in (3):

$$W = \frac{66 \times 5^2}{2 \times [480 - (66 \times 5)]} = \frac{66 \times 25}{2(480 - 330)} = \frac{1,650}{300} = 5.5 \text{ minutes (a)}$$

5 Using the formula in (3):

$$W = \frac{66 \times 5^2}{2 \times [540 - (66 \times 5)]} = \frac{66 \times 25}{2(540 - 330)} = \frac{1,650}{420} = 3.93 \text{ minutes (d)}$$

IV. 1 E   4 A
    2 I   5 P
    3 A

V. Advanced Medical Devices

Year (1)	PV Discount Factor at 14% (2)	Investment Cash Outflows (3)	PV of Investment Cash Outflows (4) = (2) × (3)	Cumulative PV of Investment Cash Outflows (5)	Product Cash Inflows (6)	PV of Product Cash Inflows (7) = (2) × (6)	Cumulative PV of Product Cash Inflows (8)
19_3	1.000	---	---	---	---	---	---
19_4	0.877	$(1,000)	$(877)	$(877)			
19_5	0.769				$500	$384.5	$ 384.5
19_6	0.675				800	540.0	924.5
19_7	0.592				300	177.6	1,102.1

$$\text{BET} = 2 \text{ years (through 19\_5)} + \frac{\$877.0 - \$384.5}{\$540.0} = 2 + \frac{\$492.5}{\$540.0} = 2.91 \text{ years}$$

Alternatively, BET can be computed as follows:

Year (1)	PV Discount Factor at 14% (2)	Cash Outflows (3)	Cash Outflows (4)	Net Cash Flows (5) = (3) − (4)	PV of Net Cash Flows (6) = (2) × (5)	Cumulative PV of Net Cash Flows (7)
19_3	1.000	---	---	---	---	---
19_4	0.877	---	$(1,000)	$(1,000)	$(877.0)	$(877.0)
19_5	0.769	$500	---	500	384.5	(492.5)
19_6	0.675	800	---	800	540.0	47.5
19_7	0.592	300	---	300	177.6	225.1

$$\text{BET} = 2 \text{ years} + \frac{\$492.5}{\$540.0} = 2.91 \text{ years}$$

Note that "year 0" under BET is when the initial concept for the project is approved by management, not when the initial investment occurs.

VI. Huntington Industries

1. Direct materials costs $100
   Forgone contribution margin on lost sale,
     $0 because machining has more capacity
     than assembly   0
   Loss from producing a defective unit in machining $100
2. Direct materials costs $100
   Forgone contribution margin on lost sale,
     $300 − $100   200
   Loss from producing a defective unit in assembly $300
3. The answers in parts 1 and 2 are related to the theory of constraints. Under TOC, the objective is to maximize throughput contribution, which is equal to sales dollars minus direct materials costs. In this case, Huntington Industries should focus on improving quality first in the assembly department because poor quality (defective units) there is more costly. That is, because machining has more capacity than assembly, forgone throughput contribution only occurs from poor quality in assembly.

CHAPTER 24

INVENTORY MANAGEMENT AND JUST-IN-TIME

MAIN FOCUS AND OBJECTIVES

The cost of goods sold often accounts for more than 70% of total costs in retail companies. In manufacturing companies, materials costs typically exceed 50% of total costs. Not surprisingly then, companies need to focus considerable attention on inventory management. Your overall objective for this chapter is to understand the importance of accounting information for inventory management in retailing and manufacturing companies. Nine learning objectives are stated in the textbook (p. 832).

Give special attention to:

- the five categories of costs pertaining to inventory
- computing economic order quantity, reorder point, and safety stock
- just-in-time purchasing
- the distinction between materials requirements planning and just-in-time production

You may already be familiar with many of the ideas in this chapter from other courses. However, in those courses the applicable costs are assumed. Management accountants help decide what costs should be included in the computations (the relevant costs) and help estimate the amounts of the costs.

REVIEW OF KEY TERMS AND CONCEPTS

A. Managing goods for sale in retail companies is important because cost of goods sold constitutes by far the largest cost item, and net income typically is a very small percentage of sales.
  1. For management purposes, five categories of costs pertaining to inventory are distinguished:
    a. **Purchasing costs**: the amount paid for acquiring the goods themselves plus freight or transportation; these costs (i) are affected by quantity discounts and the supplier's credit terms and (ii) are usually the largest of the five categories.
    b. **Ordering costs**: costs incurred in preparing and issuing a purchase order plus special processing, receiving, and inspection costs related to the number of orders processed.
    c. **Carrying costs**: costs of holding inventory; these costs include storage (such as space rental and insurance) and the opportunity cost of the investment tied up in inventory.

d. **Stockout costs**: costs arising when customer demands cannot be met from inventory; these include costs of expediting an order to a supplier and, if sales are lost, the opportunity cost of forgone current and future contribution margin.

e. **Quality costs**: the four categories of costs of quality are prevention costs, appraisal costs, internal failure costs, and external failure costs; these costs are described in section A(4) of Chapter 23's outline (p. 293).

2. Data in these cost categories pertaining to inventory are becoming more reliable and timely because of advances in information-gathering technology.

B. In purchasing merchandise, retailers must decide *how much to order* and *when to order*.

1. The **economic order quantity (EOQ)** is the optimal size of a purchase order to place for replenishing inventory.

a. When five assumptions are met (see textbook pp. 833-34):

$$\begin{matrix} \text{Total relevant costs} \\ \text{for determining EOQ} \end{matrix} = \begin{matrix} \text{Total relevant} \\ \text{ordering costs} \end{matrix} + \begin{matrix} \text{Total relevant} \\ \text{carrying costs} \end{matrix}$$

Computation of EOQ is illustrated in the textbook (p. 835). Carefully study this example and related Exhibits 24-1 and 24-2.

---

b. Exhibits 24-1 and 24-2 show the tradeoff between the annual carrying costs and the annual ordering costs, as the order size changes.

c. *Total relevant costs will be at a minimum (the EOQ level) where total annual ordering costs and total annual carrying costs are equal.*

d. The quickest and most accurate way to compute EOQ is by formula:

$$\text{EOQ} = \sqrt{\frac{2DP}{C}}$$

where D = Demand in units for a specified time period
P = Ordering costs per purchase order
C = Costs of carrying one unit in stock for the time period used for D

e. Using these symbols, total relevant costs (TRC) for *any order size (Q)* can be computed as follows:

$$\text{TRC} = \frac{DP}{Q} + \frac{QC}{2}$$

f. *The EOQ model can be easily adapted for production situations.*
   (1) This adaptation is called economic production run quantity (EPRQ).
   (2) The only change in the variables is P = setup costs per production run (instead of ordering costs per purchase order).

g. *See Practice Test Question III (items 1-5) and Problems IV (part 1) and V.*

2. The **reorder point** is the quantity level of inventory on hand that triggers a new order being placed.

a. When there is *certainty* about both demand and lead time to receive an order, no stockouts occur.

(1) Under those conditions,

$$\text{Reorder point} = \frac{\text{Sales per unit}}{\text{of time}} \times \frac{\text{Purchase-order}}{\text{lead time}}$$

(2) This situation is illustrated in Exhibit 24-3.

b. When there is *uncertainty* about demand or lead time, **safety stock** is held as a buffer to guard against running out of inventory.

> **Exhibit 24-4 gives a detailed example of computing the optimal level of safety stock (160 units). As the level of safety stock changes, note the tradeoff between stockout costs and carrying costs of safety stock.**

---

(1) The optimal level of safety stock minimizes the sum of annual stockout costs and annual carrying costs of safety stock.

(2) *See Practice Test Question III (items 6 and 7) and Problem IV (parts 2 and 3).*

C. Obtaining accurate estimates of the cost parameters used in the EOQ decision model is a challenging task.

1. The relevant annual carrying costs consist of both *outlay costs* such as insurance costs and the *opportunity cost of capital* (the interest forgone by investing capital in inventory).

a. Most internal reporting systems do not formally record opportunity costs.

b. Therefore, users of the EOQ model cannot rely exclusively on the accounting system for all the components included in the carrying costs of inventory.

2. Opportunity costs, from forgone contribution margin on current and future lost sales, are also relevant in estimating stockout costs.

3. Because predicting costs is a difficult task for managers, it may be helpful to compute the *cost of a prediction error* in the EOQ decision model.

a. See the three-step approach used in the textbook example (p. 839).

b. Fortunately, the total relevant costs for determining EOQ are *rarely sensitive to small variations in cost predictions*.

c. For example, Exhibit 24-2 shows that the total relevant cost curve is relatively flat for order sizes ranging from 400 to 600 units.

4. Since opportunity costs are used in the EOQ *decision model*, they should also be used in *performance-evaluation models*; otherwise, purchasing managers (to obtain lower unit purchase prices) will favor purchasing larger order sizes than would be optimal.

D. There is growing interest in just-in-time purchasing systems.

1. **Just-in-time (JIT) purchasing**: the purchase of goods or materials such that delivery immediately precedes demand or use; in the extreme case, a retailer or manufacturer would hold no inventories.

2. Exhibit 24-5 shows how EOQ is reduced by various combinations of two changes:
   a. Decreases in ordering costs of each purchase order.
   b. Increases in carrying costs of inventory.
3. The analysis presented in Exhibit 24-5 supports JIT purchasing; however, *do not assume that JIT purchasing policy is always guided by the EOQ decision model.* Why? Two reasons:
   a. Because the model assumes a constant order quantity, but fluctuating demand would require differing order quantities.
   b. Because the model does not consider three of the five categories of costs pertaining to inventory — purchasing costs, stockout costs, and quality costs.

Two useful exhibits illustrate relevant cost analysis:
- **Exhibit 24-6 shows that a JIT purchasing policy is favored at Video Glore over the current purchasing policy.**
- **Exhibit 24-7 highlights that a higher level of quality and on-time delivery by Sontek more than offsets the lower purchasing costs offered by Denton.**

---

4. Changes that result from moving toward JIT purchasing include smaller and more frequent purchase orders, fewer suppliers for each item, long-term contracts with suppliers, less inspection of orders received, and less paperwork.
5. These changes substantially reduce the ordering costs per purchase order.
6. *See Practice Test Problem VI.*

E. Two basic types of systems used to manage materials inventories in manufacturing companies are materials requirements planning and JIT production.
   1. **Materials requirements planning (MRP)**: a system that considers first the amount and timing of finished goods demand, and then determines the derived demand for materials, components, and subassemblies at each stage of production.
      a. MRP is carried out on a *centralized "push-through" basis* that emphasizes *demand forecasts*.
      b. An overview of MRP is given in Exhibit 24-8.
      c. Management accounting can play an important role in MRP:
         (1) By supplying accurate and timely information on all inventories.
         (2) By providing estimates of setup costs, downtime costs, and carrying costs of inventories. (*Note that setup costs in production situations are analogous to ordering costs in purchasing situations.*)
   2. **JIT production**: a system in which each component on a production line is produced immediately as needed by the next step on the production line.
      a. Three features of JIT production:
         (1) The production line is run on a *decentralized "demand-pull" basis* that responds to *actual customer demand*; this feature is often implemented by a *Kanban* system, as explained in the textbook example (p. 846).

(2) Emphasis is placed on minimizing the setup time and the manufacturing lead time for each unit.

(3) The production line is stopped if parts are absent or defective work is discovered; such action creates an urgency about correcting these problems.

b. The underlying philosophy of JIT is simplifying the production process so that only essential activities that add value to the product are conducted.

c. Some JIT adopters have extended this simplification to their internal accounting system. (The use of backflush costing is discussed in section D of Chapter 19's outline, pp. 243-44.)

d. JIT adopters make heavy use of nonfinancial performance measures in the day-to-day control of operations at the plant level.

> **Exhibit 24-9 summarizes the effects Hewlett-Packard reported from adopting JIT at several production plants.**

PRACTICE TEST QUESTIONS AND PROBLEMS

I. Complete each of the following statements.

1. For management purposes, what five categories of costs pertain to inventory? _____ _____ _____ _____. Which of these cost categories are considered in the EOQ model? _____ _____

2. What do each of the letters in the EOQ model stand for?

   D = _____ _____

   P = _____

   C = _____ _____

3. The estimated minimum inventory quantity needed as a buffer against expected demand during purchase-order lead time is called _____.

4. The relevant carrying costs for inventory consist of both outlay costs and _____ _____.

5. The purchase of goods or materials such that delivery immediately precedes demand or use is called _____.

6. _____ is a system that considers first the amount and timing of finished goods demand, and then determines the derived demand for materials, components, and subassemblies at each stage of production.

7. Ordering costs in purchasing situations are analogous to _____ costs in production.

8. A system in which each component on a production line is produced immediately as needed by the next step on the production line is called _____.

II. Indicate whether each of the following statements is true or false by putting T or F in the space provided.

____ 1. The largest category of costs pertaining to inventory is usually quality costs.

____ 2. Stockout costs include the forgone contribution on current and future lost sales.

____ 3. EOQ is the optimal level of inventory.

____ 4. EOQ minimizes the total relevant annual carrying costs of inventory.

____ 5. An example of a cost pertaining to inventory that usually would not be relevant to the decision of how much to order is the salaries of stockroom workers.

____ 6. The optimal level of safety stock is determined by considering carrying costs of safety stock and stockout costs.

____ 7. The reorder point would decrease if the ordering costs per purchase order increase.

___ 8. The total relevant costs for determining EOQ usually are not sensitive to small variations in cost predictions.

___ 9. JIT purchasing policy should be guided by the EOQ decision model.

___ 10. Adopting JIT purchasing would likely result in fewer suppliers for each item and in more paperwork.

___ 11. Under JIT production, the production line is stopped if parts are absent or defective work is discovered.

___ 12. JIT production systems usually entail more detailed accounting records.

III. Select the best answer for each of the following multiple-choice questions and put the identifying letter in the space provided.

___ 1. (CMA adapted) The carrying costs pertaining to inventory include:
   a. insurance costs, incoming freight costs, and storage costs.
   b. insurance costs, incoming freight costs, and setup costs.
   c. incoming freight costs, setup costs, and quantity discounts lost.
   d. setup costs and opportunity cost of capital invested in inventory.
   e. storage costs and opportunity cost of capital invested in inventory.

___ 2. (CPA) Barter Corporation has been buying Product A in lots of 1,200 units, a four months' supply. The cost per unit is $100; the ordering costs are $200 per purchase order; and the annual inventory carrying costs for one unit are $25. Assume that the units will be required evenly throughout the year. What is the EOQ?
   a. 144
   b. 240
   c. 600
   d. 1,200

___ 3. (CPA) Garmar, Inc., has determined the following for a given year:

EOQ in units	5,000
Total annual ordering costs	$10,000
Ordering costs per purchase order	$50
Costs of carrying one unit for one year	$4

What is Garmar's estimated annual demand in units?
   a. 1,000,000
   b. 2,000,000
   c. 4,000,000
   d. cannot be determined from the information given.

___ 4. (CPA adapted) A manufacturer expects to produce 200,000 widgets during the fiscal year ending June 30, 19_5 to supply a demand that is uniform throughout the year. The setup costs for each production run of widgets are $144. The cost of carrying one widget in inventory is $0.20 per year. After a batch of widgets is produced and placed in inventory, it is sold at a uniform rate and inventory is exhausted when the next batch of widgets is completed. The quantity of widgets (to nearest hundred widgets) that should be produced in each run in fiscal year 19_5 to minimize total costs is:
   a. 12,000.
   b. 12,500.
   c. 16,000.
   d. 17,000.
   e. 19,000.

___ 5. (CPA) For its EOQ model a company has ordering costs per purchase order of $10, and annual costs of carrying one unit in stock of $2. If the ordering costs per purchase order increase by 20%, and the annual costs of carrying one unit in stock increase by 25%, while all other considerations remain constant, EOQ will:
   a. remain unchanged.
   b. decrease.
   c. increase.
   d. either increase or decrease depending on the reorder point.

___ 6. (CMA) The amount of inventory that a company would tend to hold in safety stock would increase as the:
   a. sales level falls to a permanently lower level.
   b. annual costs of carrying a unit decrease.
   c. variability of sales decreases.

d. cost of running out of stock decreases.

e. length of time that goods are in transit decreases.

___ 7. (CPA) The Hancock Company wishes to determine the amount of safety stock that it should maintain for Product No. 135 so as to result in the lowest costs. Each stockout costs $75 and the annual carrying costs of each unit of safety stock are $1. Product No. 135 will be ordered five times a year. Which of the following will produce the lowest cost?

a. A safety stock of 10 units, which is associated with a 40% probability of running out of stock during the purchase-order lead time.

b. A safety stock of 20 units, which is associated with a 20% probability of running out of stock during the purchase-order lead time.

c. A safety stock of 40 units, which is associated with a 10% probability of running out of stock during the purchase-order lead time.

d. A safety stock of 80 units, which is associated with a 5% probability of running out of stock during the purchase-order lead time.

IV. Given for a merchandise item of Catalina Stores:

Total annual demand in units	3,000
Relevant carrying costs per unit per year	$5
Relevant ordering costs per purchase order	$300
Inventory level when each order arrives	zero
Maximum daily usage	80 units
Average daily usage	70 units
Minimum daily usage	60 units
Lead time for receipt of the item	22 days

1. Compute the total annual relevant costs at the EOQ level.
2. Compute the minimum safety stock needed to be certain a stockout will not occur.
3. Compute the reorder point.

Check figures: (1) $3,000 (2) 220 units (3) 1,760 units

V. (CMA) Gerstein Company manufactures a line of deluxe office fixtures. The annual demand for its miniature oak file is estimated to be 5,000 units. The annual cost of carrying one unit in inventory is $10, and the setup costs to initiate a production run are $1,000. There are no miniature oak files on hand, and Gerstein has scheduled four equal production runs of this file for the coming year, the first of which is to be run immediately. Gerstein operates 250 business days per year. Assume that sales occur uniformly throughout the year.

1. If no safety stock is held, compute the estimated total carrying costs for the miniature oak file for the coming year.
2. If two equal production runs are scheduled for the coming year rather than four, compute the amount of change in the sum of annual carrying costs and setup costs.
3. Compute the number of production runs that would minimize the sum of carrying costs and setup costs for the coming year.

Check figures: (1) $6,250 (2) $4,250 increase (3) 5

VI. Quinn Electronics stocks and sells repair components for television sets. Quinn implemented a JIT purchasing policy in January 19_4. One year later, Sandra Lansing is evaluating the effect that the policy has had on financial performance. She finds the following information:

Average inventory declined from $400,000 to $200,000. Pre-JIT insurance costs of $40,000 declined by 40% (due to lower average inventory).

Pre-JIT, 5,000 square feet of warehouse space was leased for $10,000. The lower average inventory allowed Quinn to sublet 40% of the space at $2.50 per square foot.

The JIT purchasing policy leads to stockouts on 5,000 parts. Quinn's policy is to handle stockouts with rush orders at a cost of $4 per unit.

Quinn's required rate of return on investments in inventory is 15%.

Compute the cash savings (loss) from the JIT purchasing policy for 19_4.

Check figure: $31,000 savings

CHAPTER 24 SOLUTIONS TO PRACTICE TEST

I. 1 purchase costs, ordering costs, carrying costs, stockout costs, quality costs; ordering costs, carrying costs; 2 demand in units for a specified time period, ordering costs per purchase order, costs of carrying one unit in stock for the time period of demand; 3 safety stock; 4 the opportunity cost of capital invested in inventory; 5 just-in-time (JIT) purchasing; 6 Materials requirements planning (MRP); 7 setup; 8 just-in-time (JIT) production.

II.

1	F	5	T	9	F
2	T	6	T	10	F
3	F	7	F	11	T
4	F	8	T	12	F

Explanations:

1 Purchase costs, the amount paid for acquiring the goods themselves plus freight or transportation, are usually the largest of the five categories of costs pertaining to inventory. (F)

2 Stockout costs also include the costs of expediting an order to a supplier. (T)

3 EOQ is the optional size of a purchase order to place for replenishing inventory. (F)

4 EOQ would minimize the total relevant costs, which are the sum of total annual ordering costs and total annual carrying costs. The minimum occurs where total annual ordering costs and total annual carrying costs are *equal*. (F)

5 Such salaries would be irrelevant for EOQ because they would not differ (at least in the short run) on the basis of how many purchase orders are placed per year. (T)

6 See Exhibit 24-4. (T)

7 Reorder point = Sales per unit of time × Purchase-order lead time. Therefore, a change in the ordering costs per purchase order would have no effect on the reorder point. (F)

8 The truth of this statement can be illustrated by the fact that the total annual relevant cost curve in Exhibit 24-2 is relatively flat for order quantities ranging from 400 to 600 units. (T)

9 To understand the full costs and benefits of JIT purchasing, it is necessary to move outside the confines of the EOQ model because that model (i) assumes a constant order quantity, but fluctuating demand would require differing order quantities and (ii) does not consider three of the five categories of costs pertaining to inventory—purchasing costs, stockout costs, and quality costs. (F)

10 Adopting JIT purchasing would likely result in fewer suppliers for each item and in *less* paperwork. Other changes include smaller and more frequent purchase orders, long-term contracts with suppliers, and less inspection of orders received. (F)

11 Such action creates an urgency about correcting these problems. (T)

12 The underlying philosophy of JIT production is simplifying the manufacturing process so that only essential activities that add value to the product are conducted. Some JIT adopters have extended this simplification to their internal accounting systems, such as by using fewer journal entries. (F)

III.

1	e	4	d	7	c
2	b	5	b		
3	a	6	b		

Explanations:

1 Of all the costs listed in the answers, the carrying costs are insurance costs, storage costs, and opportunity cost of capital invested in inventory. Incoming freight cost and quantity discounts lost are purchasing costs. Setup costs in production situations are analogous to ordering costs in purchasing situations. (e)

2   Demand in units per year $= 1{,}200 \times 3 = 3{,}600$;

$$EOQ = \sqrt{\frac{2(3{,}600)(\$200)}{\$25}} = \sqrt{\frac{\$1{,}440{,}000}{\$25}} = \sqrt{57{,}600} = 240 \text{ units (b)}$$

Note that the cost per unit of $100 is not *explicitly* used in this computation. *Implicitly*, however, the required annual return on the investment of $100 per unit is included in the costs of carrying one unit in stock for one year.

3   Let $D = $ Annual demand in units

$$5{,}000 = \sqrt{\frac{2D(\$50)}{\$4}}$$
$$25{,}000{,}000 = \frac{\$100D}{\$4}$$
$$25{,}000{,}000 = 25D$$
$$D = 1{,}000{,}000 \text{ (a)}$$

Alternatively, total relevant costs will be at a minimum (the EOQ level) where total annual ordering costs and total annual carrying costs are equal:

$$\frac{D(\$50)}{\$5{,}000} = \$10{,}000$$
$$\$50D = \$50{,}000{,}000$$
$$D = 1{,}000{,}000$$

4   Setup costs in production situations are analogous to ordering costs in purchasing situations.

      Let EPRQ $=$ Economic production run quantity

$$EPRQ = \sqrt{\frac{2(200{,}000)(\$144)}{\$0.20}}$$
$$EPRQ = \sqrt{\frac{\$57{,}600{,}000}{\$0.20}}$$
$$EPRQ = \sqrt{288{,}000{,}000}$$
$$EPRQ = 17{,}000 \text{ widgets (rounded to nearest hundred widgets) (d)}$$

Note that a production run is, in effect, an *internal* purchase, whereas the two previous questions deal with *external* purchases.

5   These changes in the variables in the EOQ model can be thought of as an example of sensitivity analysis. Assuming any figure for annual demand (say, 90,000 units), the effect of the changes on EOQ is as follows (rounded to nearest unit):

Before changes:

$$EOQ = \sqrt{\frac{2(90{,}000)(\$10)}{\$2}}$$
$$EOQ = \sqrt{900{,}000} = 949 \text{ units}$$

After changes:

$$EOQ = \sqrt{\frac{2(90{,}000)(\$12)}{\$2.50}}$$
$$EOQ = \sqrt{864{,}000} = 930 \text{ units}$$

Therefore, the changes cause EOQ to decrease. The reorder point, which is mentioned in choice (d), has no bearing on the answer. (b)

6 See Exhibit 24-4. If annual carrying costs were less than the present $5.20 per unit, total carrying costs (and, therefore, total costs) would decrease; the level of safety stock would tend to increase. (b)

7 Safety stock should be set at the level that would minimize the sum of annual stockout costs and annual costs of carrying safety stock. The following computations (in the format of Exhibit 24-4) for the four alternative levels of safety stock show that total annual costs are lowest when safety stock is 40 units:

	Level of Safety Stock	Prob. of Stockout Occurring	Costs per Stockout	Orders per Year	Expected Annual Stockout Costs	Annual Carrying Costs ($1 per unit)	Total Annual Costs
a.	10 units	0.40	$75.00	5	$150.00†	$10.00	$160.00‡
b.	20 units	0.20	$75.00	5	$ 75.00	$20.00	$ 95.00
c.	40 units	0.10	$75.00	5	$ 37.50	$40.00	$ 77.50 (c)
d.	80 units	0.05	$75.00	5	$ 18.75	$80.00	$ 98.75

†0.40 × $75.00 × 5 = $150.00; ‡$150.00 + $10.00 = $160.00

IV. Catalina Stores

1. $\text{EOQ} = \sqrt{\dfrac{(2)(3,000)(\$300)}{\$5}} = \sqrt{\dfrac{\$1,800,000}{\$5}} = \sqrt{360,000} = 600 \text{ units}$

Let TRC = Total relevant annual costs at the EOQ

$\text{TRC} = \dfrac{DP}{Q} + \dfrac{QC}{2} = \dfrac{3,000(\$300)}{600} + \dfrac{600(\$5)}{2} = \$1,500 + \$1,500 = \$3,000$

2. $(80 - 70) \times 22 = 220 \text{ units}$

3. $220 + (70 \times 22) = 220 + 1,540 = 1,760 \text{ units}$

Or, $80 \times 22 = 1,760 \text{ units}$

V. Gerstein Company

1. Number of units per run = 5,000 ÷ 4 = 1,250 units

Total carrying costs per year = (1,250 ÷ 2) × $10 = $6,250

2.

	4 Runs	2 Runs
Carrying costs		
[(5,000 ÷ 4) ÷ 2] × $10	$ 6,250	
[(5,000 ÷ 2) ÷ 2] × $10		$12,500
Setup costs		
$1,000 × 4; $1,000 × 2	4,000	2,000
Total relevant costs	$10,250	$14,500

Increase due to fewer runs $4,250

3. Economic production run quantity = $\sqrt{\dfrac{2(5,000)(\$1,000)}{\$10}} = \sqrt{\$1,000,000} = 1,000 \text{ files}$

Number of production runs = 5,000 ÷ 1,000 = 5

VI. Quinn Electronics

	Policy	Previous JIT Policy
Required return on investment		
15% × $400,000; 15% × $200,000	$ 60,000	$30,000
Insurance costs		
$40,000; $40,000(1 − .40)	40,000	24,000
Warehouse rental		
$10,000; $10,000 − (5,000 × .40 × $2.50)	10,000	5,000
Stockout costs		
5,000 × $4		20,000
Total relevant costs per year	$110,000	$79,000

Difference in favor of JIT purchasing policy $31,000

CHAPTER 25

SYSTEMS CHOICE: DECENTRALIZATION AND TRANSFER PRICING

MAIN FOCUS AND OBJECTIVES

This chapter and the next deal with various issues related to designing management control systems. This material is a blend of cost accounting (narrowly defined), strategic management, operations management, economics, and organization behavior. Your overall objective for this chapter is to understand how the combined effect of these subject areas influences the degree of decentralization in an organization and the transfer pricing method chosen. Nine learning objectives are stated in the textbook (p. 860).

Keep in mind that this material is "softer" (less number crunching) than most other chapters in the textbook. Nevertheless, the concepts are important.

Give special attention to:

- the benefits and the costs of decentralization
- the three general methods for determining transfer prices
- the impact of different transfer prices on the three criteria of goal congruence, management effort, and subunit autonomy
- the international tax issues that arise when a multinational company transfers goods between divisions located in different countries
- the general guideline for transfer pricing

Studying this chapter can be frustrating because there is no "best" way to determine a transfer price. It is desirable to concentrate on the pros and cons of each transfer-pricing method.

REVIEW OF KEY TERMS AND CONCEPTS

A. The degree of decentralization in an organization should depend on a comparison of the benefits and the costs of decentralization.
   1. The essence of **decentralization** is the freedom for managers of subunits at lower levels of an organization to make decisions; the term *subunit* refers to any part of an organization.
   2. An important reason for this freedom is information asymmetry.
      a. *Information asymmetry* exists when one particular manager has more and better information about factors that affect the performance of his or her subunit than do other managers.
      b. Example: a division manager has more and better information about his or her customers and improvements in product quality than does top management.

3. Total decentralization means minimum constraints and maximum freedom for managers to make decisions at the lowest levels of an organization.
4. Total centralization means maximum constraints and minimum freedom for managers to make decisions at the lowest levels of an organization.

> **Question**: From top management's standpoint, how much decentralization is optimal in an organization?
> **Answer**: Conceptually, the degree of decentralization chosen should maximize the excess of its benefits over its costs. In practice, these benefits and costs can seldom be quantified, but the cost-benefit approach helps managers focus on the central issues.

5. **Benefits of decentralization**:
   a. Creates greater responsiveness to the demands of a subunit's customers, suppliers, and employees.
   b. Leads to quicker decisions by subunit managers.
   c. Increases motivation of subunit managers because they have more control over their own destiny.
   d. Develops an experienced pool of management talent.
   e. Sharpens the focus of managers of smaller subunits.
6. **Costs of decentralization**:
   a. Leads to *suboptimal decision making* (also called *dysfunctional decision making*), which arises when a decision's benefit to one subunit is more than offset by the costs (or loss of benefits) to the organization as a whole.
      (1) Suboptimal decisions may occur when there is a lack of goal congruence or when no guidance is given to subunit managers concerning the effects of their decisions on other parts of the organization.
      (2) *Suboptimal decisions are most likely to occur when the subunits are highly interdependent*; interdependence exists when the decisions made by one subunit will affect the decisions and performance of other subunits.
   b. Other costs of decentralization include duplication of activities, decreased loyalty of subunit managers toward the organization as a whole, and higher costs of gathering information.
7. Decisions on sourcing are likely to be decentralized, while decisions on long-term financing are likely to be centralized.
8. Some organizations impose restrictions on the ability of subunits to outsource products or services that are available from internal subunits, and thereby limit decentralization.
9. Responsibility center choices, such as cost centers, profit centers, and investment centers, are compatible with either centralization or decentralization.
   a. For example, *profit centers* (subunits for which both revenue and costs are reported) normally are associated with high decentralization.
   b. However, divisional profit centers can be centralized as when outsourcing restrictions are imposed.
10. Regardless of the responsibility center choices, the types of reporting units frequently used by companies are geographic, functional, product-line, and customer; in

particular, accounting information on product-line profitability and customer profitability is of special interest to marketing managers.

11. *See Practice Test Question III (item 2).*

B. When a product or service demanded by one subunit of an organization is supplied by another subunit of the same organization – **a transfer-pricing situation** – two interrelated decisions must be made:

Decision 1: Should the product or service be outsourced (bought from an external supplier) if it can be insourced (bought from an internal subunit)?

Decision 2: What transfer price should be used in the case of insourcing?

> **The basic purpose of transfer pricing is to motivate subunit managers to make decisions that are optimal for the organization as a whole.**

1. *Three general methods for determining transfer prices* (discussed below):
   a. Market-based transfer prices
   b. Cost-based transfer prices
   c. Negotiated transfer prices
2. The choice of a transfer price can sizably affect the operating income and return on investment of individual divisions.
3. Division managers are quite interested in the setting of transfer prices, especially if their compensation is directly affected by division income or return on investment.
4. **Three behavioral criteria** can help in choosing a transfer price:
   a. *Promotion of goal congruence*: goal congruence exists when each subunit manager acting in his or her own best interest takes actions that automatically result in achieving the organization goals established by top management.
   b. *Promotion of a sustained level of management effort*: effort is exertion toward a goal. For example, sellers are motivated to hold down costs of supplying a product or service, and buyers are motivated to use inputs efficiently.
   c. *Promotion of a high level of subunit autonomy in decision making*: autonomy is the degree of freedom to make decisions. (Note that this criterion is applicable *only* if top management favors a high level of decentralization.)
5. The Horizon Petroleum example in the textbook (beginning p. 865) illustrates that if both the buying and selling divisions act in their own best interests, *their decisions can be suboptimal.*

> **Carefully study the Horizon Petroleum example; start with the overview in Exhibit 25-1. This example demonstrates the use of cost-based and market-based transfer prices. Be sure you understand key Exhibit 25-2 before proceeding.**

6. *Special notes on Exhibit 25-2*:
   a. Total company operating income of producing, transporting, and refining 100 barrels of crude oil is $800, *regardless of the transfer price used.*
   b. However, division operating incomes *differ dramatically* under the three transfer-pricing methods.

c. Each division would choose a *different* transfer-pricing method if its sole objective were to maximize its own division operating income.

7. Exhibit 25-2 shows that the choice of a transfer-pricing method can affect *how a company's operating income pie is divided among individual divisions*.

8. Subsequent sections of the chapter illustrate that the choice of a transfer-pricing method can also affect *the size of the operating income pie itself*.

9. *See Practice Test Question III (items 3 and 5) and Problem IV*.

10. As explained in the Horizon Petroleum example (p. 868), managers should always take into account the income tax implications of alternative transfer pricing methods such that taxable income is minimized in the higher-taxed jurisdiction.

C. International tax issues arise when a multinational company transfers goods between divisions located in different countries.
1. Multinational companies must consider additional factors in setting transfer prices:
   a. Different income tax rates in various countries.
   b. Income or dividend payment restrictions.
   c. Tariffs, customs duties, and risks associated with movements in foreign-currency exchange rates.
2. See the textbook example (p. 868) and related discussion of new Internal Revenue Service regulations concerning multinational transfer prices.
3. Note that the January 1993 IRS regulations limit companies' ability to manipulate multinational transfer pricing by requiring the transfer price to approximate an "arm's length" price.
4. *See Practice Test Problem V*.

D. Under some conditions, **market-based transfer prices** lead to optimal decisions.
1. Favorable conditions for using market prices:
   a. Intermediate market is perfectly competitive.
   b. Interdependencies of subunits are minimal.
   c. There are no additional costs or benefits to the company as a whole of using the market instead of transacting internally.
2. In using market-based transfer prices under these conditions, companies can meet the three criteria of goal congruence, management effort, and (if applicable) subunit autonomy.
3. If a temporary distress price prevails in the market, the supplier division should generally meet this price as long as it exceeds the incremental costs of supplying the product or service.

E. Many organizations use **cost-based transfer prices**.
1. In some cases, market prices do not exist or are difficult to obtain.
2. Full-cost transfer prices are frequently used in practice; however, this method can lead to suboptimal decision making, as explained in the Horizon Petroleum example (pp. 870-71).

Question: Why do so many companies use full-cost transfer prices when those prices can lead to suboptimal decision making?
Answer: Because they yield relevant costs for long-run decisions, even though short-run decisions may suffer.

---

3. Some companies use a transfer price equal to the variable costs of a product or service plus a prorated share of the contribution to companywide operating income.
   a. This proration can be negotiated.
   b. In the textbook example (pp.873-74), proration is based on *budgeted variable costs* of the respective divisions.
   c. This approach to setting transfer prices requires that the subunits share information about their variable costs.
   d. *See Practice Test Problem VI.*
4. Because a single transfer price may not be satisfactory, dual transfer prices can be used.
   a. *Dual pricing*: the use of two separate transfer-pricing methods to price transfers between subunits.
   b. Dual pricing is not widely used, even though it reduces the goal-congruence problems associated with a pure cost-based transfer-pricing method. Why? Because top management has three concerns:
      (1) The manager of the supplying subunit would not have sufficient incentive to control costs.
      (2) The subunit managers would not receive clear signals about the level of decentralization desired.
      (3) Subunit managers would have less incentive to gain knowledge about the marketplace.

F. There is no all-pervasive rule for transfer pricing that leads to optimal decisions for the organization as a whole.
   1. Why? Because the three criteria of goal congruence, management effort, and subunit autonomy must be considered simultaneously.
   2. However, the following **general guideline** yields the minimum transfer price that the seller can accept and be as well off as under the next best alternative:

$$\textbf{Minimum transfer price} = \begin{array}{c}\textbf{Additional outlay costs}\\\textbf{per unit incurred up to}\\\textbf{the point of transfer}\end{array} + \begin{array}{c}\textbf{Opportunity costs}\\\textbf{per unit to the}\\\textbf{supplying division}\end{array}$$

   a. "Outlay costs" here means cash outflows that are directly associated with the production and transfer of products or services.
   b. "Opportunity costs" here means the maximum contribution forgone by the supplying division if the products or services are transferred internally.
   c. *This minimum transfer price is a starting point for negotiations, not a recommended transfer price.*
   d. The general guideline is applied to four specific situations in the textbook (pp. 875-76).
      (1) A competitive intermediate market exists and the supplying division has no idle capacity.
      (2) A competitive intermediate market exists and the supplying division has idle capacity.
      (3) No market exists for the intermediate product.
      (4) No competitive intermediate market exists and the supplying division has idle capacity.

> **A helpful three-step approach for transfer-pricing situations:**
> *Step 1:* **Apply the general guideline to obtain the minimum transfer price.**
> *Step 2:* **Determine if the buyer subunit will buy at whatever transfer price is set.**
> *Step 3:* **Verify that the buyer's decision is in the best interest of the company as a whole.**

PRACTICE TEST QUESTIONS AND PROBLEMS

I. Complete each of the following statements.

1. The essence of _____ is the freedom for managers of _____ at lower levels of an organization to make decisions.

2. _____ exists when one particular manager has more and better information about factors that affect the performance of his or her subunit than do other managers.

3. Conceptually, the degree of decentralization chosen by top management should maximize the excess of its _____ over its _____.

4. _____ arises when a decision's benefit to one subunit is more than offset by the costs (or loss of benefits) to the organization as a whole.

5. Three behavioral criteria that can help in choosing a transfer price are _____ _____ and _____.

6. The choice of a transfer-pricing method can affect how a company's operating income pie is divided among individual divisions as well as the _____ of the operating income pie itself.

7. Using the general guideline, the minimum transfer price that the seller division can accept and be as well off as under the next best alternative is equal to _____ _____ per unit incurred up to the point of transfer plus _____ _____ per unit to the supplying division.

II. Indicate whether each of the following statements is true or false by putting T or F in the space provided.

___ 1. The degree of decentralization in an organization depends primarily on the number of profit centers.

___ 2. The benefits of decentralization include improved management motivation and decreased costs of gathering information.

___ 3. Suboptimal decisions are often associated with a lack of goal congruence.

___ 4. Decentralization is likely to be most beneficial or least costly when an organization's subunits are interdependent.

___ 5. One way to limit decentralization is to impose restrictions on the ability of subunits to outsource products or services that are available from internal subunits.

___ 6. Profit centers are not incompatible with high centralization.

___ 7. The choice of a transfer price can sizably affect the operating income of individual divisions.

___ 8. If top management imposes insourcing, total company operating income will be unaffected by the transfer-pricing method used.

___ 9. Compared to domestic companies, multinationals must consider additional factors in setting their transfer prices including different tax rates in various countries and promotion of goal congruence.

___ 10. Recent IRS regulations limit companies' ability to manipulate multinational transfer pricing.

___ 11. Full-cost transfer prices are frequently used in practice to help avoid the pitfalls of suboptimal decision making.

___ 12. The minimum transfer price computed under the general guideline formula represents a recommended transfer price.

III. Select the best answer for each of the following multiple-choice questions and put the identifying letter in the space provided.

_____ 1. (CMA adapted) Which of the following is decentralization least likely to accomplish?
   a. provide a pool of management talent
   b. shorten decision-delay time
   c. heighten goal congruence
   d. increase motivation of subunit managers

_____ 2. (CMA adapted) A subunit of an organization is referred to as a profit center if it has:
   a. authority to choose its markets and sources of supply.
   b. authority to choose its markets, sources of supply, and significant control over the amount of invested capital.
   c. authority to make decisions over the most significant costs of operations including choice of the sources of supply.
   d. authority to provide specialized support to other subunits within the organization.
   e. responsibility for combining the direct materials, direct manufacturing labor, and other factors of production into finished goods.

_____ 3. (CPA) In a decentralized company in which divisions may buy goods from one another, the transfer-pricing system should be designed primarily to:
   a. increase the consolidated inventory costs.
   b. allow division managers to buy from outsiders.
   c. minimize the degree of autonomy of division managers.
   d. aid in the appraisal and motivation of management performance.

_____ 4. The transfer-pricing problem is most difficult in organizations that are:
   a. highly decentralized with many interdependencies among subunits.
   b. highly centralized with many interdependencies among subunits.
   c. highly decentralized with few interdependencies among subunits.
   d. highly centralized with few interdependencies among subunits.

_____ 5. (CPA adapted) Mar Company has two decentralized divisions, X and Y. Division X has always purchased certain component parts from Division Y at $75 per unit. Because Division Y plans to raise the price to $100 per unit, Division X desires to purchase these parts from external suppliers for $75 per unit. Division Y's costs follow:

Y's variable costs per unit	$70
Y's annual fixed costs	$15,000
Y's annual production of these parts for X	1,000 units

If Division X buys from an external supplier, the facilities Division Y uses to manufacture these parts would be idle. What would be the result if Mar dictates that Division X buy from Division Y at a transfer price of $100 per unit?
   a. It would be suboptimal for the company because X should buy from outside suppliers at $75 per unit.
   b. It would be more profitable for the company than allowing X to buy from outside suppliers at $75 per unit.
   c. It would provide higher overall company operating income than a transfer price of $75 per unit.
   d. It would provide lower overall company operating income than a transfer price of $75 per unit.

_____ 6. A helpful first step in setting a transfer price is to determine the opportunity costs per unit to the supplying division and to add:
   a. fixed costs incurred up to the point of transfer.
   b. market price in the intermediate market.
   c. additional outlay costs per unit incurred up to the point of transfer.
   d. budgeted variable costs per unit.

IV. Given for Division A of Galloway Manufacturing Company:

Costs of manufacturing 5,000 units of a certain part:

	Total	Per Unit
Variable costs	$200,000	$40
Fixed costs	40,000	8

1. Compute the advantage (disadvantage) to the company as a whole if there are no alternative uses for Division A's facilities, and if Division B purchases 5,000 units of this part from an external supplier at a market price of:
   a. $43 per unit.
   b. $36 per unit.
2. Compute the net financial advantage (disadvantage) to the company as a whole if there are alternative uses for Division A's facilities by other Galloway operations that would otherwise require additional outlay costs of $26,000, and if Division B purchases 5,000 units of this part from an external supplier at a market price of:
   a. $43 per unit.
   b. $36 per unit.

   Check figures: (1a) $15,000 disadvantage (1b) $20,000 advantage (2a) $11,000 advantage (2b) $46,000 advantage

V. Empire Company has two divisions. Division A is located in the United States where the income tax rate is 40%. Division B is located in Korea where the income tax rate is 30%. Division A produces an intermediate product at a variable cost of $100 per unit, and then transfers the product to Division B where it is finished and sold for $500 per unit. Variable costs in Division B are $80 per unit. Fixed costs in each division are $75,000 per year. Assume 1,000 units are transferred annually and that the minimum transfer price allowed by the U.S. tax authorities is the variable cost. Also assume that operating income in each country is equal to taxable income.

1. What transfer price should be set in order for Empire to minimize its total income taxes? Show computations.
2. If Empire desires to minimize its total income taxes, what is the amount of tax liability in each country?

Check figures: (1) $175 per unit (2) U.S. $0, Korea $51,000

VI. (CPA) Ajax Division of Carlyle Corporation produces electric motors, 20,000 of which are sold to Bradley Division of Carlyle and the remainder to outside customers. Carlyle treats its divisions as profit centers and allows division managers to choose their sources of supply and to whom they sell. Corporate policy requires that variable cost be used as the transfer price for all interdivisional sales and purchases. Ajax Division's estimated sales and manufacturing cost data for the coming year, based on the full capacity of 100,000 units, are as follows:

	Bradley	Outsiders
Sales	$ 900,000	$8,000,000
Variable costs	(900,000)	(3,600,000)
Fixed costs	(300,000)	(1,200,000)
Gross margin	$(300,000)	$3,200,000
Unit sales	20,000	80,000

Ajax has an opportunity to sell the 20,000 motors to an external customer at a price of $75 per unit on a continuing basis beginning in the coming year. Bradley can purchase its requirement of 20,000 motors from an external supplier at a price of $85 per unit.

1. Compute the net gross margin advantage (disadvantage) to Ajax Division if Ajax drops the sales to Bradley and adds the new customer for the coming year.
2. Assume instead that Carlyle permits the division managers to negotiate the transfer price for the coming year. The managers agreed on a tentative transfer price of $75 per unit, to be reduced based on an equal sharing of the additional gross margin to Ajax resulting from the sale to Bradley of 20,000 motors at $75 per unit. Compute the actual transfer price for the coming year.

Check figures: (1) $600,000 advantage (2) $60 per unit

CHAPTER 25 SOLUTIONS TO PRACTICE TEST

I. 1 decentralization, subunits; 2 Information asymmetry; 3 benefits, costs; 4 Suboptimal decision making (dysfunctional decision making); 5 goal congruence, management effort, subunit autonomy in decision making; 6 size; 7 additional outlay costs, opportunity costs.

II.

1	F	5	T	9	F
2	F	6	T	10	T
3	T	7	T	11	F
4	F	8	T	12	F

Explanations:

1 The degree of decentralization in an organization should depend on a comparison of its benefits and its costs. (F)

2 Under decentralization, the costs of gathering information increase. The benefits and costs of decentralization are listed respectively in sections A(5) and A(6) of the chapter outline. (F)

3 Suboptimal decisions also occur when no guidance is given to subunit managers concerning the effects of their decisions on other parts of the organization. (T)

4 Decentralization is likely to be most beneficial or least costly when an organization's subunits are *independent*. When the subunits are highly *interdependent*, suboptimal decisions are most likely to occur because the decisions affecting one subunit influence the decisions and performance of another subunit. (F)

5 Imposing restrictions on outsourcing limits decentralization because the freedom for managers of subunits at lower levels of an organization to make decisions is reduced. (T)

6 Profit centers normally are associated with high decentralization. However, profit centers can be highly centralized, as when outsourcing restrictions are imposed. (T)

7 See Exhibit 25-2. (T)

8 See Exhibit 25-2; total company operating income is $800, regardless of the transfer price used. (T)

9 All companies need to consider the promotion of goal congruence in setting their transfer prices. Compared to domestic companies, multinationals must consider several additional factors in setting their transfer prices: different income tax rates in various countries, income or dividend payment restrictions, tariffs, custom duties, and risks associated with movements in foreign-currency exchange rates. (F)

10 The January 1993 regulations limit a multinational company's ability to manipulate the amount of taxable income in a particular country by requiring the transfer price to approximate an "arm's length" price. (T)

11 Although full-cost transfer prices are frequently used in practice, this method can lead to suboptimal decision making in the short run, as explained in the Horizon Petroleum example (pp. 870-71). The main rationale for using full-cost transfer prices is that they yield relevant costs for long-run decisions. (F)

12 The minimum transfer price computed under the general guideline formula is a *starting point* for negotiations between the buying and selling divisions; it is *not* a recommended transfer price. (F)

III.

1	c	4	a
2	a	5	b
3	d	6	c

Explanations:

1 A cost of decentralization is suboptimal decision making. One reason this phenomenon occurs is that the goals of subunit managers may not be congruent with top management goals. For example, a division manager, who is acting to maximize divisional operating income, might decide to buy a component part from an outside supplier instead of one of the company's own divisions.

This decision could decrease operating income of the company as a whole. (c) Note that answers (a), (b), and (d) refer to benefits of decentralization.

2 Profit centers are subunits for which both revenues and costs are reported. Profit centers normally are associated with high decentralization, but they can be highly centralized. Answers (c) and (e) refer to cost centers (the revenue aspect is not mentioned) and (b) refers to an investment center. (a)

3 In designing a transfer-pricing system, three behavioral criteria should be considered: goal congruence, management effort, and subunit autonomy. These criteria are central to the motivation of division managers and appraisal of their performance. Answer (a) is incorrect because, under generally accepted accounting principles, inventory cannot be carried at more than its cost in consolidated financial statements. Therefore, when transfer prices exceed costs, which is often the case, intracompany (interdivisional) profit must be eliminated from inventory. Answer (b) is incorrect because allowing division managers to buy from outsiders should not be the *primary* purpose of designing a transfer-pricing system. Sometimes it may be more profitable to outsource, and other times it may be more profitable to insource. Answer (c) is incorrect because a transfer-pricing system seeks to optimize (as distinguished from minimize or maximize) the degree of autonomy of division managers. (d)

4 The transfer-pricing problem is the greatest in organizations that are highly decentralized with many interdependencies among divisions. The reason is that, under conditions of considerable freedom in decision making, decisions made by one subunit will affect the decisions and performance of other subunits. (a)

5 If transfers are dictated at $100 per unit, Division X would pay Division Y 1,000 × $100 = $100,000. This transaction is intracompany (interdivisional) in nature (that is, money is taken out of one corporate pocket and put into another). Therefore, *the $100,000 will have no effect on operating income of the company as a whole*. Assuming the fixed costs of Division Y are avoidable, the effect of purchasing internally on the operating income of the company as a whole would be:

Total relevant costs of external purchase,		
1,000 × $75		$75,000
Deduct total relevant costs of internal purchase:		
Avoidable outlay costs,		
1,000 × $70	$70,000	
Opportunity costs to the supplying division	-0-	70,000
Difference in favor of purchasing internally		$ 5,000

Therefore, operating income of the company as a whole would be $5,000 higher if Division X buys from Division Y. Given that transfers are dictated, *this conclusion will hold regardless of the transfer price used*. The reason is that the transfer price itself, being money taken out of one corporate pocket and put into another, is not relevant to an analysis for the company as a whole. Of course, performance evaluation of the subunit managers would likely be affected by the transfer price used. (b)

6 This formula is presented in section F of the chapter outline. (c)

IV. Galloway Manufacturing Company

1.

	(a)	(b)
Variable costs per unit, $200,000 ÷ 5,000	$ 40	$ 40
External market price per unit	43	36
Net advantage (disadvantage) per unit	$ (3)	$ 4
Multiply by number of units	× 5,000	× 5,000
Net advantage (disadvantage) to the company		
as a whole	$(15,000)	$20,000
(The fixed costs are irrelevant.)		

2.

	(a)	(b)
Net advantage (disadvantage) as above, before considering alternative use of facilities	$(15,000)	$20,000
Advantage from alternative use of facilities	26,000	26,000
Net advantage to the company as a whole	$ 11,000	$46,000

(The fixed costs are irrelevant.)

V. Empire Company

1. To minimize its total income taxes, the company should report no operating income in the U.S. This result will occur if the transfer price is set at full cost: $100 + ($75,000 ÷ 1,000) = $175 per unit.

2. Using the $175 transfer price from part 1, the company's tax liability in the U.S. is $0 and in Korea is $51,000:

Division A (U.S.)		Division B (Korea)	
Sales, 1,000 × $175	$175,000	Sales, 1,000 × $500	$500,000
		Tranferred-in costs,	
Variable costs,		$100,000 + $75,000	(175,000)
1,000 × $100	(100,000)	Variable costs, 1,000 × $80	(80,000)
Fixed costs	(75,000)	Fixed costs	(75,000)
Operating income	0	Operating income	170,000
Income tax	0	Income tax (at 30%)	(51,000)
Net income	$ 0	Net income	$119,000

VI. Carlyle Corporation

1. In making this decision, the manager of Ajax Division needs to determine the difference between the total relevant gross margin of selling externally and of selling internally. The variable manufacturing costs per unit are $3,600,000 ÷ 80,000 = $45. Assuming the fixed costs of the Ajax Division are unavoidable:

Total relevant gross margin of external sale, 20,000 × ($75 − $45)	$600,000
Total relevant gross margin of internal sale, 20,000 × ($45 − $45)	-0-
Difference in gross margin to Ajax Division of selling externally	$600,000

Alternatively, this answer can be obtained by comparing the financial statement results for the 20,000 units in question:

	Internal Sale (the Present Situation)	External Sale
Sales, given; 20,000 × $75	$ 900,000	$1,500,000
Variable costs	(900,000)	(900,000)
Fixed costs	(300,000)	(300,000)
Gross margin	$(300,000)	$ 300,000

Difference in favor of external sale   ⌐ $600,000 ⌐

2. Two steps are used to obtain the answer. First, determine the amount of additional gross margin that would result from the internal sale at $75 per unit: $20,000 \times (\$75 - \$45) = \$600,000$, or $30 per unit. Second, reduce the tentative transfer price of $75 by an equal sharing between the divisions of the additional gross margin (that is, a 50%:50% split): Actual transfer price $= \$75 - .50(\$30) = \$60$ per unit

```
┌─────────────────────────────────────────────┐
│                  CHAPTER 26                   │
│                                               │
│            SYSTEMS CHOICE:                    │
│    PERFORMANCE MEASUREMENT                    │
│      AND COMPENSATION                         │
└─────────────────────────────────────────────┘
```

MAIN FOCUS AND OBJECTIVES

This chapter focuses on the role of performance-evaluation measures as a central component of management control systems. Various aspects of performance evaluation and compensation arrangements are discussed. The problems encountered in decentralized companies are emphasized, especially those organized into divisional investment centers. Your overall objective for this chapter is to understand the importance of using multidimensional performance-evaluation measures. Ten learning objectives are stated in the textbook (p. 890).
Give special attention to:

- the five interdependent steps for choosing among accounting-based performance measures
- two accounting-based performance measures relating income to investment: return on investment and residual income
- the tradeoff between the benefits of performance-based incentives and the costs of imposing uncontrollable risk on a manager
- recent actions by the SEC and FASB regarding executive compensation

Be sure to distinguish between measuring performance of the manager of an organization subunit (such as a division) and measuring performance of that subunit as an economic investment. The former is used in decisions on compensation and future job assignments. The latter should be a prerequisite for allocating resources within an organization.

REVIEW OF KEY TERMS AND CONCEPTS

A. Performance-evaluation measures (hereafter referred to as performance measures) are a key part of management control systems.
1. A given performance measure has three characteristics:
    a. Financial or nonfinancial
    b. Internal or external
    c. Long run or short run

> A management control system should include four types of information that can be used in performance evaluation:
>
> | Type of Information | Example(s) of Performance Measure |
> |---|---|
> | 1. Financial/internal | Operating income, return on investment (ROI) |
> | 2. Financial/external | Stock price |
> | 3. Nonfinancial/internal | New product development time, manufacturing lead time |
> | 4. Nonfinancial/external | Market share, customer satisfaction |

2. Some companies use a report called *the balanced scorecard*, to emphasize different performance measures.
    a. The balanced scorecard often includes measures of profitability, customer satisfaction, innovation, and efficiency/quality/time.
    b. This approach avoids overemphasis on a single performance measure and highlights tradeoffs among the measures that managers face.

B. In the design of management control systems, **five steps are used for choosing among accounting-based performance measures**:

Step 1: Select a variable(s) that represents top management's financial goal(s). Examples: operating income, net income, ROI.

Step 2: Define the items included in the variable(s) selected in step 1. Example: "investment" can be defined as total assets or stockholders' equity.

Step 3: Specify the measures to be used for the items included in the variable(s) selected in step 1. Example: historical cost, present value, or current cost can be used to measure assets.

Step 4: Select a target against which to gauge performance. Example: all divisions probably will not have the same budgeted ROI.

Step 5: Specify the timing of feedback, which depends largely on the level of management that is receiving the feedback and on the sophistication of the organization's information technology. Examples: weekly, monthly, or quarterly reports.

> **The issues considered in each of these five steps are interdependent. The resolution of these issues will depend on how top management views the cost-benefit tradeoffs among the three behavioral criteria of goal congruence, management effort, and subunit autonomy.**

C. Three key accounting-based performance measures are return on investment, residual income, and return on sales.

> **These measures are illustrated by the Hospitality Inns example in the textbook (beginning p. 892). Exhibit 26-1 provides the data for the illustration.**

1. Return on investment (ROI) is computed as follows:

$$\text{ROI} = \frac{\text{Income}}{\text{Investment}}$$

   a. ROI has conceptual and practical appeal because it blends into a single number all of the major elements of profitability — revenues, costs, and investment.
   b. However, ROI should be used with caution and in conjunction with other performance measures.
   c. ROI is also called accounting rate of return or accrual accounting rate of return.
   d. Under an approach known as the *du Pont method of profitability analysis*, the ROI computation is divided into two components:

   Investment turnover × Income-to-revenue (sales) ratio = ROI

$$\frac{\text{Revenue}}{\text{Investment}} \times \frac{\text{Income}}{\text{Revenue}} = \text{ROI}$$

   e. Using the du Pont method, the textbook example (p. 894) shows that ROI can be increased by decreasing costs, increasing revenues, or decreasing investment, while holding the other two factors constant.
   f. *See Practice Test Question III (items 1-3).*
2. Residual income is computed as follows:

Residual income = Income − Imputed interest charge for investment

   a. The objective of maximizing residual income induces a desirable expansion of an organization subunit as long as it earns a rate of return in excess of the imputed charge for investment.
   b. In contrast, the objective of maximizing ROI may induce managers of highly profitable organization subunits to reject projects that, from the standpoint of the organization as a whole, should be accepted because they are expected to yield ROI in excess of the required rate of return on investment.
   c. These likely effects on managers' behavior from using ROI versus residual income are explained in the textbook (p. 895).
   d. *See Practice Test Question III (item 4) and Problem IV.*
3. Note that in computing ROI and residual income, different companies use different definitions of "investment," including total assets available, total assets employed, working capital plus other assets, and stockholders' equity.
4. Also note that in using ROI or residual income, performance evaluation of *a manager* should be distinguished from performance evaluation of *an organization subunit*, such as a division of a company.
   a. For example, the most skillful manager may be assigned to the weakest division.
   b. Therefore, a manager would usually be more appropriately judged by comparing his or her performance against a budget target rather than against other divisions.
5. **Return on sales (ROS)** is computed by dividing income by revenue (sales). ROS is a synonym for the income-to-revenue (sales) ratio component of ROI in the du Pont method of profitability analysis.
6. Exhibit 26-2 shows that companies around the world differ in terms of the performance measures they emphasize.

D. There are several *measurement alternatives* to consider when evaluating the performance of organization subunits: present value, current cost, and historical cost.
  1. Present value is the asset measure based on discounted cash flow estimates.
     a. In general, a new asset should be acquired if its net present value is positive or zero.
     b. Similarly, a currently held asset should be disposed of if the present value of its future net cash inflows is less than the current disposal price.
  2. Current cost measures for assets are a means of reducing the comparability problems that arise with historical cost measures.
     a. *Current cost* is the cost today of purchasing an asset identical to the one currently held; it is the cost of purchasing the services provided by that asset if an identical asset cannot currently be purchased.
     b. The Hospitality Inns example from earlier in the chapter is used to illustrate the computation of current costs (pp. 898-99).

  > **Exhibit 26-3 uses a six-step approach for computing ROI based on current-cost information. Carefully study each step.**

     c. This illustration shows that current-cost ROI can be much different from historical-cost ROI.
  3. Historical-cost measures are used more often in practice.
     a. As a result, there has been much discussion about the relative merits of using gross book value (original cost) or net book value (original cost minus accumulated depreciation).
     b. Those who favor gross book value claim that it helps comparisons among divisions. In contrast, if net book value is used, the constantly decreasing denominator can increase ROI as an asset ages, and thereby make comparisons among divisions misleading.
     c. Others favor net book value because it is more consistent with amounts shown in conventional financial statements.
     d. *See Practice Test Problem V.*

E. For evaluating the performance of managers, individual components of a management control system should be consistent and mutually reinforcing.
  1. Goal congruence problems can arise where there is a conflict between the measures used to evaluate a manager's performance and the decision models advocated by top management.
  2. For example, accrual accounting measures are often used for evaluating the performance of managers, while capital budgeting decisions are often based on discounted cash flow methods.
  3. Such conflicts can be avoided if performance evaluation is based on a comparison of predicted cash flows and/or accrual amounts with the corresponding actual results.
  4. The budgets used in these cases should be carefully negotiated with full knowledge of the pitfalls of historical-cost accounting.

F. The basic principles for evaluating employees' performance are applicable in three contexts: for a manager of an individual facility, at the individual activity level, and at the total organization level.

1. *For a manager of an individual facility*, his or her total compensation usually includes a combination of a salary and a performance-based component.

   a. This compensation arrangement should strengthen the link between goal congruence and management effort.

   b. However, performance-based compensation places more risk on managers. Why? Because actual results depend to some extent on factors that managers cannot control.

   > *Question*: **In designing compensation arrangements, what important tradeoff should be considered?**
   >
   > *Answer*: **The tradeoff between the benefits of performance-based incentives and the costs of imposing uncontrollable risk on a manager.**

   c. **Moral hazard** describes situations in which an employee is tempted to put in less effort (or report distorted information) because (i) the employee's interest differs from the owner's interest and (ii) the employee's effort cannot be accurately monitored and enforced.

   d. Incentive compensation arrangements are most likely to be cost-effective where three conditions are met:

      (1) The owner and manager have different goals (for example, the owner wants income and the manager is work averse).

      (2) The owner cannot observe the manager's actions.

      (3) The manager has considerable control over the actual results used to evaluate his or her performance.

   > *Question*: **What dictates the size of the incentive component relative to the amount of salary?**
   >
   > *Answer*: **It depends on how well the performance measure captures the manager's ability to influence desired results.**

   e. *A good performance measure changes significantly with changes in the manager's performance but is not much affected by changes in factors beyond the manager's control.*

   f. A helpful textbook example (p. 903) illustrates that where managers have no control over investment and revenues, using an ROI-based performance measure can be costly and ineffective; using cost-based incentives would be desirable in this case.

   g. Benchmarking a manager's performance against the best levels of similar performance that can be found inside or outside of the company can be cost-effective. Why? Because, in effect, this approach "cancels" the common noncontrollable factors and provides better information about a manager's performance.

h. *See Practice Test Question VI.*

2. *At the individual activity level*, most employees perform multiple tasks and sometimes work in teams.
   a. The textbook example of an auto repair shop (p. 904) discusses the potential conflict between the quantity of repair work and the level of customer satisfaction.
   b. Team-based incentive compensation encourages employees to work together to achieve common goals.

3. *At the total organization level*, executive compensation plans are based on financial and nonfinancial information.
   a. A major issue in designing these plans is choosing the mix of base salary, annual incentives, long-run incentives, and fringe benefits.

   > **To avoid managers having a myopic focus on the short run, long-run incentives are necessary.**

   b. Three factors emphasized by designers of executive compensation plans:
      (1) Achievement of organization goals
      (2) Administrative ease
      (3) Likelihood that those affected by the plan believe it is fair
   c. Executive compensation practices at some of the largest U.S. companies have been under strong criticism in recent years.
   d. Two factors critics believe have contributed to excessive executive compensation:
      (1) Improper accounting for stock options given to executives.
      (2) Inadequate disclosure to stockholders of the details of executive compensation plans.
   e. At the time this edition was written, *the FASB has agreed in principle to change the accounting requirements for stock options*; it has proposed that companies record as a cost in their income statements the fair market value of the options on the date the options are given.
   f. In October 1992, *the SEC issued new rules* requiring more detailed disclosures of the compensation of top-level executives, the principles underlying executive compensation plans, the performance criteria used, and how well the company's stock performed relative to other companies in the industry.

4. Managers in all organizations bear environmental and ethical responsibilities.
   a. Socially responsible companies are increasingly setting targets to reduce pollution and measuring their environmental management performance against these targets.
   b. Subunit managers are ethically responsible for reporting reliable performance numbers, and top management should unequivocally and frequently communicate an absolute intolerance for manipulation of accounting reports.

PRACTICE TEST QUESTIONS AND PROBLEMS

I. Complete each of the following statements.

1. Three characteristics of performance-evaluation measures are _____ _____ _____.

2. Some companies use a report called the _____ to emphasize different performance measures that often include profitability, customer satisfaction, innovation, and efficiency/quality/time.

3. Of the five interdependent steps used in choosing among accounting-based performance measures, what is step 5? _____ _____.

4. Under the du Pont method of profitability analysis, the two components of the ROI computation are _____ _____.

5. Residual income is equal to income minus _____ _____.

6. _____ is the cost today of purchasing an asset identical to the one currently held; it is the cost of purchasing the services provided by that asset if an identical asset cannot currently be purchased.

7. In designing compensation arrangements, there is a tradeoff between the benefits of creating _____ and the costs of imposing _____ on a manager.

8. _____ describes situations in which an employee is tempted to put in less effort (or report distorted information) because (i) the employee's interest differs from the owner's interest and (ii) the employee's effort cannot be accurately monitored and enforced.

9. What two organizations have recently taken important action regarding executive compensation issues? (use initials) _____

II. Indicate whether each of the following statements is true or false by putting T or F in the space provided.

___ 1. A company's market share is an example of nonfinancial/external information.

___ 2. In the design of a management control system, the five steps used for choosing accounting-based performance measures involve issues that are interdependent.

___ 3. ROI is equal to income divided by investment turnover.

___ 4. There is considerable uniformity in how companies define the numerator and the denominator in the ROI computation.

___ 5. The objective of maximizing ROI may induce suboptimal decision making by division managers.

___ 6. Companies around the world are remarkably similar in terms of the performance measures they emphasize.

___ 7. In general, it is desirable to use the same criteria in evaluating performance of the division manager and performance of the division as an economic investment.

___ 8. Conflicts between decision models and performance evaluation models can be avoided if performance evaluation is based on a comparison of predicted cash flows and/or accrual amounts with the corresponding actual results.

___ 9. Performance-based compensation arrangements tend to reduce the risk borne by managers.

___ 10. A sufficient condition for moral hazard to exist is that the employee's interest differs from the owner's interest.

___ 11. The salary component of total compensation dominates when only weak measures of performance are available.

___ 12. Using an ROI-based performance measure for a manager of a Marriott hotel could be both costly and ineffective.

___ 13. Benchmarking a manager's performance against the best levels of performance that can be found inside or outside of the company can be cost-effective.

___ 14. A factor that critics believe has contributed to excessive executive compensation is improper accounting for stock options given to executives.

___ 15. Top management should unequivocally and frequently communicate an absolute intolerance for manipulation of accounting records.

III. Select the best answer for each of the following multiple-choice questions and put the identifying letter in the space provided.

___ 1. Roma Bottling Co. has an investment of $3,000,000, an income-to-revenue ratio of 4%, and an ROI of 12%. Its revenue is:
   a. $360,000.
   b. $9,000,000.
   c. $1,440,000.
   d. $12,000,000.
   e. none of the above.

___ 2. See item 1. The investment turnover is:
   a. 5 times.
   b. 4 times.
   c. 3 times.
   d. 2 times.
   e. none of the above.

___ 3. (CMA adapted) A company's ROI would be increased if:
   a. sales increased by the same dollar amount as costs and total assets increased.
   b. sales remained the same and costs were reduced by the same dollar amount that total assets increased.
   c. sales decreased by the same dollar amount that costs increased.
   d. sales and costs increased by the same percentage that total assets increased.
   e. none of the above.

___ 4. Fletcher, Inc. has a residual income of $180,000 and an operating income of $500,000. If the imputed interest rate is 16%, the amount of investment is:
   a. $320,000.
   b. $3,125,000.
   c. $8,000,000.
   d. $2,000,000.
   e. none of the above.

___ 5. See item 4. ROI is:
   a. 5%.
   b. 10%.
   c. 15%.
   d. 20%.
   e. none of the above.

IV. Given for the Canning Division of Mason Company:

Investment	$4,500,000
Income	990,000

1. Compute residual income, assuming interest is imputed on investment at 18%.
2. If a proposed project is expected to have a 20% ROI, would it tend to be accepted if:
   a. Performance evaluation is based on ROI? Explain.
   b. Performance evaluation is based on residual income? Explain.

   Check figure: (1) $180,000

V. Given for a milling machine of Rochelle Company:

Investment in machine	$200,000
Annual net cash flow from operations	$38,344
Useful life of machine	10 years

1. Assuming that the accrual accounting model is used as a basis for performance evaluation, compute the ROI as follows (use straight-line depreciation with no terminal disposal price):
   a. First year using gross book value as the investment base.
   b. Sixth year using gross book value as the investment base.
   c. First year using average net book value during the year as the investment base.
   d. Sixth year using net book value at the beginning of the year as the investment base.
2. If the accrual accounting model is used to make performance comparisons among divisions, which basis would be preferable, gross book value or net book value? Explain.

   Check figures: (1a) 9.17% (1b) 9.17% (1c) 9.65% (1d) 18.34%

VI. Endicott Inc. sells electric motors in the industrial market. The company has decided to develop a compensation plan for its salespersons. Three options are being discussed: (1) fixed salary only, (2) sales commissions only, (3) mix of fixed salary and sales commissions. What factors should be considered in designing this plan?

CHAPTER 26 SOLUTIONS TO PRACTICE TEST

I. 1 financial and nonfinancial, internal and external, long run and short run; 2 balanced scorecard; 3 Specify the timing of feedback; 4 investment turnover, income-to-revenue (sales) ratio; 5 an imputed interest charge for investment; 6 Current cost; 7 performance-based incentives; uncontrollable risk; 8 Moral hazard; 9 SEC, FASB.

II.

1 T	5 T	9 F	13 T
2 T	6 F	10 F	14 T
3 F	7 F	11 T	15 T
4 F	8 T	12 T	

Explanations:

1   The table in section A of the chapter outline shows the four types of information in a management control system and gives examples of related performance-evaluation measures. (T)

2   These five steps are listed in section B of the chapter outline. The resolution of these issues will depend on how top management views the cost-benefit tradeoffs among the three behavioral criteria of goal congruence, management effort, and subunit autonomy. (T)

3   ROI is equal to income divided by investment. Investment turnover is equal to revenue divided by investment. (F)

4   There is considerable diversity in the definition of these components. For example, two measures frequently used for income are operating income and net income. Investment could be total assets available, total assets employed, working capital plus other assets, or stockholders' equity. When any of the choices involving assets are selected, another issue that must be decided is whether to use gross book value or net book value. (F)

5   The objective of maximizing ROI may induce managers of highly profitable organization subunits to reject projects that, from the standpoint of the organization as a whole, should be accepted because they are expected to yield ROI in excess of the required rate of return on investment. (T)

6   Exhibit 26-2 shows that companies around the world differ in terms of the performance measures they emphasize. (F)

7   The division manager would usually be appropriately judged by comparing his or her performance against budget targets. The performance of the division as an economic investment depends on its long-run profitability. This distinction is important to keep in mind because the most skillful manager may be assigned to the weakest division. (F)

8   The budgets used in these cases should be carefully negotiated with full knowledge of the pitfalls of historical-cost accounting. (T)

9   Performance-based compensation arrangements place more risk on managers because actual results depend to some extent on factors that managers cannot control. (F)

10   The statement accurately describes one of the two necessary conditions for moral hazard to exist. The other is that the employee's effort cannot be accurately monitored and enforced. (F)

11   The truth of this statement is illustrated by government bureaucrats who are paid all or almost all of their compensation in the form of salary. (T)

12   See the textbook example (p. 903). Using cost-based incentives would be desirable in this case. (T)

13   This approach can be cost-effective because, in effect, the common noncontrollable factors tend to be canceled. (T)

14   At the time this edition was written, the FASB has agreed in principle to change the accounting requirements for stock options; it has proposed that companies record as a cost in their income statements the fair market value of the options on the date the options are given. (T) Note that another factor that critics believe has contributed to excessive executive compensation is

inadequate disclosure to stockholders of the details of these plans. In response, the SEC issued new rules on this matter in October 1992.

15 The statement describes an ethical responsibility of top management. Subunit managers are ethically responsible for reporting reliable performance numbers. (T)

III. 1 b   4 d
     2 c   5 e
     3 b

Explanations:

1 Income = 12% × \$3,000,000 = \$360,000; Revenue = \$360,000 ÷ 4% = \$9,000,000 (b)
2 \$9,000,000 ÷ \$3,000,000 = 3 times (c)
3 To answer this question, use assumed amounts. Suppose the present ROI is 20% as follows:

$$\frac{Sales}{Investment} \times \frac{Income}{Sales} = ROI$$

$$\frac{\$1,000,000}{\$500,000} \times \frac{\$1,000,000 - \$900,000}{\$1,000,000} = 20\%$$

Using assumed amounts for the changes specified in the question, the effects on ROI in each of the answers can be calculated as follows:

(a) Sales increased by \$300,000, which is the amount that costs and total assets increased:

$$\frac{\$1,300,000}{\$800,000} \times \frac{\$1,300,000 - \$1,200,000}{\$1,300,000} = 12.5\%$$

(b) Sales remained the same, costs decreased by \$60,000, and total assets increased by \$60,000:

$$\frac{\$1,000,000}{\$560,000} \times \frac{\$1,000,000 - \$840,000}{\$1,000,000} = 28.6\%$$

(c) Sales decreased by \$50,000, costs increased by \$50,000, and total assets remained the same:

$$\frac{\$950,000}{\$500,000} \times \frac{\$950,000 - \$950,000}{\$950,000} = 0\%$$

(d) Sales and costs increased by 15% and total assets increased by 15%:

$$\frac{\$1,150,000}{\$575,000} \times \frac{\$1,150,000 - \$1,035,000}{\$1,150,000} = 20\%$$

ROI increases under answer (b).
4 Imputed interest = \$500,000 − \$180,000 = \$320,000; Investment = \$320,000 ÷ 16% = \$2,000,000 (d)
5 \$500,000 ÷ \$2,000,000 = 25% (e)

IV. Mason Company

1. \$990,000 − (18% × \$4,500,000) = \$990,000 − \$810,000 = \$180,000
2. (a) ROI = \$990,000 ÷ \$4,500,000 = 22%; the proposed project would be rejected because it decreases overall ROI.
   (b) The proposed project would be accepted because it increases residual income by \$180,000, as shown in part 1.

V. Rochelle Company

1. Annual net cash flow from operations $38,344
   Deduct annual depreciation, $200,000 ÷ 10   20,000
   Operating income $18,344

   (a) and (b) ROI on gross book value for each year: $18,344 ÷ $200,000 = 9.17%
   (c) Net book value at the end of first year = $200,000 − $20,000 = $180,000
   ROI on average net book value during the first year = $18,344 ÷ [($200,000 + $180,000) ÷ 2] = $18,344 ÷ $190,000 = 9.65%
   (d) $18,344 ÷ (0.50 × $200,000) = $18,344 ÷ $100,000 = 18.34%

2. Gross book value would be preferred as a basis for comparing division performance. The increasing ROI on net book value (from 9.17% to 18.34% in six years) could possibly be deceptive, given a constant operating income ($18,344 per year).

VI. Endicott Inc.

The basic tradeoff to consider is between creating incentives and imposing risk. Compensation based on sales commissions creates incentives for the salespersons to work hard but they also bear risk because total sales are affected by some factors outside their control. For example, a salesperson may work hard but noncontrollable factors (such as a recession, strike at a customer's plant, etc.) may cause sales and the salesperson's compensation to be reduced. A fixed salary, independent of sales performance, does not impose any risk on the salesperson but it also creates no incentives. For this reason, many companies use a mix of salary and sales commissions—the salary component reduces risk while the commissions component creates incentives.